FOR A HUMANE
ECONOMIC DEMOCRACY

FOR A HUMANE
ECONOMIC DEMOCRACY

Ota Sik

Translated by
Fred Eidlin and William Graf

PRAEGER

PRAEGER SPECIAL STUDIES • PRAEGER SCIENTIFIC

New York • Philadelphia • Eastbourne, UK
Toronto • Hong Kong • Tokyo • Sydney

Library of Congress Cataloging in Publication Data

Sik, Ota, 1919-
For a humane economic democracy.

Translation of: Humane Wirtschaftsdemokrataie.
Includes index.
1. Comparative economics.   I. Title.   II. Title:
Economic democracy.
HB90.S5513   1985   330   85-6470
ISBN 0-03-064186-1 (alk. paper)

Published in 1985 by Praeger Publishers
CBS Educational and Professional Publishing, a Division of CBS Inc.
521 Fifth Avenue, New York, NY 10175 USA

© 1979, 1985 by Ota Sik

56789 052 987654321

Printed in the United States of America on acid-free paper

INTERNATIONAL OFFICES

Orders from outside the United States should be sent to the appropriate address listed below. Orders from areas not listed below should be placed through CBS International Publishing, 383 Madison Ave., New York, NY 10175 USA

Australia, New Zealand
Holt Saunders, Pty, Ltd., 9 Waltham St., Artarmon, N.S.W. 2064, Sydney, Australia

Canada
Holt, Rinehart & Winston of Canada, 55 Horner Ave., Toronto, Ontario, Canada M8Z 4X6

Europe, the Middle East, & Africa
Holt Saunders, Ltd., 1 St. Anne's Road, Eastbourne, East Sussex, England BN21 3UN

Japan
Holt Saunders, Ltd., Ichibancho Central Building, 22-1 Ichibancho, 3rd Floor, Chiyodaku, Tokyo, Japan

Hong Kong, Southeast Asia
Holt Saunders Asia, Ltd., 10 Fl, Intercontinental Plaza, 94 Granville Road, Tsim Sha Tsui East, Kowloon, Hong Kong

Manuscript submissions should be sent to the Editorial Director, Praeger Publishers, 521 Fifth Avenue, New York, NY 10175 USA

PREFACE

In this book, I describe the model of a new economic system. I began work on the basic principles of this model in the 1960s while I was directing the State Economic Reform Commission of the Czechoslovak Socialist Republic (CSSR). Above all, a recognition that market relationships among independent enterprises are essential at the present stage of development of industrial societies gave rise at that time to my criticism of the Soviet economic system (which was also forced upon the CSSR) and led me to work toward a fundamental reform of that system. I developed the conception of market relationships among collective enterprises within an overall macro-economic skeleton-planning and state regulation of the market which, of course, presupposed the abolition of centralized, regimented planning and state-bureaucratic management of the economy. At the time, I also saw the advantages of private entrepreneurial initiative but wanted to see it confined to the sector of small-scale businesses, trades, and handicrafts, as well as small-scale services. After the extremely negative experiences of the Soviet system of planning, I was concerned with reconstructing a functional and effective economic order, but without returning to a capitalist economic system.

As is well known, despite enthusiastic support for these reformist goals by all segments of the population, they were suppressed by means of the military intervention of August 1968 and the return of restorative political forces in the CSSR. The great experiment, which was to demonstrate the possibility of economic development not only without capitalist contradictions, but also without state monopolism and bureaucratic domination, was strangled at the moment of its birth. For my own part, there was no other alternative than to leave the country in order at least to preserve and develop further the theory underpinning this practical attempt. In the months and years of its practical activity, the Czechoslovak Reform Commission prepared a host of concrete proposals and materials in order to realize the many necessary changes and modifications of the economy. We did not have time to write a theoretical work which would explain and justify the new model in all its functional interdependencies. Even the comprehensive reform proposal that was adopted politically had, of necessity, to appear in the form of a concrete economic-political program and a catalogue of measures, which however lacked any profound theory. Thus, although our reform proposals were indeed the result of years of intensive analysis, theoretical considerations, discusssions, and ideal standardizations, they were not theoretically formulated in all their complexity. We were simply overwhelmed, in terms of the availability of time, by the practical requirements of reform.

My subsequent teaching post at the St. Gallen Graduate School of Economics, Law, Business and Public Administration enabled me to devote myself to theoretical work once again, and I have concentrated and placed a high priority on theoretical economics. A renewed concern with the problems of Western economic practice and theory strengthened a conception I had already developed, which saw the capitalist market-economic system as less and less adequately meeting the needs of future societal and human development. But, the greatest danger to humanity lay in replacing this capitalist system with the Communist system of planning. It became increasingly clear to me that a third, non-capitalist, non-communist way was needed for the economies of the industrially developed countries, and that the basic principles of the Czechoslovak reform conceptions offered the right starting point. So I had to lay out my renewed theoretical work more broadly than before. In order to do this, I needed to buttress my work with an analysis of Western economic theory and practice, which required many years of patient work. Only then was I able to concentrate on further developing, deepening, and refining my original reform ideas. Above all, completely new insights from Western economies enabled me to modify my ideas fundamentally in several areas so as better to adapt them to the needs of countries with differing economic systems.

It was possible, with the assistance of the Schweizerischer Nationalfond zur Foerderung der wissenschaftlichen Forschung, Bern, to finance a small research team which helped me especially in the analysis of Western reform experiment. I would like to thank the Nationalfond for this. I would also like to express my thanks here to the Swedish Arbetslivzentrum, Stockholm, which hastened the completion of this book through the provision of a leave semester. I have shortened the present English translation to half the length of the original German edition. The large (800-page) size of the German version put off many potential readers, since it required too much of an investment of time on the part of the reader. It also turned out that the mathematical mode of expression used in economic theory, which I used to some extent in my German edition, caused great difficulties for those not trained in economics. Since I wanted very much to address an audience consisting not only of economists and specialists, I have, in making abridgments for the

English edition, effectively eliminated all mathematical formulas and, to some extent, made the verbal explanations more understandable. By doing this, I hope to have made this edition, more than the German edition, accessible to more people who are politically interested and who feel a shared responsibility for the further development of society.

During the past year, I have worked on an analysis of the economic crisis of the 1970s as manifested in the particular case of the Federal Republic of Germany. I was interested in an empirical demonstration of my assertion that the processes of distribution of the national income in the capitalist economic system come continually into conflict with the development of productivity, and that severe economic crises result from this. This analysis reconfirmed the soundness of my ideas about economic distribution planning aimed at resolving crises; their significance and the preconditions for them are discussed in this book.

If this book helps to prevent other nations from ever having to go through the difficult experiences which befell my people; if systems of bureaucratic domination are prevented from emerging and those in existence are dismantled as soon as possible, then this book will have served its purpose. Only when as many people as possible try to avoid sticking their heads in the sand when confronted by threatening developmental tendencies can they also become free creators of their future.

INTRODUCTION

Environmental pollution has reached threatening proportions. In many areas the forests are gradually dying out, the seas and oceans are becoming polluted, the air in the cities is full of carbon dioxide, foods are saturated with poisons, more and more varieties of plants and animals are being destroyed. These and similarly alarming reports reach us daily. Scientific studies are accumulating information about the devastating consequences of an uncontrolled explosion of industry, which conjure up visions of a planet approaching destruction. A growing number of people, particularly young people, are taking these warnings very seriously, and, seeing their future threatened, are searching for ways to alter the course of events.

Efforts are being made in many places, through citizen initiatives and protests, to bring pressure to bear on politicians, bureaucracies and the economy; and in some countries environmentally-oriented green parties have already been formed. But this struggle to contain the kind of economic growth that is hazardous to man and nature appears futile in light of rising unemployment in all Western industrial countries and the fear that many people have of losing their jobs. The microelectronic revolution is driving an increasing number of people out of production and is threatening their livelihood. In an economic system where technological advance is not able to make allowances for the threat it poses to society, the immediate insecurity and existential fear of many people makes them blind and deaf to the perversion of the environment.

An apparently intractable contradiction emerges here, especially in light of the fact that the Marxist attempt at solving the economic problems of capitalism can be regarded as a failure. Although the socialist countries have eliminated unemployment, this has been only at the expense of very low worker productivity, ludicrously high-production costs, and a great deal of superfluous, useless production which squanders labor and material without creating any use-value. The losses in efficiency caused by the completely bureaucratized Communist economy are immense. As a result, many of the people's basic needs are not satisfied. Their standard of living lags far behind that of the workers in industrialized capitalist countries and their economic dissatisfaction can only be held in check with the help of an enormous machinery of repression.

However, the pressures generated by this dissatisfaction do force the Communist rulers to expand production constantly and extensively, irrespective of the costs, in order to show an annual growth in production. Furthermore, the growing arsenals behind which the holders of power believe themselves to be more secure can only be produced at scandalously high expense. But, in the final analysis, these military endeavors have to be realized by sacrificing the satisfaction of the people's needs, since inefficient production makes it impossible simultaneously to ensure both military strength and a higher standard of living. The politically motivated expansion of production thus cannot afford to take account of the consequences to the environment, and consequently the pollution of nature is comparatively more severe than in the Western industrial countries.

It is therefore all too understandable that the majority of working people in the West find the Communist trade-off for full employment to be too high. This suggests the basic dilemma of our times. If under Communism the elimination of the market-controlled private development of production can only result in economic losses, supply shortages reminiscent of wartime, abandonment of a broad satisfaction of needs, and a lack of popular political participation, then the majority of workers will consider it more advisable to come to terms with the socially undesirable consequences of this capitalist economy than to struggle to transform it into Communism. But this would seem to suggest that there is no way out of the anti-nature obsession with production of the economy. As soon as people's interest in protecting the environment by cutting back on production begins to conflict with their interest in private profit or in preserving jobs and increasing their real income, their interest in ecology will take second place. The development of production, whose driving force is a socially-uncontrolled private decision-making system, cannot be overcome by political campaigns and citizens' initiatives.

But there is a feasible way out of this basic dilemma. If it were possible to maintain a demand-oriented development of production, in which the factors of production were utilized to optimal advantage and innovatively developed, that is, to preserve the advantages of private, market-oriented production while overcoming its socially uncontrolled, short-sighted, and ruthless course, then people's fears of losing their jobs and livelihood would be eliminated. At the same time, people's interest in their environment would increase and would no longer be repressed by considerations of work and income. A democratically determined development of the relationships between private consumption, satisfaction of public needs, improvement of the environment, equilibrium maintenance, and full employment in production, could be secured by a regulated, planned distribution of the national income which, however, would not stifle the market incentives of production.

Economically, one can conceive of a planned regulation of the division of national income so that private and public needs-satisfaction, improvement of the environment, and the full employment, secured by investments would develop in a balanced manner. Such a system of regulation would not require replacement of the market mechanism by the bureaucratic planning of production. The market demand for differing macro-goods groups (goods for private consumption, for the meeting of public needs, for institutions to protect the environment, and for capital goods) would no longer depend upon income divisions determined by the distribution struggle between business, unions, and the state, a struggle which is blind to the needs both of society and of the future. Rather, it would depend upon a regulated income distribution, established by democratic consensus, that would respect the need for economic equilibrium. This regulated development of demand would not stifle the market incentives of enterprises and their sole responsibility for a maximally effective development of production. It does, however, presuppose overcoming the struggle over distribution between entrepreneurs who are exclusively interested in profits, and unions which are exclusively interested in wages.

The antagonism between wage and profit income constitutes the basis of the social struggle over distribution, and leads to distributive consequences which make balanced economic development impossible and, in the final analysis, (though with short-term exceptions), full employment as well. The alienation of wage earners from capital and profit, as well as their growing pressures for increases in wages and consumption leads, in conditions of stagnating or falling capital productivity, to falling rates of profit, which makes it all the more difficult to increase investments in quantities sufficient to ensure efficiency and full employment. The reaction of predominantly profit-oriented entrepreneurs to this development is to introduce new labor-saving technologies that hold out the promise of increasing not only their rate of profit but also their share of the market. In several industrial countries this development is further aggravated by monetarist and supply-side economic policies. These have been adopted with the aim of raising the efficiency of productive capital, displacing inefficient enterprises, increasing rates of investment, and accelerating technical advancement. The result is sharply rising unemployment which is regarded, even by many economists and politicians, as an inevitable precondition of technical advancement, structural change, and increases of efficiency in production. It is only too obvious that under these circumstances environmental considerations will be pushed into the background.

The image of man underlying this policy proceeds from the assumption that wage earners' interest in job security and increasing their wages will prevent a rise in the efficiency of production through technical advancement and the flexible restructuring of corresponding needs. According to this view, only under the threat of unemployment and with state intervention in the process of income distribution to favor profits, is it possible to ensure the required development of investment and rise in efficiency. The one-sided interest of the wage recipient is assumed to be unalterable, and hence economic compulsion and pressures are believed to be necessary to counter this interest. For the same reason, a socially regulated distribution of income favoring a balanced, highly efficient economic development guaranteeing full employment is held to be pure utopia.

These economic notions cannot be overcome with arguments grounded in social ethics, since people's one-sided interests in wages and job security, like their alienation from capital and profit, are a reality. Neither can these interests be eliminated through moral-political influences. However, it would not be considered utopian to impute capital and profit interests to the wage earners once they have a real share in the ownership of the capital of their enterprises. By means of capital- and profit-sharing, as well as worker codetermination, they will acquire an interest in the effective development of production and investment, as all experiments with enterprises of this kind demonstrate. Only this kind of development of interests can create the crucial preconditions for overcoming the social antagonism of wage and profit interests and the struggle for income distribution.

On the basis of the capital, profit, and investment interests of the employees of all enterprises, it would actually be possible to realize an economically rational distribution of the national income; and together with these democratically determined goals, economic and social development could be achieved under conditions of macro-economic equilibrium and full employment. In the process, neither the activities of private enterprise nor the indispensable market mechanism would be eliminated. On the contrary, the market mechanism should then work much better than it does in contemporary capitalism. One of the most important aims of the democratically regulated development of the economy would be the protection and improvement of environmental conditions, which would no longer threaten people's employment interests.

The humanization of working conditions within enterprises, as well as the development of the entire economy along these lines, can be accomplished. The ensuing chapters are devoted to a more concrete description and substantiation of a more suitable economic system.

CONTENTS

FOR A HUMANE
ECONOMIC DEMOCRACY

1

NEEDS AND INTERESTS

CLASSIFICATION OF NEEDS

The satisfaction of most human needs is <u>economically limited</u>. This means that needs-satisfaction depends upon presently available and past accumulated labor (capitalized in the means of production), as well as upon prevailing relationships of distribution and exchange. Apart from this, however, there also exists a broad range of needs that are <u>not economically limited</u>. Therefore, needs should be divided first of all, into two broad categories: those which are <u>economically limited</u>, and those which are <u>not economically limited</u>.

This basic classification of needs cannot be equated with the distinction between material and non-material needs, since the satisfaction of many non-material needs is today still economically limited. The development of individual as well as social services and activities with which certain needs can be satisfied--for example, educational needs, artistic needs, and security needs, and the like--not only requires the labor associated with services, but also buildings, furnishings, tools, consumer goods, etc. for the people employed in them. Therefore, the needs which these activities can satisfy, must also be included among the economically limited needs.

The significance of this classification is not only related to its economic aspects, but must also be accepted by individuals. To be sure, people as individuals may harbor the most diverse wishes and dreams, and their latent needs will always precede their effective, operative needs. However, as soon as they express or become aware of needs that they want satisfied immediately, (whether as individuals or as communities, states, etc.), these will be needs which they can satisfy either immediately or in the foreseeable future, given the exigencies of their economic situation (employment/income situations), and/or there will be a development of needs the fulfillment of which is not economically limited. Before we further examine this development of needs, we will present a more broadly conceived classification of needs in order that we might better understand

the   distinction   between   economically   limited   and
non-economically limited needs.

Needs Classification

Primarily economically limited needs

Individual material needs	(food, clothing, shelter, furnishings, heating, lighting, transportation, money, means of production, places of production, etc.)
Reserve and health needs	(provision for old age, sickness, unemployment, care of children, securing of leisure time, medical services, care of the sick, etc.)
security needs	(community defense, protection of property, administration of justice, protection from crime, employment and income, security, securing peace, etc.)
needs for spiritual development and activity	(information, knowledge, education, faith, religion, art, entrepreneurial activity, etc.)
needs for social services	(community administration, neighborhood organization, city planning, water supply, sewerage, urban sanitation, environmental protection, public transportation, etc.)
needs for diversified physical activity	(creative, diversified work, arts and crafts, games, competition, wrestling, sports, tourism, etc.)
needs for environmental protection	(reduction of noise, air and water pollution, maintaining the safety and soundness of the soil, food, plants and animals, preserving the variety of species, biotopes, etc.

Primarily non economically limited needs

needs for physical- psychological satisfaction	(sexual needs, needs for the development of imagination, for meditation, for the exercise of power, etc.)
social needs	(love, friendship, attention, group activities, communication, community, association, common weal, etc.)

needs for rest	(sleep, recreation, relaxation, release from work up to and from a certain age, etc.)
needs for self-affirmation	(respect, recognition, praise, standing, admiration, prestige, usefulness for society, self-development, etc.)
need for social activity and a share in decision-making	(right to vote, initiative, responsibility, opportunities for public criticism and to effect change, cooperation and codetermination, self-government, etc.)

Since the categories have necessarily been simplified, they can capture only similar essential traits, while some overlap cannot be avoided. If this list manages to highlight important differences in interrelationships and developmental tendencies, then it can contribute toward a deeper understanding of the phenomena concerned. Of course, phenomena such as human needs can only be construed as phenomena which, although widespread, are not present in every individual nor in every group.

Here, it is not so much a matter of categorizing and classifying needs per se, since this process can obviously be carried out from the most diverse points of view. What does seem important to us is to distinguish between the two above mentioned groups: economically limited and non-economically limited needs. The classification employed here attempts to emphasize more strongly the extent of economically limited needs to counter other more oversimplified conceptions. At the same time, we will describe somewhat more concretely what is meant by non-economically limited needs. This will pave the way for the conceptions of reform that will follow later. The economic domain has so far been restricted to the satisfaction of economically limited needs. As we will see later, this is no longer sufficient, even though the economy's main task will have to remain the satisfaction of economically limited needs.

The view that, just because he always sets his goals starting from himself, the individual has to behave egoistically, is a false one. The individual, as the recipient of all sensory impressions and the creator of all thoughts and conceptions, can do nothing else but proceed from himself, [1]

---

[1] ". . . individuals, since they can do nothing else, have

even though in doing so, he does not always direct needs-satisfaction exclusively to his own advantage. His capacity to make sacrifices for the good of those he loves, to suffer for them, and indeed, in extreme cases, even to give his own life, is a reality. His social needs are thus not primarily egoistic needs, even though their point of departure always remains the individual, and even though the relationships between different people will display differing degrees of altruism.

Naturally, the individual also satisfies, for example, his sexual needs, his needs for recognition and for praise from those he loves, his friends or his community. In this sense, many needs are bound up with each other in a contradictory manner, and every categorization and grouping is an artificial division of what in reality constitutes an indivisible totality. The group of social needs expresses the concrete existence of more or less intense, altruistic needs, that is, the complicated and contradictory satisfaction obtained when one can give joy and satisfaction to other people even at the cost of one's own privation and suffering.

We have here categorized needs which all people have to a greater or lesser extent. Even though the concrete manifestations, structures, and intensities of these needs are different for each individual, it can be said that these groups of needs are manifest in most individuals. Moreover, there are needs which, although widespread, cannot simply be considered universal needs, and only more profound psychological research can determine whether or not they are universally valid. Among these are, for example, the need to exercise power, to dominate other people, to oppress, to exploit, etc.

It is now more apparent that the satisfaction of the needs contained in the first seven groups depends first and foremost on the economic conditions of the individuals and societies concerned, and therefore can only be realized to the general extent to which they can be secured for a certain period of time with the help both of all available labor in the broadest sense of the word and all available natural resources and energy sources. At all levels of human development and in all social systems, the great majority of people have always had to expend a relatively large amount of working time in order to produce, using the forces of nature, the goods and services that satisfied their needs, needs which are constantly developing in quantity, quality, and structure. The satisfaction of these needs is not only

proceeded from themselves. . . . K. Marx, Die deutsche Ideologie, Werke, vol. 3, p. 228.

the result of, but also at the same time a new impetus for the development of human work activity. Economically and socially conditioned differentials in the development of needs within different societies leads to differing ways of ordering the development of needs.

To understand better how this ordering takes place, we must distinguish between latent needs, which manifest themselves as pure desires, wishes, and longings, and effective needs, which call forth immediate activity and effort for their satisfaction. Effective, real needs develop in people, not in isolation, but always in conjunction with an estimation of which activities, how much effort, work, trouble, and time will be required for their satisfaction. In a market economy, an estimation of the income needed for the satisfaction of economically limited needs will also emerge immediately. This is of course--and economists know this well--an estimation of utility on the one hand, and required performance, labor, and expenditure on the other.

This internal contradiction within every person can hardly be overlooked, even by psychologists, whether it occurs in a primitive natural economy where the individual satisfies his needs directly with his own labor, or in a market economy, where he must make some contribution in order to obtain economic use-value (needs-satisfaction) from others. Special note should be made of this point, since purely psychological explanations of needs, transformations of needs, gradations of needs, etc., consistently tend to regard all these as independent of economic developments, or not to see them as dependent on economics. Such explanations do not adequately distinguish between those needs that are economically limited and those that are not, between the generalized needs of an average person and the basically different needs of members of unequal social strata. They have by no means sufficiently worked out the differences between needs that can be satisfied because they are secured in terms of income or free time, and needs that arise as desires, wishes, or longings, which may be politically articulated, but cannot for instance be satisfied due to the individual's economic position; these needs do not therefore trigger any appropriate activity and thus do not become manifest as real, effective needs.

The fact that we abstract from the contradictory character of human beings' evaluation of their needs-satisfaction, brings us no closer to a deeper understanding of them. A psychologically more profound explanation of what, for example, the concept of utility means to economists can provide us with a better understanding. Psychology has developed various theories which attempt to explain the essence of these needs. We cannot devote sufficient attention here to judging whether homeostatic

theory, stimulus-response theory, cognitive theory or any
other theory[2] furnishes the most correct explanation of
needs. From economic observations and experiences and
above all from experiences with the socialist system--which
truly must be regarded as a phenomenal social experiment
as yet insufficiently exploited by the various scholarly dis-
ciplines--a theory has developed which most nearly resem-
bles psychological stimulus-response theory, but which emphasizes more strongly the social conditioning of the
development of needs.

The socialist experience shows that one must not underestimate the relative independence (relative autonomy
vis-a-vis economic conditions) of the development of needs
in people. Although recognition of this relative independence must not lead back to an exaggerated negation of the
power of economic conditions to condition needs, the socialist experience demonstrates convincingly that qualitatively
as well as quantitatively, human needs evolve under the influence of the most diverse factors external to the economic
system.

Yet for all that, it is not only latent needs that are
involved here, but also their transformation into new needs,
some of which are so strong that they lead the people in
droves to further activities and pursuits, that--in addition
to official work, which is insufficient to meet their needs--
satisfy these needs. These activities include moonlighting,
black-market trade, prohibited private small-scale production, large-scale theft from state enterprises and collective
farms, trade in currency, and stepping up of consignments
from Western countries. All these activities are generally
thriving and to some extent even increasing, and they demonstrate how relatively independently developed needs are
satisfied.[3]

This phenomenon will be dealt with later in greater detail. A deeper analysis of it leads, however, to the more
general conclusion that people's needs always arise in the
form of objectively evoked, subjectively colored conceptions
of objects which, when insufficiently available or totally ab-
sent, produce negative feelings of uneasiness and tension.[4]

---

[2] Cf. H. Thomae, ed., Allgemeine Psychologie, Handbuch
der Psychologie, vol. 11, Motivationen (Goettingen,
1965), p. 19ff. Cf. also O. Neuberger, Theorien der
Arbeitszufriedenheit (Stuttgart/Berlin, 1974), p. 23ff.

[3] See Manifest der demokratischen Kommunisten, in Der
Spiegel 1 (1978), p. 19ff, and 2 (1978), p. 26ff.

[4] B. Dietrich, and H. Walter, Grundbegriffe der psycholo-

According to stimulus-response theory in psychology, feelings of uneasiness can develop either from too intense stimulation, caused by deprivation of the most diverse objects (things, persons, occupations impressions, etc.), or from insufficient stimulation, caused by satiation, unvaried and monotonous needs-satisfaction, or boredom. Man strives for an optimal level of stimulation,[5] both following decreases of overly intense stimulation through overcoming deprivations, and following enhanced stimulation through the development of new needs and their satisfaction. As one approaches an optimal level of stimulation either as a result of a lowering of stimulation, or of various increases in stimulation, positive feelings of pleasure, of satisfaction are produced. Certain kinds of needs-satisfaction and changes in the level of stimulation evoke desires of differing degrees of intensity. Man has striven and will always strive for comfort, satisfaction, relief of boredom, and increased pleasure.[6]

Whether needs-satisfaction lowers or raises stimulation, its objects are always socially conditioned, transmitted, and shaped. Object-related needs are determined not only by socially conditioned production, but also by customs, traditions, moral conceptions, and ideologies prevailing in society, in short by thoughts and emotions emanating from the environment. Therefore, these needs are always bound up with the socially conditioned value judgments of the individual. People's value judgments express their biologically-based needs, as well as being the psychical results of the social influences which modify and further develop their needs. Those objects which man needs appear valuable to him, but his needs are in turn influenced by values that are decisively influenced and determined by the society in which he lives. Needs evoke conceptions of value; however, new socially-created conceptions of value will always give rise to new needs. Although social influences do encompass economic influences, the former are nevertheless broader and more complex, in that, for example, education, religion, moral principles, politics, the effects of the mass media, etc., play an essential role in them.

---

gischen Fachsprache (Munich, 1972), p. 43.

[5] Cf. D. E. Berlyne, Conflict, Arousal and Curiosity (New York, 1960), p. 200ff.

[6] T. Scitovsky, Psychologie des Wohlstands (Frankfurt/M, 1977), p. 71.

Needs can therefore never be understood as a mere reflection of the economy. The immediate as well as the larger social environment, membership in certain groups, the psychosis of the time, all affect people's value judgments and hence the development of their needs. It also happens that human dissatisfaction is produced when one cannot use, enjoy, or own a qualitatively special object (thing, person, relationship, activity, environment, impression) which many other people or people elsewhere (in other countries) have come to take for granted. If the non-satisfaction of certain needs is subjectively felt very intensely, negative feelings of dissatisfaction can transform themselves, in a complex manner, into fear, pain, torment, tension, etc.

The lack of need-objects is always bound up with more or less concrete desires for these objects, or sometimes with indeterminate and vague conceptions of such objects (need simply for variety, for more or better things, etc.). Such desires for concrete objects, as well as objects less concretely understood, can be termed latent needs. Among these, those which seem capable of being satisfied in the foreseeable future by means of various activities (or better, by means of various expenditures) will be transformed into effective needs. The satisfaction of the need thus results in the alleviation of the negative feeling, its metamorphosis into a positive feeling, a feeling of satisfaction, of well-being, even of pleasure.

As needs develop further, however, they are not only numerous, varied, and persistent in their qualitative and concrete nature, but they also evoke negative feelings of varying intensity. Their satisfaction then results in positive feelings of varying intensity. These differences alone--differences in the emotional intensity of all needs and needs-satisfaction--are an important factor in the emergence of hierarchies of needs. As we will see later on, these differences also play a role in the transformation of efforts aimed at the satisfaction of certain needs into interests. Without a doubt, under conditions of physiological hunger, we will be disposed to hasten to include the need for nourishment (along with a number of other fundamental needs) among the basic needs. However, when a need for certain delicacies, (for example, for gourmet treats) is at stake, certain reservations will be rightly expressed, since here once again we are faced with the difference between individual and social hierarchies of needs. For certain individuals (for example, gourmets), the preparation and consumption of delicacies becomes their greatest need, and indeed becomes their strongest interest. Accordingly, this individual or specific hierarchy of needs cannot be the expression of an objective social hierarchy of needs even though it exists objectively.

But is there then anything at all like a social hierarchy of needs, if the needs-hierarchies of individuals will always be different? Certainly there will be social groups whose hierarchies of needs--though not identical in detail--are very similar in their basic ordering of values. This means that among those belonging to the same group, different needs will display roughly the same differences of intensity. This difference in intensity with which both needs and needs-satisfaction are experienced, as well as the differences bound up with this as needs recur after having been satisfied and the variable decreases in their intensity, have long been recognized by economists, even prior to the theory of marginal utility. Yet this again brings us to a realization that the hierarchical ordering of needs cannot be explained in and by the needs themselves, that is, solely in terms of the differing intensity of feeling which they, and the satisfaction of them evoke; rather, the differing expenditures which the satisfaction of needs exacts from people's human needs plays an equally decisive role.

This concept of expenditure will not be further analyzed at this point since it will be discussed further later on and in a different context. For the time being, it is sufficient to state that the concept of expenditure in a market economy, given the presence of economically limited needs, always appears directly as incomes, and these incomes (however they may have been generated) contrast with the price of goods. However, these incomes are highly differentiated, and economically limited needs can, for the most part (with the exception of social services which are largely state financed), be satisfied only within the limits of this income. There will thus be a different ordering, not only of the parameters of the overall needs-satisfaction of the different income groups, but also of their hierarchical arrangement (the structure of demand for them).

It is precisely when we make a distinction between economically limited and non-economically limited needs, that it becomes apparent that all people, irrespective of their income, harbor a host of non-economically limited needs. Indeed, they are often even more strongly manifest among precisely the low-income earners as compensation, as it were, for unattainable economically limited needs. It would also be difficult to understand why certain needs would not begin to emerge, on a large scale, at very low levels of economically limited needs-satisfaction. Examples of such needs would be social needs, (needs for friendship, love, community, etc.); or needs for self-affirmation (recognition, praise, respect, etc.); or needs for tranquility. One might further mention a number of needs that are only slightly economically limited, such as those for religious activities, acquisition of information, and the like. This, in fact, corresponds to actual historical developments.

Even at the lowest levels of meeting individual material needs, reserve needs develop, as do needs for faith, for art, for play, social needs, needs for tranquility, for self-affirmation, for public activity, and for codetermination. Only the growing alienation of man in advanced societies, particularly in the capitalist and socialist era, has retarded, or made quite impossible, the development of different kinds of needs, especially needs for social activity and a share in decision-making, on the part of a large part of the population.

Different kinds of needs, and economically non-limited, thus arise simultaneously at different levels of material living standards. Diverse, slightly economically limited or non-economically limited needs develop at low levels of material development, or at least relatively no less so than at the higher levels. However, we might distinguish and classify needs, a hierarchical ordering within the category of economically limited needs is far more apparent than the distinction between them and non-economically limited needs. The economically limited needs,--and among them, individual material needs--represent a far broader and qualitatively constantly changing spectrum of needs than the group of so-called basic physiological needs. Therefore, we can outline a hierarchy of economically limited needs, both for particular individuals (assuming that we select a representative sampling of all income groups and that we question them properly), and the further development of society; and in the process we can distinguish between individual material interests and the broader group of economically limited needs.

The reason lies in the fact that the development of effective needs depends, above all, upon the development of income, which, when it grows in real terms, always increases the growth of needs in the direction of relatively expensive objects, and hence toward more economically limited needs. If this economic constraint did not exist, a great many people would very quickly extend their needs to encompass goods and services which today must be considered luxury items; they would not be content for long with the consumption of basic goods. There is absolutely no reason why only certain segments of the population, rather than all families, should want the use of a modern apartment or even a comfortably furnished house. We are not at all concerned, in the present context, with the question of whether this is economically possible and whether some day architecture and city planning will not take completely new directions. Our concern is only to show clearly where the true bases of the current structure of needs are to be found, to establish what their predominant dimensions are, and to ensure that there be no illusions about the develop-

ment of needs <u>as</u> <u>such</u>. Irrespective of which goods we use
as examples, we will always find that, starting from the
lowest standard of living--the subsistence level, where, for
example, the need for food (in whatever form) is really a
fundamental need--within a social group, a hierarchy of individual needs for material consumption, reserve health, security, etc., will take shape. This hierarchy can no longer
be explained in terms of the needs themselves, but rather
primarily in terms of the fact that they are economically
limited.

Not only the reality of capitalist society, but also that
of socialist society shows that no amount of education, public moral suasion, planning of consumption, etc., can prevent the emergence of effective needs on the part of those
segments of the population among whom such <u>effective</u> needs
were not present at a particular time solely because they
were economically limited. As soon as certain needs are
present in latent form, they will always become effective
needs the moment a rise in income or the overcoming of
various other limitations on needs (for example, too little
free time, etc.) allows it. This is not to say that all individuals would develop the same needs, and certainly not
that the present hierarchy of needs could not develop much
differently under different social conditions. It is only that
in presently existing social systems the development of
needs is primarily economically limited, and that any suggestions that the limits of growth of material needs have
been reached, even in the wealthiest countries, are not
correct.

If for instance the real income of below-average income
groups could rise more rapidly, their consumption would
accordingly rise more rapidly. The structure of this consumption would naturally also change rapidly. The most
rapid increase would of course occur in the consumption of
those goods whose use is today increasingly economically
limited.

Obviously, at the highest level of needs-satisfaction
(among the highest income earners) relative satiation begins
to appear not only of individual material needs, but also of
reserve, security, and other economically limited needs,
precisely because there is little which those belonging to
these levels cannot economically afford. Such material satiation, or even oversatiation, can actually pave the way toward non-economically limited needs and raise the significance of some of these. But even among high income
groups, material satiation is only <u>relative</u>. As soon as relatively higher economic demands emerge, for example, in
the train of new goods or services, the interests of many of
those who appeared satiated will again move in this direction.

Just as in the past, therefore, material needs will change qualitatively and grow quantitatively in the foreseeable future. The intensity of the individual needs will change, not so much due to the satiation of other needs or groups of needs, as to the gradual transformation of the conditions of human life resulting from social changes. Simplified schemata of a hierarchy of needs cannot precisely capture a reality undergoing a process of transformation.

When the intensity of different needs changes as a result of social changes, this does not necessarily indicate satisfaction of another group of needs. But it often occurs as a result of changed productive and economic conditions, different forms of settlement, the emergence of cities, states, and religious institutions--in other words, on the basis of changed economic and social conditions. As we reflect on history, we are struck not by a substitution of one group of needs for another, but by the rather complementary, reciprocal relationship among them, and by the fact that, in the process, intensity naturally varies. Within the individual groups, needs are constantly shifting in their relative positions so that some attain a level of relative satisfaction and others therefore grow more rapidly. Economics has also long been aware of the phenomenon of differing elasticity of demand for goods. In a relatively saturated market, sales of certain goods cease to be affected by lower prices, or may even decline. In other markets, the demand for goods can increase dramatically despite more or less fixed prices. Similar movements also occur, however, within the other groups of non-economically limited needs.

Not only can we draw conclusions about the behavior of individuals (for example, about their behavior in buying goods, as described by the theory of marginal utility) from the fact that needs of differing intensity exist, and that their degree of intensity changes with degree of needs-satisfaction but we can also draw important socio-economic and socio-political conclusions as well. In different social systems, differing systems of need satisfaction are also built up. Certain needs or groups of needs are more prevalent, others are not; some are more fully and better satisfied, others more poorly and less adequately.

If, as is the case nowadays, different social systems exist contiguously in time, their respective needs-development will no longer occur as the isolated product of one or the other system, but instead, they will influence each other reciprocally. They transcend, so to speak, all state boundaries, including the boundaries of countries with different systems or that may even be hostile toward each other. Needs have become palpably internationalized, and the mass media, intensive communications, trade relations, tourism, and cultural exchange have been among the prime causes. If certain needs are then less adequately satisfied in one system than in the other, this will in time evoke much stronger negative reactions and a much stronger demand for the fulfillment of the needs implanted from the other system than would have been the case in the absence of a view across the frontier.

In the socialist system of Soviet bloc states, the satisfaction of individual material needs and of societal decision-making needs (right to vote, opportunities for public criticism and change, codetermination, etc.) are retarded in comparison with the West. But in the Western capitalist system it is, above all, needs for guaranteed income and employment, for better medical and social insurance, for more comprehensive child care, or, more generally, for security and for a stronger sense of community, that are thought to be inadequately fulfilled.

The intensity of such desires in East and West is growing as an awareness spreads among the people that the satisfaction of certain needs is better and more possible in the other system. Vehement demands for the greater satisfaction of these needs very often lead to absurd attempts to demand greater satisfaction of the new needs without altering the manner in which the existing needs are satisfied, thereby overloading the objective capabilities of the system.

This fact leads us to the demand for realistic systemic reform.

If we were in a position to measure the intensity of needs or the strength of positive perceptions and feelings in the satisfaction of needs, then we would be able to determine reliably what part certain needs should play in the totality of needs-satisfaction. The physical and mental effort which people have to exert altogether or on average in order to satisfy their needs, is also hard to measure. At present, and certainly under the conditions of a new system, the present (and possibly the past) as well as the desired future proportion, of the broad groups of needs and the conditions for their satisfaction must be ascertained and measured. They would also have to be--as will be described below in greater detail--secured in terms of incomes policy.

Five important conclusions can be drawn from what has been said:

1. In terms of the national economy, further increases in the development of individual material needs are to be expected, since all attempts to limit this development of consumption must fail, given the still sharp social differentials within industrial societies. To be sure, the rate of this increase could develop differently, and would have to be regulated differently in different countries.

2. The falling propensity to consume and rising tendency to save as noted in Keynes's economic theo-
   ry--an essential component of the explanation of
   crises--[7] cannot be attributed to a slackening
   growth of needs on the part of a large part of the
   population. This tendency has other causes (to be
   dealt with later on), which again are particularly
   bound up with the differing economic limitations on
   needs-satisfaction.

3. The accelerated growth of needs for security, spiritual satisfaction, community, communication, job
   satisfaction, social activity, codetermination, etc.,
   which can be observed today, must not be regarded as the manifestation of a prior satiation of individual material needs, nor is it concentrated only
   among the highest income groups. Indeed, it is
   relatively stronger among some social groups whose
   material consumption is lower. It is thus caused
   by social transformation, a point to which we will
   return later.

4. Human needs cannot be changed at the behest of
   rulers, power groups, or planning systems. Real
   needs, as they form under the influence of economic, political, social, and cultural developments,
   should thus be better perceived and acted upon.
   Facilitated by a broad democratization of the economic decision-making process, the rate of development and the financing of the changed needs can
   be systematically affected.

5. The development of needs is perceptibly growing
   into an international phenomenon even while it is
   crossing the boundaries of different systems. The
   more the people in one system become aware that
   certain needs are better and more completely fulfilled in the other system, the more intensive become their demands for the satisfaction of those
   needs which are not adequately satisfied in their
   own system. The systemic limits on the better satisfaction of needs will become increasingly obvious
   thus accelerating new movements for systemic reform.

---

[7] An outstanding overview of the different explanations of
crises is given by G. V. Haberler, Prosperity and Depression (Cambridge, Mass., 1937).

We will now turn our attention to several questions relating to the development of needs in contemporary capitalist systems, and to current theoretical reflections about them, in the light of the socialist experience.

THE DEVELOPMENT OF NEEDS IN THE CAPITALIST SYSTEM

In general, the satisfaction of needs is regarded as the self-evident aim of all economic activity, and the quest for the most effective means of realizating these aims constitutes one of the main tasks of the economic sciences. Recently, however, the question has arisen as to whether needs-satisfaction might not be better accomplished in an economic system organized differently than in current systems. Related to this, are the questions as to whether maximization of needs-satisfaction should be sought at all, whether the reasonable satisfaction of needs can be equated with maximum consumption, and whether the latter in any case is desirable.[8]

The topicality of this problem, which is widespread in the West, arises from an observation of negative developmental tendencies in both systems, and it is not surprising that in a certain sense the issue raises doubts about the whole idea of meeting needs. Under capitalism the principle of profit maximization leads to the one-sided, exaggerated development of individual needs. The imposition of producer interests (that is, for the great majority of goods, by highly concentrated, oligopolistic, and monopolistic concerns) clearly leads to attempts to influence consumers

---

[8] Cf. G. Bodenstein and H. Leuer, eds., Geplanter Verschleiss in der Marktwirtschaft (Zuerich/Frankfurt, 1977); W. Michalski et al., eds., Industriegesellschaft im Wandel, Probleme, Loesungsmoeglichkeiten, Perspektiven (Hamburg, 1977). See also W. Ophuls, Ecology and the Politics of Scarcity: Prologue to a Political Theory of the Steady State (San Francisco, 1977); E. Hoedl, Wirtschaftswachstum und Umweltpolitik: Umweltpolitik als Begrenzung oder Voraussetzung fuer wirtschaftliches Wachstum (Goettingen, 1975). Cf. A. Sauvy, Zero Growth? (Oxford, 1975). Cf. E. Fromm, Haben oder Sein (Stuttgart, 1976), p. 156. Cf. F. Hirsch, Die sozialen Grenzen des Wachstums. Eine oekonomische Analyse der Wachstumskrise (Hamburg: Reinbek, 1980). Cf. O. Herrera et al., eds., Grenzen des Elends (Frankfurt a.M., 1977).

through advertising and sales devices. In particular, the outcome of the manipulation involved here is that the large producers shape popular needs.[9] To be sure, a large number of scholarly works[10] have made the population aware of the fact that continued unchecked growth of production will cause a dangerous depletion of natural resources and perversion of the environment. But despite these insights, the population cannot exert any influence on the growth of production. Given the existing capitalist system, therefore, there can be no change in the manipulation of consumption. In an unchanged system, the pressure to consume, to which not only capitalist entrepreneurs are subject, but also the working people and unions (allegedly to ensure growth in employment) will increasingly come into conflict with the obverse development, namely the shrinking of natural and ecological conditions of production and life. Under the present system, only acute catastrophes can halt this development, which would have devastating consequences for millions of people. The measures that would have to be taken in such catastrophic situations, spontaneously and under pressure, would produce much greater losses than would a series of timely and planned sacrifices.

Manipulation by monopolies and oligopolies primarily affects the sphere of individual consumption. It overstimulates consumption at the expense of meeting social needs. Of necessity, however, a growing proportion of human needs cannot be met by individual incomes, but must be satisfied with certain social resources, which today primarily signifies state resources. In addition to growing needs for social security, these include in particular

---

[9] Cf. J. K. Galbraith, Gesellschaft im Ueberfluss (Munich/ Zurich, 1959), p. 171. et seq. Cf. V. Packard, The Hidden Persuaders (New York, 1957).

[10] See D. H. Meadows and D. L. Meadows, The Limits to Growth, A Report from the Club of Rome's Project on the Predicament of Mankind (New York, 1972); M. Mesarovic and E. Pestel, Menschheit am Wendepunkt. 2. Bericht an den Club of Rome zur Weltlage (Stuttgart, 1976); D. Gabor et al., Das Ende der Verschwendung, Zur materiellen Lage der Menschheit. Ein Tatsachenbericht an den Club of Rome (Stuttgart, 1976); H. Gruhl, Ein Planet wird gepluendert. Die Schreckensbilanz unserer Politik (Frankfurt, 1975); and H. C. Binswanger, W. Geissberger, and T. Ginsburg, eds., Der NAWU-Report: Wege aus der Wohlstandsfalle (Frankfurt a.M., 1978); H. C. Binswanger, H. Bonus, M. Timmerman, Wirtschaft und Umwelt (Stuttgart, 1981).

infrastructural needs, medical, social, and cultural needs, as well as needs for education, environmental protection, and the like, whose dimensions must increase along with the advance of individual consumption, and indeed, must increase faster in relation to it. Ensuring that these needs are met by means of taxes and similar kinds of state revenues and expenditures must be regarded as no more than a necessary evil under conditions of forced individual pressure to consume. The productive resources required to bring about overstimulated development of individual consumption are objectively lacking for a more rapid development toward the meeting of social needs. The redistribution of state finances is thus impeded by the partially manipulated development of individual consumption. The decision of the people, though not consciously made, concerning the relationship between individual and social needs-satisfaction in the context of inflation (to which, incidentally, it has contributed), will always lead spontaneously to a tendency toward the disproportionate satisfaction of individual needs.

However, the socially guaranteed development of consumption and life becomes more significant as industrial production and living standards rise. The introduction of more tranquil and healthier housing and living conditions, for example, requires completely new developments in city planning and transportation technology, increased hygienic measures, better sanitation, afforestation, water procurement and purification, and secure energy supplies. Only a small part of all this can be financed by individual incomes. Left entirely to the market, this development would lag increasingly behind the growing number of vital needs. But the free market cannot bring about the satisfaction of such needs as greater existential security, medical and social services, preventative health measures, complex, technically advanced methods of examination and treatment, the general expansion of education, development of cultural activities and broadening of interests.

The notion that many of these services can be produced and sold in the same way as goods is obviously unrealistic. If this were attempted, it would deepen discrepancies in the provision of medical, social, and cultural services among the different strata of society and impede the socially necessary furthering of qualitatively new conditions of life, as well as the reorganization of the growing amount of leisure time in the advanced industrial countries. Services in these areas of need, which the state or other social institutions provide free of charge or at greatly reduced prices, are more practical and less expensive than any kind of tied subsidies for socially weaker strata, which have to be controlled and bureaucratically administered.

This is not, however, to dispute justified criticism that the bureaucratic phenomenon is expanding to a dangerous degree in the state, economy, and society as a whole, as well as the need to curtail it. On the contrary, such objections must be strongly underlined. In all domains in which state service institutions can be replaced by market-based enterprises without severe social consequences, an attempt should be made to do so. In socially significant areas of social services, however, the bureaucratic phenomenon cannot be brought under control by expanding the market , and the appropriate course here ought to be seen as the thorough democratization of decision-making processes and controls in society.

The problem of the bureaucratization and uncontrollable explosion of costs in the state service sectors is also dealt with in detail in the NAWU Report.[11] We regard its position on the future development of social services, a position reached on the basis of an analysis of developmental tendencies, as more realistic. The need for social services that cannot be satisfied through purely market activities, will grow in the future. Nevertheless, ways of avoiding bureaucratic nationalizations should really be sought, while social services should be prevented from reverting to profit-oriented production for the market. Decentralization and the formation of small networks, as proposed by the NAWU Report, might be one feasible possibility.

Yet even decentralized increases in services carried out in small, overseeable and directly controllable domains (small networks, communes, consumer cooperatives, etc.) imply a redistribution of incomes generated in the primary sectors which, taking place purely spontaneously and unplanned, could only create greater disproportions and disruptions in circulation within an economy. If the macro-economic interrelationships between production, income distribution processes, and consumption (of goods as well as services) within the economy are ignored and their implementation left exclusively to the spontaneous initiative of market producers or decentralized communities, without these interrelations being respected and purposefully and democratically regulated, at least in their overall macro-economic dimensions, then it will be increasingly difficult to avoid faulty distribution, disruptions of circulation and reproduction, and undesirable and threatening developments in living conditions.

---

[11] Cf. Binswanger, Geissberger, Ginsburg, Der NAWU-Report, p. 242. et seq.

All these growing problems require fundamental solutions, and the confused procrastination with which they are
treated in the industrialized countries has led to mounting
popular dissatisfaction, frustration, citizens' initiatives,
radicalization, and partly violent resistance. It is becoming
more and more vividly apparent that the market mechanism,
increasingly distorted by monopolies, with its uncontrollable, one-sided demand for growth, its manipulation of individual needs, its existential insecurities and fears for the
future, and its failures to meet social needs, as well as
the disastrous ecological consequences of the unregulated
development of industry, are the principal causes of the
growing aversion to the market mechanism in general.
They reinforce not only Marxist anti-market theories, but
also give rise to non-Marxist ideas about the fundamental
reeducation of man within a new society, whose long-range
goal would be to overcome society's obsession with acquisition completely and create a readiness to give up all forms
of property in order to be whole. [12]

However understandable the reasons for their origin
may be, these theories are illusory. As partially applied
by Marxist regimes, they have already had severe consequences upon people. It is precisely in the light of the
experiences of Communist planning that there must be a
careful examination of precisely which lessons are to be
learned from the deficiencies of the capitalist market mechanism just described. What must be determined is whether
the market mechanism itself has to be eliminated, as Marxist
theory requires, whether the exaggerated development of
needs and people's interest in acquisition are to be overcome, or whether in the final analysis social control and
regulation of the growth of consumption and its basic orientation would be the better solution.

The Marxist conception, which does away with the
market and substitutes a social plan to determine the development of production and consumption, has been in practice
for decades in the Soviet bloc states. Planned decision-
making about the development of production and consumption will always be accomplished by a social organ about the
growth of highly aggregated production groups. Even if
we ignore the fact that in reality it is a bureaucratic planning apparatus that determines the dimensions of planning--
since the population in the East neither possesses the necessary information about possible alternatives, nor can it
influence the planning apparatus--this kind of planning for
the meeting of needs is always decisively characterized by
two factors: First of all, needs cannot be objectivized into

---

[12] See Fromm, Haben oder Sein, p. 167.

true and false,[13] reasonable and unreasonable alternatives.
Nor can they be differentiated into basic needs and secondary needs.[14] Arbitrary procedures do occur.   Second, it
is not possible to determine the right quantities of demand
for the production of each individual consumer good.
    Even if the bureaucratic character of planning could be
overcome, and if there existed democratic planning or, as
some socialist theories demand, planning by workers' councils,[15] there could still be no direct voting about the kinds
of goods that should be produced and those that should not
be produced because they were thought to be superfluous
or prompted by false needs. As long as quantitatively differentiated consumption is necessary--and this necessity will
be dealt with in detail below--no majority can decide whether certain concrete minority demands ought or ought not to
be recognized. Quantitative income differentials can be
democratically determined, as can their magnitude and gradations. What cannot be determined, however, is the con-
version of this income into actual consumption, and hence
the qualitative character of determining and meeting individual needs. If a planning body--even a democratically
elected one--were to decide that a certain kind of clothing,
housing, entertainment, etc. was reasonable or unreasonable, this would not only amount to a violation of individual
freedom of decision, but would also be an arbitrary decision
lacking objective criteria.
    There are, of course, scientifically ascertainable cri-
teria for evaluating the harmfulness to health or society of
certain consumer goods, and these might perhaps be extended to many other kinds of consumption. In fact, for
many such cases there already are limitations or prohib-
itions on production in the capitalist market economy.
Here, individual freedom of decision is rightly restricted in
the interests of the individual himself or of society. Nevertheless, this kind of social assessment and regulation of
individual freedom of decision cannot be carried over to the
development of needs in general, since wherever the emergence and satisfaction of a need is prevented contrary to
the potential of the economy, without a clear recognition of
the negative consequences to the individual or society, this

[13] See H. Marcuse, Der eindimensionale Mensch (Neuwied
    and Berlin, 1968), p. 25.

[14] See E. Mandel, Marxistische Wirtschaftstheorie (Frank-
    furt a.M., 1968), p. 704ff.

[15] See A. Carlo, Politische und oekonomische Struktur der
    UdSSR, 1917-1975 (Berlin, 1972), p. 84.

represents arbitrary bureaucratic violation of the individual by a social power-political organ, no matter whether it is of democratic or authoritarian origin.

The experiences of the Soviet bloc states demonstrate the weaknesses of such solutions. When the planned production of consumer goods and services does not adequately meet the needs of the people, with respect to quality, variety, and innovation, this contradiction cannot be done away with by education, moral suasion, and political propaganda. Human striving for needs-satisfaction, for possession, then becomes even greater than in the capitalist system. This manifests itself in an excessive admiration of Western consumption, in youth's imitation of Western styles of dress, in the chase after Western currency which can be used to buy Western goods in special stores, in the thriving black market, in increasing thefts of materials and embezzlement in state enterprises, in the growth in corruption, in the people's longing for especially scarce goods, such as cars, apartments, home furnishings, and cottages.

All this in fact confirms what Marx foresaw. Overcoming people's interests in material prosperity, in the acquisition of things, in the improvment of opportunities for consumption, is unthinkable under conditions of a relative scarcity of most consumer goods. The scarcity of such consumer goods is manifest in the fact that, even in the most well-to-do industrial countries, their usage must be limited and differentiated by means of the price structure. In this way great differences inevitably arise between individual social strata, precisely in the use and consumption of expensive goods. If this limitation did not exist, an unacceptably large percentage of consumer goods and services would not be available in quantities sufficient to satisfy all needs. Regardless of the system of distribution employed, these goods would end up going only to a select group of consumers. Yet as long as these great differences exist in the potential for the satisfaction of human needs, there will be a strong demand for the meeting of those needs which cannot yet be satisfied. Envy and jealousy, a desire for that of which one has been deprived, will thus remain.

Of course, under certain conditions, for example under the influence of certain ideological or religious ideas, groupings of people (albeit mainly young people not yet integrated into the economic system or excluded from it by unemployment) will emerge and establish new self-sufficient business and housing collectives. These young people will primarily form agricultural cooperatives where they can develop a completely reorganized style of work and production oriented toward the group and its needs.

This back to man and nature movement is a completely understandable reaction to the technical and anti-humane perversion of our time and to the existing systems. Not only does it appear as a new alternative to many young people, but it really is such an alternative. It is a concrete manifestation of the revolt against the old values and needs, and it actually replaces the old scale of values with a new one. However agreeable and worthy of support this movement may be, and however much we might hope that these and similar business and housing collectives will develop further, nevertheless, we cannot see it as a real alternative or even the beginnings of an alternative to the present system. The capacities of this economic form to provide sustenance are simply insufficient for the dense population of the industrial countries--even if the entire population were to reduce its material needs drastically, which is hardly a realistic idea.

As we have already suggested, contemporary economic and social systems are not immutable. Indeed, the present work seeks to indicate how they have to be changed. These changes cannot, however, be based either on unrealistic conceptions of production or on conceptions involving the reduction of people's needs. The feeding of mankind is today no longer possible without industrial production. This industrial production itself creates material needs, which no amount of education, ideology, or religion can drive out of people's minds. We must, however, meet only those new, non-economic needs and interests that grow spontaneously out of the given relationships, interests which are becoming increasingly widespread and which are causing people to search for new forms of cooperative work and social coexistence.

Our currency is not revolutionary wishful dreaming that would change the lives of people overnight and set them on a new course, but rather institutional changes in popular will-formation, goal-determination, and decision-making techniques in economy and state, with which the people's new and growing needs and life expectations could prevail, free from manipulation by established power elites. We will now examine further these needs and the preconditions under which they can be realized.

NEEDS AND WORK

Needs-satisfaction is, at the present stage of development, dependent upon human labour and the available means of production. For the time being, we will ignore the means of production and turn to the decisive productive force, human labour. Even in the most advanced industrial states, human labor still takes up a great deal of time. The working day is still long, and leisure time does not give most people much opportunity for self-development--it is barely sufficient for rest and the regeneration of the labor force for the next working day. Only given those long hours of work as well as the existing division of labor and intensity of work, can needs be satisfied on the scale to which people have become accustomed. Basically, they do not want to give up this needs-satisfaction; on the contrary, they are attempting to increase it.

For the bulk of the working population, work is strenuous, tiresome, monotonous--a lifelong burden which is performed in this form only because it is the basic requirement for earnings, for the standards of consumption and living they seek.[16] This is not to say that people are lazy and passive by nature, but rather that most would not do that work, day after day, as they are today obliged to do, if their livelihood could be assured in some other way. They would choose activities richer in variety, would attend to their hobbies, develop sporting, cultural, and entertainment activities valued and respected by society or social groups. They would strive for self-realization in line with their abilities. I assert this despite sociological surveys[17]

---

[16] See H. W. Sievert, Arbeit-und Berufseintellung junger Industriearbeiter, in Th. Scharman and E. Roth, eds., Vom Proletarier zum Industriebuerger (Bern/Stuttgart/Wien, 1976); E. Pieroth, Die 8 Stunden am Tag. Eine sozialkritische Studie (Muenchen, 1974); U. Bierkner et al., eds., Schichtarbeit. Schicht-und Nachtarbeiter-Report (Frankfurt, 1973) M. Osterland et al.,Materialien zur Lebens-und Arbeitssituation der Industriearbeiter in der BRD. Ein Forschungsbericht (Frankfurt, 1973); H. Kern and M. Schumann, Industriearbeit und Arbeiterbewusstsein. Eine empirische Untersuchung ueber den Einfluss der aktuellen technischen Entwicklung auf die industrielle Arbeit und das Arbeiterbewusstsein (Frankfurt a.M., 1970); and P. Mueler-Seitz, Industrielle Schichtarbeit in betriebswirtschaftlicher Sicht (Berlin, 1976); C. Offe and M. Stadler, eds., Arbeitsmotivation (Darmstadt, 1980).

indicating that many people mention all kinds of things other than earning money. But these surveys prove nothing.
On the one hand, the real reason for work--that is earning
money--is often intentionally concealed by an atmosphere of
social hypocrisy. On the other hand, earning money is for
many such a self-evident fact that nothing more is thought
or spoken about it. It thus seems subjectively more important to the respondent to give some socially useful activity
or one that has prestige and manifold implications. Given
the present division of labor and lifelong rigid subordination to work, most people cannot develop any abilities and
specialized knowledge other than those needed for their occupation. For this reason, they often cannot even conceive
of any activities and ideas of social usefulness other than
those pertaining to their accustomed work. However, if it
were possible for them to occupy themselves in a different
way, without any worries or economic compulsions, they
would certainly not decide, for instance, to stand for eight
hours a day in the factory next to the same machine, continuously pushing the same levers. This apparently speculative, or at least not readily demonstrable line of argument
is significant in that it stands opposed to the usual moralizing arguments common to both economic systems, that is, to
those also unproven contentions about work motivation and
work morale which are allegedly supported by various simplified methods of testing. The assertion that people do
not work for money alone, or even primarily for money,
conceals the fact that, except for a relatively narrow class
of people, the bulk of the population is economically compelled by the prevailing rigid division of labor to do work
which they would not do under completely different conditions.
      Scitovsky simplifies greatly[18] when he cites arguments
to the effect that people work purely for pleasure, and
tries to establish this using the example of volunteer work
by retired people. Of course people need to remain active.
Retired people in particular, who in their final years feel
superfluous and lonely, attempt to overcome this state of

---

[17] See F. Herzberg, B. A. Mausner, and B. B. Snyder-
     man, The Motivation to Work (New York, 1959), p. 81;
     E. Throsrud, and F. Emery, Mot en ny bedriftsorgani-
     sasjon (Oslo, 1972), p. 66, et seq. cited in F. Vilmar,
     ed., Menschenwuerde im Betrieb (Reinbek bei Hamburg,
     1973), p. 268; O. Neuberger, Messung der Arbeitszu-
     friedenheit (Stuttgart, 1974), p. 103.

[18] Cf. T. Scitovsky, Psychologie des Wohlstands, pp. 83
     and 87.

affairs by working for society. For some people, their hobbies are quite sufficient. Yet many others either have not been able to develop a hobby before retirement or cannot, even if they have such a hobby, alleviate their agonizing loneliness. They therefore try to capitalize on every opportunity for volunteer work, even outside their fields of specialization, in order to gain a feeling of social usefulness and to cultivate more active contacts with fellow workers.

However, one cannot infer from the human need for active, socially useful activity that people would carry out all the tasks required by the present division of labor, to the extent required today, without pay differentials. Even housewives carry out their unpaid work primarily because it is necessary for the family's standards of consumption and living under the given division of labor. Many housewives, desiring recognition for their work, press for an interesting job with more independence.

There are, to be sure, some very interesting jobs, which become the real pleasure and essence of individuals' lives. But this cannot obscure the fact that the overwhelming majority of people do not have such feelings. If they did not have to depend on earnings and had an entirely free choice, people would neither carry out all those activities nor as many of them as are presently necessary for consumption under the prevailing division of labor. However, as long as people do not give up a certain level of consumption, namely that ensured solely by the division of labor, different jobs will remain attractive in different ways. Society can only seek realizable ways of limiting alienated labor, as will be shown later.

This observation leads us to the conclusion that differentiated payment for work on the basis of a complex evaluation of that work cannot be eliminated, so long as the relatively rigid division of labor cannot be changed.

This is not to say that for many people other factors and considerations apart from pay are not important in the choice of job. This is merely to state that, in the absence of certain income differentials, the performance of much socially important work and hence the meeting of needs required today could not be assured.

Now if this differential development of income gives rise to differences in society's needs-satisfaction, the gradually increasing limitation of needs directed at the lowest incomes would then be justified. Although this would of course ensure that people's purely economic interests would remain the dominant ones, it is at the same time the basic condition for securing not only all jobs within the parameters of the division of labor, but also the growth of work incentives and the qualitative progress of human labor.

All countries that, on the basis of simplistic socialist ideas, have temporarily ignored these necessary interrelationships and introduced leveled wages, have always abandoned this practice after a brief interval. It has been demonstrated first, that purely moral initiatives and incentives cannot replace material rewards, and second--at least during a certain period of development--the intellectually more demanding jobs must be better paid than the primarily physical and intellectually less strenuous jobs. Yet for all that, it is also conceivable that, at very advanced stages of industrial growth, physically difficult, unpopular, or disparaged jobs will be more highly paid than various activities of a primarily intellectual nature. Yet, these too will be differentially evaluated jobs, the socially significant implementation of which can be ensured only by means of differential payments.

Contrary to all theories that regard material rewards as something peculiar to capitalism, which will be overcome by the transition to socialism (theories which even today haunt the minds of young people in the West), socialism has produced a completely different set of experiences, which are more relevant than all arm-chair theories. It has been proven that people are basically unwilling to do more difficult work for society or to increase their performance and effort in order to acquire higher job qualifications, if they do not receive a correspondingly higher income and thus are unable to meet their needs at a higher level. This has nothing to do with capitalist profit seeking, but is the expression of a necessary, work-equivalent development of income, so long as work itself has not become part of the self-interest of the majority of the people.

Labor researchers in East and West have come to recognize the need to differentiate wages according to objective, measurable differences in people's intellectual and physical work load, and therefore to develop different systems of work evaluation. This research into work and the evaluation of work is on the right track, even though it has not captured all aspects of wage differentiation (that is, amount of gradation and changing wage differentials) that are important for the socially necessary development of work. They attempt to generalize on the basis of assessments derived from general data about the subjective evaluations and decisions of millions of people.

So far, however, we still do not have an adequate scientific explanation of how the average minimum and maximum wage levels are established at the various levels of economic development. Wage levels are also interrelated with the division of gross income into wages and gross profit (or in Marxist terms, wages and surplus value) in the economic micro- and macro-spheres (division of the national income).

Neither the Marxist labor theory of value, nor the neoliberal theory of marginal productivity afford a plausible explanation of how wage levels are determined in a capitalist system. But there can hardly be a practicable theory of optimal wage development in a capitalist system, since the wage level is necessarily the result of a struggle between opposed interests, between wage earners and capital owners.

Work-dependent income and income from capital depend on entirely different conditions, and their respective developments are in opposition to each other. Thus, the coexistence of these two factors does not permit the working people to develop an interest in the use-value their labor creates, but rather generates pronounced wage interests on the one hand and capital interests on the other. The creation of use-value (needs-satisfaction) through labor can be assured only indirectly through the immediate interest in profit maximization of the owners and managers of capital. However, the fact that profits are maximized by means of the monopolistic manipulation of needs and the one-sided distortion of needs, to the detriment of the long-range vital interests of the people, quickly produces an awareness that this mechanism alone cannot guarantee the optimal development and satisfaction of needs. It would have to be replaced by workers' participation in decisions relating to the formation of needs and to labor, as well as the reciprocal relationship between these two factors.

This participation in decision-making is not, however, to be observed in the Communist practice of planning production and consumption, with its rejection of the market mechanism. Replacement of the market mechanism by bureaucratic decision-making in the processes of production, investment, distribution, and consumption has led to an even more profound alienation of the working people from work, working conditions, and the product of their work. Communism has replaced manipulation of the development of needs by capitalist monopolies and oligopolies with bureaucratic interference in consumption by means of centralized decision-making and totally monopolistic state enterprises. This does not make the strong wage interest of the working people disappear. Rather, it may have developed even more strongly than under capitalism. It is, moreover, accompanied by a disinterest in the formation of state capital, in the growth of the means of production, and in investment activity, among other things. The political bureaucracy is not capable of changing this development of interests by means of education and moral appeals so long as the fundamental characteristics of the system remain.

The satisfaction of economically limited needs will continue to develop in a differentiated manner and will necessarily be bound to different work outputs as long as this satisfaction depends essentially upon human labor--labor which, under the given division of labor, most people perform only for economic needs-satisfaction. Under these conditions, economic needs, or people's efforts toward increased satisfaction of them, are the most common driving force of economic activity. Needs-satisfaction will therefore remain one of the people's basic criteria for the evaluation of economic and social systems for a long time to come.

People will, in the final analysis, always strive for optimal satisfaction of their ever-changing needs; this, of course, applies to economically limited needs as well as non-economically limited ones. As individuals, they will also have to come to terms, within the given social context, with the degree of needs-satisfaction which they have been able to realize on the basis of their partly inherited, partly self-created social positions. As members of social and political groups, movements, and organizations, they will always tend to support or become involved in such political activities as might help bring about changes in society, which they think will better fulfill their needs.

Conceptions of social change, which might serve to bring about a better satisfaction of human needs, have been developed since time immemorial by philosophers, social scientists, and politicians. The less utopian, the more closely linked to reality, and the more oriented to the experiences and ideas of the masses these concepts of change have been, the greater have been the prospects for their realization by strong political movements. Before we demonstrate concretely the ways in which the present economic and social systems impede a better satisfaction of human needs, as well as the changes in these systems which might help substantially to improve needs-satisfaction in the near future, we would like to formulate very generally and synoptically what is meant nowadays by the system-dependent satisfaction of needs. First, however, let us list some typical contemporary deficiencies, without indicating which of them are more typical of capitalist or communist systems:

1. Production does not adequately take into account, either structurally or qualitatively, the economically limited needs of the people, and people as consumers do not have sufficient opportunity consciously and consistently to determine production;

2. More needs could be satisfied from the existing labor and productive potential, but production is developing in such a manner that this potential is inadequately utilized, or factors of production are left idle;

3.   Existing needs could be satisfied with much less ex-
     penditure of the labor of the whole of society, or
     more needs could be satisfied with a given expen-
     diture of labor, if production were to develop eco-
     nomically, in a technically more progressive man-
     ner, and without unnecessary wastage of labor and
     means of production;

4.   Production involves a superfluous growth in needs
     at the expense of important groups of needs; these
     may be needs in general or certain groups of
     needs, and the people do not have the opportunity
     to influence directly the reciprocal relationship be-
     tween production and the growth of needs, or the
     inner structure of this growth;

5.   There is too great a difference in different social
     groups' opportunities for consumption. Needs
     could be satisfied in a more balanced way, without
     thereby weakening the motivation necessary for la-
     bor and production or lowering the overall level of
     the meeting of needs;

6.   Economic development forces a one-sided satisfaction
     of economically limited needs and prevents a better
     satisfaction of more rapidly growing non-economi-
     cally limited needs both without and within the do-
     main of production.

It is to be expected that these, or similar, system-dependent means of needs-satisfaction, as they come increasingly into conflict with the needs of the majority of the
people, will produce demands for systemic changes that
might be expected to overcome these deficiencies.

At the present stage of development, however, especially in the industrially developed countries, it has become
more and more apparent that the mere satisfaction of needs
is no longer enough, and that within the economic domain
as well, the significance of the satisfaction of various non-
economic needs is constantly increasing. Let us first take
a general look at the changes in recent decades that have
brought about a sharp rise in non-economic needs and aspirations.

THE SIGNIFICANCE OF NON-ECONOMIC NEEDS

We have attempted to present the reality of human needs-formation and the necessity of increasing the satisfaction of economically limited needs in society. We have stressed from the outset that a host of non-economically limited needs always develops alongside the economically limited ones, and very often--in the case of inadequate satisfaction of the latter--even play a compensating role. People need not only food, clothing, and shelter, and not only more and better material goods. They also need love, friendship, community, a sense of belonging, recognition, and respect. They long for security, safety, tranquility, and peace. Not only are these universal and enduring human values; they also have different concrete manifestations, different intensities, and different rankings so that, at different stages of development and under certain social conditions and relationships, various non-economic needs can grow in significance.

The present era is characterized not only by unprecedented advances in science, technology, and productivity, which have allowed popular consumption in the industrialized countries to rise extremely rapidly, but also by the fact that it has encumbered ever broader segments of the population with hitherto unimagined psychological pressures, insecurities, and feelings of anxiety. A comprehensive analysis of this psychological development cannot be given here. Instead, we would merely like to draw attention to the social interrelationship between such negative psychological manifestations and the development of science, technology, and the economy. Systemic reform ought to strive for positive changes in this direction as well.

The two opposing systems--capitalism and socialism -- naturally contain different factors which produce increasing insecurity and fear among the people, even though a few of these negative psychological mass phenomena do occur in both systems, thus giving them an ostensibly global character. In enumerating the most important factors which unnerve people and produce feelings of stress and anxiety among a growing number of people in the Western industrial countries (the corresponding factors in the Communist states have already been dealt with in detail in my book, The Communist Power System, the following would have to be mentioned first and foremost:

1.   Possible loss of job or status;

2.   Possible misuse of science, possibilities of war and looming escalations of violence;

3. Loss of faith, values and close human relationships.

Regarding possible loss of job or status, the capitalist system affords too few possibilities of foreseeing and influencing its own future development, too few possibilities of providing for man's security through work, too few possibilities for participatory decision-making by the broad sectors of the population concerning the future organization of their work, their status, their enterprise, the economy, and the economic policy of the state. The cyclical development of the economy brings about recessions, crises, unemployment, and bankruptcies. Rationalization measures and technological improvements are carried out without regard for human destinies. The development of the people's education and continuing education is not coordinated with technological progress in production. Youth unemployment and the redundancy of older people are manifestations of this lack of coordination. What is required of the people very often exceeds their potential for growth--job rotations, transfers, and terminations are carried out, for the most part, in an impersonal and authoritarian manner. All these experiences produce stress and fear of competition and crisis, which become most pronounced among those people who, for various reasons, cannot keep up with increasingly ruthless competition.

Regarding possible misuse of science, possibilities of war and looming escalations of violence, the pace of scientific and technological progress is constantly accelerating. Although new discoveries in the fields of physics, chemistry, biology, etc., are making possible a rapid increase in the needs-satisfaction and living standards of the people, they have resulted in an excessive and increasing squandering of natural resources, a perversion of the human environment, and a continuing threat to human existence. People feel increasingly insecure as doubts are raised about certain kinds of energy use, once thought to be safe, but now invoking the prospect of an uncontrollable catastrophe. With mounting reservations, they are viewing the terrible consequences of the increasing use of chemicals in agriculture and food production. They sense the threat to life posed by the possible abuse of biological knowledge. The growing danger to human life through peaceful economic developments, which cannot be sufficiently controlled by the population, as well as the even greater dangers of the possible outbreak of war, are making the people's need for security into an increasingly stronger interest. Two world wars have already caused such incredible sacrifices and sorrow that a large part of the world's population today, having lived through one or both wars, cannot forget their terrible memories.

Regarding <u>loss</u> <u>of</u> <u>faith</u>, <u>values</u> <u>and</u> <u>close</u> <u>human</u>
<u>relationships</u>, technological progress and scientific enlight-
enment lead to loss of faith.   Earthly sorrows and fears
were easier to bear when the hope of justice and life after
death fortified the people.   Constraints in this life were
taken as a personal test willed by God, which would one
day be rewarded by the glory of the transcendent kingdom,
and were thus freely accepted.   The relentless disintegra-
tion of these beliefs resulting from the rise of scientific
knowledge and information buried these hopes of life after
death, and confined people's expectations of happiness to
the period of their lives on Earth.   The loss of higher, divine values was bound to produce a demand for greater
needs-satisfaction in the Here and Now.   The gain in pleasure in this life came increasingly to be identified as the experience of happiness.   Pressure for increased consumption
and material security in this life is the necessary form of
expression of this kind of rational development.
    This development goes hand in hand, however, with
the spiritual impoverishment of the people.   Man needs recognition and support as a suffering being, either from God
or his fellow men.   He needs affirmation of the value of his
existence and the meaning of his life.   When divine support
begins to wane, human recognition becomes all the more important.   The greater the intellectual development of men,
the greater the significance attributed to close human relationships.   And yet, technological-economic progress occurs
within a context of competitive struggle and increasingly
intense individualistic pursuit of success and status.   Men
alienate each other and fall into loneliness, fear, and despair.   The socialist vision of the future once gave new
hope to many, and was, for a time, able to compensate for
the transcendental loss of faith.   But the Soviet perversion
of socialism and the disillusionment bound up with it, the
inability of socialist movements to give people new, more
humane social perspectives, amounts to the disappearance of
the last remaining great hopes.
    Thus, the result of twentieth century technological and
scientific progress has been a very dichotomous development
of man.   On the one hand, it has made it possible to overcome hunger and has led to an unprecedented rise in the
living standards of broad strata of the population.   Material enrichment has made life easier and increased life's
pleasures; and people will react to any attempts to downplay the significance of this satisfaction of needs with in-
comprehension. Yet at the same time, alienation, spiritual
impoverishment, loneliness, and despair are increasing as
the expression of the lower level of satisfaction of important
non-economic human needs.

Growing socio-economic insecurity causes the human need for security to increase constantly and in new forms. Although the development of public health, social security, and unemployment insurance, among other things, is one manifestation of increasing security, at the same time it causes people's fear of illness and unemployment to develop into an ever stronger fear of failure in an environment of success. Social pressures, uncertainty about the future, and the limits of one's own will evoke new insecurities and fears, which demand new forms of protection and security.

The perils of war, threats to the environment, and the escalation of force cannot be eliminated by law and order politicians and fascist regimes. The reversion of human beings into spineless, manipulated puppets of bureaucratic state power is hardly a conceivable future solution to great social problems, in view of this century's fateful experiences of fascist and communist systems. The need for broader and deeper democratization, for more popular codetermination at the work place and in the enterprise, in the development of the national economy, in the future orientation of politics and the state, in the social organization of their lives--all these are needs that the people are feeling more and intensely. To be sure, narrow-minded and power-hungry politicians do temporarily prevail now and then with their demagogy. But the growing demand for a new and more profound democratization of social life can no longer be repressed.

The need for further democratization of society is of course a political need, and this means that political ideas and programs, as well as organizations, are necessary. New political ideas are generated predominately by individuals or small groups (mostly intellectuals), mainly in reaction to broader social and/or economic needs and interests which emerge among different social groups on the basis of certain objective developments. Ideas about, and movements for codetermination, capital-sharing by wage earners, and further-reaching experiments geared to these ideas and movements in many enterprises, citizens' initiatives, environmental movements, movements for economic democratization in church circles, etc. are expressions of differing political reactions to growing new social and other non-economic needs. This political development will be examined more closely at the end of this book. Here, we merely note in passing that only further political developments can confirm whether, and which, concrete conceptions of democratization (for example, those developed here) truly correspond to the needs of broad strata of the population, and can become a practical force for social change in the form of political organizations and groupings. However, it would be most difficult to deny the existence and prevent the spread of the social and security needs underlying them.

Neither can the democratization of scientific knowledge among ever-broader social strata be curbed any longer. The negative effects of this development, such as loss of faith, hedonistic one-sidedness and spiritual impoverishment cannot be overcome by a rollback of human understanding. Although religious movements will continue to fill the menacing emptiness in the lives of many people and give them a higher sense of meaning, in the long run, the crucial influence of scientific knowledge and enlightenment goes hand in hand with the need for new relationships among people and opportunities for self-realization. The less the members of coming generations look to God for confirmation of the value of their existence, the more important will be those other forms of human togetherness in which the individual achieves fulfillment and with whose activities he can identify. People's lives, and above all the lives of young people, are increasingly lived in spontaneously emerging interest groups.

The feeling of belonging to groups with a goal orientation similar to his, prevents loneliness and continually provides the individual with confirmation of his importance to others. The individual's interest in the group and its activity thus often becomes a stronger motivation for his activity than the general, still predominately economic motivations can be. The group gives the individual a needed sense of security, of usefulness to others and of their recognition of him. In it, he can develop his abilities and initiatives and overcome his insecurities. In this social unit the relationships between the individual and larger social units are evident. Groups therefore may be an important step on the way to overcoming alienation.

The formation of groups of this kind, as well as far-reaching democratization in the state and the economy, in the enterprises and economic system, in partial spheres, and in economic policy decisions, undoubtedly correspond to the increasingly strong non-economic needs of contemporary man. Not to satisfy them would be to produce dangerous neuroses, frustrations, alienation, hopeless fears, and the escalation of force in society. The repression of these human needs in fascist and communist totalitarian systems, by means of state snooping into private affairs, persecuting individuals for their beliefs, creating a uniform ideology, and brutal repression, only leads to a deepening of human alienation and isolation. But these regimes can only temporarily delay man's struggle for more democracy and self-determination. Sooner or later, even in totalitarian states, the many unsatisfied needs and interests of the people will break the totality of the state and lead to far-reaching democratization.

The satisfaction of non-economic social needs for community, group affiliation, job satisfaction, social activity, a
share in decision-making, and self-affirmation must not be
allowed to come into conflict with the satisfaction of further
growing economic or economically limited needs. All notions
to the effect that economically limited needs have already
been satisfied, or even that their growth and their satisfaction ought to be limited, are products of a sectarian way
of thinking which is foreign to the people.

Only if society can develop in such a way as to guarantee more purposefully the meeting of all human needs,
both economic and non-economic, will it be successful in the
long term. The interests of the majority of the population
are undoubtedly best served by a humane democratization of
the economy, one which places the determination of how to
meet economic needs in the hands of democratically elected
representatives of the people. And, to state it clearly
once more: in the process of reforming the system, growing
non-economic needs must not prevail at the expense of the
principle of efficiency in society. On the contrary, reform
must be seen as the way to increase efficiency and hence
better to satisfy all human needs.

Furthermore, people's interests are an important form
in which they express certain needs-developments. To ful-
fil these needs is one of the strongest motivations of their
economic and political activities. Socio-economic reform
can thus prevail only if it is in the interests of broad social strata. To our explanation of the role of needs in contemporary developments, therefore, we will now add an
analysis of the role of interests.

THE SIGNIFICANCE OF INTERESTS AND DIFFERING
   INTERPRETATIONS OF THEM

In both systems, the problem of interests remains the
most ignored and concealed domain of human activities. Although economic and political interests in particular are
among the most significant motivations of human activity,
since they give rise to crucial incentives,[19] the ruling
classes of the moment apparently pay least heed to this
fact, or even consciously disregard it, for reasons related
to their own interests. The problems of interests are thus
approached in very different ways and are consequently
also very differently interpreted. Depending on whether

---

[19] Cf. O. Sik, The Third Way (New York, 1976), p. 52 et
seq.

they are examined by economists, political scientists, sociol-
ogists, philosophers, or psychologists, interests have been
explained in terms of varying substance or emphasis. It
cannot be the task of this work to present a history of the
explanation of this concept. It seems more important to us
to approach those problems which are bound up with the
greatest difficulties in explaining interests.

It has been primarily economists who have stressed the
important role of selfish economic interests in economic activity and economic relationships. Ever since the Physiocrats, they have drawn attention to the conception of ego-
oriented interests as the dominant manifestation of interests
in general.[20] The economists cannot be reproached with
paying primary attention to economic interests, since these
are their proper object of research. It would of course be
preferable if they were to grasp the interrelationships between these and other interests, such as political ones.

However, one pronounced flaw in economic theory is its
insufficiently differentiated understanding of economic interests, which gives rise to a too general view of economic
motivations and of conflicting activities in the economy. Of
course one might object here that the study of the differentiation of interests belongs to psychology, not economics. But psychologists cannot get a hold on the problem
because the differentiation of economic interests primarily
reflects people's different positions in the economic environment and the existence of the most diverse economic processes. Surely, it is chiefly the task of economists to illuminate more concretely the interrelationship between
economic processes and interests.

To link our understanding of interests with the satisfaction of existing needs is the unavoidable step that will
bring us closer to a recognition of the essence of interests.[21] Man can have an interest in the satisfaction of material as well as spiritual interests, egoistic as well as altruistic, passive as well as active--in short: however we
enumerate or categorize these needs, the satisfaction of
each one of them can also become the interest of an individual. Although the linkage of interests and needs is here
stressed as fundamental to our understanding of interests,
this does not mean that interests and needs can be equated. Not every meeting of needs can be equated with the
interests of the individual. If we keep in mind the scale of

---

[20] Cf. G. Myrdal, Das politische Element in der national-
oekonomischen Doktrinbildung (Bonn/Bad Godesberg,
1976), p. 24.

[21] Cf. Sik, The Third Way, p. 43 et seq.

needs in its entire breadth, it becomes clear that a person's interest is never equivalent to all his needs. Moreover, it is not the need as such that becomes an interest, but rather its satisfaction. It is not the need, but its satisfaction (satiation) that produces a positive feeling (comfort, satisfaction, desire) in the person. Thus, while the need (hunger, thirst, cold, tiredness, etc.) gives rise to a negative feeling (discomfort, fear, pain, despair, loneliness, etc.) in the person, satisfaction of the need overcomes--at least temporarily--negative feelings and induces positive feelings. The strength, intensity, and duration of the effects of these positive feelings vary, however. Not all needs-fulfillment, therefore, gives rise to an interest, but only that which evokes an especially intense feeling of desire.

Thus, only those need-satisfactions become human interests, which evoke very strong feelings of desire, which also express themselves in a very strong, relatively persistent, or constantly recurring orientation of will and activity toward the attainment of these need-satisfactions, that is, the realization of interests. The interests are again hierarchical however--there are stronger and weaker interests, and interests of shorter or longer duration. Since at the present stage of development almost all objects of need (not only things for everyday needs, but also cultural objects, services, sporting activities, etc.) can only be had for money, the procurement of money, which in economic terms means the earning of income, becomes one of the strongest economic interests for most people. In other words, the economic interests (that is, interest in economic activities and/or in the results of economic activities) generally continue to be the strongest; and of these the interest in income is the most intense.

This general characterization does not suffice, however, since within the interest in income there are clearly substantial differences between certain social strata. Just as botanists cannot halt their investigation and explanation at the point of describing the specific phenomenon tree if, within this group of phenomena, essentially different kinds of trees exist and must be understood, so too economics cannot and does not come to a stop at the phenomenon of income. It attempts, first and foremost, to explain different kinds of income (salaries, profits, interest, pensions, etc.). It then only vaguely demonstrates that these different kinds of income are among the most important indications of people's differing positions in the economy (and hence in their economic relationships), out of which develop completely different income interests on the part of the different social strata.

Nor is this situation altered by the fact that individuals alternately or even simultaneously may draw different kinds of income. The relatively long-term existence of such differing levels of economic status, kinds of income, and economic interests cannot be disputed. The Physiocrats had already recognized these fundamental differences. If these differences are not as strongly emphasized nowadays, and if there is a preference for speaking of a rank-ordering of incomes (thus allowing qualitative income differentials to disappear into simple quantitative rankings), this is primarily an expression of an aversion to Marxist approaches and conclusions, and thus another ideological development.

Economic interests are here regarded, on the one hand, as given and indisputable. On the other hand, they must be morally condemned in public and in terms of the interests of society, or at least consciously repressed. There is apparently nothing more about them that needs to be explained. They are the negative, albeit unavoidable, side of man, and thus a kind of lightning rod to be used by all politicians when social failures occur. They then need only to inveigh against the lack of public morality. To be sure, economists since Adam Smith have taken note of economic interests as a motive of economic activity, and their compensating influence underlies the theory of perfect competition. But they have never gone beyond this most general characteristic, since this might lead them into the Marxist waters of materialism, and thus into a contradiction with moral philosophy, religion, and efforts at political unification. This problem thus became a taboo. It has been simply factored out, since it contradicts the moralist doctrine.

Every specific social mode of production requires concrete interests in the economy that motivate economic actions and processes so that the economy can function and develop further. These interests govern people's productive activities, economic cooperation, exchange and distribution processes, and thus constitute the imperceptible background to the most diverse economic dimensions and relationships. Economic relationships occurring with lawlike regularity emerge and can consequently be understood only from the parallel interests of members of large social groups with the same economic effects. The basic cause of most of the unresolved problems and debates is the failure of economic theory adequately to observe and differentiate this background of interests which underlies economic processes.

The debate between the respective advocates of the labor theory of value and the theory of marginal utility can be prolonged to infinity so long as economists fail to pay heed to all the diverse interests manifest in the parallel activities of producers and consumers, as well as in the contradictory behaviors of different social groups, and which are evident in the recurring economic dimensions and relationships of certain eras. What Ricardo and Marx, for example, called value, and saw as the reification of work, is in reality the objective expression of a general interest, and of the behavior of producers. This interest was naturally different among small producers in the Middle Ages (labor equivalence) than it is among large capitalist manufacturers (capital valorization).

The theorists of marginal utility have placed the subjective evaluation of goods at the center of their economic observations. But in so doing, they have neglected the peculiarities and differing socio-economic interests and their contradictory nature. They have overlooked the interest-governed behavior of consumers as such (which, to be sure, only represents one side of the exchange relationship) and have tried instead to develop a universal, all-determining economic theory out of a partial economic aspect. They were bound to wind up in a dead end, since they ignored the decisive interests of producers, interests which cannot be explained by consumers' evaluations of the utility of goods, and which cannot be reduced to a common denominator with them.

Modern behavioral scientists certainly pay attention to the motivations underlying different kinds of economic behavior. As is the case in all detailed psychological research, however, their approaches have become atomized and as a result the individual behavior is broken down and investigated according to the most diverse points of view. But these approaches preclude the specific commonality of interests and manner of behavior of those large socio-economic groups that are distinguished by the antagonism of their economic interests. Most probably, the desire to dissociate themselves from Marxism plays a decisive role in this. The result, however, is that economic understanding has regressed to a state inferior to that of the Physiocrats.

Only an understanding of economically dependent interests and the interests that determine the economic behavior of large social groups makes possible a correct understanding of economic patterns. For these patterns are nothing but the theoretical reflections of the dominant mode of behavior of people at the same economic level under given economic conditions, whose concrete interests compel this behavior. Essentially, one finds a number of recurring processes, since people do behave rationally in accordance with their interests. But because opportunities for the individual to acquire knowledge and information are always limited, distorted, and insufficient, people are compelled to grope toward the kind of behavior most advantageous to themselves. It thus follows that a series of wrong, deviant actions produces an approximate, average, and, in the long run, patterned mode of behavior; it is the average, the common, the ever newly created average value of the most diverse activities of the millions. Economic laws are thus always only very general and long-term tendencies evolving out of the movements of similar innumerable individual economic phenomena.

Only in this way can one understand value-equivalence in the pre-capitalist exchange of goods or the establishment of a national economic average rate of profit in early capitalism. Just as the exchange of goods, according to labor value, could only be an approximate, tendential result of a very long-range division of labor among the different occupations, so a rate of profit is also established that only tends toward the same rate as a result of constant long-term groping by the owners of free money capital toward the most advantageous investment of their capital. But the development of demand for specific kinds of goods is also a very approximate and tendential expression of the interests of individual consumers in maximizing their utility and balancing their marginal utility, given existing prices of goods and different incomes.

Insofar as the members of different social groups in the economy think in terms of concrete advantages, then, the same economic interests are objectively present and continue to play a decisive role in people's activities. For this, there is a kind of negative proof: the attempt by socialist economic policymakers to ignore group interests (partial interests) in practice and to negate them in theory has led to enormous economic losses and to the perversion of economic activities in the socialist countries.

Although we have been emphasizing the existence and role of economic interests today, as well as for the foreseeable future, this does not mean that we underestimate the significance of non-economic interests in a future economic system. Our emphasis is only intended to counteract the kind of idealism that underestimates economic interests, since it will always resemble thinking prevalent in the socialist states. To the world's moralists, these economic interests are the beginning of all evil, and every social utopia presupposes the overcoming of private interests and their subordination to society's interests as the basic condition for the functioning of a New Society.

The notion that economic interests have to be eliminated as a motivation of human activity has become nothing short of a universal trait of social utopias of all orientations. But idealistically and philosophically inclined utopianists, on the one hand, see the prerequisite of their renewal of society as the reeducation of man to do good, to practice abstinence and frugality, and to bring about his transcendental and altruistic orientation, all with the help of religion, ethics, and education. On the other hand, the Marxists believe that in their utopia they will be able to overcome economic self-interest by eliminating private own-ership of the means of production and market relationships as the capitalist foundations of the motivation of economic activity. Let us now look at the further development of this theory under the conditions of the socialist system.

THE CONCEPT OF INTEREST AS IDEOLOGY

Socialist practice has so far not managed to eliminate economic interests, even though it has ostensibly done away with capitalist relationships. This being the case, material interests can henceforth be seen as the manifestation of capitalist remnants in people's heads which, with the help of a gradual socialist education, must be dispelled. Until this happens, however, material incentives must still be tol-erated and utilized.

However, the fact that economic interests emerge out of given economic relationships, that they are a necessary manifestation of the given conditions of work and consump-tion, that they are socially structured, and that a mecha-nism of demonstration and confrontation is thus necessary in both the economic and political domains--all this cannot be admitted. The relationship between economic conditions and interests cannot be consistently thought through, nor can implications for the system be drawn from it. This re-lationship cannot be officially accepted, because to recog-nize it is to call the system itself and its rulers into ques-tion. The moment it ceases to fit into the political bag of tricks, the materialist way of thinking is quickly thrown overboard.

Political interests in silencing antagonistic interests and conflicts of interest, as well as in manifesting the uniform interest of the entire population are thus crucial to an in-terpretation of the concept of interests under socialism. The existence of the interests of a ruling political bureauc-racy, as opposed to the interests of the rest of the popula-tion, is to be kept secret, and this ideological limitation in-fluences any explanation of the essence of interests. Thus, what is involved is only a different and even starker kind of manifestation of ideological penetration when, in Marxist analyses of interests,[22] (1) interests are equated with

---

[22] Cf. W. W. Radajew, Oekonomische Interessen im Sozialis-mus (East Berlin, 1974).

needs satisfaction; (2) individual interests are detached from class interests; and (3) the social structure of interests under socialism is concealed. In particular, the last mentioned item conditions the previous two mistaken conceptions.

The most significant Soviet works concerning the problem of interests lack any discussion of the problem of interests in the socialist system. For this reason their explanation of the general concept of interest is so diluted that questions about the specific nature of interests in different social systems cannot arise at all. They regard the concrete interests of individual persons as their own, entirely subjective affair, a matter, at most for individual psychology, while the interests of the class are an objective category--independent of these individual interests.

This absolute separation of the universal aspects of the interests of the members of a social stratum or class from the differing concrete shapes which these interests assume in the individual, serves only to justify the claims of Marxist parties to a monopoly over the representation and defense of class interests. It does not matter which concrete interests the workers may be pursuing, what shape economic and political interests may really take, even those of a large majority. Rather, the only important thing is that their interests should be represented by the Communist parties. If a large or even overwhelming number of these workers should happen to pursue interests other than those that the Communist parties raise to the level of fundamental interests then it is not that the interests are false or oversimplified, but rather that the workers have just not yet reached an understanding of their own interests.

In reality, however, there is no interest of a particular social group which does not sooner or later actually become manifest as the concrete interest of a large part of the membership of this group. It is entirely possible to forecast the development of interests of a social group, that is theoretically to formulate interests which have not yet become manifest among a majority of the members of the group but will become so after a certain time under certain conditions. However, if this development of interests does not take place after a relatively long period, then the theoretical formulation of these interests was wrong. It remained merely a theory. In this case, concrete interests have developed differently and the theory requires correction. Here, it is of no use to point to the wrong development of the presupposed conditions. For precisely in the event that conditions do not develop in the manner presupposed, this presupposition is also false and the formulation of interests remains at best a pure hypothesis.

The interest of a social stratum or class will, therefore, sooner or later be concretely manifest as the interest
of a majority of the members of this stratum or class.   Otherwise the interest would amount to an untenable theoretical
assertion.   Of course, the fact that actual class interests
exist is not only expressed as more or less equivalent to
the economic interests of the class members, but also as
displaying the same social interests (interests in the satisfaction of the needs for community, needs for solidarity,
needs for belonging to the given class, etc.) and political
interests (interest in the common struggle for political demands, for power, etc.).   Class interest is a complex, com-
posite, and generalized interest that combines different
characteristic individual interests.   As such, however, it
must--if not immediately, then at a certain level of develop-
ment--be pursued by the majority of members (of the part
of society characterized as a class) as their own interest.
Without a strong-willed pursuit of certain needs-satisfac-
tions, people's interests do not exist, neither their egoistically nor their collectively oriented interests.
    Though official Soviet Marxism may assert that the
working class in the capitalist states has an objective interest in eliminating capitalism, establishing a proletarian state
(the dictatorship of the proletariat), nationalizing the means
of production, and introducing dirigiste central planning,
among other things, this objective interest is, for the time
being, nothing more than a theoretical assertion.   It is not
selected and generalized from an aggregation of the workers' individual interests, as objectivity would require.   On
the contrary, such a procedure is indignantly rejected as
an un-Marxist, subjectivist procedure.   This objective interest is derived from the economic patterns of capitalism,
from which the workers' struggle against capitalism and
from which socialism presumably must necessarily emerge.
But all these are no more than theoretical views which naturally cannot, as such, simply be rejected.
    An analysis of the capitalist system, which would ex-
pose its contradictions and barriers to development, cannot
be rejected a priori as a methodological procedure.   Neither
can one reject out of hand the implications of this for the
development of an interest within significant social strata or
classes, say an interest in a fundamental change in the political and economic system, or in the outline of a new social
system which would eliminate the faults of the old system.
This will also be done in the present work, and it is my
view that the social sciences should not hesitate to undertake critical analyses of the system and to make proposals
for fundamental change, if they would avoid degenerating
into ideological apologies for the system.   But each theoretical analysis, and all the conclusions drawn from it (even

concerning the development of interests), can for the time being only claim to be a relatively grounded theoretical hypothesis. Whether or not it is correct will only become apparent through the further development of the analyzed system itself and of the interests of its broad population.

However, as soon as one party lays claim to a monopoly of truth for its theory while rejecting any fundamental modification of this theory as a hostile revision, as soon as critical confrontations between this theory and reality are suppressed within a certain sphere of influence and the gap between theory and reality is simply ignored, then this is the expression of an unscientific ideologization of the theory and its transformation into a sheer article of faith.[23] If theoretical assertions are advanced about the interests of the working population, but then these interests cannot be discerned in reality among a majority of the same population, even after generations, then the theory is not correct.

One party can naturally take the position that the interest of party members expresses the future interest of the workers or even a majority of the working population; but it happens that the development of a corresponding consciousness can take quite a bit longer. Democracy must tolerate even a viewpoint of this kind as long as this party only seeks to influence and accelerate such a development of interests through its activities and politics under democratic conditions. However, as soon as it takes its conceptions of interests to be the sole truth and believes it has to make its interest prevail by force, even before it becomes apparent in a democratic way that this is the manifest interest of a majority of the population, then that party is acting against the actual and differently oriented interests of a majority of the population. Should its attempts in fact succeed due to favorable power relationships (insufficient or badly organized resistance, chaotic conditions in the country, etc.), the party must then set up a dictatorship of the minority against the interests of the majority. This fact cannot be obscured by any sophism invoking objective and subjective interests.

If such a power seizure results in a dictatorship of the minority over the majority that has to be maintained for decades because it does not eliminate the clash of interests between the established rulers and the majority of the population, the simplest way of concealing this tension is a resort to ever increasing sophistry. This includes the

---

[23] O. Lange, Entwicklungstendenzen der modernen Wirtschaft und Gesellschaft. Eine sozialistische Analyse (Wien, 1964), p. 180.

assertions that the party rules in the name of the whole working class, that the established power represents not only the interests of this class, but also those of the farmers and intelligentsia allied with it, and that there exists a socialist community of all working people. Yet for all that, contradictions between the interest of society and the interests of individuals cannot be completely denied, since the different interests of the members of society do still come to light here and there.

Even Radajew explains the existence of contradictions between society and individual interests under socialism in a similar way, though he does not go beyond the interests of the ruling political bureaucracy. To be sure, he does see the individual members of society as having an interest in being paid for their work, in the satisfaction of their personal needs, and in the product for itself. But this interest is, as it were, only one aspect of their own interest, the other aspect being the interest of society as a whole-- which in a sense is also their own interest as well. That is to say, the product for society again belongs to the working population exclusively and is used only in their interest.[24] Exploitation therefore no longer exists, and all the working population are equal as owners of the means of production, as working people and in their equality of access to the sources of subsistence.[25]

In reality, under socialism the appropriation of the means of production and the meeting of needs takes place within a context of crass antagonisms of interests between the ruling, all-determining bureaucracy and the rest of the people, who are deprived of all decision-making functions. Party and state control over the results of production, facilitated by plans for production, distribution, and finances, leads to a situation in which the majority of society, namely the productively active people, have no influence over production, distribution, and product utilization. Planning is done by bureaucratic institutions, is totally alienated from the workers, and does not take their interests into account. The working people cannot evaluate the plans, have no opportunity to choose among alternative plans, and regard the whole decision-making process as outside their actual sphere of action. They regard the submission of the enterprise's production plan at enterprise assemblies as a formal act which gives them no real possibility of changing the plan.

---

[24] See Radajew, Oekonomische Interessen.

[25] Ibid., p. 220.

Economic alienation of the working people has not decreased, but in fact increased. The people do not understand why, despite regular plan fulfillment--according to official reports--their living standards remain below those of the people in capitalist countries, even in the industrially advanced communist countries. They also do not understand why there is inflation in their planned economies. They cannot understand why their production continues to lag behind production in the capitalist countries, nor why the dependence of many branches of their economies on capitalist countries continues to grow rather than decrease--in agricultural production for instance.

In place of capitalist control over the social results of work, control by the bureaucracy now prevails. This in no way represents social appropriation, and thus one must continue to speak of a growing contradiction between the highly socialized means of production and the state-bureaucratic mode of appropriation. One consequence of this contradiction is that neither production nor the distribution of products corresponds to the real interests of the population. This is also the main reason why the bureaucratic ruling class does not allow democratic conditions and free expression of the people's interests, and can rule only with the help of an absolute dictatorship and a repressive political system.

Private capital has been eliminated, to be sure, but has been replaced by state capital, represented and administered by the party bureaucracy. Exploitation of the working strata has not been eliminated, but rather has further increased. The surplus product created by people engaged in production is relatively greater than capitalist surplus value,[26] and its utilization serves primarily to preserve the overgrown party and state-bureaucratic apparatuses, as well as to cover the great economic losses induced by bureaucratic decisions. Rising exploitation is concealed by bureaucratically determined statistics: neither data concerning the number of officials in the party and state apparatus, nor those concerning the size and utilization of the surplus product may be made public.

It is not only the power of the bureaucracy over the non-bureaucratic strata, but also their living conditions that distinguishes them socially from the people. Under economically backward conditions, in which persistent scarcity prevails--too few apartments, furnishings, means of transportation, modern consumer commodities, various foodstuffs, services, etc. in relation to demand--privileges are intentionally established for the power bureaucracy, which are

---

[26] Cf. Sik, The Third Way, p. 224ff.

manifested in preferential allocation of all scarce goods and in widespread corruption. The highest political functionaries are accorded levels of consumption and living conditions entirely comparable to those of the grand bourgeoisie in the West. To be sure, in comparison to the Western upper classes, they are much better able to conceal their privileges (for example, by confidential income levels, distribution of goods in special stores, large and strictly isolated resorts, etc.).[27] Yet some information nonetheless does reach the people. For this reason, social antagonisms between the people and the party bureaucracy are increasing. The interests of the political bureacracy develop in a manner antagonistic to the interests of the rest of the population.

The apologetics for the political system, as well of the economic system under socialism necessitate the transformation of interest theory into ideology. In particular, it is officially insisted that the socialist economic system is incompatible with the market mechanism, meaning that the need for it cannot be demonstrated so long as the deficiencies in the prevailing theory of interests are not exposed.

The system of centralized, dirigist planning, that liquidates the market mechanism, is also based, among other things, on the conception that under the conditions of state property and a socialist state, no antagonistic interests can exist between the state planning and management bodies on the one hand, and the state enterprises on the other. The unity of the interests of all the working people also means harmony of interests between the collectivity of the enterprise and management and the interests of the superior state organs. Consequently, the central plans and politico-economic directives should also basically correspond to the goals and efforts of the enterprises.[28] If there were problems in the domain of planning, they could only be poetic problems, not conflicts of interest.[29]

It is characteristic of Marxist theory that, although it admits of impediments to the development of socialism in the formation of socialist consciousness, in order to eliminate

---

[27] Cf. Sik, The Communist Power System(New York, 1981), p. 105 et seq.; see also, R. Bahro, The Alternative in Eastern Europe (London, 1978).

[28] W. Ulbricht, Zum oekonomischen System des Sozialismus in der DDR, vol. 1 (E. Berlin, 1968), p. 103.

[29] See I. I. Kusminow, Abriss der politischen Oekonomie des Sozialismus. Methodologie (East Berlin, 1976), pp. 410-11; see also K. U. Brossmann, Komplexe Grund-fondsplanung (East Berlin, 1977).

these impediments, it calls for the development of an <u>un-</u>
<u>derstanding</u>, among all working people if possible, of the
economic regularities of the socialist system, its developmental requirements, common social interests, state goals
and plans, the unity between state planning goals and the
interests of all members of society, etc.   The development
of a socialist consciousness among all members of society is
thus understood as a continuing process of understanding
and hence the result of a process of education that brings
about not only a deeper understanding of state goals and
plans among the people, but also an incentive for each individual in his work, in the preparation of common plans,
and in their fulfillment and over-fulfillment.   Officials proceed from the assumption that there are no specific interests peculiar to a majority of individuals or production collectives and contrary to the interests of the community.
Thus everything depends upon how well the understanding
of the broad masses of working people develops, how their
socialist consciousness takes shape.   And then it will be
possible to bring about the socially required activity of all.

It is, of course, also officially admitted that contradictions exist between the interests of particular individuals
and the interests of society.   However, these contradictions
are regarded as insignificant obstructions, as contradictions
between individuals attempting to assert their egoistic interests at the expense of the majority of society and thereby to win advantages. What is involved here is thus always
a problem of morality, an offense against the rules of socialist morality, not merely an offense against the laws in
force and hence a direct violation of the law which can be
relatively easily determined and punished.

It is true that moral rules are important in those
spheres of human behavior in which behavior cannot be legally specified, and are thus constantly evolving.   In these
spheres, it is possible to initiate activities that might develop more to the benefit of the community, just as they
might develop more to the benefit of the individual and to
the detriment of the community.   What is no longer correct,
however, is the official view that the dissemination and re-
inforcement of socialist morality is primarily the result of a
growth of socialist consciousness.   This development of
consciousness is understood as the population's constantly
growing awareness of economic regularities, community interests, and planning goals.   Out of this awareness grows
an understanding of which socially useful activities can actually best promote one's own interests and society's interests in the long run.   People's understanding also increases
with respect to those activities which, on the contrary, will
harm the community and themselves in the long run.

This theory can be recognized as mere theory and cannot contribute to the solution of serious problems in socialist economic practice. After all, it builds upon unrealistic, purely abstract, intellectual premises. It proceeds from the assumption that there exist certain rules of behavior in economics which, first of all, show clearly what kind of behavior or action is bad, harmful, in short immoral, and which is good, useful, and moral. And second, these rules would be voluntarily observed by the majority of workers, having developed spontaneously as their own intrinsic morality. In reality, however, there is not and cannot be any such morality. With such a moral solution, the dominant ideology attempts only to bridge those fundamental gaps in socialist economic theory that it is incapable of filling scientifically. It is important to establish this, not only to point out the flaws in socialist economic theory and practice, but also to expose as misguided several new socialist theories in the West, insofar as they are again based upon conceptions of a new socialist morality.[30]

To begin with, traditional moral rules, which the people have held, accepted and widely observed since time immemorial, have been expressed as such simple and broadly understood rules of behavior that they can, for this very reason, be understood and passed on by the vast majority of the people without any special theoretical training. In the second place, they must commend behavior that, in their experience, has served people's immediate interests in preserving and strengthening their narrower or broader community, and they must condemn any behavior that contradicts these interests. Moral rules have only worked effectively in interest groups--from the narrowest to the broadest--where the members of these communities have recognized that what was identified as morally bad really did cause harm to the community, and what was considered morally good was really useful to it. The confrontation between generally understandable moral principles and the positive or negative consequences of certain actions for the community have thus had to be immediately apparent and convincing to everyone. This presupposes that the individual sees moral principles as right and, furthermore, knows that other members of society also think the same way and that they too would recognize and condemn individual transgressions in like manner. Then and only then can morality have a concrete effect on society.

---

[30] For example, the theories of A. Carlo, _Politische und oekonomische Struktur der UdSSR (1917-1975)_ (Berlin, 1972).

In a very broad and internally complex economy in which the division of labor is well advanced, however, morality can no longer operate in this way. In fact, the members of a national economy constrained by the state may well form a community. But the contradictions arising from the immediate interests of the diverse narrow groups within this political unit will be so pronounced that their community of interests will be definable only in abstract terms, and will be unfathomable and uncontrollable to the individual. Only where he can immediately and empirically perceive a unity of interest, will the individual also adhere to the unwritten rules of common procedure. Such units of common interest will, as a rule, be work groups or, in certain respects, enterprise collectives. The interest units of unionized professional groups, trade associations, or even wage earners in general, which become conscious units of common interest as a result of wage conflict under the conditions of a capitalist market economy, cannot work in the Communist system, where there is no wage conflict and hence no broad-scale solidarity.

Interest units thus form, not on the basis of abstract theories or political pipe dreams, but only as a consequence of real interests of people who, because of perceptible actions and results, recognize empirically that they have a commonality of interests (strikes, citizens' initiatives, struggles against quota increases, etc.). To judge by experience so far, the overriding economic interest of an absolute majority of all working people in the socialist system is their interest in maximizing their income (that is, income in the form of wages, salaries, premiums, profit sharing, and other forms, including under-the-table income) while expending as little effort as possible. Since the division of labor, working conditions, and labor intensity have not changed in comparison with what prevails in the capitalist system, and moreover, since the technical conditions of production have remained relatively backward, work is still a burden for the majority of people, and is seen mainly as a pre-condition for obtaining income. This interest in income leads to common action among work or production collectives, aimed at general income maximization with a minimum of work expenditure. Such interest units have also led spontaneously to the development of special moral rules which--in contrast to propagandistic moral ideologies--exert a real influence within these production communities.

Work and production collectives, rather than the individual worker, are responsible for production and monetary income in industrial society, despite the formal persistence of money-goods relationships. Under capitalism, the collective worker--a designation which Marx used in explaining

capitalist production[31] --has taken the place of the individual producer of the Middle Ages and continues to exist, in
socialist production, as the enterprise collective.   It is the
enterprise managements, who in the final analysis, have to
determine the concrete development of production, given the
varying differing quantity and quality of central, planned
global tasks.   It is they who have to transform global planning tasks into the detailed structure of production (quantity and quality of all products), production variables, production   organization,   production   technology,   the
development of productivity and costs, etc.   In the course
of this concrete determination of production, the enterprise
managements act first and foremost as representatives of
the interests of the production collectives, since (1) its
support for their function is of crucial significance, (2) the
managers of the enterprises are pursuing the same interests
as the production collective as a whole, and (3) the interests of the higher supra-industry organs (central adminis-
trations, general directorates or directorates of peoples'enterprises   or   trusts,   or   ministries)   harmonize   with   the
interests of the enterprises.   The concrete determination of
the development of labor and production by the management
of the enterprise is thus governed to a decisive extent by
an interest in maximizing the income of the enterprise collective while increasing productivity only when absolutely
unavoidable.
     It is of fundamental importance here that decisions
concerning the concrete development of production by the
managements of enterprises be made under conditions no
longer influenced by the market mechanism or that such influences be basically constrained and perverted.   However,
central planning does not replace the positive function of
the market mechanism; nor can it be replaced under the
given context of interests.   The interests of the enterprise
collectives simply no longer tend automatically toward social
interests as a result of income losses or gains, but rather
are pushed the other way around, into conflict with them.
Particularly for this reason, the structure of production
develops in a way that bypasses the structure of consumer
needs, and thus uses up factors of production (expenditure
of labor, means of labor, objects of labor) at a rate relatively much higher than capitalist production.   For the same
reason, it lags behind the technical progress and productivity increases achieved by the capitalist system and cannot be compared with it in terms of product quality and in-
novativeness.   The   mere   fact   of   having   rejected   the

---

[31] K. Marx, Das Kapital, vol. 1 (East Berlin, 1973), p.
531.

functions of the market mechanism has pushed socialist production into second place. Later on, we will deal more extensively with the need for a market mechanism and in particular with ways and means of mitigating its capitalist
defects.

By way of conclusion, then, it can be said that all notions to the effect that people's economic interests, that is,
primarily their interest in maximization of monetary income,
can be eliminated or reduced at the present stage of development by means of moral-political appeals, educational efforts, theoretical appeals to reason, etc., are utterly unrealistic, as they ignore or oversimplify the sources of
these interests. So long as a life long, rigid division of
labor, great differences among various work activities, a
relatively long work day, preponderantly monotonous, rep-
etitive, and fragmented work, authoritarian systems of management and control on the job, etc., prevail--in short, alienated work, which not even today's actually-existing
socialism has been able to overcome--the overwhelming majority of the people will do this work mainly in order to
earn income. And as long as this income necessarily limits
needs-satisfaction in an economically discriminating manner,
interest in income maximization will be one of the most important interests as far as a large majority of the population are concerned.

However, under the given division of labor, labor creates real income only if it actually produces optimal use
values for other people. Since this is today no longer the
concern of individual producers, but rather of large work
collectives and/or production enterprises, then there must
be some mechanism which forces these enterprises, through
the economic interests of their workers, to efficiently
produce use-values for consumers. The market mechanism
is precisely the mechanism by which the creation of the income of the enterprises is brought into a relationship with
their creation of use-value. The socialist planning system
could in no way completely replace this market mechanism,
since it has not shown itself capable of creating a reciprocal, flexible relationship between the concrete income of the
enterprises and the actual needs-satisfaction of consumers,
and hence of organizing the economic interests of the enterprise workers toward a maximally efficient creation of
use-value through their collective work. Rational recognition of the necessity of this orientation, which for the time
being remains indispensable, means at the same time recognition of the necessity of a well-functioning market mechanism. We will deal later with how this market mechanism
could be better organized, and how it could be freed from
the deficiencies it displays in the capitalist economic system, deficiencies which impede a more consistent formation

of income in relation to the level of efficiency of use-value creation.

Although in this chapter we have demonstrated above all the continuing need for economic interests at the present stage of the development of labor and consumption, (thus countering the constantly recurring illusions about the elimination of the market mechanism), this does not imply that the actual kinds of economic interests existing under capitalism cannot and should not be changed. If, in the first place, economic interests are characterized primarily by the ways in which people acquire their incomes, and if fundamentally different kinds of income formation also give rise to fundamentally different economic interests; and if then, in the second place, existing conflicts between certain economic interests--above all conflicts between wage and profit interests--are recognized as the principal causes of basic defects and disruptions in the capitalist economic system (as will be shown later in greater detail) then the question must also arise as to whether, and how the antagonism inherent in these kinds of economic interests can be changed. What is at stake, therefore, is not merely illusionary attempts to eliminate economic interests as such, but rather a search for ways and means of changing the kinds of economic interests that the people have, so that these would continue to lead the people to create use-value as efficiently as possible, yet at the same time would overcome the social antagonism between wage and profit interests. The chapters that follow are devoted to this problem.

2

THE NEED FOR ECONOMIC DEMOCRATIZATION

OVERCOMING THE UNILATERAL DEVELOPMENT OF CONSUMPTION

We have already demonstrated that individual needs grow considerably faster than human labor and production can satisfy them. The satisfaction of many needs is thus subject to economic limitations. Work, with its alienating division of labor, is a heavy burden for the majority of people which is often borne only because it is the basic precondition for the satisfaction of needs. In other words, most human needs must be met out of individual incomes acquired through labor or in the marketplace. Whenever sudden departures are made from this principle, the socially necessary development of labor and production is inevitably disrupted and needs cannot be satisfied on a broad scale. Adherence to the basic market principle of needs-satisfaction does not mean, however, that one does not see the increasingly obvious deficiencies in the particular form of needs-satisfaction in the capitalist system nor that one ought not to search for ways of overcoming them.

One difficulty of this system is that it produces a large number of goods which could be replaced by others that would last longer and/or would have a greater use-value. But they are not replaced because the transition from the first type of goods to the second would apparently create insoluble problems. It would be an ideological oversimplification to attempt to explain the failure to effect fundamental changes in production--for example, a changeover from short-lasting to long-lasting cars requiring far fewer repairs--merely in terms of the profit-making interests of the owners of capital. Indeed, there are large automobile companies which, although no longer private property, have no more interest in introducing such long-lasting vehicles than do privately owned firms. At first glance, one is struck by an immediate realization that the transition to longer-lasting products would mean a sharp decline in production and rapidly rising unemployment.

This fact gives rise to an overriding interest on the part of wage earners, one which is much stronger than their interest in the growth of profits (though the latter is of course present as well), and which is directed against these innovations and changes in production. Therefore, so long as the transition from short-lasting to long-lasting manufacturing methods and the substantial attendant decline in production is still accompanied by the creation of conditions which produce unemployment and other negative social consequences, then changes in production of this kind will always be extremely difficult to realize. In cases where immediate interests in maintaining wages and employment are bound up with the entrepreneurs' profit interests in resisting certain changes in production because these changes would in fact run counter to these interests, all rational arguments in favor of these changes are bound to fail.

Not infrequently, the existing system of production involves goods which are not absolutely essential to the satisfaction of people's needs, or which might be better replaced by other goods. Yet, as already demonstrated, addressing the problem with dirigist planning methods is no solution, since this would undermine the market mechanism and market interests; it would lead to bureaucratization and ultimately to intolerable losses and to inadequate satisfaction of people's broad and real needs. No central planning organ can presume to decide which goods are necessary for needs-satisfaction and which are superfluous.

However, if on the basis of objective analyses it could be established that changed socio-economic conditions could provide opportunities for substitution in production, which made it possible to reduce production and realize labor and material savings without lessening or qualitatively worsening needs-satisfaction at the same time, then two possible solutions would be conceivable. Either there would be further needs still inadequately satisfied, which would require structural changes in production, that is, changeovers to labor-reducing products on the one hand and expansion of more needed kinds of production on the other (we will demonstrate further in the following that the market alone is often not adequate to provide for such structural changes; or there would in fact be no other production possibilities able to compensate for the reduction in labor, perhaps because no further needs existed--which is extremely dubious. In this event, a reduction in work time would of course be necessary. Despite less work, people could continue to satisfy their needs at their accustomed level, since they could then utilize a large number of products for a much longer time and would not have to replace many of them so often.

The question then, is why the market mechanism alone cannot bring about certain structural changes, even though it is precisely in this area that its advantages are obvious when contrasted with dirigist planning. In the first

instance, naturally, one should mention the growth of monopolies that constricts the market. If highly concentrated
giant enterprises such as monopolies or oligopolies so dominate certain branches that they are able to forestall any
competition which would pose a threat to their established
mode of production, then there is only a very small hope
for fundamental structural changes. The introduction of
entirely new, revolutionary products which would not only
totally substitute for existing products and force them out
of the market, but would also paralyze entire productive
units and drastically reduce employment in entire branches,
is impossible where oligopolies exist and act in concert. In
order to counter this, first, a far more consistent anti-
monopolistic policy would be necessary than in the present
system; and second, a systematic, long-term and well-pre-
pared restructuring would be required, which would mean
retraining thousands of people in order to safeguard existing jobs or create new ones.

The second and more important reason why necessary
structural changes are hindered is due to income formation
and occurs when individually- and socially-financed needs
enter into competition with each other. In the development
of capitalism so far, individual incomes have not been sufficient to satisfy a whole range of needs, and as we have already demonstrated, the needs that tend to expand are
primarily those which must be financed by social institutions, primarily by the state. However, as long as the
broad strata of society are not in a position really to reflect
on these social needs, to discuss them and decide on them
democratically from among alternative proposals, they will
remain detached from them.

The more bureaucratic and opaque are the decisions
made in these areas, the more alienated from them the
population will be. Under such alienating conditions, one's
own personal income is always of more direct concern than
social income, whose use-value cannot be adequately quantified in concrete terms and indeed often cannot be assessed
at all. Consequently, aversion to increases in taxation--ac-
companied moreover by more and more incomprehensible and
bureaucratized tax systems--is only a natural manifestation
of the alienation between the individual and society.

This understandable antipathy on the part of the population toward any tax increase is further aggravated by
the demagogy of many politicians. On the one hand they
attribute all the blame for the growth of inflation to the
state, but fail to mention such pressing problems as the
pollution of the environment, the proliferation of vehicles on
the roads, the constant threats to health, increasing as-
saults on tranquility and sleep, etc. On the other hand,
however, as soon as the degeneration of the unbridled and

unplanned industrial agglomeration and urban development begins to make itself felt in social frustration, acts of violence and criminality, the same politicians call for the strengthening of the state and the enlargement of its repressive institutions and armies in order to create order-- quite ignoring the increased taxation necessary to bring these measures about. Instead of gearing their actions to the complexity of the situation and combating the real causes, (if only by using increased financial sources,) they wage a one-sided struggle against the symptoms of the problem, but with little prospect of success.[1]

Thus, while society will continue to generate relatively more needs that will have to be met from social resources, the satisfaction of these needs will be constrained by heavier tax levies. Relative tax increases alone cannot solve this problem. What is lacking is not only money, but above all productive capacity, the means of production, and labor power which are all committed, to a questionable extent, to the manufacture of superfluous products--superfluous in the sense that they serve to satisfy artificially-induced, manipulated needs. Once these needs have been aroused, in whatever manner, they are transformed into actual needs and require income for their satisfaction. However, citizens are only willing to give up a certain percentage of this income for taxes, since they are largely alienated from that part of the needs-satisfaction process paid for by the state.

In this way, a vicious circle evolves. New individual needs are constantly being created in order to maintain and increase production and work. Rising incomes must be geared toward, and expended for, these growing needs. People do not want to surrender an increasing percentage of their incomes for taxes because they see their personal needs as more important than social needs. If these personal needs were not artificially induced, they would not grow so rapidly. But they are expanded because as they grow, so too do production, jobs, wages, and profits. And so it goes. Within the existing system, in which the proportions between people's individual and social consumption are not evaluated, discussed, and decided beforehand, it is impossible to break out of this circle. But the fact of individual consumption, which is induced and exaggerated, and social consumption, which lags, has increasingly serious

---

[1] In this context the negative example of many cities, for instance, New York, comes to mind. Here, induced individual consumption is coupled with a gradual decline in living conditions since not enough funds are available for urgent and increasing social-municipal needs, and a great deal of what is available goes up in bureaucratic smoke.

effects on people's lives.[2]

If the linkages among all the spheres of society are not constantly analyzed, and if no long-term development alternatives are worked out for the basic orientation of production, for overall income distribution, and for the major areas of social consumption and then submitted to the people for discussion, people will primarily be concerned only with their short-term personal goals. Many politicians will then consider it opportune to adopt this frame of mind, and will no longer see any possibility of presenting more fundamental alternatives.

The actual process of favoring individual over social needs is, however, often not seen as a reaction to the existing social system, as an actual expression of the alienation of the individual from the state and society. This phenomenon is much more readily ascribed to eternal human egotism or alternatively the inability of the broad masses to understand the complicated requirements of the economy and the state. This predisposition leads to the conclusion that only state agencies can make decisions concerning taxation, state revenues and expenditures, economic policy directives, etc., and that their decisions must be more or less imposed upon the people.[3]

Notions that imply that the people simply do not want to make decisions about long-term, complex, and difficult problems of development, but would prefer to leave them to trained experts, are widespread in both West and East. Communist and anti-communist ideologies harbor a deep-seated negative attitude about the capacity for judgment of the broad strata of the population, and they differ from one another only in respect to which intellectual elite they would entrust with the leadership of society and the powers to make decisions about its development. Both cling to elitist notions because they are convinced that only select

---

[2] J. K. Galbraith formulates this phenomenon in his famous thesis of public poverty, private riches. A current and revealing discussion of this thesis is found in L. Boeckels, B. Scharf, and H. P. Widmaier, Machtverteilung im Sozialstaat. Untersuchungen zur These: Oeffentliche Armut bei privatem Reichtum (Munich, 1976). See also C. F. von Weizaecker, Wege in der Gefahr (Munich and Vienna, 1977), p. 68, which however emphasizes not the reality of the more rapidly growing social needs, but instead the significance of the service sector as prerequisite to job security. This corresponds to the undifferentiated conception of labor in Weizaecker's work.

[3] See F. A. Hayek, The Road to Serfdom Munich, 1976).

leadership groups are in a position to make decisions regarding social needs,   state revenues and expenditures,
and both political and economic policy development.   These
decisions are then announced to the people as if they were
the only possible correct ones, and information of this kind
is presented in very general terms while not many of the
problems involved are mentioned as they would arouse too
many doubts.   Any broad discussion of alternatives is considered not only redundant but dangerous.

   In reality, however, the reasons why the broad masses
are disinterested in state activities, state fiscal problems,
and political and economic policy decisions run much deeper.   They are not manifestations of a fundamental disinterest of the people in the grand issues of their society's development; rather they are the consequence of decades of
experience which show that whenever truly different alternatives regarding economic and social developments are not
presented to the people for their choice and decision, all
decisions will in the end be made by small, powerful political groups or powerful political machines.

   Even in political democracies, as governments alternate
and one party grasping for power is replaced by another,
so little changes in the direction of the economy and in economic policy that people have simply given up hope that it
ever will.   Whether under conservative-bourgeois or social-
democratic governments, all Western industrial states have
been beset by the same problems of inflation and crisis; of
course, problems of transportation, housing, social assistance, children, and the aged are much discussed before
elections, but then nothing, or very little changes in the
situation.   The people more and more come to feel that they
can depend only on what they struggle for and get themselves on an individual basis, or on what, as their own, is
in their sphere of personal decision-making.   Their attitudes toward other people, toward society, and toward the
state become increasingly indifferent.

   In a totalitarian communist system, where people have
long recognized their powerlessness in social decision-making, they are utterly excluded from participation and completely disinterested in public issues.   They know very well
that they cannot change anything in the national economic
plans, the state budget, the welfare system, or housing
and transport conditions, and that all criticisms, which
must always be directed at the same responsible political
organs, will not only not bring about any changes in existing abuses but will more likely result in trouble for them
and their children in the form of disadvantages and repression.   The result must be political resignation and increased
individualism characterized by extreme consumerist orientations.   The degradation of the people to the level of mere

accessories at mass rallies, of applause-makers at ostentatious displays of mass enthusiasm, and the fact that these are organized by omnipotent machines with their systems of control and retribution--a fact which has long since penetrated into the consciousness of each and every worker--makes a mockery of the socialist ideal of freedom.

It is therefore discouraging when many young people in Western industrial states, in protest against democracy's inability to come to grips with its growing economic and political problems, seek a cure-all in authoritarian systems of government. It is not only leftist movements that believe that Marxist avante-gardes must fight on behalf of the still-immature people, then maintain their interests long after the revolution and enforce these interests with the methods of power politics. Resurgent rightist and neofascist movements also see salvation in a strong arm capable of maintaining law and order and of replacing endless discussions with decision-making by intelligent men. However much they may fight each other, both these groups have one basic attitude in common: they are convinced of the infallibility of their own ideas and conceptions of society. They believe they have already found the recipe to cure all of society's problems, and they see themselves as the liberators of the people.

In reality, all opponents of democracy, whether of the left or right, can be characterized by their disdain for ordinary people and by an unlimited desire for power, even though both sides make much of the freedom to which they aspire, be it of a nationalist or socialist stamp. Without democracy, however, no human freedom exists. However loudly one may proclaim freedom, if he does not emphasize that one of its basic conditions is pluralism of ideas and interest groups as well as tolerance toward dissenters, then he is a demagogue.

In its practicable form, the interest of society cannot be anything but a compromise among many different interests--a compromise which incorporates as many interests as possible and which does not suppress the interests of the minority. The latter must have an ongoing opportunity to obtain information and to express themselves in order that they too might eventually be able to form a majority. Only under such conditions can new ideas arise at all, can mistakes be found, can one discover what factors work against the interests of the majority of the population, can one recognize the causes of deficiencies and prepare new proposals. In an authoritarian system, mistakes made by leading politicians are not to be exposed, nor may they be criticized, and thus one finds it all the more difficult to overcome them. Such systems thus always, sooner or later, end up in a blind alley.

Even if the advocates of Western democracy agree with this political conception of democracy, their agreement does not go so far as the application of these democratic principles to economics and economic policy decision-making. And yet the solution to the mounting difficulties of the highly developed industrial societies must be sought in economic reform. While the economy itself is becoming more and more socialized, and is increasing in complexity, it is no longer just the individual person, but the individual plant, the individual enterprise, that have become mere cogs in a huge machine comprising the national economy and, increasingly, the world economy--developments which are creating an ominous situation for all people. Yet the responsibility for economic decision-making remains concentrated in the hands of a few people. For the most part, there are no alternative proposals for different possibilities of development, for instance those that include the larger contexts and different socio-economic consequences for democratic decision-making by the people's representatives. On the contrary, decisions are made on the basis of proposals, presented without alternatives, for fundamental changes which would no longer be within the powers of the elected parliamentarians. Hence, even in the Western democracies economic policy decision-making is increasingly left to anonymous bureaucratic machines. The contradiction between labor, which is largely socialized, and decision-making, which is done by small power elites, is growing and increasingly approaching the stage of absolute Communist bureaucratization.

The resolution of this contradiction must be sought and found in new ways of democratizing the economy. Not only the preservation of political democracy but its extension into the economy is the way to realize the real interests and develop the responsibility of broad strata of the population on behalf of a development which determines and enters into the lives of everyone to a decisive degree. This is to say that small elites should not decide everything that affects the lives of the masses, but that actual ways and means must be developed for them to examine alternative possibilities of development, and these should include broad political discussions throughout all of society. In this manner it would be possible to arrive at the alternative which enjoys the support of the majority.

In particular, changes in institutions, decision-making structures and mechanisms in the social micro-spheres and macro-spheres should promote the awareness, manifestation, confrontation, and eventual mutual adaptation of differing interests, as well as create conditions for a more consistent discovery and implementation of mutual, long-term interests. Although this cannot mean the elimination of all conflicts of interests, it should better facilitate a conscious, peaceful

solution to them. Not by concealing clashes of interests
and by suppressing interests, but only by baring actual
differences of interests, by respecting minority interests,
and by the maximum possible voluntary harmonization of
different interests can a more humane society develop.

Of course there will never be one development alternative that meets the interests of everyone, and it will also
be impossible to prevent mistakes being made in the national
economy. Nevertheless, the alienation of the economy and
the state from the citizens can only be overcome gradually,
and a sense of responsibility for the great, vital decisions
can only be increased among more and more people through
democratic elections and democratic decision-making systems. The drift toward bureaucratization can no longer be
stopped merely by isolated popular initiatives aimed at preventing developments which directly threaten people--initia-
tives, incidentally, which can all too readily be abused by
political demagogues--but by broad, regular, and institutionally safeguarded discussions about all fundamental economic alternatives, including opportunities for democratic
decision-making. Majority decision-making on the part of
the people, within a pluralist process of group formation
that provides for the possibility of alternative decisions
while ensuring the exclusion of economically and/or politically privileged strata or classes, can open the way to
overcoming people's narrowly egoistic, socially alienated
thinking in both the macro- and micro-economic spheres.

Under these circumstances, the competition between individual and social income development and needs-satisfaction will no longer--or less and less--clearly turn out to the
advantage of the former. Four things are already evident
to many people today: that fundamental improvements in
urban development, housing, the traffic and transport systems, and in environmental and health protection are necessary; that stressful conditions must be eliminated while
tranquility must be increased; that long-term employment
prospects must be assured; that comprehensive social security is increasingly important to their lives and must at
least be equated in significance to individual consumer
goods. Once the possibility exists of knowing in advance
the consequences of alternative developments of social
needs-satisfaction, of comparing needs with each other and
judging them more comprehensively, then more and more
decisions will be implemented that favor various fundamental
changes in social life, possibly even at the cost of slower
growth in individual consumption. It is obvious that, hand
in hand with all this, state revenues and expenditures
would have to meet the democratically determined social satisfaction of needs.

Only a development of this kind can overcome the one-sidedness of capitalist consumption. Even if individual consumption does continue to grow, it will no longer be promoted as mindlessly and wastefully as it is today, namely in order to increase the number of jobs and the level of wages and profits by means of new, manipulated, and artificially-induced consumer behavior. If the increasingly important fulfillment of social needs is consciously expanded by means of the planned, long-term restructuring of production, not only will more constant production and employment be secured by a growth which corresponds to the supply of labor, but superfluous increases in consumption will also be eliminated. Although individual consumption and hence the impulse to increase individual income will for some time retain their crucial significance, the increased production of enterprises could be oriented, in relatively increasing proportions, to the systematically regulated tasks of the state without restricting competition among producers.

CONFLICT BETWEEN WAGE AND CAPITAL INTERESTS

In the capitalist system, and even more so in the communist system, the working person is profoundly alienated from the means of production operating in society. The places of production, the enterprises and plants, the material situation, the energy resources, etc., with the help of which huge worker collectives produce what millions of people need for their lives - this whole gigantic production machinery has now become, for most people, a stranger phenomenon than it was for the Luddites at the beginning of the Industrial Revolution. Although they are the crucial foundation of labor, income, and hence of life in general, the working people not only have no decision-making powers concerning the basis of production, they also regard it with complete disinterest.

Naturally, blue- and white-collar workers have an interest in the preservation of their places of work, since this is a precondition of employment and income. But the ways in which the growth of the enterprise takes place, investments are made, the structure of production changes, sales are made, efficiency is developed, profits grow and are used, and the products are evaluated by consumers--all this, for most workers in these enterprises, is outside their responsibility and thus lies beyond their interests. Whether in family-owned enterprises, in large corporations, or in nationalized plants in communist systems, blue- and white-collar workers everywhere see themselves as mere wage earners and nothing more.

The owners alone, whether individual families, a few shareholders, a large number of stockholders, or the state, have the right to determine the development of the enterprise. They alone decide on the continued existence, expansion, or closing of the enterprise, its production goals, production equipment, and the amount of work to be done. They are responsible for the enterprise's external dealings, and they decide on the disposition of the results of production, in which they have a direct interest. Quite generally, we may state that ownership of an enterprise represents the continuous appropriation by the owners of new means of production and results of production. It is expressed in the owner's right to decide on or dispose of the results, processes, and means of production.

Decision-making powers can be transferred by the owners to their appointed production heads, executives, directors, and managers. But these are all responsible to the owners, even though in many large corporations the former's responsibility is becoming more and more formal, so that real decision-making power lies in the hands of management. This does not however alter the fact that only a small group of people decide on the enterprise's development and hence on the work of thousands, while employees are excluded from the whole process.

State property, in a socialist system, is represented as the property of the whole society. However, this is only an abstract and empty claim that contrasts with the real power of disposition. The population has no possibility of directly or indirectly determining the development of the plant or of production; they receive no information and have no opportunity to intervene or to effect change. They cannot even gain influence by means of political elections. Nor do they have anything to say about the appointment of directors or other leading functionaries of the plant. The production collectives have just as few rights. They are consulted only in order to get their advice on how to better increase production. They do not even have the right to express their views on wage regulations or to fight for higher wages.

The party bureaucracy alone has the decisive power over state operations. All elections within the party organs are purely formal and do not call the party machine's basic decisions into question. Here again, therefore, the workers in the enterprise see themselves as mere wage earners vis-a-vis a completely alien owner who, moreover, behaves in such a despotic manner as to preclude any form of wage struggle.

The owners of the enterprises always have the right of disposition over the results of production, which in a commodity economy primarily means disposition over the proceeds derived from the sale of commodities. Once the current reproduction of capital (ersatz investments) has been achieved, what is left is actual gross income. And both private and state owners have an interest in maximizing this gross income. The further division of income into wage and capital income is the basis of a struggle between wage earners and capital owners in which each side attempts to gain a maximum return for itself. The nature of the income division changes, as has been described, hand in hand with the development of capitalism. The specific interest of the owners of capital or the owners of enterprises is therefore directed toward the maximization of capital income, whereas that of the wage recipients is concentrated on the maximization of wage income. The fact that the amounts of wage and capital income depend upon the division of gross income--a process determined by power--produces the contradiction between wage and profit interests.

If the wage earners are not owners of the enterprises, if they have no rights of disposition and decision-making, they will only be interested in set wages negotiated prior to the completion of production. For them it is a matter of payment for work carried out, quite independent of its social results, over which they have no decisive influence. The owners determine the course of their work activity, control it, and must pay the workers in accordance with the agreement. With respect to forms of wages tied to increases in productivity (piecework, job-work, etc.), the situation is no different. These still represent payments for work done and are thus fundamentally different from profits, in which those aspects of the entrepreneurial economy are concentrated that are not susceptible to wage-earner influence. Even where private firms do have an interest in allowing their employees a share of the profits--in order to provide them with an interest in increasing these profits--this may be seen as only a supplementary incentive. This contradiction between wage and profit interests will exist as long as the ownership of the enterprises remains alienated from the working people. Therefore, there will also be no socially optimal division of the gross income so long as this situation prevails.

THE ECONOMIC RESPONSIBILITY OF THE PEOPLE

Our analysis of the two systems has demonstrated that neither can fulfill one requirement in particular which today confronts humanity and which will be crucial to its fate: societywide democratic decision-making about the future development of the economy, in the course of which the responsibility hitherto enjoyed by narrow power strata could be transferred to the broadest strata of the population.

Never before has such a strong pressure been exerted by the people on their political representatives to effect rapid, maximum increases in wages and consumption. Under the conditions of Western bourgeois democracy, trade unions and trade union functionaries--and many politicians working in the same direction--legitimate themselves by fighting for these wage and consumption interests. Developments of this kind lead to new forms of inflation and jeopardize the capitalist drive for profits which has for ages ensured the rapid, productive, and effective rise of the capitalist market economy.

The unconquerable individual interest in consumption, artificially promoted by a system of competition and unrestricted striving for profit, and transformed in the context of political power interests into the decisive criterion of political legitimation efforts, is the concentrated expression of human economic alienation in both systems existing today. The more rapidly the forces of production develop and consumption increases, and the further and more suggestively information is disseminated about new and pleasant life chances, the stronger will be the struggle for increased consumption and the elimination of consumption differentials within society. What is here disregarded are the conditions of social equilibrium as well as the ecological, social, and individual consequences of such consumerist strivings. Moral indignation toward people's consumerist materialism and toward their weak moral reactions, appeals against the consumerist drives and pressures as well as appeals against consumerism and for the renunciation of consumption--all these are futile, as they historically always have been. For they do not reveal the real cause of the development; they only polemicize against its symptoms.

This one-sided development of needs cannot be transformed without changing social conditions. For this reason, economic and political relations must change. As long as the overwhelming majority of the population remain working and consuming subjects, while responsibility for the development of investments, growth of production and consumption, orientation of economic development, etc. rests with narrow and exclusive decision-making organs, the result can only be mass disinterest in the economic processes and unbridled consumerism.

It will however be more and more difficult to invest enough to sustain full employment and growth while at the same time holding down inflation. As long as pure market incentives on the one hand and bureaucratic planning incentives on the other continue exclusively to determine economic development, there will hardly be any chance to harmonize economic growth with investments, raw materials and energy sources; to lower individual consumer wastage in order to meet better social needs; to halt the increasing environmental pollution produced by industrial exploitation and profiteering industrial agglomerations; to overcome the great differences in economic levels among various parts of the globe and countries; and to stop the insane losses resulting from armaments and threats to life.

In the capitalist market economy, the alienated drive to consumption and profits inhibits a development of production and consumption that would correspond to the long-term interests of society. In the bureaucratic planning system, mindlessly exaggerated investment quotas are used to attempt a growth in production aimed at reconciling the controversial consumption interests of the people with the military power interests of the rulers. But the less the ineffective production system is able to meet the people's growing consumption interests, and the more insecure the ruling bureaucracy thus feels, the more will it attempt to bolster its power with economic plans increasingly remote from reality.

The short-term profit interest in the market economy and the long-term power interest in the planned economy, given an increase in the mindless pressure to consume and the growing economic alienation of the masses of the people, could quite possibly lead to a world catastrophe. Some politicians who are partially aware of such dangers do attempt to prevent the worst by making moralistic and thus less effective appeals. Most however underestimate the dire scientific warnings about the future and instead pursue opportunistic political goals; indeed many even retreat into a cynical après nous le déluge attitude.

In this situation, only systemic reform could provide a solution by overcoming the economic alienation of the working strata of the population. No doubt this can happen only through democratization of decision-making in both the macro- and micro-spheres of the economy. This democratization must however make use of individual needs and interest incentives to guarantee that economic initiatives increase, rather than lower, efficiency and which orient the development of production in a more humane direction: Democratization, efficiency, and a more humane orientation of production --these are the slogans that summarize the requirements of any reform of the economic systems. They must therefore be seen as the basic criteria of any such reform. [4]

In the process of effecting such reform, it would of course be necessary to retain those components of the system which today already promote the development of the three basic criteria; the other components of the system, which impede it, would have to be changed. At the same time it is a matter of introducing completely new basic features of various kinds into the two existing systems. Even if this systemic reform could be implemented over a relatively long period of time, through a gradual sequence of changes in institutions, processes, and modes of action, it would have to be understood and pursued in all its complex inner logic, since all economic, process-related system components are linked to each other, and none of them will function properly without the others. Indeed, without a proper linkage, the results may be often transformed into the opposite of those intended.

Thus, the profit motive, for instance, will promote a socially necessary effective development of production only if coupled with enhanced competition among independent enterprises. If, on the other hand, collective enterprises are given an interest in profits while a monopolistic organization of production without competition continues to exist (as is the case, for example, in the economy of the GDR), then the profit motive would produce even more antisocial modes of operation and development of production. Or if competitive relations are implemented while at the same time no instruments exist to prevent a monopolistic development of profit or income on the part of a few large enterprises (as for instance in the Yugoslav economy), then income differentials will arise that do not match productivity. This leads workers in non-monopolistic plants to attempt to adjust their own income level to that of the monopolies, even where this cannot be justified in terms of their productivity. This then gives rise to inflation. Therefore, before turning to an examination of specific models, we will summarize some interconnections between certain basic processes that will have to be taken into account in any reform attempt.

First and foremost, at the present stage of development, that is, given the still rigid division of labor which for the most part binds people all their lives to whatever spheres of professional activity they are in, and given the fact that differences among the working people, as far as

---

[4] On the connection between democracy and efficiency, see also W. Brus's argument in his Sozialisierung und politisches System (Frankfurt/Main, 1975), p. 202 et seq.

their creativity and self-realization are concerned, are still substantial, economic incentives to work must be retained. This cannot be understood as only monetary payments to individual persons for their work, but above all money incomes for individual production collectives. Here it must be noted that, at the existing stage of the development of labor, only the market mechanism, via its income-formation process, is able to compel the production collective (which alone makes decisions on the concrete development of production) to seek a development of production optimal for society.

This method of developing income, which is dependent upon social utility and the efficiency of entire production collectives, is expressed in its most acute form in profits. Wages, on the other hand, least express this social labor orientation. Where competitive pressure exists, profits will increase directly as the enterprise more consistently and more flexibly produces in accordance with needs, turns out better and more useful products, utilizes its factors of production more economically, and is able to increase its productivity while relatively lowering its costs of production through technological progress. In the case of an enterprise whose activities less successfully meet society's demands, its profits will decline relatively or disappear completely. Wages, in contrast, express only remuneration for a certain quantity of work of varying qualification within the plant. They do not react, at least not directly, to changes in the social utility and efficiency of the whole plant.

As long as the private capitalist ownership of the enterprises accords responsibility for the success of production only to the owners and the functionaries appointed by them, whereas this responsibility is basically denied to the entire production collective, direct income formation by the collective in accordance with market results is not necessary and basically impossible. As long as this is so, the workers' wage demands will also be made independently of market results and indeed, repeatedly in the face of them. The indifference of the working masses toward market results and profits, as well as the investments made on the basis of these, together with growing consumption-oriented wage pressures, must eventually, as we have seen, jeopardize the overall development of the economy.

If this economic alienation is to be overcome and responsibility for a socially useful and effective development of production and investment is to be really democratized, the incomes of working people must be tied in greater measure to the market results of enterprises in the form of their substantial participation in profits. Shared material responsibility of this nature, tying the incomes of all workers at least partially to the market results of the enterprise, is again inconceivable without the democratization of control and decision-making rights affecting the development of the enterprise. Worker participation in the market results of the enterprises and democratization of powers of disposal and decision-making rights in the enterprises amount to the democratization of the enterprises' ownership.

Participation in decision-making is in turn not conceivable without the collective being given coresponsibility for capital- and profit-sharing. Otherwise it would be a one-sided development which ignored the economic interconnections. The German trade unions' efforts to achieve codetermination, for instance, are susceptible to this kind of danger. For this reason we will now examine this aspect more fully.

PARTICIPATORY DECISION-MAKING IN THE MICRO-SPHERE

Codetermination is supposed to lead to employee equality in the enterprise. The representatives of the wage earners (the term wage earners or Lohnempfaenger, is more precise than employees or Arbeitnehmer, since they in fact carry out work, or sell their labor) in top-level decision-making boards, or in supervisory or administrative councils, where decisions are made about fundamental intra-enterprise policies, are supposed to have parity representation. Codetermination is regarded as a step toward the goal of comprehensive economic democratization. The advocates of codetermination in the enterprise expect it to provide better insights into the enterprises' economic development. Moreover they see it as an opportunity to implement the wage-earners' interests quickly and consistently.

While codetermination certainly does contribute to economic democratization in the micro-sphere, as long as all the other basic features of the system remain intact, above all the contradiction between wage and profit interests, it is no solution to the problems cited. It may even create new difficulties. Just as the Marxist theory of socialism, which, by ignoring the problems of interests, has resulted in a diseased system, this movement, which begins with different theoretical premises and different goals, is similarly threatened with a setback if it fails to take the problems of interests into account.

Marxist and non-Marxist oriented persons who, as advocates of the interests of the workers, would like to transcend capitalism in a revolutionary or reformist manner, repeatedly begin with the assumption that the roots of all the evils of capitalism lie in the profit motive (greed). The contradiction between wage and profit interests, they believe, must be resolved by eliminating profit interests. And even if such interests cannot perhaps immediately be done away with among businessmen, in no event should workers acquire an interest in profits. For this would only increase their egotistical and invidious profit interests. The workers should struggle only for a fair wage and their interest is said to be equal pay for equal work, an interest which unites them in solidarity beyond the confines of the enterprise. An interest in profit, on the other hand, would encourage intra-company egotism and break the wage-solidarity of the workers. These arguments, and similar ones, are made, for example, by many trade union functionaries who, though rejecting the Communist system, subjectively fight with the deepest conviction for the workers' interests.

Many continue to believe that the individualism, egotism, or communal divisions among the people can be transcended by deploying education, organization, moral codes, or consciousness-formation to stress their commonalities, communalism, or ties. We have already demonstrated several things: that human beings always harbor both ego-oriented and communally-oriented needs; that they develop both egotistical and altruistic interests; that the concrete form of their needs and interests changes as society, and their position within it, changes; that the intensity of their interests changes with their overall development; and that the eternal contradiction between egotism and altruism thus cannot disappear. All attempts to overcome people's ego-related interests by means of education, moralization, ideology, or politics, are bound to fail.

It would be depressing if all the important experiences and insights gained from the Eastern socialist experiment were ignored or understood only superficially in purely moralizing terms (the bourgeois morals of the bureaucrats are the cause of it all). Views like this, however, are disseminated by those who want to keep the worker from developing any interest in profits, who see profit interests as only evil capitalist interests. Such views permit of only two conclusions: either a development toward dirigist economic planning which logically would have to regress behind what, for example, in Hungary is already considered self-evident; or an attitude that, although today one cannot get by without profit interests, these are peculiar to the capitalists and should not be shared by the workers. However, this second attitude, held by many non-communist socialists, trade unionists, and moralists, means adhering to the contradiction between wage income and capital income, between wage interests and profit interests.

Yet if this contradiction is not overcome, all the rules of codetermination and participatory decision-making in the enterprise cannot eliminate the struggle for income distribution. The wage-earners' representatives in the administrative organs will in all important decisions always be guided only by the interests of wages and labor--which is of course expected of them. This however does nothing to change the workers' disinterest in investments, in structural changes in production, in increased efficiency, in necessary reductions in production, in retarding wage growth, etc. In short, the wage earners are still alienated from the socially necessary development of the economy. They thus view this development from the perspective of their one-sided, short-term interests, since it largely occurs outside, and frequently conflicts with, these interests. Profit remains the alienated basis not only of investment but also of capitalist consumption. Any regulation of wages, especially one which might favor profits and investments, will be resisted.

At the same time, codetermination must be regarded as a restriction on entrepreneurial initiative as far as businessmen are concerned, since they are still responsible for the development of their capital and do not always just make profits but also sustain losses. If the workers raise objections which do not emanate from the interests that must be crucial to the success of an enterprise engaged in market competition, they can in fact retard or even block decisions vital to the enterprise (rapid structural changes, reductions or changes in production). This explains the employers' struggle to secure at least a voting majority (by means of nominating the chairman and others) in the negotiations for intra-company parity codetermination in the German Federal Republic. The position of many trade union functionaries, namely that the interests of the wage earners (that is, their social interest) must be taken into account in all decision-making, has thus not been logically thought through.

The crucial interest of working people is oriented toward a maximally crisis-free, continuous, and secure economic development in which unemployment, inflation, and environmental pollution do not occur. New horizons in living standards, reduction in hours of work, lowering of stress, and overcoming labor alienation--these are the workers' interests. Developments of this kind are not possible without maximum efficiency in production, without constant structural changes and market adaptations, without innovations, technical progress, and the highest efficiency of investments. It is therefore no longer enough for the vast majority of the population to be concerned only about the realization of their immediate work, wage or consumer interests while responsibility for the long-term development of capital is left to a relatively small group.

But mere participatory decision-making in the enterprises' highest organs by no means implies a genuine assumption of responsibility. A purely moral responsibility is no longer sufficient. Lessons ought to be learned here from the socialist countries' experiences. Decision-making in collective organs, which does not have long-term material effects on the members of such organs, leads to collective irresponsibility. Popularity contests with the aid of short-sighted and overly hasty resolutions also occur when functionaries are rated and elected from below. Bureaucratism will predominate when functionaries are appointed by superior power groups. The first tendency was devastatingly revealed in the Russian post-revolutionary period and was sharply criticized by Lenin[5] (for whom the elimination of the soviets introduced a purely power-political solution); the second is part of the daily routine in all commissions charged with evaluating investment plans and other fundamental economic measures and with preparing appropriate proposals.

Functionaries who are not made directly responsible for the consequences of their decisions, that is, who stand to lose neither their positions nor their incomes, will always have a rather lax attitude toward the necessary decisions, and indeed may pursue secondary intentions that are primarily politically motivated and damaging to the economy. Naturally, all this can be rejected out of hand as unprovable. And the fact that it is formally unprovable has always made it difficult to reveal the bureaucratic essence of all decision-making procedures in the Communist system and to deduce from this its momentous lack of efficiency vis-a-vis capitalist decision-making. But even without formal proof, practical experiences are available and ought to be heeded. Attention ought also to be paid to the fact that the one-sided glorification of individualism in the West--ignoring the long-term human motivations and modes of behavior--when applied in practice, may have consequences just as ominous to society as a whole as does the Communist ideology practiced in the East bloc states.[6]

This does not mean however that democratization of the economy is not necessary. On the contrary, nothing can so decisively counteract the threat of bureaucratization and

---

[5] See V.I. Lenin, Werke, vol. 30 (East Berlin, 1974), p. 300.

[6] See O. Sik, The Communist System of Power (New York, 1981).

increased alienation as economic democratization. But it must be understood as democratization not only of rights but also of duties, of responsiblity, of the material conse- quences of all decisions. The employees must become collec- tive owners or co-owners of the enterprises. As such they, like the private owners of today, would share in profits and losses. We will return once again to the concrete forms and institutional problems which arise in this context. For now, only a few words about the principle itself and its ground- ing are in order.

Existing joint-stock corporations already represent a step on the road to the democratization of capital owner- ship, although the step is admittedly a small one which has not solved two difficult problems. First, this form has not prevented the concentration of large blocks of shares or stock majorities in the hands of a few owners. In this way democracy has been completely undermined in many joint- stock corporations. In reality, the great mass of small shareholders in such corporations have essentially nothing to say. They often do not even attend the more or less formal general stockholders' meetings. They are manipulat- ed by the large shareholders at the pleasure and in the in- terest of the latter. The second and, in the context of the above mentioned difficulties of capitalism, even more impor- tant problem is the fact that nothing has changed in the situation of the overwhelming majority of wage earners. For them share-capital remains alienated ownership; their rela- tionship to it is purely one of labor and wages.

The logical extension of the step already taken toward the democratization of capitalist ownership must therefore be a search for ways of overcoming the two deficiencies cited. First, it would be a matter of decentralizing the concentra- tion of property rights in the hands of a few so that de- mocracy could become a reality rather than a farce. Sec- ond, all wage earners must become owners of their companies if they are to overcome their alienation. This will not be achieved, however, by large enterprises occasionally selling or giving their employees a few shares in the com- pany. This changes their position very little. They re- main mere wage earners who basically have no decision- making rights. Economic democracy is not thereby strengthened but remains bogus democracy. And profit- sharing is so minimal that it plays a smaller part than, for example, interest from the bank accounts of small savers. Most owners of such company shares tend instead to con- sider how they can someday profitably sell the shares in order to come into money quickly and hence increase their consumption.

The problem then is to find forms of capital participa- tion for employees which would in time give them the feeling of being genuine collective owners with corresponding decision-making rights as well as tangible participation in profits and losses. Only in conjunction with such developments would the actual situation of working people, and thus their interests and consciousness, begin to change. Instead of being mere wage earners they would evolve into co-worker/co-owners whose wage interests would be tied to capital income interests. A growing interest in profit, fostered by profit-sharing would, as experience shows, produce an interest in capital development, in the company's investment activities, in the development of its production and business affairs, and in its efficiency, leadership, etc. Disinterest and indifference would, in time, and on the basis of accumulated experience, give way to participation in the activities and development of the company.

As we shall also see, ownership should not be individualistic, for instance in the form of individually alienable employee shares, since this would not overcome the already cited deficiencies in democracy. It is not a matter of creating in employees the psychosis of the small owner who thinks only of profits, speculations, advantageous sales, or capital accumulation. Nor is it a matter of the obvious goal of helping people become better off. This could be achieved relatively easily with the aid of trans-enterprise employee investment funds. Neither in the first case nor the second, however, does the relationship between the people and their enterprise change. They shouldn't think only of the interests they would receive from an employee investment fund, similar to a bank savings account, nor indeed should they think only of how they could advantageously alienate their shares in order to increase their consumption rapidly. Above all they should become responsible co-owners of their enterprises, guided by their individual profit and consumption interests to identify with the interests of the enterprise, its efficiency, its investment needs, and its development. It is a question of working out a form of ownership which would aid the employees of an enterprise to start from, then go beyond their self-evident and unavoidable individual material interests, and to develop a long-term interest in the enterprise, in its economic relations, and ultimately in the entire economy.

One cannot condemm this as intra-company egotism, for an interest in the maximum efficiency of one's own enterprise often best serves the interest of the population as a whole. If the aim is not to perpetuate the contradiction between wage and profit interests with all its capitalist consequences, then each employee must have a direct interest in profits and hence in the efficiency of the enterprise. A wage earner who is disinterested in the development of profits is in reality disinterested in the social results of his labor. He will be interested only in doing his work according to the rules and getting paid for it. His interest does not however include such questions as whether the enterprise supplies consumers with really useful products, whether it consistently improves the quality of these products, whether it employs the latest technology to attain maximum productivity, whether its structure of production is flexible, or whether it is generally developing its production with maximum efficiency, profitability, and therefore with mounting returns. This is ultimately true of both systems.

Any search for a way of transcending the inherent contradictions and alienating phenomena of these two systems must allow the working people themselves to assume responsibility for the social use and efficiency of their labor. The general framework for this consists of market mechanisms, macro-economic planning, and market regulation.

Any objections here ought not to be to the effect that employees would develop a greater interest in the profits and efficiency of their enterprises, but rather that these profits must not be made through activities harmful to society and not related to performance, as is so frequently the case in capitalism. To the extent that the development of profits really reproduces socially useful activity on the part of the enterprise, the employees' interest in profits can only be evaluated positively. However, the moment that profit increases can be achieved continuously at the consumers' expense, with the aid of advantages disproportionate to performance, with a monopoly position and the like, such profit interests would have antisocial effects.

This however is no longer the problem of capital participation and profit interest itself but of the above-mentioned deficiencies of the capitalist market or its monopolistic limitations and other imperfections. Possibilities of overcoming these, and the problem of market regulation, are issues which will concern us later. It must only be clearly seen that under certain conditions, which as yet have to be created, the interest of company employees in the development of the enterprise and of profits can and should become a socially positive and desirable interest.

WHY PROFIT-FORMATION AND PROFIT INTERESTS?

However, if it is asserted that the incomes of employees with a share in capital formation should be tied, by means of profit-sharing, to the enterprise's market results, the question persists: Why should the employees receive any wages at all? Why should their entire income not simply represent a percentage of the distributable market income of the collective enterprise? Even if we set aside the possibility of merely partial workers' capital-participation in capitalist firms and conceive of enterprises completely under collective employee ownership, the incomes of these co-worker/co-owners should be formed only in part as profit-sharing and largely as firmly fixed wages. But we cannot support any transition to a scheme of incomes based entirely on the market-determined income (gross income) of the enterprise--as is the case, for example, for cooperatives or, basically, in the Yugoslavian system as well--without a universally valid method of determining wages that runs horizontally through the national economy.

In Yugoslavia, efforts are being made to realize the Marxian socialist principle of from each according to his abilities to each according to his work, and this is supposed to be achieved by the self-administering organs (workers' councils) of the plants themselves through their autonomous distribution of the enterprises' market-determined income. This achieves a better linkage between individual income and the social utility and efficiency of the plant's collective work than is the case in the Soviet socialist system. The market mechanism and the self-interest of the Yugoslavian plants lead to more demand-conforming and effective production activities than can be accomplished by Soviet dirigist planning. For this reason, Yugoslavian income distribution better corresponds to the socialist principle of work than does Soviet dirigist wage planning.

Despite the fundamental advantage of Yugoslavian income formation from the aspect of the socialist work principle, some deficiencies have appeared which make it difficult really to implement this performance principle, thus contributing to income formation not in line with performance. Such deficiencies are created above all by the separation of the plant's gross income into wages and profits--a dichotomy which has been combated solely in ideological terms. Wages and profits are regarded in Yugoslavia as capitalist categories, and since there are no longer wage earners--but now associate producers--in the socialist enterprises of Yugoslavia, these categories have also been eliminated.

The socialist plant collectives are formally independent in the distribution of their incomes. No central organ has the right to pass regulations respecting this distribution

process. In reality, however, their right of disposition is
limited, for indirect social influences affect this distribution
process. Thus the distribution proportions (quota spans)
for remuneration funds and entrepreneurial funds, for the
amounts of personal incomes, and the like are worked out
on the basis of so-called social consultations within each
branch of the economy, the communes, and regions (with
the help of economic chambers, trade unions, and other social organizations). Enterprises that oppose these consultations quickly come under pressure.[7] They are subjected to
political influence exerted by the trade unions and the Party (League of Communists) and to administrative intervention; their funds are blocked by the banks and every possible economic sanction is applied against them.

The system is too vague, however, and too exposed to
chance events and arbitrary interference. It cannot guarantee a really performance-related development of plant and
personal incomes. This is not to say that differences in
income formation ought not to exist; they are indeed necessary because plant collectives do of course perform differently (in terms of productivity, quality, economic efficiency, flexibility, etc.) However, income differentials often
arise that do not correspond to differences in performance,
but instead develop from the monopolistic position of large
enterprises, from a company's domination of branch production (decisive share of production) and/or of the market,
from the exclusiveness of products, of markets, and the
like. In these cases, the performance-related development of
income is undermined. And precisely such income differentials are necessarily present in Yugoslavia as well, since
the income system itself makes impossible any distinction
between income differentials of this nature and income differentials which properly reflect performance. They induce, as already mentioned, a stronger upward pressure on
wages and wage struggles in plants which cannot derive
monopolistic incomes and which in this way produce arbitrary income formations and inflationary pushes.

At the same time, the Yugoslavian income system, by
allowing the plants the freedom to determine their own income distribution, prevents an overall social harmonization
between consumption-oriented incomes and the production of
consumer goods. The practice of very vaguely orienting
income distribution through particular social consultations
cannot alter this situation appreciably. In fact, the quotas
of personal incomes and investments from gross income are

---

[7] See M. Drulovic, Arbeiterselbstverwaltung auf dem Pruef-
stand Erfahrungen in Jugoslawien (Bonn/Bad Godesberg,
1976), p. 90 et seq.

very different in the various branches and plants. Their
respective developments are even more diverse, with the
result that a balanced development of the national economy
is not possible. The macro-economic imbalance is manifested
in recessions and, most especially, in the form of massive
inflation. Consumption-oriented income continuously grows
faster than production. As prices increase, the enterprises' incomes may also grow, and these produce the funds
for investments.

However, the actual investment quota is too low in relation to the existing labor supply, so that the basis of
production is not broadened rapidly enough to be able to
absorb fully the available labor force. And although the
Yugoslavian system produces greater pressures toward
technical progress and productivity increases, than does
the Soviet system--a positive feature--it requires labor-saving investments in particular with the result that the essentially inadequate investments create even fewer new
jobs.

One serious problem here, however, is the fact that
the workers' collectives in economically weaker and mainly
non-monopolistic enterprises orient their demands for higher
personal incomes in terms of the average personal incomes
of the economically strong and often oligopolistic or monopolistic enterprises. They demand the same personal incomes
as are paid there, and the workers' councils and directorates in these enterprises yield to this pressure because
they fear that otherwise qualified, skilled workers would
move to better paying enterprises.

In enterprises with a low gross per capita income,
therefore, higher personal incomes detract from investments. Since in this case extra-political pressure on income
distribution remains too vague and, moreover, since there
are no sufficient criteria for personal income formation, this
practice on the part of the weaker plants has grave economic consequences. For the weaker plants cannot overcome the causes of their economic weakness only on the
strength of their own inadequate investments. They merely
worsen them. Some of these plants attempt to finance investments by taking up credits, and this causes even
greater difficulties for a large number of them. The authorities attempt to lend a helping hand, in the form of subsidies, to many plants thus threatened with bankruptcy. This
is especially so for the larger plants who provide irreplace-
able jobs for many workers. But in this way productively
inadequate income is generated on a large scale, which
drives inflation upward.

Though we may have criticized certain aspects of the
Yugoslavian income system, this must not be taken as a
critique of the Yugoslavian system in general. On the contrary, we regard this system as the first significant attempt

at overcoming, in a completely new and unique way, both the sterile Soviet state-bureaucratic system and the capitalist system. As far as efficiency, the spirit of innovation, flexibility of the structure of production, and product diversification are concerned, the Yugoslavian socialist market system has already by far surpassed the Soviet system and demonstrated the importance of market initiatives taken by independent collective enterprises vis-a-vis centrally directed state enterprises.

Though this system nevertheless still has to struggle against difficulties and suffers above all from high rates of inflation along with inadequate job security, this in our view is an expression of certain systemic deficiencies. We have already mentioned one such deficiency that appears particularly important. On the one hand, the Yugoslavian system, under the influence of Marxist anticapitalist ideology, has discarded certain economic processes which cannot yet be eliminated at the present developmental stage of labor and needs (for example, the already mentioned necessity for labor-equivalent wages and performance-stimulating profits). On the other hand, this system, influenced by its understandably anti-Stalinist, anti-bureaucratic, anti-Soviet ideas, has failed to effect the socially necessary central direction of the national economic distribution system (income from investment, consumption, individual consumption, social consumption). For this reason it is unable to adequately prevent macro-economic disruptions of a capitalist nature (inflation, investment weaknesses, underemployment) and thus loses the advantages of its progressive self-administering system. In this way the system lays itself open to attacks by the dogmatic centralists.

In accordance with the Yugoslavian experience, what must be sought is a system of ownership which overcomes the alienation between employees and their enterprises and produces the democratization of will-formation in the enterprise's decision-making organs. On top of this, it is also necessary to establish a direct interest on the part of the co-workers in the efficiency of investment and production relating to the enterprise's market-derived incomes. At the same time however, this must not eliminate the separation of income into wages and profits. For this would mean the loss of any basis for measurable comparisons of labor quantities and intensities as well as the proper ratio between performance and profits. Without the existence of wages and profits, neither full employment nor macro-economic equilibrium can be accomplished.

It is an ideological prejudice to state that the categories of wages and profits are unique to the capitalist economy. Many socialists hold similar views with respect to the category of the market. While the Yugoslavs have overcome their prejudice toward the market and recognize the existence of a socialist market, they do persevere in an ideological prejudice toward wages and profits. Wages however are not just the expression of the purchase of labor power by alien capital owners. If this capital alienation can be overcome, wages can develop into a form of distribution which would ensure equal payment for equal quantities of work while simultaneously respecting the requirements of the qualifications, preparation, and reproduction of the labor force. At the same time, this horizontally equalized wage basis provides an opportunity of better recognizing, in the generation of profits, the causes of their differentiation. Some of the ways of creating the necessary co-workers' interest in a maximally effective and needs-oriented development of production and investment would be certain measures (to be demonstrated later) against monopolistic profit increases not in accordance with performance and employee profit-sharing in a process of performance-related profit differentiation.

With the aid of macro-economic planning and a corresponding centralist incomes policy, the distribution of the entreprises' profits can then be regulated. Such policies would ensure both the maintenance of the plant collective's own interest in the optimization of the enterprises' income and a macro-economically balanced development between consumer-oriented income and the production of consumer goods. As well, the necessary differences in co-worker profit-sharing between capital-intensive and labor-intensive branches can be consciously regulated only if the profit category is present. There exist of course macro-economic interconnections which an individual enterprise alone is not able to comprehend fully and to respect. Therefore the distribution process in the enterprises can only occur independently, within a certain basic framework regulated by society as a whole. In this way democratization in the micro-sphere of the enterprise is linked to decision-making processes in the macro-sphere of the national economy.

SUMMARY OF THE GOALS OF SYSTEM REFORM

On the basis of the preceding analysis, let us now attempt to summarize in point form those basic preconditions of a modern national economy which cannot be eliminated in the foreseeable future and which would therefore confront the new system:

1. Industrial mass production cannot be abandoned, since otherwise peoples' basic needs could not be met.

2. The rigid division of labor, coupled with relatively
    long working hours will, for the same reason, con-
    tinue to exist for some time.

3. The division between management and employees can
    be attenuated, but not completely eliminated for
    some time to come.

4. The principle of efficiency must be retained, since
    the relative scarcity of goods will not be overcome
    in the foreseeable future.

5. The existence of economic incentives is necessary,
    since a large part of mankind performs, and will
    continue for some time to perform, the work allot-
    ted it in particular as a precondition of consump-
    tion.

6. The credit system, including interest, cannot be
    abandoned for a long time, since the risk-laden use
    of savings must be tied to the material interests of
    the user.

7. The tying of risk-related decision-making to oppor-
    tunities for success cannot be abandoned because
    otherwise the losses resulting from bureaucratic
    decision-making would mount, and would have to be
    borne by society.

8. All economic decisions must be made by persons who
    will feel the economic consequences in their own in-
    comes.

However, the application of these principles does not
necessarily mean that the following relations, which are
particularly characteristic of the capitalist system, must be
retained:

1. the socially divided contradiction of profit and wage
    interests;

2. the alienation of the working people from the owner-
    ship of capital;

3. the alienation of the working people from control
    over the managers of the economy.

These three specific relations of the capitalist system
are not necessarily bound up with the previously mentioned
requirements of an economy at its present stage of labor

and consumption relationships. On the contrary, if they can
be overcome in future, a more effective, harmonious, and
humane economy should be possible.

What then are the basic requirements of a modern
economy which--as the preceding analysis has shown--can-
not be guaranteed by the systems presently in existence?
By furnishing a concise answer to this question, we can at
the same time fix the goals which any structural policy reform of the existing systems would have to aim at. By simultaneously emphasizing the decisive obstacles to the implementation of these basic requirements, we will reveal the
systemic changes which must be regarded as preconditions
for attaining these future goals.

First, the efficiency of the economy should and could
be greater than it is in the existing systems.   In the
broadest sense of the word, the issue here is the capacity
of the economic system fully to utilize the potential production resources to create use value and optimally to promote
new and more effective factors of production. This promotion of efficiency is however often simplified and wrongly
understood, and because of this misunderstanding, combated. The greatest misunderstanding arises from the identification of efficiency with growth. The effort to achieve optimal effectiveness is then rejected by all those who
believe--rightly or wrongly--that they have to combat the
striving for growth today. Since we will later treat growth
separately, here will only deal with the actual problem of
efficiency.

Under today's conditions it is necessary to ensure potentially maximum efficiency, quite irrespective of whether
production is to increase more slowly, more rapidly, or not
at all. The preconditions for an increase in efficiency are
therefore of a qualitative rather than quantitative nature.
Not by longer hours of work or intensification of labor, but
on the contrary by a better utilization of the existing factors of production and by qualitative progress, should future hours-of-work reductions and work-lightening measures
be facilitated. Whatever goals society sets for itself,
whether increased or better structured or more balanced
consumption, whether more healthy ecological living conditions, whether increased and restructured leisure time--for
all these things maximum economic efficiency is needed if
they are not to remain idle pipe dreams.

In the capitalist market economy the basic causes of
efficiency loss must be sought in the fact that, without
macro-economic planning and regulation, the market mechanism cannot prevent cyclical macro-disruptions with their
periods of inflation and crisis and their growing monopolies.
In the socialist economy, by contrast, the absence of the
market mechanism and the inability of the dirigist planning

system to replace it produces great efficiency losses. The
new economic system must therefore achieve greater economic efficiency by means of a new kind of linkage between
the market mechanism, macro-economic planning and market
regulation.

Second, the new system should facilitate a continuous
macro-economic equilibrium. In any highly socialized production process where the division of labor is very advanced, the fundamentally different income groups (based
on consumptive, investive, and state-utilized incomes) always originate in subsystems other than those whose products they pay for. For this reason the direction of their
proportional distribution cannot be left to the market
mechanism. The market system, as essentially an intrinsic
steering system, operates according to the principle of trial
and error. Its ability to effect rapid and flexible changes
in all production decisions the moment the immediate deficiencies in the sales trend become apparent, enables it to
avoid excessive losses and to adapt production rapidly to
market demand and the competitive situation.

Since the individual managers of production operate
under the pressure of their own material profits and losses,
they will be interested in as rapid reactions and changes as
possible in order to keep losses to a minimum. Their capacity to adapt rapidly to the demand structure, to incorporate
potential innovations in technology and products, to quickly
fill gaps in the market, to saving resources at a greater
rate, etc., means that the instrinsic steering organs of the
market economy system cannot be replaced by the market-
indifferent partial organs of a centralized planning system.

The picture is quite different, however, with respect
to the distribution processes by which the various income
groups evolve.

Although these distribution processes are regulated by
the market mechanism, the principle of trial-and-error has
completely different effects and consequences. The individual intrinsic management boards cannot directly grasp
certain things, and certainly cannot change them by means
of flexible decision-making reactions. Among these are the
problems of whether the totality of wage and profit incomes
generated in innumerable independent enterprises are relatively too high or too low, whether they will produce a
surplus of consumer goods or investment goods in relation
to the mass of different products, or trigger a crisis or inflation. Error here signifies a macro-economic disproportion
which not only is expressed as a crisis or wave of inflation
but also can only be overcome by crises. Crisis is a form
of temporarily overcoming macro-economic distributive disproportions, and is therefore inevitable in a system in
which all mistakes in decision-making can only be corrected

ex posto facto by the intrinsic management boards. The advantage of this management system, so far as the micro-production structure, production efficiency, and technical progress are concerned, is here transformed into a great disadvantage.

In order to overcome the disadvantages of periodical crises and inflationary pushes without losing the advantages of the market mechanism, the system of intrinsic production management must be augmented, in an adequate manner, by an extrinsic, systematic management of the distribution processes. The distributive proportions between the gross income produced and the three large income groups (consumptive, investive, and state-utilized incomes) should be planned from the outset so as to ensure the harmonious development of individual consumption, social consumption, and investments. However, this regulation of the distribution process should be done in such a way as not to restrict the intrinsic management boards' interest in maximizing their income through production decisions made on their own initiative. Macro-economic planning of the distribution process thus has nothing to do with the notion of planning as a substitute for the market mechanism. It ought to replace the market mechanism only where its own trial-and-error method produces great economic disadvantages and losses.

But in order to plan for the maintenance of the macro-economic equilibrium, what is required is not only the institutional implementation of a planning system with its own organization, methodology, information-acquisition, and realization instruments, but also the overcoming of those conflicts of interest which have until now dominated the struggle for income distribution. If one analyzes all attempts at economic planning in the Western states as well as the attempts at so-called concerted action in the German Federal Republic, one consistently finds that their basic weaknesses do not only, nor even primarily lie in the difficulties of production processes but chiefly in the insurmountable conflicts of interest in the struggle for income distribution and development. So long as the contradiction between wage and profit interests exists, it would be impossible to plan for income distribution capable of harmonizing the development of consumption and investment. For this reason the elimination of this conflict of interests by means of overcoming the alienation of the working people from capital is a precondition for the planned balance in macro-economic development.

Third, the new system should facilitate the conscious influencing of future consumption and quality of life on a macro-economic scale. This must not be understood as the centralized planning of the individual consumption structure. A centralized command system over the internal structure of future individual consumption must be rejected, since this leads to the bureaucratic strangulation of needs-satisfaction. Not even the branch production structure ought to be centrally and quantitatively (proportionally) fixed because this would preclude the flexibility of unpredictable marginal shifts between branch productions. On the basis of their own interests, the enterprises must pursue a policy, not of meeting certain centrally planned branch production proportions, but of achieving the most flexible adaptation of current production to market demand--even if this eventually conflicts with the enterprise's previous production plans.

However, as far as the macro-proportions of consumption --or in broader terms the future quality of life--are concerned, they ought to be part of the sphere of democratic decision-making by the whole population. By such macro-proportions we mean the proportion between total individual consumption and total social consumption, and within social consumption the proportions between their most important individual sectors (health system, social system, education, sports and recreation, arts, housing culture and urban planning, environmental protection, etc.). Even in a market system, these macro-proportions are not determined by the market mechanism but above all by the state budget. Taxes and other state revenues determine how much of individual incomes is left for the sphere of individual consumption, and the state's expenditures basically determine the scope of the individual sectors of social consumption, that is, that consumption which completely or for the greatest part must be financed from overall social funds.

We have seen, however, first, that state determination of the macro-proportions takes place independently of any democratic choice among alternatives on the part of the population, and second, that it is always only the residue of heavily manipulated, monopolistic individual consumption. Only where macro-economic planning is used and the population is able to choose from among several variants to determine future developments, right from the phase of plan preparation and selection by means of public discussion (through elected representatives and finally through political choice), will it be inclined to identify with the overall development. The development of social consumption can then compete, right from the outset, with individual consumption rather than being only the residue of the individual consumption already produced and defended.

In particular, the establishment of the pace of growth of overall consumption on the basis of potential growth in production, given full employment and the desired proportion between work and leisure, together with the desired regeneration of the human environment, should in future be the result of a democratic choice from among alternatives. Not only democratization and humanization in the sphere of work but also the conscious expansion and reorganization of leisure can promote people's activity, self-development, and interest enrichment, and may lead to a more rapid overcoming of their social alienation. The enrichment of human life is thus not conceivable without a planned restoration of the human environment and living conditions. For this reason, what is at stake here is more than the planning of the development of consumption. It is planning for the future quality of life, in the wider sense of the word, that would help to reduce society's obliviousness toward the future and increase the fulfillment of needs for security.

Fourth, the new system should see to it that income formation is related to performance. In the capitalist system a large percentage of incomes does not correspond with people's contribution to society, but as capital incomes, forms essentially differentiated incomes which are performance-related only to a relatively minor degree. Only a small portion of profits, which are often styled as enterprise incomes, can be regarded as an equivalent remuneration for current entrepreneurial activity and/or entrepreneurial risk. This percentage cannot however be equated with the percentage of capital income utilized for consumption, since the consumptive share can come about without any corresponding performance (for example, in the case of inherited capital and the like) or can substantially exceed performance-equivalent income (for example, in the case of increasing consumption at the expense of potential investment) or can be derived from monopolistic profits.

In the socialist system, incomes develop according to the measurement of hours of work, hierarchies of qualifications, and the fulfillment of plans. Yet one cannot designate these as performance-equivalent incomes for they are produced without a linkage to the qualitative, use-value related results of labor. Since in the absence of the market mechanism there is no possibility of comparing and measuring the various use-values, the labor productivity and intensity of different branches also cannot be compared. Also noncomparable are all endeavors taken on the initiative of the various branches and plants and their quite different structural adaptations to needs, improved quality, cost-savings, etc. As a result, the socialist system is characterized by equal payment for unequal performance and unequal payment for equal performance on a large scale--a system in which working people's interest in efficient production for needs-satisfaction is minimal.

The new system should thus aim at an income mechanism which consistently produces substantially more performance-related incomes than is the case in the old systems. Performance must not be regarded merely as

relatively continuous labor activity; it also involves unique
ideas and initiatives that could provide new benefits for society. This includes individual entrepreneurial initiative, to
locate gaps in the market, or to discover new opportunities
of production. All this must continue to be motivated by
special incomes. The continued deployment of funds subject
to risks should have real effects, in terms of both profits
and of losses, on the incomes of those persons who decide
how to use these funds.

The wage system requires a more consistent application
of the results of comparative labor research, including democratic decision-making about alternative wage increases and
wage differentials. Together with wages, profit-sharing
would have to create sufficient interest on the part of all
employees of market enterprises in the optimization of their
profits. This however requires the centralized regulation of
profits to restrict nonperformance-related, monopolistic
profits and to enhance the relationship between performance
and profit differentials.

Income distribution in the new system should thus realize the following basic goals, which are not only different
but also in some measure contradictory:

1. Harmonization of differently utilized income groups
    (income for individual consumption or social con-
    sumption and investments) with the corresponding
    production groups (equilibrium principle);

2. Creation of equal basic incomes for equal work
    functions and equal quantities of labor (solidarity
    principle of remuneration);

3. Creation of differing incomes for different use-value
    of work results and different work efficiency
    (principle of performance-related wages);

4. Stimulation of entrepreneurial initiative and activity
    by means of income incentives without violation of
    the principle of performance-equivalent income
    (principle of entrepreneurial stimulation).

The new system, with the aid of various preconditions and
measures, would have to facilitate the realization of these
principles of distribution.

Finally, the new system should unify the interests of
capital and consumers. Interests in the most effective use
and expansion of capital, of the accumulated value of which
forms society's basis of production, have so far developed
only on the part of owners of private capital. The working
strata of the population have been alienated from capital,

and they have not only been indifferent toward its growth but have seen it as obstacle to increased wages and consumption. Throughout a long historical stage of development, the interests of the owners of capital were sufficient to ensure an effective and rapid development of capital in society. In the struggle for the division of the newly created values they were strong enough to assure themselves of large profits from which to form net profits and expand capital at a historically accelerated pace. The struggle for wages could not jeopardize this development of investment and capital.

In recent decades, however, a basically new situation has evolved which is increasingly threatening the further development of capital as the economic basis of all spheres of society. Economic, as well as political, cultural, and ideological developments have produced such a strong consumption drive among people that the narrow interests of capital are too weak in the face of it. The wage struggles carried out by the strengthened trade unions--and sometimes even against them--together with rapidly growing state expenditures, have led to consumption patterns in which the necessary development of investment is only possible amid new kinds of more rampant inflation. Declining technical stimuli, decreasing risk-readiness, and falling productivity finally led to a worldwide economic crisis which has turned out to be of uncommonly long duration.

It is increasingly evident that the narrow interest of capital in society is no longer sufficient to resist the one-sided wage and consumption interests of broad sectors of the population. The latter's alienation from capital, their disinterest in and lack of responsibility toward the development of the basis of their own existence cannot be overcome by moralistic sermonizing and political mobilization. More and more people are concerned about growing consumer euphoria, lack of perspectives, dissoluteness, and an escalation of violence and demoralization. Admittedly an understanding of the common essence of all these phenomena--most recently of people's alienation from society and ways of overcoming it--is still spreading too slowly. However, the movement for codetermination in the most diverse spheres of life and particularly in the sphere of production is one expression of this growing awareness. At this point it is clear that the basis of decision-making processes and of capital responsibility must be widened, although it is still not understood that this responsibility must go hand in hand with an actual capital interest. Without such an awareness, the broadened decision-making basis could easily turn against capital development.

What happens when direct capital interests are ignored and liquidated and decision-making processes are bureaucratized, has been demonstrated by the Communist system. The alienation of the working people from their enterprises and their labor has, if anything, increased still further. Certainly, low work morale, increasing thefts in the enterprises, moonlighting, black marketeering, corruption, and alcoholism point in this direction. People's immediate experience is that decisions about production, production results, distribution of products and incomes, appointment to management functions, work allocation, daily necessities, etc. are taken by a narrow stratum of political bureaucrats and cannot be changed. This experience shapes their indifferent and hostile attitude toward the economy. Official propaganda efforts cannot alter the picture.

The new system should transform the working people into real, social owners of their enterprises. Their enterprises are the collective places of production whose communal labor produces those results that must be useful within the market mechanism, and that produce income for their creators. Only when the employees in this collective production really participate in the market results, when they personally experience success and failure in terms of their incomes, when they sense the importance of more, and more effective investments, when they are able, with the aid of information and accounting, to understand the complicated enterprise machinery, and finally when they achieve the certainty that they too can influence the development of the enterprise via their elected representatives, only then will they increasingly have a feeling of co-ownership.

Profits need no longer be regarded as alienated income. They can now be seen as a foundation of collective investment and of one's own share in success. Then the social contradiction between wages and profits will disappear.

The actual capital owner is whoever can appropriate the results of capital-utilization and decide on the deployment of capital. The moment the production collective becomes the actual capital owner, the consumption interests of its individual members can be linked to the profit and capital interests of the whole collective and thus promote the socially necessary capital development. The enterprises would transform themselves into co-worker societies.

These then are the basic requirements of the new system which, if realized, could bring about economic, human, and social advantages vis-à-vis the systems in existence today. The most important conditions for realizing them are:

1.   formation of co-worker societies;

2.   implementation of macro-economic distribution planning;

3. planned regulation of the market.

EMPLOYEE-OWNED ENTERPRISES AND ENTREPRENEURIAL INITIATIVE

THE NEUTRALIZATION OF CAPITAL

The desired systemic reform will require some form of ownership of the enterprises and of productive capital in general, that decisively reduces the alienation of the working people from their enterprises and counters their disinterest in capital, tendencies inherent in both systems. This must constantly be kept in mind when the correct methods and forms of reaching the goal are at stake. In current political developments, there are forces which appear to aim at the same goal but which, due to the vague terms in which their goals are set, could produce results that would not lead to a genuine overcoming of capital alienation.

In Europe in recent decades, very different conceptions of codetermination, capital-sharing, and formation of wealth, have developed in the economic practice of experiments undertaken by many enterprises, in various political programs, as well as in the objectives of many trade unions. While many have already been implemented as isolated experiments, others are still no more than theories and/or political or trade union programs. As a basis for the present work, these ideas or experiments were examined in detail, analyzed, and a typology constructed. All these findings cannot be reproduced here, since this would expand this book excessively.[1] For this reason, we will consider some of these existing conceptions only in order to help explain a number of problems and interrelationships, namely those which involve important differences.

---

[1] Cf. U. Gaertner and P. Luder, Ziele und Wege einer Demokratisierung der Wirtschaft (Ph.D. diss., Hochschule St. Gallen fuer Wirtschafts-und Sozialwissenschaften; Diesenhofen, Switzerland: Verlag Ruegger, 1979), Part B.

It seems important to us, in the context of overcoming alienation, to indicate that this goal cannot be attained simply by increasing the assets of the working people. The conceptions advocated by liberal parties in particular, which, as in the German Federal Republic, have already resulted in practical legal measures, are aimed exclusively at a general formation of employee assets under conditions that remain otherwise unchanged. Alienation can only be reduced once the wage-earners' attitudes toward economic activity and the production goals in the enterprises have changed. It is a matter of abolishing the social antagonisms between wage and profit interests, since otherwise the struggle for the distribution of income (and thus macroeconomic disruptions as well, with all their consequences) cannot be eliminated.

This cannot, however, be attained through mere asset-formation among workers. If a certain percentage of profits is put aside for employees and lodged in supra-enterprise capital funds, there is no change in existing relationships. All this does is legally create savings that earn interest for their owners which they can perhaps withdraw after a certain term and use for purposes of consumption. Even if the use of these savings for consumption is prevented (for example, by means of a long-term or permanent locking-in of these amounts), there will be no change in the relationship between employees and capital, and their exclusive interest in wages. Even if carried out in a thorough manner (which would not, however, square with liberal ideas), this method of using trans-enterprise capital funds would be so anonymous and so foreign that it would be almost tantamount to the nationalization of investment funds.

Even if we imagine a consistent, though in practice unfeasible, transformation of all profit shares used for net investment into workers' assets and their concentration in trans-enterprise investment funds, the employee's basic position would not be changed, even after decades. However large the portion of capital that employees could formally acquire through the investment funds, it would be just as foreign to them as, for example, state property is in the Communist states. They would have no influence at all on its development; the individual would know nothing about the investment of his capital, and basically would only be interested in the interest accruing from it. But even this would be regarded as a supplement to wages, and from the quantitative point of view alone wages would still constitute their main interest. And this interest would still have to be secured on the basis of trade union struggles, since the social antagonism between wages and profits would not be eliminated by the fact that employees received interest on capital.

We can therefore see that the vagueness of the end gives rise to vague means, which cannot contribute to the elimination of the difficulties of the present-day capitalist system. It is not a question of making the working people wealthier in the sense that they would be able to consume more as a result of having more assets. Irrespective of to whom productive capital in its anonymous form (mentioned above) might belong, only that part of the gross product not needed for gross investment and reserves could be consumed. And, whether this consumable part is distributed by means of wages or partly through interest from alienated capital makes no difference in the attitude of employees toward the enterprises, toward investments, or toward capital. Change will not be brought about by shares of anonymous capital, of productive value invested somewhere in the national economy, which only earns interest or dividends. Rather, it will be a concrete, experiential proprietory relationship with each and every institution of production in which a person works, the results of which have a direct, decisive influence on his personal income level, and in whose existence he ultimately has an emotional involvement.

But even the notions held by many trade unions of supra-enterprise capital funds to finance investments underestimate the significance of interests in investment activities. The investor has to invest with the intention of realizing as great a profit as possible from his investment, as well as living with the threat of losing income or even going bankrupt as the result of a poor investment. Where this interest is lacking, where the person or persons making investment decisions is not the same as those who will receive income from future production, investment decisions will, first of all, be made as bureaucratically as they are in the communist system; and second, the workers will be as totally indifferent to them as they are under capitalism.

The working man must be given the opportunity fully to identify his effort, his output, his fate with his enterprise in the broadest sense of the word. A very important idea noted by Daniel Bell[2] is that genuine owners have a direct and psychological interest in the fate of their enterprises. This cannot, however, be said about the dispersed stockholders of large concerns. The enterprise is only a living social institution for its workers, not for its stockholders. Many workers devote a substantial part of

---

[2] Cf. D. Bell, The Corporation and Society (Paper delivered at the international seminar, Socialism in Changing Societies, Tokyo, 1972), 29.

their lives to their enterprises. It thus means more to
them than an anonymous capital investment. However, the
fact that the development of their incomes depends more on
increases in wages negotiated or fought for by their unions
than it does on the economic results realized by the enterprise is an impediment to workers' full identification with
their enterprises. Further impediments to this identification are that vital changes in the enterprise are determined independently of labor, that labor represents merely
a controlled, passive cog in the great human machine, that
labor sees managerial activity as merely demanding and controlling, which is why it can never be trusted. If fundamental changes could be effected in this relationship, not
only would the resulting identification of millions with their
enterprises release new motive forces, but in particular it
would bring about a significant socially-oriented enrichment
of people's interests. Starting from an awareness of the
existence of a broad scale of human needs and interests,
one should also regard people's places of production as areas of activity where differing needs can and must be satisfied. In the determination of such needs, two opposed
mistakes are constantly made. One consists of equating all
needs and interests, which ignores the intensity of economic
interests and their enduring, long-range priority over and
above many other needs and interests. The other consists
of a one-sided consideration of exclusively economic interests, together with ignorance about the significance of many
other needs and interests. Applied to the places of production, overcoming these mistakes means recognizing the
necessity for a long-range increase in effectiveness, since
only highly effective production can ensure the working
people of a growing real income, which continues to figure
among their strongest interests.[3] Simultaneously, however,
the satisfaction of many additional, and increasingly strongly manifested needs of people in production will become
significant. Among these are, first and foremost, the
need for job satisfaction, self-realization, and identification
with one's immediate environment.

---

[3] If research on the psychology of motivation and work-satisfaction has not yet arrived at clear-cut conclusions either regarding the position of interest in wages in the
overall scale of interests and needs of working people,
indirect researches support our plausibility assumption.
See E. Walter-Busch, Arbeitszufriedenheit in der Wohls-
tandsgesellschaft (Bern/Stuttgart, 1977). See also O.
Neuberger, Messung der Arbeitszufriedenheit. Verfahren
und Ergebnisse (Stuttgart etc., 1974).

In the long run, satisfaction of these non-economic needs in enterprises cannot take place at the expense of effectiveness, since this would lead to economic losses. Only losses in efficiency and accompanying losses in income (for example, in comparison with other enterprises) very rapidly show that satisfaction of the need for income continues to figure among the strongest of human needs. As long as this need is satisfied, it is often taken for granted, no longer gets special consideration, and many other needs suddenly become more prominent. Thus, when the working man believes that he has a relatively good income and that his work is justly compensated, his other needs gain in significance, and he also strives for their satisfaction in the workplace.

Recent scholarly research suggests that greater job satisfaction and conditions in which man can develop and realize himself more actively, with greater variety and initiative, not only do not run counter to the principle of effectiveness but, on the contrary, actually increase economic efficiency. This insight also plays an important role in the demand for a new proprietory relationship between the working people and their enterprises and in the overcoming of their alienation from these places of production. It proceeds from a recognition of the fact that the working man is interested in raising the efficiency of the enterprise and ought to bear a share of the responsibility for it. In the process, his job satisfaction will increase and new possibilities will emerge for active participation in the decision-making processes of the enterprise. The latter in particular will then create conditions under which man no longer sees the enterprise only as a place where labor is compelled by economic forces, but as an institution with whose social functions he can identify. Thus not only the mere creation of assets is at stake here, but rather the construction of a property relationship between hitherto mere wage earners and their enterprises.

To forge such a relationship between the working people and their enterprises and to overcome their exclusive interest in wages is the goal of the employee-owned enterprise, which we will summarily designate the humanization of these production communities. On the basis of recent analyses of existing experiments in participation, the employee-owned enterprise represents a synthesis of those usable elements of reform initiatives, which would best conform to the basic requirements of systemic reform. We do not intend to develop concrete organizational forms, since these would have to be adapted to the respective peculiarities of different industries and enterprises. Rather, we will set down the principles which, in the context of the complete conceptualization of the system, should prevail in the domain of the organization of production. But before doing this, we will have to address ourselves to the prob-lem-complex of entrepreneurial activity.

Among proponents of the market economy, skepticism regarding employee capital-sharing implies, above all, a fear that it could lead to employees holding a majority of capital shares. This is seen as a threat to free enterprise and as a move toward socialism. For this reason, special care is taken, in the process of capital-sharing, to prevent a takeover of property by a majority of the workers in private capitalist firms. Many entrepreneurs who on their own initiative have implemented employee profit-sharing or capital-sharing think along similar lines. In the present work, we are attempting to avoid or counter purely ideolo-gical discussions and arguments. We are concerned with the solution of prevailing fundamental economic and social problems and the overcoming of those relationships and processes that are dangerous and threatening to the fur-ther development of humanity. As soon as one moves from a concrete discussion about relationships, causes and ef-fects, to a discussion about isms, objective, scientific ar-gument stops and ideology begins. We will attempt, using as objective a line of argument as possible, to address those readers who are willing to reflect without prejudice upon existing economic and social relationships, and to consider changing certain processes on the basis of the ad-vantages and disadvantages they offer.

Of course the moment one begins to evaluate and criti-cize advantages and disadvantages, one notes that no clear-cut conclusions exist, since all processes are internally contradictory. As authors, we are of course striving to formulate our evaluations so that they will conform to the interests of a majority of the people in the industrially ad-vanced countries. Since, however, we do not have the possibility to test this, we can only present our views for general criticism.

We must now attempt to evaluate the advantages and disadvantages of these processes and perhaps find solutions which, even while changing certain processes, would not completely lose their existing advantages. We would also like to try to proceed in as differentiated a manner as possible, in order to avoid schematic interventions. What seems crucial to us, in any case, is to overcome wage-earners' alienation from capital and the conflict between wage and capital interests, which give rise to struggles over distribution. As long as this situation prevails, it is difficult to imagine how the cyclical tendency of capitalism, with all its consequences, can be overcome. However, the solution will very probably be different in large concerns than in medium-sized or small enterprises, different in cor-

porations   than   in   small,   individually-owned
enterprises--both in terms of form and time.   What seems
most important to us is to work out a   form of property
which would facilitate a politically-programed, gradual transition to the neutralization of capital ownership.

By neutralization of capital ownership we mean the
creation   of a form of property in which the capital ownership of an   enterprise would neither be tied to individuals
nor divisible among individuals.   The owner would be the
production collective of an existing or newly established
firm.   The collective, designated as an assets-management
association, would not have the right to divide the   capital
among its members.   It would constitute only the interest
base   for the juridically (statutorily) determined administration of   capital by an elected body.   The assets-management
association   would administer the capital in trust and leave
the effective management to the   enterprise-management association utilization of productive.   Individual power of control over capital and individual capital accumulation--as well
as the possibilities for influence bound up with these--could
no longer   arise.   We will call enterprises which function on
the basis of neutralized capital co-worker/co-owner enterprises.

As opposed to our earlier conceptions of the individual
right of workers to a share in the ownership of the collective capital of the enterprise (which would also be docu-
mented by individual securities or certificates), we have,
due to certain   reservations, gone over to the conception of
an individually   neutral, that is neutralized capital.   If
captial is related to individuals, this could give rise to difficulties in the mobility of the work force,   since in the
course of   refunding or buying back the certificates in the
event of a worker's voluntary change of jobs, differences in
the capital value of individual firms would produce obstacles
to job change, as well as highly speculative moves to other
firms.   A model was discussed which, by neutralizing capital, would help to overcome wage-earners' alienation from
capital and yet not hamper the necessary mobility of the
work force.

Capital neutralized in this way does not, however,
mean that economic interests cannot be utilized optimally.
Economic interest in capital efficiency arises through   appropriation by the members of the co-worker/co-owner enterprise of certain sums of   profit derived from the use of
capital.   In a co-worker/co-owner enterprise, the production collective simultaneously constitutes   an institution of
production which, to a certain degree, realizes   the organization of production, its management, division,   interplay,
etc.   We will call this organization of production an enterprise-management association.   A co-worker/co-owner enter-

prise thus consists of a capital-administration association and enterprise-management association. The respective production collective (personnel) constitutes the social basis of both, which alone has the right to elect, control, and possibly even recall both associations.

The purpose of the enterprise-management association is the organization and development of production and marketing, and thus also utilization of available capital in order to realize optimal profits. As we will see later, profits will always be distributed so that a percentage of them will be paid to the individual members of the employee-owned enterprise (the production collective) for their personal use. The greater the profits realized by the employee-owned enterprise, the greater the profit shares paid to each worker. In this way, all members acquire an interest in a maximally effective utilization of capital, production, and development of capital. Before we deal with this organization in greater detail, we would like to show why we see the co-worker/co-owner enterprise as the most appropriate form from the point of view of its gradual though programed emergence and spread.

It is a form of property which originates without expropriation of the former owners. It makes possible the formation of neutralized capital from the profits of existing firms in a predetermined period of time, fixed by a statutory determination of the corresponding share of profit. The share of profit used to constitute the neutralized capital is not lost to the firms, but rather continues to constitute their own capital, which can be utilized for net investment; only the form of its ownership changes. At the same time, this facilitates a differentiation during the period of time for the constitution of the neutralized capital in the large corporations, as distinct from private companies, medium-sized family enterprises, and small firms. This temporal gradation and the differentiation of the percentages of profit for constitution of the neutralized capital is especially necessary since entrepreneurial interests in the small and medium-sized enterprises must be preserved.

In large corporations, the expansion of neutralized capital can proceed relatively rapidly, since entrepreneurial activity has long since devolved from the owners of capital to appointed managers. Innovations, as well as risk and often creative initiative, are assumed by managers who are not owners of these firms at all, or who own only a small share in them. It is sufficient that their interest in a maximally effective development of the enterprise is secured by means of individual profit-sharing. The emergence and rapid increase of neutralized capital out of relatively greater profit shares--also intended for the net investment of these enterprises--would not greatly affect the activities of

management. On the contrary, as we will see, this
activity could be better concentrated on the future requirements of the economy, since in an enterprise completely
owned by co-workers enterprise, conflicts between outside
stockholders and trade unions (which often involve the
managers as well) would cease.

If there were a desire further to accelerate the transformation of corporations into co-worker/co-owner enterprises, all net investments, indeed all gross investments
could be invested in the form of neutralized capital. The
capital newly created each year would thus rapidly build up
the capital of the employees' assets-management associations. To be sure, dividends paid to the former stockholders would then stagnate or possibly shrink. In any
case, the share of profit to be paid to private owners for
their own use can be regulated in different ways, which
we will discuss later.

In small and medium-sized enterprises where the owner
also performs managerial functions and in which private
property remains one of the motivations of entrepreneurial
activity, the formation of neutralized capital could take
place more slowly and only above a certain level of profit.
More important, however, would be to equalize the profit
shares (shares for personal use) of workers in these enterprises (which would continue to be private, or partly
private) with the shares of workers in the co-worker/co-
owner enterprises.

One system of profit-sharing, in accordance with a
scheme to be explained later, would represent a strong incentive for the participating workers. If this incentive did
not exist in small and medium-sized enterprises, these enterprises would experience difficulties in attracting workers with at least minimal qualifications. It might therefore
be important for the state to substitute selective tax relief
for profit-sharing in cases of enterprises with slowly growing neutralized capital or no neutralized capital at all. Another possibility would be to tie tax relief to the selective
formation of neutralized capital.

The same rules would apply to all newly established
firms, which would continue to come into being through
private initiative, as well as to existing employee-owned
enterprises; we will discuss this later. Up to a certain
level of profit, there would be private enterprises without
capital neutralization, but with profit sharing for the
workers. Then, at a certain level of profit, the legally obligatory formation of neutralized capital from the fixed
percentage share of profit would begin. However, in enterprises established with the help of the neutralized capital
of co-worker/co-owner enterprises (for example, by the
merger of several employee-owned enterprises) or employee-

owned banks--this will also be explained later--or finally in those established by the state, the capital would have to be completely neutralized from the outset, thus giving rise to new co-worker/co-owner enterprises.

In this way, valuable private entrepreneurial initiative will not be frustrated, either by maintaining existing firms, or by privatly re-establishing them. And yet, neutralization of capital would be programed to develop selectively and temporally. From year to year, a growing portion of the capital would become the collective property of the enterprise workers. This would overcome their alienation from capital in a controlled manner: and as a result of planned profit sharing, the struggle over distribution of income would be overcome from the first day (of the official decision) onward. Depending on the progress of the re-establishment of private firms there would of course always exist a private sector alongside the sector of the employee-owned enterprises, including the small private enterprises which would be left intact. This would, however, be advantageous, since it would not frustrate private, creative initiative and would, at the same time, (through general worker profit-sharing and through the obligatory formation of neutralized capital beginning with a certain level of profit) also guarantee elimination of the antagonism between wage and profit interests. Thus, the economically planned distribution of income and maintenance of equilibrium would then also be realizable.

DECISION-MAKING STRUCTURES IN CO-WORKER/CO-OWNER ENTERPRISES

Everyone organized in a co-worker/co-owner enterprise will automatically be a member of the assets-management association as well as the enterprise-management association. The neutralized capital of a co-worker/co-owner enterprise will be managed by the assets-management association with the help of the elected assets-management council. The assets-management council will be elected at the general meeting of the assets-management association, and is responsible to it. The assets constitute capital in the sense that they are to be used productively and effectively, and should yield optimal profits. For this purpose, the assets-management association will place the assets at the disposal of the enterprise-management association which, for its part--represented by management (executive board, management, etc.)--is responsible for the effective utilization of capital assets.

We refer here to neutralized capital, since no individual property rights to this capital exist, and even the general meeting of the assets-management association of the enterprise-management association does not have the right to decree the disbandment of the association and distribution of its assets among its members. Externally, the co-worker/co-owner enterprise is responsible to the extent of its assets. Even in the event of insolvency, whatever assets are left over (after all debts are paid) cannot be divided among the members of the assets-management association, but would have to be used for public purposes (for example, for charitable purposes). An individual employee in the enterprise is thus a co-owner of the collective assets only as a member of the assets-management association, and this only so long as he remains a co-worker. Once he ceases to be a co-worker--for whatever reason--he can no longer be a member of the assets-management association and thus cannot be a co-owner.

The enterprise-management association is the actual productive organization of the co-worker/co-owner enterprise. Its task is to ensure the productive development of the enterprise. The general meeting of the co-worker/co-owners would have a function similar to that of the general meeting of a corporation. It would be the legal authority of the co-worker/co-owner enterprise, and in general its tasks would be: adoption and revision of the bylaws of the enterprise-management association; election of the members of the supervisory council; periodic evaluation of the activities of the supervisory council; evaluation of the enterprise's annual accounts; discharging the supervisory council and the executive; introduction of proposals for the firm's operations; possible criticism of the activity of the supervisory council and removal of its members; etc.

In a completely employee-owned enterprise, the supervisory council is the elected body representing the interests of the co-worker/co-owners. It appoints the executive or management of the enterprise and controls its activity over the long run. In the event of poor results (in comparison with other firms), it has the right to arrange for a professional analysis or scrutiny of management's activities and if necessary, to replace the management board. It determines the rules for the division of the profit-sharing funds. And it has to decide whether the enterprise is to participate financially in newly established ventures.

Otherwise, however, the supervisory council has no right to intervene in the day-to-day operations of management, since the latter bears full responsibility for management of the enterprise. The main task of the supervisory council is to assure effective management of the enterprise in the long run and to safeguard the interests of the co-worker/co-owners. At periodic general meetings and through other channels of information, the supervisory council has to inform the co-workers about the enterprise's basic developments, problems, and successes. It also has to receive their criticisms and suggestions, and implement them where necessary.

The supervisory council would be elected for a period of about five years, about the period of a middle-range macro-economic plan. Its members could not be members of the executive or management. Members would for the most part be elected co-worker/co-owners of the enterprise. To some extent, however, specialists who enjoyed the confidence of the co-workers could be elected from outside. The number of members of the supervisory council would depend on the size of the enterprise, but ought not to be more than 15 to 17. A person could be elected for a maximum of two terms, in order to prevent the emergence of a new aristocracy of functionaries. The re-election of half the members at the end of each electoral term, while leaving the other half to continue their functions through the second electoral term, would ensure the requisite continuity of experience and work of the supervisory council. Some form of material incentive might be considered for the members of the supervisory council--for instance, a one-time compensation related to the development of profits--thus giving them a stake in the long-term effectiveness of the enterprise.

The executive, or management, would be chosen by the supervisory council. Irrespective of how management might be constituted (depending on the size and kind of the enterprise), it should always be independent and fully responsible for all its decisions concerning the development of production, investment, and the enterprise as a whole within the framework of the statutes of the enterprise. Only for capital investments for new ventures, fundamental re-organizations, unavoidable layoffs of co-workers, etc., would it have to seek the permission of the supervisory council. To manage the firm, professionals could be hired who were not from the enterprise itself. The managers' terms of office would not be limited and would depend on their work. Their style of management should not be authoritarian, but rather democratic, in the same way as the democratic system of management--to be dealt with later-- that we recommend for the entire co-worker/co-owner enterprise. Concrete labor, wage, and social policies would be established within the framework of economic regulation in yearly contracts between management and the unions (their function will also be explained).

Every member of the co-worker/co-owner enterprise would be entitled to membership in the assets-management association and the enterprise-management association. He would enjoy all the rights that derive from these memberships, in particular the right to vote in elections to the assets-management council and supervisory council, the right to information and to oversee the economic development of the firm, the right to criticize and have this criticism taken into account, the right to profit-sharing within agreed-upon rules, to active participation within the democratic system of management, to participation in organized economic training, etc.

A co-worker who leaves the enterprise of his own will ceases to be a co-owner. However, he automatically becomes a co-owner again in whatever other employee-owned enterprise he might join.

The possibility of co-worker layoffs for economic reasons (production cutbacks, reorganization, etc.) cannot be completely ruled out under the new system, even in co-worker/co-owner enterprises; but this could only take place with the permission of the supervisory council. Changes in the structure of production and measures aimed at technological modernization should, however, be prepared well in advance. For as these changes were implemented, expandable production programs would have to be found, so that no workers would have to be laid off. As we will see, the entire production collective can democratically decide to accept temporary losses in profit, rather than simply decreeing layoffs, in order to create new opportunities for production, to carry out retraining, and hence in the long term to make up for losses in efficiency. It is to be expected that under conditions of macro-planning, there would be no general crises as well as no crises within individual sectors of the economy, and that layoffs for economic reasons would be rare. A maximum amount of material security, assistance in finding new jobs, possible compensation for retraining and relocation costs, etc., would be taken for granted in the new system.

The unions would also have a role to play in the co-worker/co-owner enterprise, although their social function would differ greatly from what it is in capitalist firms. The interests of the supervisory council would, after all, be aimed at the long-range development, efficiency, and results of the enterprise. This would also be true of management. The co-workers would thus continue to need an organization to look after and represent their short-term interests, such as problems in the workplace, compensation, social and cultural requirements. It would naturally no longer be necessary to fight for these interests against outside owners of capital. Thus, the forms and methods of protecting employees' interests would also change. Nevertheless, someone would have to pursue these immediate interests and keep an eye on the possiblities for their realization, especially when annual contracts are made with management. (The unions' remaining tasks will be examined later.)

In the enterprise-management association there would thus be a three-way jurisdictional division among unions, management, and supervisory council, which would protect both the short-term and long-range interests of the co-worker/co-owners in a new interplay of forces and mutual control. The new ownership form, the new organization, and the new authorities should help to realize their interests in steadily rising income, job security, a fair wage, job satisfaction, active codetermination, identification with the collective, and self-realization.

In large enterprises and concerns these authorities would of course have to be organized in two or three tiers, or in other words, through a system of representation. In large enterprises consisting of relatively independent units, there would have to be supervisory councils to head the units, as well as a representative supervisory council at the top of the enterprise. In the case of concerns comprised of several enterprises there would have to be yet another supervisory council at the head of the concern's management. The organization of the assets-management association would probably be coordinated by more or less centralized or decentralized associations. The problems of this kind of organization cannot be dealt with here, since such an analysis would have to take account of the great variety of concern organizations, which would go beyond the scope of this work. It will be assumed that an explanation of the basic principles of an employee-owned enterprise should make it possible to apply these principles to the various actual organizational forms of large concerns, and this would not be a difficult task for the appropriate specialists.

As we have stressed, our system of democratic decision-making and promoting co-workers' identification with their enterprises requires maximum decentralization and economic independence of the sub-units. The larger a trust is, and the more levels of co-worker/co-owner representation it has, the more important it becomes to bring the levels at which profit is calculated (profit centers) into proximity with sub-enterprises that can be readily overseen, and the more important the democratic management system becomes--which will be dealt with shortly. Only where the co-workers can readily oversee the economic results, where they can evaluate the activities of the representative bodies, and where collective property is tangible can the co-workers really identify with their enterprises and acquire an interest in its development.

In enterprises where neutralized capital would be in a minority position and where the old share capital or private capital of individual owners would still have a significant influence, representation of wage earners in the supervisory council would remain minority representation, or the increase in this representation would depend on either the goodwill of the owners or, as in some countries (for example, West Germany), on codetermination regulations established by law. When there is a preponderance of representatives of private capital, or even proportional representation, the antagonism of interests between wage-earners and owners of private capital cannot be fully overcome. As long as the distribution of profits depends essentially on the will of private owners of capital, the struggle of union-organized wage earners for wage increases cannot be eliminated.

If, however, the new system could be politically effected within a framework of democratic legality--which is our starting assumption--this would also mean a new ordering of the relation within the remaining private, and predominantly private capitalist firms as well. In the new system, neutralization of capital would, as already mentioned, be a politically programed process, which could take place at varying rates. In any case, there would always be a more or less broad sector of enterprises with private (small enterprises) or partly private and partly neutralized capital in this system. In the politically accepted new system, however, these firms would also be subordinated to rules governing the distribution of profits and parity representation of co-workers.

As soon as wages in such private or partly private enterprises developed in conformity with a balanced and planned development of wages at the level of the national economy, and the sharing of co-worker profits also corresponded to the planned sharing of profits (how this would be possible will be explained), the antagonism between profit interests and wage interests would be basically broken down. The struggle for wage increases would not take place, or would no longer be supported by the unions participating in the macro-economic plans. In the process of fixing wages and sharing profits in this way, remuneration for labor in private enterprises and co-worker/co-owner enterprises would be basically equal, and the remaining profits of private entrepreneurs would have to be regarded as a desirable incentive to entrepreneurial activity.

On this basis, there should no longer be any difficulty in introducing proportionally constituted bodies in private and partly private enterprises (in small and medium-sized enterprises there would be no supervisory councils) in which co-workers, together with private entrepreneurs or their representatives, would evaluate and make decisions about fundamental questions regarding the development of the enterprise.   Under such conditions, the question of the chairman's affiliation--which is a bone of contention in reg- ulating proportional codetermination under conditions of op- posing profit- and wage-interests--should no longer play a crucial role.

INCOME DISTRIBUTION

The principles of income distribution that have been explained   will   be   realized   within   the   entrepreneurial sphere.   The   actual   distribution   of   incomes   within   co- worker/co-owner enterprises, as   well as in private and partly private enterprises, will have to conform   to planned specifications for income distribution (distribution   formula) and the wage agreements at the level of the national   econ- omy.   In harmony with this planned incomes policy, each enterprise will have a free rein for actualization and a rela- tively   independent decision-making scope with regard to income distribution, which will then naturally reveal differ- ences between employee-owned   enterprises and private en- terprises.   We would like, first of   all, to show how this distribution would take place in a co-worker/co-owner en- terprise.

We will proceed from the assumption that these enter- prises will realize different incomes from their activity on the market.   For the time being let us set aside the ques- tion of which measures would ensure that these   differences in market income would correspond only to differences in performance, since this problem will be dealt with later on. We are thus assuming that the income of the enterprise corresponds to its performance.   This consists of wages (established by the enterprises according to supra-enter- prise wage   agreements) and gross profits.   There are also corresponding   regulations for the distribution of profits.

As already explained, at the end of the year all enter- prises   receive from the   competent state institutions the functional wage scales negotiated according to sector, on a national-economic level, with the   basic wages set for the coming year.   These basic wages represent monetary com- pensation for a certain   quantity of labor (working time), of a worker appropriate to his functional position in the wage   group   scale   of   the   sector   concerned.   The   total amount of all forms of work-wages, time-wages, and incen- tive-wages (piecework, premium wages) has to correspond to the   agreed upon basic wage.   Incentive-wages must be set so that the incentive-wage realized at a socially average intensity of labor corresponds to the fixed time-wage for the given wage group. Higher incentive-wages will then correspond to increased quantities of labor (labor intensity). In this way, wages will ensure the formation of basic incomes throughout the entire national economy according to the principle equal wages for equal quantities of labor in equivalent work functions.

Apart from wages (time-wages and incentive-wages) there are other supplementary forms of wages (premiums, bonuses, honoraria, commissions, gratuities), whose allocation and amount would be determined by the enterprises themselves. However, these supplementary wage forms can no longer be counted among the basic work-wages determined and controlled at the national economic level. In this sense, they would already have to be regarded as forms of compensation to be paid out of profits, and the amount of profit available for profit-sharing would be reduced by this amount. The enterprises will thus utilize these forms only in as much as they are truly necessary and optimal. That part of gross income which exceeds work-wages constitutes gross profit. Net profit, or what remains after deducting taxes and interest on outside capital, is divided according to a planned distribution formula between the profit-sharing fund and the surplus income to be used for purposes of the enterprise (for net investments, reserve funds, etc.). Only the profit-sharing fund can be used for personal income, and it must not be overdrawn, since otherwise it is impossible to ensure a planned equilibrium at the national-economic level. Thus all supplementary wage forms must be drawn from it.

This division of gross income could be represented as follows:

gross income
- work-wages (time-wages and/or incentive-wages)

= gross profit
- taxes and social contributions
- interest on outside capital

= net profit (tax balance profit)
- profit-sharing fund (supplementary wage forms, profit-sharing)

= surplus enterprise income (net investments, reserve funds, savings, new ventures)

The profit-sharing fund of a particular enterprise is determined by the enterprise management according to a formula which we will be able to explain only in the context of macro-planning (see Chap. 4). The supplementary wage forms, which are paid out continuously, are drawn in advance from the account of planned and anticipated profit-sharing funds. The sum for profit sharing is calculated by subtracting the annual or semi-annual profit-sharing fund from net earned profit. This is then divided among the co-worker/co-owners according to the decision of the supervisory council of every employee-owned enterprise acting on its own. Here are a few possible ways of dividing such profits:

1.   indiscriminately to all co-worker/co-owners;

2.   according to differences in wages;

3.   according to performance, whether of the individual co-worker or of the entire group;

4.   according to the number of years of service to the enterprise.

Of course, these aspects lend themselves to additional differing combinations and quantifications, which must be left up to the individual enterprises and which will above all require empirical experience.

An important part of this will be the already noted establishment of cost- and/or profit-centers in smaller, overseeable enterprise units (divisions) within large concerns.   The better the individual co-workers can see the cost- and/or profit-calculation, the stronger is the influence of profit-sharing on the activity of the co-workers in the direction of efficiency and cost reduction.   Of course, where increased interest in cost reduction could lead to an unmanageable deterioration in the quality of enterprise units, other, more useful stimuli would have to be found.

It should always be kept in mind that an increase in the co-workers' interests in profit is a socially necessary interest if (and only if) profit increases are for the good of society.   If profit is an expression of real savings in costs, if the job satisfaction of the working people increases along with their growing use of consumer goods and improving working conditions, then the profit interest corresponds to the struggle for humanization of the the economy.   However, should an increased interest in profit produce an interest in dimished product quality or give rise to growing rivalries and high-stress levels at the work place, the profit interest as such must not be condemned, since the economy cannot function effectively without this interest; but the concrete forms and conditions of the profit interest would have to be thought through anew.

The objection that the newly created interest in the development of profit within the employee-owned enterprise would necessarily encourage individualism, is incorrect: on the contrary, it can even deepen communal thinking.   The individual alone cannot increase profits, but only the entire production-collective concentrated at the profit center.   By the same token, the individual receives only a fair share of the jointly earned profits, so that there is a growing sense of everyone's responsiblility for the results of common work.   The highly egoistically-oriented interest in wages is more likely to be weakened. If then an interest in collective profit is accompanied by group work and a democratic system of management, interest in work and job satisfaction will increase. Management will not be more difficult, but rather easier.

Nor does the system of capital neutralization and co-worker profit-sharing conflict with the necessary flexibility of the labor market. Because of the fact that a co-worker in a new enterprise automatically becomes a co-owner as well, job changing will involve essentially the same conditions as those prevailing in the present market economy. Naturally, all wage earners will seek to join those enterprises which attain relatively high profits. But these enterprises will take on new co-workers only when they see

improved   market   prospects.   Moreover,   these   new
co-workers would then have to contribute toward increased
productivity, since their   marginal product would have to
ensure recovery not only of their own wages, but also of a
profit ratio at   least commensurate with the existing wage
level.   In such   cases, however, it would be desirable that
the new labor power migrate   from other less productive
enterprises.

If the high-profit enterprises did not have   suitable
market prospects, however, they would   not take on any
new   co-workers.   Co-workers in enterprises with   lower
rates of profit will then make comparisons, thus leading
them to exert stronger pressure on the management of their
own enterprises in order to bring about a growth in profits
by means of improving efficiency.   But all this is part of
the positive effects of the market mechanism.

It is repeatedly claimed that differences in   profit cannot be equalized by the performance and efforts of the
production collective alone, and consequently that they are
caused by objective factors independent of men's work.   We
will deal with this problem   later, in connection with the
regulation of the market.   It must be   stressed here, however, that precisely those greater differences   in the rate
of profit which cannot be eliminated by the performance   of
the production collective can also be ascertained and largely
done away with by means of market regulation.   The remaining differences in profit   would thus depend essentially
on the performance of individual   employee-owned enterprises, and should function as a socially indispensible motivation for increases in efficiency.   Wherever   this objective
criterion of profit and the profit motive do not   exist, not
only do greater losses in efficiency occur, but income formation is also less equitable.

The co-workers of employee-owned enterprises will be
interested   not only in an optimization of profits, but also
in the   preservation of their enterprises.   In the event of
bankruptcy of their enterprise, not only would they lose
their jobs, but most would   probably also lose their profit
shares for the preceding weeks or months.   If an employee-
owned enterprise got into difficulties   and operated at a
loss, all co-workers would of course be directly affected in
that they would lose their profit shares.   Some of the   co-
workers would try to get off the sinking ship.   Given a division   of profit which took into account one's length of
affiliation with the enterprise, however, precisely the   most
experienced and qualified co-workers,   as well as those involved in management, would attempt to save the enterprise
and would spare no effort to do so.

An unavoidable bankruptcy would then   naturally take
place subject to the same   legal conditions as   prevailed in

the previous market economy. However, since
macro-planning could prevent general crises, such bankruptcies should be exceptional cases. On the contrary, on
the basis of experience with existing enterprises with collective capital property, intense efforts of entire production collectives for structural changes, innovations, reorganizations, cost reductions, etc., hold out the promise of
greater success than enterprises in which the co-workers
are alienated from capital.

In private or partly private enterprises--which would
nevertheless be subject to centrally planned profit-sharing
for co-workers--calculation of the profit shares of the co-
workers from out of net profits would have to take place
in the same way as in employee-owned enterprises. Whenever private owners simultaneously performed the functions
of directors or other management personnel, they would be
paid a normal salary for the exercise of these management
functions. In addition, they would have the right to appropriate and dispose of the net profits remaining after
deducting profit-sharing funds. The remaining profit
should assure them a relatively high sum for purposes of
consumption (entrepreneurial risk incentive), as well as
make possible the requisite net investment.

In enterprises exceeding the statutorily determined
level of profit, this net investment would then, as already
stated, ensure the formation of neutralized capital. The
transformation of net investment into neutralized capital
would not, however, retard the initiative of private entrepreneurs since, in the first place, the neutralized capital
will not be taken out of the enterprise, and second, any
growth in it would increase the profit shares for the private entrepreneurs as well as for the co-workers. In
Chapter 4 we will deal with planning the division of profits
in private enterprises.

In the case of small enterprises (handicrafts, minor
services, etc.), the quality of private property should be
preserved up to a fixed level of profit. Private initiative
and the owner's own work are irreplacable in such small
enterprises. The point is demonstrated, first and foremost, by the experience of the Eastern bloc states. There,
co-worker profit-sharing is almost certainly impossible without deliberate tax relief. Only after a certain level of sales
and profits has been reached would net investment also be
transformed into neutralized capital administered by the
co-workers. Since the small producers would not cease to
be private owners of their capital, the initial neutralization
of new capital would not retard growth in small enterprises
either.

OPTIMIZATION OF PROFITS

In a market economy all productive enterprises represent smaller or larger forms of production cooperation whose purpose is to create use-value for society in the most efficient way, and to yield monetary value, and hence income, for owners and producers in exchange for this use-value. These external and internal purposes of an enterprise mutually condition each other and represent two sides of the same coin. However, in an enterprise where the division of labor is well advanced, the creation of use-value for completely unknown consumers is a largely alienated activity as far as the producers are concerned. In it they see only the economically necessary condition for the generation of their income. Maximization of this income is thus seen as the real aim of their productive activity although, from a purely empirical point of view, the owner of every enterprise is aware that the greatest possible creation of use-value with minimal means (labor and means of production) represents the necessary precondition for income maximization.

In a market economy, private entrepreneurs must endeavor to maximize profits. But this is not primarily an expression of their subjective greed; rather it is an expression of the objective requirements of historically given market conditions. Profit maximization expresses above all the socially imposed minimization of production costs in relation to the necessary creation of use-value.

The point is, however, that profits can be maximized not only as a result of the greatest possible efficiency in production, but also in other ways. Some other possible ways of maximizing profits are lowering wages, cartel agreements, and monopolistic control and limitation of production. In such cases, however, profit maximization is no longer a manifestation of a socially desirable maximization of efficiency, but rather of social processes that are wholly undesirable to society. Instead of revealing this clearly and unequivocally, and simultaneously saying openly that the capitalist economic system has no criteria for distinguishing and separating the socially necessary from the undesired factors of profit maximization, critics of the capitalist system cast aspersions on the maximization of profit itself. But if even defenders of the private market economy are beginning to have doubts about the maximization of profits, this problem will have to be clarified here. Otherwise, goal-setting within the employee-owned enterprises could come into conflict with the interests of society.

This is primarily a question of identifying and eliminating the antisocial processes of profit maximization. So far, we have explained how the tendency to increase profits at the   expense of wages can be eliminated with the aid of neutralized   capital, employee-owned   enterprises   and   a planned incomes policy.   Below, in the context of the ex-planation of the regulated   market mechanism, we will show ways of counteracting the tendency to increase profits by means of monopoly, rather than efficiency and   perform-ance.   As a result of all these   changes and measures, in-creases in profits should reflect increases in efficiency. Then the question arises as to whether, under such   condi-tions, we should continue to speak of the necessity of max-imizing profits.

     With respect to the new system, we have so far only used the term profit maximization.   But what does this mean?   Certainly, it must not be taken to mean, say, that the principle of efficiency should be eroded.   We have   al-ready shown clearly enough that, for the foreseeable fu-ture, no society can forego any opportunity to maximize the efficiency of its production.   We have already stated that the crucial prerequisite in planning reductions of working time or in reducing or freezing growth is the highest possi-ble degree of efficiency.[4] However, so long as market rela-tionships do exist, such maximization of efficiency ought to be expressed as maximum   profits as well.   Profits should always be maximal,   whether achieved through optimal utili-zation of means of   production, maximal worker productivi-ty, technical progress, or better organization of work, or in other words, through relatively minimal input   (costs of production), increases in production, improvement of prod-ucts, higher use-value of new products, or in   short maxi-mal output (proceeds and/or turnover).

     If, nevertheless, we do not use this term, it is not because we do not feel that this kind of maximization of profits should not be attempted, and certainly not because of moral reservations about increasing profits in this way. We speak only of an   optimization of profits, since in the employee-owned enterprises,   apart from a strong interest in maximal efficiency, there will be other co-worker needs and interests.   The satisfaction of these needs must be re-spected.   In particular, their already-mentioned needs, for job satisfaction and co-worker participation in decision-mak-ing processes, take on a much greater significance.   To pay attention to these is to humanize the production pro-cess.   These additional needs may clash with the interest in efficiency, although this   does not mean that they are en-tirely contradictory.   However, in individual cases they can mutually constrain each other, permanently or temporarily.

----

[4] Cf. O. Sik, Argumente fuer den dritten Weg (Hamburg, 1973), p. 37ff.

Thus, for example, a rotation of co-workers from one task to another within the work group can, in individual cases, temporarily lead to a decline in worker productivity and thus in profits, although generally and in the long run, worker productivity should rise, or at least remain constant. But as we will see later, the existence of such contradictions should not be a reason for abandoning job rotation.

In general, this must be understood as follows. The simultaneous realization of the interests of efficiency and the humanization of the production process in an employee-owned enterprise should, over the long term, produce a rise, rather than a drop, in efficiency. On the other hand, in individual conflict situations, certain processes can be given priority over more efficient solutions because they are more humane. The existence of these differing interests in an employee-owned enterprise--which in individual cases can be parallel, yet contradictory--mirrors the differing goals which an employee-owned enterprise, with its democratic system of management, has to pursue. Of course every limitation of efficiency means that profit would turn out to be lower than its potential maximum.

An optimal development of profit should therefore be attainable from the outset with the aid of macro-economic planning, market regulation, and micro-economic plant management. As we will see later, micro-economic optimization of profit should guarantee the profit quota and surplus-income quota that the community needs for the optimal development of net investment, corresponding to the macro-plan adopted. The plant managements of the employee-owned enterprises and of the private enterprises will strive to achieve increases in profit by means of maximal efficiency, but if possible not by sacrificing the equally important goal of humanizing the production process. Whenever humanization has a long-term detrimental effect on efficiency because of its connection with more general and fundamental questions of the organization of production, a democratic decision of the production collective in question will have to be obtained. If on the basis of information concerning all consequences and possible alternatives, a majority of the collective consciously rejects a rise in income (rise in profit) in favor of humanization of production, this would have to be accepted by the enterprise's management.

EMERGENCE OF DIFFERENT SECTORS OF THE ECONOMY

It is clear that an economy based on a division of labor, mass production, and the exchange of goods must function under relative shortages of productive resources, pressures for economic efficiency, and economically limited needs-satisfaction. As long as these exist, profit will be a concentrated criterion of efficiency in enterprises that produce goods. This will be so, irrespective of how the form of property, and hence the form of appropriation and disposition of profits, is arranged. As indispensable as the profit criterion is to goods-producing enterprises, this is far from signifying that there must be a profit criterion in all institutions where people work together for other people. In highly developed capitalist economies, there is already a very broad sector of activities which employs many people and creates use values for society that are not oriented toward the profit criterion. These include the state administration, security and defense agencies, the public education system, to a large extent public medical services, social security, and others.

These institutions will naturally not disappear in the new system, and is is rather to be expected that the public sector, its activities, and hence the number of people employed in it will expand. This will mean, however, that an ever growing number of people will not be able to orient their activities according to the profit criterion. We have already mentioned elsewhere why these institutions cannot show a profit.

Just because a society decides democratically to maintain or even expand certain agencies of social needs-satisfaction, whose outputs are not sold and which are not profit-oriented, this of course does not mean that there can be no profit-sharing for co-workers in this broad sector of activities. This raises the question as to whether great privileges would go to those employed in production, and whether the attractiveness of employment in institutions without profit-sharing would therefore decrease. This question and this objection are justified, and we will have to resolve this problem in some way other than by introducing profits and profit-sharing.

We will see later how the growth of both wages and profit-sharing can be planned, and how national wage scales can be worked out with the help of the trade unions. But for now we can anticipate that the approximate growth of the profit in the economy and of profit-shares paid out to co-workers by goods-producing enterprises can be forecast and planned. This means that the approximate level (as a national economic average) of per capita profit-sharing in the productive sector can be predicted. Thus the growth of average wages in the domain of non-goods-producing services can also be calculated in advance. Co-workers in the public service sector would thus receive on average as high a wage, according to plan, as co-workers in production did in the form of wages and profit-sharing.

There are, however, further important economic service institutions whose ownership form we must deal with separately: banks and private insurance companies. These involve services which, although they must be included in the goods-producing sector, are located so to speak on its margin, at the point of intersection with the public service sector. The hierarchical summit of the banking system-- central bank, federal bank, state bank, or whatever it may be called in various countries--differs in many ways from profit-oriented goods-production. It is not by chance that banks have been nationalized in most industrial countries. From a certain point of view, they actually constitute a peak institution which rather more performs a service in the public interest than concentrates on its own profit interest, most particularly in the issuance of currency and regulation of the money supply for the national economy. In this respect the central bank has a superior position-- vested with the power of the law--compared to the commercial banks.

In the new system, there would be little change in the business activity of the banks, since their activities are preponderantly bound up with the market mechanism, which would be preserved or even more consistently developed. The credit system would continue to exist. The task of the banking system in the redistribution of income and the allocation of capital would be more broadly and deeply adapted to the market mechanism. Regulation of the money supply would still be necessary.

It must be recognized that people have an interest in interest and will always have it so long as current conditions of scarcity continue to exist. The interest of lenders in a maximal interest yield, constrained to whatever extent may be economically necessary by the opposed interest of borrowers, similtaneously assures a maximally efficient utilization of credit. This conforms to society's interest in making use of the totality of disposable capital and all factors of production as efficiently as possible. In the absence of this economic interest, what develops is the mere bureaucratic distribution of savings, capital and resources, as well as antisocial squandering and wastage of labor and resources, which no moralistic assertions and no amount of mobilization can overcome.

Since amassing savings, creating credit, allocating credits, and all other monetarily valued services can take place only through a specific banking system, it is also necessary for the individual banks (as parts of the system) to develop an interest in the most efficient use of credit. This in turn conforms to their own profit interest. Experiences in the East bloc states show most clearly that credits allocated without a profit interest on the part of the lender will, in the final analysis, be distributed in a purely bureaucratic manner. Here, we have no intention of getting into a discussion about the similar lack of interest, on the part of borrowers in the Eastern enterprises, in the most efficient possible use of credit. But even if such an interest were sufficiently present, the banks, as purely bureaucratic institutions, are not interested in allocating credits to those enterprises which would make the best use of them for the good of the whole society.

The banks must therefore develop their own profit-oriented interest in an effective allocation of credit. One can envision the same distribution of profit and the same formation of neutralized new capital in the case of banks as in the productive sphere. First of all, profit-sharing in banks and savings institutions should develop an interest on the part of co-workers in the growth of profit, since this would intensify their interest in the efficiency of credit allocation. Second, for reasons of macro-economic equilibrium, bank profits, like other profits, would have to be subdivided into parts for consumption and investment.

The difference between the deployment of neutralized capital in banks and productive enterprises will, however, be substantial. This is due simply to their different economic functions. While in the productive sphere, newly formed neutralized capital would be used preponderantly for net investment within the productive enterprise itself, for in banks it would be just the reverse. Here, only a relatively small part of net profit can be expended for new bank buildings or branch banks. Most of it has in the past been turned either into supplementary liquid capital, used for purposes of additional credits or the acquisition of securities, or into industrial capital realized by the acquisition of stocks or the establishment of industrial enterprises. Concerning the previous form of the stock corporation, as well as establishment of new enterprises by banks or by existing industrial enterprises, the following is to be said about the new system:

Today's large concerns finance their investments primarily out of their own resources[5] and the diffusion of

---

[5] The proportion of self-financing of German enterprises (f)

stock capital is already taking place relatively slowly. In
the system we are advocating, in which the development of
profit will be regulated by the plan, self-financing would
predominate because it would ensure the required net investment. Changes in the structure of production could
basically be realized through the credit system or, in extraordinary cases (in the energy sector and similar
projects with long periods of amortization), with government subsidies. The formation of neutralized capital in
existing corporations should lead to a gradual, programed
transfer of outside shares into the neutralized property of
the enterprise collective. This could take place either by
means of a buy-back of stocks by the enterprise, or with
the assistance of the state. Basically, this would amount to
a long-range transformation of shares into neutralized enterprise property. The stock corporation as a form of
ownership would gradually wither away. In future, therefore, we should not expect the transformation of the liquid
capital of banks into stock capital.

The founding of new enterprises (small or medium-
sized), in which the private entrepreneur is the head and
motive force and would also continue to be the leading force
of the entrepreneurial development, should not only continue intact, but be encouraged in every possible way. Private ownership of founding capital would be guaranteed.
From a certain level of net profit upwards, however, neutralized capital would then be created for the co-workers
out of a fixed portion of profits. However, with large enterprises founded on the initiative of established enterprises, industrial enterprises, banks or insurance companies, this is, even at present, not a matter for private
initiative, but is, rather, the result of a broadly organized

---

(their own resources, that is, savings including transfers
of assets plus writeoffs) in percent of gross investments.

year	f(%)	year	f(%)
1950	75.1	1967	81.8
1955	69.5	1968	79.7
1960	70.8	1969	65.3
1961	66.4	1970	65.4
1962	69.7	1971	63.2
1963	69.7	1972	63.6
1964	67.2	1973	62.1
1965	64.6	1974	71.9
1966	70.2	1975	80.5

Sources: Monthly reports of the Deutsche Bundesbank,
statistical yearbooks, and the author's own calculations.

and planned investment of capital. The founders are here not identical with the hired managers. In future, these new establishments would be accomplished immediately and from the beginning in the form of neutralized capital property. Even if enterprises, industrial enterprises, and banks continued to take the initiative, the founders should not be the owners of the new enterprises. Their invested capital would represent a long-range or open-ended credit, and the new production collective would have to pay interest to the founders at a rate higher than the normal bank interest (founder interest rate). The capital would take the form of neutralized capital and would thus be administered by the new Assets Administration, in whose administrative council representative of the founders could participate. The new owners' collective could pay off the long-term credits out of profits at its discretion--for example, for a period of time, out of net investments. In exceptional, economically justified cases, the state could accelerate debt repayment through tax relief.

The same basic principles would apply to private insurance companies as to banks. We have already discussed the profit-sharing scheme that would be required for co-workers. In insurance companies too, net profits would, from a certain level upwards, be transformed into neutralized capital. After deducting net investment needs, this newly formed capital could be transformed only into reserves and savings (or also into credit capital). It would, of course, be just as possible to use accumulated liquid capital for purposes of founding industrial enterprises (or participating in their foundation), but this would also only be in the form of long-term credits for which foundation interest rates would be paid. Here too, the division of profits would be regulated.

HUMANIZATION OF WORK

We have already shown that in the reformed system, and above all in employee-owned enterprises, apart from the principle of efficiency, the humanity principle appears as the characteristic principle of economic activity and economic organization. The humanity principle expresses in summary form the principal consideration and satisfaction of people's highly developed non-economic needs, that is, for work-satisfaction, self-realization and self-development, identification with the work group and the enterprise, security and a meaningful life perspective, codetermination in the development of the economy, etc. The guiding principle of the economic reform will be to take these needs into consideration and to create the institutional as well as

organizational preconditions for their satisfaction, for further development in micro-economic units, enterprises, employee-owned enterprises, as well as at the macro-economic
level (national economic planning, economic policy).

If we now wish to deal with the introduction of the
humanity principle into the productive organization of an
enterprise against the background of neutralized capital, we
will once again have to consider the relationship between
this principle and the efficiency principle. In our initial
theoretical discussion of fundamentals, we attempted to
show that taking into account the satisfaction of certain
non-economically limited needs does not necessarily lead
again to the opposite extreme, that is, ignoring the decisive
role of economic needs. We must now explain in more concrete terms what this means, in order to guard against
discrediting oversimplifications and dogmatic reservations.

The humanization of productive activity should, first of
all, transform the position and significance of the person in
the enterprise. Man should no longer be only a means of
realizing profits in production, but rather production itself
should also become a means for the immediate satisfaction of
important non-economic needs and for people's self-realization. In order to transform this demand from a purely
ethically-motivated desire into institutionally anchored arrangements of work, the neutralization of capital is necessary, since this would create the preconditions for the humanization of the work process. This would be manifest in
certain changes: decision-making processes; relationships
with management; work activities; solution of the problem
of labor losses.

Now, what is meant by the emphasis on the continuing|
decisive role of the efficiency principle in the economy? It
expresses the claim that the factors of production, which
are relatively scarce in relation to economic needs, will
continue to force a long-run optimization of profits in production. The humanization of production must therefore not
impede the optimization of profits. As we will see, this is
not a fundamental, long-term contradiction provided that
one does not count on an absolute maximization of profit
but instead consciously accepts democratically decided profit
reductions to enhance the humanization of production. The
optimization of profits that comes about as a result of applying these two principles includes the efficiency-related
maximization of profit.

Changes in the direction of the humanization of work
should, however, overwhelmingly bring about an increase
in efficiency in the long run. We will now examine the important changes in decision-making processes, management
relationships, work activity, and unemployment, which the
humanization of work would bring about. However, we

cannot deal separately with decision-making processes, management relationships, etc., since in the reality of the enterprise these processes are more intermeshed than they are in the world of abstract concepts. We will therefore point out some complex changes in the organization of production, the outlines of which have begun to appear in diverse developmental trends, and which have been in some measure dealt with experimentally and even theoretically, and which in our opinion would signify important humanizing changes. The following measures to reform the organization of production should be purposefully introduced or, where they already exist, should be reinforced:

- decentralization and transition to participatory decision-making processes,
- transition from control to rule-governed processes and broad programs, programmatical guidelines,
- introduction of self-steering work groups,
- dissemination of economic informational and educational activity,
- generalization of social plans.

In the first place, more than one person is involved in participatory decision-making processes. |They also include people whose activities will be subject to these, and finally, not only professional superiors. The notion of participatory decision-making within productive enterprises stands in opposition to views about the need for authoritarian decision-making in production, such as those prevailing in both the Western and Eastern economic system.

Present systems of decision-making and management proceed from the assumption that any extensive organization of production according to the division of labor principle-- one which is to achieve definite results in the shortest possible time and using relatively few resources, and one which can constantly effect changes, external adjustments, and innovations--requires decision-making that is as uniform, operational, and authoritarian as possible. This system of managing capitalist production was also adopted by Lenin in the Soviet Union, ideologically justified by him, and implemented in Soviet enterprises under the designation of the so-called one-man-management principle.

In the capitalist system, however, a broad, diversified science of productive organization, decision-making, and management systems has developed in recent decades, and has been reinforced by systems theory and cybernetics. It is at any rate not possible to describe in detail the findings and theories of the highly efficient decision-making and management systems that have accompanied this scientific development. What is important for the proposed fundamental change, in the sense of broader participation, is the consideration that decisions in production are more effective when made for subsystems that are as small as possible and as close as possible to the productive activity itself, decisions which can thus be made on a broad and concrete basis. Incidentally, this consideration corresponds to the empirically ascertainable trend toward decentralization of decision-making processes and the divisionalization of productive organization.

Greater responsibility for planning, decision-making, and management of productive activity can be brought to the actual doers or executors of specific productive activities or to other economic activities (sales, purchasing, advertising, etc.) without making impossible the necessary cooperation between these non-centrally managed activities, if more efficient decision-making and management can be developed. Decision-making bodies can possess more specific and thus more complete specialized knowledge, can more rapidly acquire richer and more flexible information about opportunities for innovation and crisis-producing aspects, establish closer and more trusting relationships with the people involved in production, and more quickly compare the actual results of their decisions with the goals envisaged. This would result in the saving of resources, in innovations in products, technology, and productive organization, in flexible arrangements of the structure of production and the raising of productivity to such a point that net gains would by far exceed all the costs and time losses of a complicated system of coordination.

This tendency toward decentralization and compartmentalization is in keeping with the creation of smaller independent enterprises and sales organizations and the establishment of centers of profit, cost, and investment within large enterprises and trusts. This will reestablish the connection between market demand and the development of production for smaller, more flexible and more easily coordinated productive units and will enhance the independence of their decision-making bodies. Apart from actual power politics and large-scale financial transactions, the only areas of activity that would remain centralized would be those which could be more efficiently developed for all divisions in common, for example, research and development, intra-enterprise training, the opening up of new markets, raw materials and energy resources, the founding and financing of new enterprises, etc. Furthermore, bringing sales and purchasing as close together as possible within smaller, more overseeable productive units makes it possible to comprehend their market performance, the development of efficiency and profit and, more specifically to foster efficiency in their productive decision-making bodies through direct profit-sharing.

In recent decades, the tendency toward decentralization of decision-making and toward the economic independence of smaller subsystems has grown stronger within
large concerns and multinationals whose capital has grown
larger. The more interest in power and expansion grows
in the centers of these mammoth capital organizations, the
more urgent becomes the delegation of decision-making authority and of responsibility for the actual efficiency of
productive and market activities to the management bodies
of smaller subsystems.

This tendency toward decentralization creates a more
participatory system of decision-making. The current trend
toward decentralization has already demonstrated how important it is to tie decision-making responsibility to actual
productive activity. The closer the decisions of smaller
productive units can be brought to market results and thus
actually closer to the domain of consumption as well, the
more readily the decision-making bodies can acquire not
only additional knowledge and better information but also a
market-oriented interest. So far, however, this tendency
toward decentralization has not called into question the
principle of the sole responsibility of the professional superior and the management hierarchy bound up with it.
The competent superiors make decisions regarding appoint-
ments to the management positions under their domain, or
at least have an influence on them.

The establishment of a participatory decision-making
body would thus signify a further development of already
existing trends. Then, even at the lowest levels (work
groups), workers/employees would be drawn into the decision-making processes relating to the activity of the work
groups. Next, the way would be paved for a grass roots
transformation of decision-making procedures, in the sense
that decisions would be made not by superiors in an authoritarian manner, but rather democratically by the participants in the decision-making process. Finally, the professional superior, appointed from above, would be
replaced--initially at least, at the lowest decision-making
level (work-group master, foreman)--by a representative
elected by the work group. Since these changes would
affect the work group first and foremost, we will discuss
them in the context of the self-steering work groups. It
is evident from the preceding discussion, however, that the
changeover to participatory decision-making would be a
substantially broader process than the democratization of
decision-making already underway, and the former would,
under certain conditions, begin to eliminate the prevailing
antagonism between managers and managed.

This changeover has not, however, been realizable
under the prevailing antagonism of interests between owners

and non-owners of capital, between appropriators of profit and wage earners. For economists, who take this antagonism as axiomatic and are theoretically imprisoned by it, participatory democracy is inconceivable in its final, qualitatively new stage. In terms of the old conceptions, it is always the private owner of capital, or at least the manager as the representative of the owners of capital, who has to establish the goals of production, and these are authoritatively handed down to the workers from top to bottom (concretized and particularized with the help of the management hierarchy). So far, it has been impossible (with the exception of certain experiments to be mentioned later) to develop the notion that now perhaps workers and employees could decide how, and with which procedures and what division of labor certain final processes of production are to be realized, and that they would even be able to elect their own work leaders or, more appropriately, their work coordinators.

It is to be expected that workers' rising interest in increasing profits will also develop their interest in cutting costs, raising productivity, and increasing surplus value on the part of co-workers. However, since the resulting profits in large enterprises (as well as in huge profit centers) will occasionally be too far removed from the work group, the profit interest generated by profit-sharing will not suffice by itself, even though it may be an important condition for the development of an interest in efficiency among the workers, and one which will grow with experience. If, however, the relationship between the workers/employees and their work were to change in a real and fundamental way, to the benefit of both the enterprise and society, as well as to their own satisfaction, it should be possible to realize the measures, proposed here, that aim at the humanization of work. We will now deal with the humanization of work, taking the example of self-steering work groups. Self-steering work groups figure in the broad conception of a participatory decision-making order outlined here and are, in fact, particularly important elements in it.

If the co-workers of all groups were to be drawn in as full, interested members entitled to participate in decision-making, this would signify a broadening of the basis of information, of problem-solving incentives and of readiness to take decisions; and it would help to produce the all-important satisfaction on the part of the co-workers themselves. Their feelings of security, of their own significance to the group and the enterprise, and their identification with them, of self-realization and self-development will grow. Work, in conjunction with other changes, can thus gradually be transformed from a forced, alienated activity to an inwardly satisfying one.[6] It is not so much a matter of recurring, routine decisions, but rather of decisions relating to purpose, innovation, and crises,[7] --cases in which an increase in the number of proposals for decision-making, for the harmonization of interests, and for a readiness to carry out projects can be highly significant to the successful development of production. The transformation of authoritarian decision-making by superiors, following discussion, into democratic voting by all participants would still require some experimentation to establish the various stages of decision-making. However, Scandinavian experiments already in progress have shown the advantages of this kind of democracy at the level of self-steering work groups.[8]

A further prerequisite of participatory decision-making is the changeover from processes of control to processes of regulation within enterprises. Where, as has been the case under a hierarchical and authoritarian system of management, superiors give detailed instructions to their subordinate subsystem managers and prescribe their activities, this does not leave any room for the latter's initiatives and endeavors to find the best possible solutions. The new processes of regulation should be formulated so as to enable them to discover their own solutions and evolve their own search techniques; this means that they should be applied not only to arrive at those occasional decisions involving

---

[6] Participation in group processes leads to the formation of group identities, affording protection against narcissistic self-isolation. It makes possible the development of latent abilities in individuals or the development of new ones. Individual self-confidence is developed not only just by means of awareness of a formal right to participate, but precisely by exercising this right. Participation thus affords the kinds of opportunities for individual development referred to in traditional discussion as the self-realization of man, as the 'ecstasy of walking upright' (Bloch). F. Naschold, Organisation und Demokratie, Untersuchungen zum Demokratisierungspotential in komplexen Organisationen (Stuttgart a.a., 1971), p. 51.

[7] See the proposed typology of decisions in F. Naschold, ibid., p. 62ff. Similar considerations can be traced back to the work of H. A. Simon, et al. See The New Science of Management, (New York, 1960), and The Architecture of Complexity, in Proceedings of the American Philosophical Society 6 (1962), pp. 467-82.

[8] See N. Maier, Teilautonome Arbeitsgruppen. Moeglich-

goals, innovations and crises, but also to include continuous productive activities in which, so far, tasks have been routinely assigned to the individual subsystems.

There should be skeleton programs indicating the chronological and result-related interrelationships among the various subsystem activities. Subsystem collectives and their managers should be motivated not only to find the most efficient ways of carrying out the activities and attaining the results of their own subsystems, but also to coordinate with other subsystems. The skeleton program would define the main stages while providing motivated individuals an opportunity to find the best possibilities of realizing their part in the system on the basis of their own cognitive processes and adapting according to their own interests. Therefore, either the production process will be regulated with the help of triggering information which intentionally leaves vague the requirements of production within a tolerable range, thus enabling those affected to provide their own interpretation and make their own decisions; or skeleton interrelationships will have to be programed which, again, motivate the subsystems to their best concretization of substance and mutual coordination. In this way, the one-sided organizational hierarchy will transform itself into a series of subsystems interlinked by loops of information feedback.

The most important humanizing change is the introduction of self-steering work groups, since these affect the work activities of the majority of the most intensely alienated workers and employees. The Scandinavian experiments have already shown the functional capacity of this important transformation in work.[9] However, only with the

---

keiten und Grenzen eines Modells zur Humanisierung der Arbeit (Meisenheim am Glan, 1977), and the literature cited therein.

[9] See E. Trist and K. Bamforth, Some Social and Psychological Consequences of the Longwall Method of Coal-Getting, in Human Relations 4 (1951), pp. 3-38; also E. Thorsrund, Demokratisierung der Arbeitsorganisation. Einige konkrete Methoden zur Neustrukturierung des Arbeitsplatzes, in F. Vilmar, ed., Menschenwuerde im Betrieb. Modelle der Humanisierung und Demokratisierung der industriellen Arbeitswelt (Reinbeck bei Hamburg, 1973), pp. 117-42; also H. Steinmann, M. Heinrich, G. Schreyoegg, Theorie und Praxis selbststeuernder Arbeitsgruppen. Eine Analyse der Erfahrungen in Skandinavien (Koeln, 1976). Also Ch. Lattmann, Die Humanisierung der Arbeit und die Demokratisierung der

creation of neutralized capital and employee-owned enterprises does the real economic foundation and completion of
this change in work emerge.   The feeling of greater job
satisfaction would be enhanced and cemented by an awareness of sharing in the ownership of the enterprise.

Instead of the individual, the self-steering work group
now becomes the responsible executor of productive tasks
assigned to it by the skeleton program or alternatively by
superordinate agencies by means of normal functional instructions. The work group's decisions about the most efficient methods of production are only taken collectively,
and it is relatively autonomous in determining the organization of its work. Naturally, it has to deliver the results
of production within the time allotted by the plan and with
the prescribed quality, and in the process it may shorten
or otherwise change the course of production in its own
interest, at its own initiative and in coordination with the
adjacent subsystems.

The leader of the group will be elected, mainly according to the criterion of who is best qualified to lead the
group. If the tasks and/or aims of the work group
change, the leader can also be changed. In time, all members of the group can be trained for group leadership and
the leadership of the group can change hands regularly.
The decision-making authority of the group leader will be
democratically legitimated by election and collective consultations about the work to be done, even though in the in-
terim, operational decisions will have to be made autocrati-
cally. In general, the leader would represent the work
group to the outside, above all in the deliberations of the
councils of the superior instances or in discussions with
other work group leaders regarding coordination and planning. In time, other members--those most suitable at the
respective time--could be delegated to attend such discussions.

The division of labor and the nature of cooperation will
be determined by the group. One of the aims is enrichment of work activity by means of the planned rotation of
jobs. The members of the group will change jobs in the
production process at set intervals. They will thereby
broaden their qualifications and experience, and to some
extent overcome the monotony of a single job. The more
diverse are the activities within the work group, given the
division of labor, the more satisfying this job rotation can
be. Although this alternation is important for increasing
job satisfaction, it must not be overestimated. It will not
overcome the great barriers set by the division of labor in

Unternehmung (Bern/Stuttgart, 1974).

society, since there is a limited scope for new opportunities and different jobs within the group. For this reason alone, the issue of remuneration for work done will always be of crucial significance.

The work group will also determine the division of wages within the group. This means that total wages for the quantitative and qualitative results of production within a given time will be paid by the firm to the entire work group insofar as this is technically feasible. The latter body--which best knows the efforts and requirements involved in the various jobs and their attractiveness--will decide on the individual distribution of these wages and on the rules for, and possible exceptions to this distribution. Where a part of profit-sharing is utilized as performance bonuses, the group will also decide on the distribution of these bonuses.

The principle of electing alternating leaders could also be gradually extended to the higher levels of the employee-owned enterprise. The respective work group leaders would constitute the executive body of the enterprise or department and would, for their part, elect the most suitable enterprise manager or department head. This person would not only be the leader of the enterprise (department), responsible along with the entire executive body for carrying out its tasks, internal division of labor, coordination, etc., but would also represent this larger subsystem at the higher level. This projected extension of the democratic election of subsystem leaders from lower to higher levels would naturally have to be considered carefully, especially with regard to professional training, qualifications, and the possible ways of taking account of these in the electoral process. The advantages and disadvantages of this system at higher levels should also be tested with the help of experiments.

The self-steering work group's contribution to the humanization process should be obvious. Not only does it affect the work of the individual, but it also makes possible his active participation in the planning and organization of work. In the final analysis, the individual is able to gain an overall awareness of the entire work process and its results, and can therefore better identify with the enterprise and better understand its economic results and how they are expressed as profits. His sense of security will increase, since the group can give him better backing in difficult personal situations as well. He can be employed precisely according to his abilities, which would increase his self-confidence and enable his personality to develop further. In this way, the efficiency of production would not only not be impaired but, on the contrary, would increase in the long run.

This process would have to be supplemented, within
the employee-owned enterprise, by the purposeful and organized expansion of economic information and education.
If capital neutralization is to be prevented from becoming a
formal affair involving a few meetings of the collective owners and mechanical profit-sharing, the economic problems of
the enterprise will have to be made understandable to all
co-worker/co-owners. The co-owner ought to be aware of,
experience, and learn to understand the plans, outlooks,
prospects, difficulties, dangers, successes, etc. of his enterprise.

In contrast to similar informational practices in contemporary large enterprises, in the employee-owned enterprise
such information would fall on much more fertile terrain.
Awareness of the direct relationship between the success
of the firm and the growth of their own incomes, the possibility of influencing the management of the enterprise
through elected supervisory councils, the right as co-owners to demand accountability and, if necessary, to bring
about a change in management--all this endows economic
information with a much greater significance. Co-workers'
readiness to take in comprehensible information would grow.
One might also expect to see an increasing demand for active economic participation, as well as new proposals and
criticisms, and a readiness to pose questions on the part
of the co-workers. Special attention would have to be
paid to the organization and utilization of their inputs.
Only in this way would co-workers begin to feel themselves
to be co-owners with a share in conceptualization, decision-
making, and responsibility.

Co-workers should in particular broaden and deepen
their economic education in order to produce cadres of future representatives. Just as the membership of the supervisory councils (or in large enterprises several levels
of supervisory councils) should change, so a broad reser-
voir of people would have to be educated who, with their
knowledge and general overview, would be capable of filling these responsible positions. Co-workers would also
welcome special courses for economic and technical economic
training, since they would now be aware of their practical
utility. In addition, there should be special courses for
workers whose learning inhibitions could be overcome in a
conducive milieu. The result of economic education could
be that a growing number of workers and employees would
gradually come to an understanding of such concepts as
costs, prices, profits, and their interrelationships within
the enterprise, as well as in the national economy. And
this, in turn, could disseminate an understanding of economic information and the firm's economic situation among
the workers, with a resultant growth in overall responsibility of the employee-owned enterprise.

A situation of this kind could create new possibilities for solving the problem of wastage of work time by means of a generalization of social plans. As we will show later in our discussion of the market mechanism, the flexible variation of the structure of production and the modernization of productive, labor-saving techniques is indispensable at the present stage of development. Therefore, circumstances will always arise which make certain workers redundant. In capitalist systems the problem has been resolved simply by means of layoffs, the consequence of which is frictional unemployment or, in times of crisis, mass unemployment. If the laid-off worker is lucky he can find a new job relatively quickly in another enterprise. However, he has no guarantee that this will happen, and all too often the difficulty of finding a new job is increased by the very fact of his being unemployed, since his plight is tacitly attributed to his own incompetence. The psychological burden imposed on people by phenomenon of unemployment is an expression of the inhumanity of the capitalist system.

Preparations for all major structural and technical changes in the enterprises will be carried on for a relatively long period. Furthermore, reductions of the work hours would not have to be effected overnight. As soon as a new attitude can evolve toward the working people in the enterprise--which would be a feature of the employee-owned enterprise--the problem of loss of jobs can be solved in a new and more humane way, without losses in income in the long run. If the necessity for changes in production and for the abolition of old work activities or jobs is recognized in good time, this should immediately trigger an organized search for production substitutes and new programs of production. Whether through new ventures by the old enterprise or through participation in other firms, the employee-owned enterprise would, in a growing economy, always have the possibility of compensating for labor-saving on the one hand or creating new jobs on the other. As we will see later on, there cannot be too little work in a reformed economic system. Even in the most extreme case, the problem could be solved by reducing the hours of work.

The problem of loss of jobs can thus be solved without resorting to degrading unemployment. This of course requires a fundamentally different attitude toward the working people; it requires timely economic prognoses and preparations for substitution; and it requires the employee-owned enterprise to be prepared to accept short-run declines in profits. Of course, when labor has to be saved, the simple laying off of co-workers is much less costly than creating new jobs, since the latter is bound up with retraining processes and many other things that cost money.

A readiness to bear such costs should figure among the crucial humanization efforts of the employee-owned enterprise. Of course, the employee-owned enterprise must also strive to minimize costs and to make up for short-run profit losses by capitalizing on new opportunities for production. Basic security for the people in the employee-owned enterprise will not only further the aims of humanization, it will bring about gains in efficiency, since it will increase the incentive to those affected.

Macro-distribution planning, dealt with in the next section, would be one of the basic preconditions for overcoming the cyclical course of the economy and the mass unemployment bound up with it, both of which lead to an unacceptable worsening of people's economic conditions.

4

MACROECONOMIC
DISTRIBUTION PLANNING

DISRUPTIONS OF THE MACRO-EQUILIBRIUM

In any advanced economic system based on the division of labor principle, there will be fundamental reciprocal linkages among the broad economic processes which in theory are also designated as macro-variables.[1] (We will speak of macro-processes for the time being and explain them later.) The reciprocal linkages require a development of these macro-processes in quantitative ratios sufficient to guarantee an economic equilibrium. In a capitalist economic system, however, the development of these macro-processes cannot be consciously regulated so as to maintain an equilibrium, since it is the outcome .of spontaneous, independent decisions made by a huge number of isolated private entrepreneurs, boards of directors, budget planners, consumers, etc.; it is produced by wage struggles and wage agreements, by governments' economic policy decisions, and the like.

No decision-making body possesses an understanding of the conditions favoring equilibrium or of the respective other isolated decisions; nor is it in their immediate interest to have such an understanding. One consequence of such a decision-making system is that the macro-processes repeatedly develop in such a way as to disrupt its equilibrium. Or in other words, recurrent macro-disequilibria develop at various intervals. They will necessarily manifest themselves in serious economic and social economic crises.

In our conception of macro-disequilibria and our evaluation of them, we depart from most Western economists' theories of crisis, boom, and cycles.[2] In particular, it is

---

[1] See, for example, G. Ackley, <u>Macroeconomic Theory</u> (New York, 1969), p. 3.

[2] The relevant literature is so comprehensive that only the most important orienting works, from different periods,

our conviction that the macro-equilibria manifest in constantly recurring general economic crises, cannot be compared with micro-disequilibria, that is, disequilibria between
the supply of, and demand for goods, groups of goods or
products of entire branches. We regard the macro-disequilibria as unnecessary plagues on humanity, in the course of
which, during certain periods, the marketing of virtually all
of production stagnates, investments in general are sharply
reduced, production must be lowered, and mass unemployment results. We reject any suggestion that they have to
be regarded as inevitable realities with which one must simply come to terms, not unlike unstoppable natural catastro-
phies.

For non-economists, we should emphasize first of all
that the cause of general market declines is not to be found
in the satiation of all the population's needs, since everyone
knows that the needs of the broadest strata of the population remain unsatisfied on a very large scale, and below-
average income recipients find that only a minimum number
of their economic needs are so fully covered that they are
unlikely to continue growing. The so-called satiation point
can therefore only express the fact of restricted purchasing
power, that is, that at certain times real wages cannot rise
or that wages are even in decline. In such cases the causes must be sought elsewhere than in a general satuation.

Although partial satiations may occur, that is a surplus
of individual goods or groups of goods, these involve micro-disequilibria or structural problems rather than general
market crises. While demand for certain products can decline, it can increase for others. And it would be difficult
to maintain that, given a general rise in the real wages of
below average income earners' their demand for products to
meet current needs, for example, certain kinds of foodstuffs, textiles, shoes, etc., would not increase further,
even in the world's richest countries.

During periods of rising real wages, therefore, structural changes in production can be relatively easily brought
about because the decline of certainkinds of production is
compensated, without triggering general crises, by growth
in other areas of production. Although necessary changes
in the structure of production can aggravate general market
crises, they do not cause them. Also, in periods of general growth, a decline in some labour-intensive branches and
expansion in some less labour-intensive branches need not

can be mentioned here: W. C. Mitchell, Der Konjunk-
turzyklus (Leipzig, 1931); G. Haberler, Prosperity and
Depression (Harvard, 1937); G. J. Tichy, Konjunktur-
schwankungen (Berlin, Heidelberg, New York, 1976).

produce mass unemployment, since there are always enough other labour-intensive branches whose needs are continuously growing and which can thus absorb extra labor power.

The general declines in production which have occurred from time to time thus cannot have been produced by a general satiation. Either there is a sudden decrease in market prospects for consumer goods--despite a large number of unsatisfied needs--or outlets for the means of production rapidly decrease. Either way, a drop in investment and production is the result. The causes of these differential declines in the market prospects of the two large productive groups must be explained.

First and foremost, I would direct attention to fluctuations in the productivity of capital. By capital productivity I mean the relationship between the value of production (output) and the value of the functional capital deployed in production (investment funds plus floating capital).[3] This relationship changes quite fundamentally in different periods. There are periods of rising capital productivity during which both the gross value of production and the net product grow more rapidly than the value of the functional capital necessary for production. There are times of equally rapid growth of both quantities, that is, of constant capital productivity. And finally, capital productivity can fall at certain times, that is, the scope of production can grow more slowly than the necessary functional capital.

The causes of these fluctuations are consequences of different trends. They may be both of a technical-economic and a purely economic character. Capital productivity, for instance, can grow with the aid of completely new techniques and technology; it can grow because existing productive capacity is better utilized when production is on the increase or because prices for raw materials and energy are falling while inventories remain constant, and the like. But capital productivity can also fall when, due to increasing competitive pressures, totally new technologies must be applied; in the process expenditures for new productive facilities will grow more rapidly, for a time, than the scope of production, as expressed in prices (but will nevertheless be profitable, since they save on labor, power, and wages). Capital productivity can drop because prices for raw materials, energy, and the like will increase, but the price increases cannot be transferred completely to the final products. It is also possible that production capacity will

---

[3] See also H. Siebert, Einfuehrung in die Volkswirtschaftslehre II (Stuttgart, Berlin, Cologne, Mainz: 1977), p. 77.

be less fully utilized, that inventories will increase, etc.

Fluctuations in capital productivity are not however the cause of disruptions in the macro-equilibrium. Rather, these must be seen as inherent in the functional distribution of the national income[4] in opposition to the development of capital productivity. Whatever the development of capital productivity at any given time, it almost always comes up against a counterforce in the form of the quota of the final investible income--against that which it would optimally require for its own development. National income is, in the final analysis, utilized partly for consumption and partly for net investment. The shares of consumption and investment in the national income make up the consumption and investment quotas and are the result of the so-called functional distribution processes. The current false development of investment quotas (which originates in the capitalist distribution processes in the context of the existing or necessary development of capital productivity) leads to reductions in investment activity to a greater or lesser degree, which immediately produces disruptions in the equilibrium (recessions, crises).

In this way, rising capital productivity would require a falling profit and investment quota and a rising consumption quota (in a certain quantitative ratio). But in practice, as soon as the profit quota rises and the consumption quota falls, given increasing capital productivity (which is common under capitalism in the absence of state countermeasures), excessive investment funds must be generated at a certain moment. A portion of the investment funds will not be utilized, which gives rise to a recessive decline in the production of investment goods or in the entire production 'process'.[5] By contrast, falling capital productivity would require rising profit and investment quotas. In capitalist practice, however, falling capital productivity usually confronts a falling profit quota and investment funds that are relatively declining. This also leads to reductions in investment activity because the relatively declining investment

---

[4] On this, see, for example, C. Roberts, Verteilungstheorie und Verteilungspolitik (Cologne, 1980), p. 68 et seq.

[5] An analysis of economic development in Germany from 1950 to 1975 demonstrates that the development of investments (usually after a brief temporal lag) quite precisely corresponds with the development of capital productivity, given the contrary development of consumption. W. Glastetter, Die wirtschaftliche Entwicklung der Bundesrepublik Deutschland im Zeitraum 1950 bis 1975 (Berlin, Heidelberg, New York, 1977), pp. 75 and 97.

funds, if utilized for investment, would produce an even lesser growth of production and profits. Under these circumstances, investments are not worthwhile, and many investors prefer to put their money into interest-bearing investments (besides, the present period is one of rising interest rates). Here again, the result is economic crisis.

In early capitalism, when trade unions did not yet exist, or were too weak and fragmented, and when the state still redistributed relatively little of the national income, the growth and size of real wages from time to time, repeatedly, fell behind the growth of production. Technical progress, and with it growing capital productivity, had the immediate result of expanding the profit quota (gross profits as a percentage of the national income) while the wage quota (despite growing average wages and employment) fell. Wages thus grew more slowly than productivity.

Wages were, and still are, always predominantly consumption-oriented income with relatively low net savings.[6] The fact that they lagged behind the development of productivity resulted in consumption rising more slowly than production and in the consumption quota falling. The profit quota grew, in contrast, and with it excessive funds for investment as well. At a certain point, this led necessarily to the overproduction of consumer goods. Producers of consumer goods had to reduce their investments, and this ultimately led to lower investments in the investment-goods branches and hence to a general economic crisis.[7] But these developments are no longer characteristic of the industrial countries, and the present economic crisis has other causes. The former crises of overproduction are no more the

---

[6] According to budgetary calculations respecting non-independent gainfully employed persons in Switzerland, in 1975 the net savings of this group were so low that interest from these savings made up only 0.4 percent of their total budgetary income (see the special issue of the periodical Volkswirtschaft (1979), p. 34). Since the Swiss non-independent gainfully employed persons' per capita incomes and savings are among the highest in the world, this means that the net savings of wage-earners in other capitalist countries are generally even lower.

[7] For more on this see O. Sik, The Third Way (London and New York, 1976), pp. 245 et seq., and A. Stobbe, Gesamtwirtschaftliche Theorie (Berlin, 1975), pp. 95 et seq. Dogmatic Marxist economics today still insist that this is the sole cause of crisis. See for instance Politische Oekonomie des Kapitalismus und Sozialismus (Berlin, 1974), pp. 254 et seq.

main characteristics. In terms of today's economic development, what is typical is not the surpassing of consumption-
oriented income by production, but the reverse: an exaggerated development of consumption. Processes of
overconsumption have become the salient characteristic and
are manifested in modern inflation and eventually in special
kinds of general economic crises as well.

In contemporary capitalism too, a growth in capital
productivity, that is, a more rapid increase in the scope of
production (output) than in functional capital (input)--
which was characteristic, for example, of most industrial
countries during the 1950s--would lead to a growth in the
profit quota. But certain counter-processes are at work
against this development. In most of the industrialized
countries, a rapid increase in employment and the emergence of strong trade unions after World War II resulted in
a substantially more rapid growth in the size of wages than
had been the case in the past. Average wages increased at
essentially the same rate as labor productivity and, during
several of the years, even more rapidly.[8] This raised the
wage quota, or at least prevented it from declining. Second, most industrial countries implemented Keynesian economic policies, which gave rise to state income redistribution favoring more rapidly increasing social consumption.

The rapid growth in consumption set off by both processes resulted in an even more rapid growth in investment
activities. Under conditions of rising capital productivity,
this growth in consumption, and hence Keynesian economic
policy as well, resulted in anticyclical effects. It ensured
that consumption would not lag so much behind the development of productivity and it prevented the generation of
excessive liquid investment funds, factors which had basically arrested crises such as those arising in early capitalism. To be sure, an excessive growth in consumption-oriented income was again produced here, in the course of
which nominal incomes, with the aid of the instrument of
credit, grew more rapidly than actual production. This was
necessarily manifested in the form of accelerating inflation.
In a market economy, the state is simply not in a position
to adapt the results of its income redistribution quickly
enough or precisely enough to the requirements of the actual development of productivity.

However, as soon as the conditions for falling capital
productivity--in contrast to the conditions of growing capital productivity--are generated, that is, when for various
reasons a given amount of functional capital value results in

[8] See O. Sik, Humane Wirtschaftsdemokratie (Hamburg, 1979), pp. 769-70.

diminishing growth in the scope of production (falling marginal productivity of functional capital), then a constant quota of wages, profits, and taxation (as a percentage of national income) leads inevitably to a falling rate of profit (yield). Yield, that is, the relationship between profits and invested capital, must drop, since net social product and national income, as well as profits (assuming a constant profit quota), grow more slowly than productive capital. Moreover, if wage and tax increases similar to those previously effected during periods of growing capital productivity are implemented, then not only the rise in inflation but also the decline in the rate of profit is accelerated. Instead of the growing investment funds necessary for a certain increase in production, fewer and fewer investment funds are formed from relatively declining profits. The results must be reduced investment activity with a regressive production of investments and, ultimately, regressive consumption.[9]

This process is further accelerated by simultaneously rising interest rates, since demand for credit grows more rapidly than the formation of savings and credit funds. Demand for credit and, with it, interest rates are driven upward on two fronts: (1) by private entrepreneurs beset by marketing difficulties and attempting to avert bankruptcy by means of increasing credit, and (2) by states with budgetary deficits which rise as tax revenues decline, and an attempt is made to compensate for this by raising still more credits. This also reduces investment activity, which is already declining, and deepens the economic crisis.

In the final analysis, both the 1974 recession and the present world wide economic crisis are manifestations of distribution processes which have occurred since the early 1970s under conditions of rapidly decreasing capital productivity-- the very reverse of what is required for this productivity to develop. Instead of rising rates of profits and investments, which, with the aid of technical modernization, innovation, and structural change, would have been required to restore rising capital productivity, the current development of wages, taxes, and consumption has led to a more and more regressive development of investments.

The monetarist anti-inflation policies, which many countries adopted in the 1970s have, of course intentionally fostered, an upward surge of interest rates. In order to counter the increasingly negative effects of interventionist

---

[9] The entire problem complex of crises and inflation is treated much more exhaustively in the German edition of this book Sik, Humane Wirtschaftsdemokratie (Hamburg, 1979).

Keynesian economic policies, the monetarists argue, the economy ought to be left largely to its own market forces; the policy of scarce money would then accelerate a healthy contraction of production. That is to say, as production falls and the market contracts, long overdue structural changes and technical modernization would be implemented. In the process, of course, all those enterprises and branches which can no longer keep pace with the greater efficiency requirements as interest rates rise, will have to be forced into bankruptcy.[10] Not only does this line of reasoning assume the liquidation of a large number of enterprises and a high level of unemployment, it also implicitly sees such developments as a means of lowering the wage quota and raising the rate of profit. Furthermore, at least in theory, it is supposed to effect a substantial decline in state revenues and expenditures. The redistribution of the national income in such a way as to favor profits and invested net income, as this policy aims to do, is intended to bring about a renewed increase in investment activity, capital productivity, and labor productivity, as well as to bring about a new boom in the economy.

Monetarist economic policies do not however eliminate the causes of economic crises, since they cannot prevent the rise of macro-disequilibria. As has already been shown, these develop through interest-determined distribution processes and the consumable and investible net income which they produce, and which, at certain times, repeatedly go against the development of capital productivity. Under conditions of rising capital productivity, excessive amounts of net investment income were once produced, but under conditions of declining capital productivity, excessive amounts of net consumptive income, as well as inadequate profits and insufficient investment incentives, are normally the rule. Either way, reduced investment activities and declining production are produced, and crisis is the result.

Monetarists will claim that maintaining a scarce money supply can prevent an excessive rise in consumption. However, they ignore the fact that at certain times net consumptive income can grow excessively, not by state redistribution and by expansion of the money supply, but by increasing the wage quota at the expense of the profit quota. But state expenditures cannot normally be reduced to the required extent, and thus create a need for further credits (with upward interest pressures). These developments in distribution, which result from a certain constellation of interests and powers, cannot be prevented solely by

---

[10] See also F. A. Hayek, Geldtheorie und Konjunkturtheorie (Salzburg, 1976), p. 101.

regulating the money supply, just as they cannot prevent an excessive increase in the profit quota and in net invested income.

In periods of rising capital productivity, Keynesian economic policy has not prevented an increase in excessive non-utilized non-invested income, and has thus not eliminated the cause of crises. But it has also been unable to prevent a decline in capital productivity, which has led to a gradual reduction in motivation to invest. This tendency has been further accelerated by a growing burden of taxation and a development of inflation caused in part by the state itself. The monetarist critique of Keynesian economic policy stresses only the latter deficiency of Keynesian policy without taking account of the differentiated effect of Keynesian policies under varying conditions of capital productivity.[11] This differential effect has not been revealed by the anti-monetarist Keynesians themselves because they too have failed to note this connection between functional distribution processes and the development of capital productivity.[12]

Although monetarist fiscal policy has been able to dampen inflation, it cannot change distribution processes or prevent the development of falling rates of profit in times of declining capital productivity. This policy will also fail to counteract rising interest rates in the intensifying crisis and will only see it as the natural remedy for excessive demand for credit. Only after a substantial decline in demand for credit--possible only after decreases in production and consumption of substantial economic and social proportions, bound up with massive company bankruptcies and staggering unemployment rates--can a gradual decline in interest rates come about. Then, investment activity can slowly begin again, reinforced by a necessity for technical reconstruction on the part of surviving enterprises. This

---

[11] In his book, Free to Choose (New York, 1980), Milton Friedman rightly criticizes the negative consequences of interventionist economic policies in the United States, which have not only produced a gigantic bureaucracy and a huge national debt, but have also been unable to prevent recession and growing unemployment. However, he does not take account of the various effects of state redistributive policy in periods of rising and falling profit rates and differing developments of capital productivity.

[12] See for instance, E. Lundberg, Stabilization Problems in an International Setting--Old and New (Kiel Institute for World Economy, 1981).

normally means a gradual business revival which need not, however, by any means lead immediately to full employment, since the new techniques will be developed on the basis of extraordinary labor-saving technology.

In conclusion, we can only express our conviction that neither Keynesian nor monetarist economic policy is capable of eliminating cyclically recurring disruptions in the macro-equilibrium of a market economy. The unregulable development of functional distribution processes in relation to differential development of capital productivity is necessarily menifested in economic crises of massive economic and social proportions, which represent one of the most pressing problems of the market economy. The waves of high unemployment, social insecurity, and fear of the future bound up with these crises may, in certain countries, lead to right-wing or left-wing political radicalization and thus jeopardize the democratic liberties of a society.

The spontaneous unregulated growth of capitalist production and consumption also results in even greater threats to the conditions of natural and human existence; and cyclical macro-disruptions, with their negative economic and social consequences, make extremely difficult, if not impossible, any attempt to combat consistently this threat to the environment. In the process, the perversion of our environment, which has become part of our general awareness, has in many places already assumed alarming forms. The pollution of rivers and lakes, of the seas, the ground water and the air in urban areas and industrial concentrations, the increasing amount of noise in these centers, the accumulation of noxious residues in foodstuffs, the dying off of whole forest areas, and the gradual clearing of the rain forests, the encroachment of the desert regions, the rapid extinction of more and more animal species--all this can no longer be deemphasized, let alone disputed. Our information about these devastating developments is based upon overwhelming scientific evidence.[13]

The political measures taken in the direction of environmental protection do not, by any means reflect the radical character which the radical destruction of the environment necessitates. The majority of the older generation tends to underrate this development, usually taking comfort

---

[13] On this, see D. L. Meadows, The Limits to Growth (New York, 1972); M. Mesarovic and E. Pestel, Menschheit am Wendepunkt (Reinbek bei Hamburg, 1977); D. Gabor, et al., Das Ende der Verschwendung (Stuttgart, 1976); Binswanger, Geissberger, Ginsburg, eds., Der NAWU - Report: Wege aus der Wohlstandsfalle (Frankfurt/Main, 1978).

in the belief that the issue has been exaggerated and that the whole affair is not as dangerous as it is made out to be. But a majority of the younger generation sees its own future as highly threatened and is much more disturbed by what it has learned about the environment. Naturally all other life-threatening developments intensify this feeling: the arms race that never ends, the manufacture of absurd quantities of world-annihilating weapons, contradictory information about the dangers in developing nuclear energy, possible abuses of the latest biological, chemical, and other scientific findings, etc. All these developments produce an increasingly emotional resistance against the entire contemporary economic and political development of society.

We cannot enter here into a discussion of all these conditions and their psychological manifestations. But if we try to answer the question of why so relatively little has been done about the destruction of the environment and why a majority of the population, and thus politicians as well, are willing to downplay or even suppress the relevant information, we then again arrive at the uncontrollable and unregulable quality of a pure market economy. It cannot be brought into line with the requirements of a healthy environment, with the potential condition of energy and raw materials, with vital humanitarian aspirations, etc.

It is not only profit interest in the most rapid possible economic growth--as is often simplistically asserted--that leads to neglect of the threat to the environment. The interests of the broad masses of the working population in a substantial increase in real wages, in job security, and in overcoming unemployment work in the same direction. These interests are even greater in crisis periods, in times of mass bankruptcies and rapidly growing unemployment. Under such circumstances, the dangers to the environment are suppressed and ignored. If ways and means are not found to link people's interests in income and consumption to their interest in a sound environment, the latter will remain the weaker interest.

The funds required by industry for investment purposes have declined greatly in the course of the past decade and thus only small amounts have been spent, and this under compulsion--when specifically prescribed and regulated by law--for environmental protection equipment. The environmental protection measures, which the state, regional, and municipal organs have to implement and finance, are even further neglected in periods of falling tax revenues and budget deficits. Enterprise managers and political authorities alike know only too well that in times of general austerity and inadequate funds they can first and foremost cut back environmental protection measures, and that in doing so they enjoy the tacit support of a majority of the population. The consequence is that more of the environment is constantly being polluted and destroyed than cleansed and regenerated.

The question thus arises as to whether the uncontrollable and unregulable development of the national economy with all its negative and threatening consequences, is to continue, or whether it is possible to overcome its negative aspects while maintaining or improving the market mechanism. We are convinced that although in economic terms a solution to the negative problems exists, its realization is dependent on the formation of a very broad consciousness throughout the population, who are in a position to generate sufficient political pressure to force steps to be taken in the direction of this solution.

It would be possible, by means of a systematic regulation of the macro-distribution processes and on the basis of transformed interests on the part of wage earners, to pursue a complex of democratically conceived economic, ecological, and social goals without having to surrender the advantages of widespread entrepreneurial initiative and the market mechanism. The advantages of a market economy can be retained while, at the same time, overcoming its negative and threatening aspects. The economic interests which motivate people such that production develops in a maximally efficient and needs-oriented way should be extended, while remaining subordinate to larger social and humanitarian ends.

THE GOALS OF MACRO-ECONOMIC DISTRIBUTION PLANNING

Macro-economic distribution planning is not intended to replace the market mechanism, as socialist dirigist planning in particular advocates. Rather, it should supplement the market mechanism in controlling the development of the economy. This is especially the case where the market mechanism can only be inadequately controlled or when it can only operate through substantial disruption of economic process. Here macro-economic planning (henceforth shortened to macro-planning) should be utilized. As the preceding analysis has shown, it is the domain of economic macro-proportions in particular in which fundamental interconnections exist, and which the responsible economic policy-making organs must deliberately respect.

What is involved here is primarily a series of interrelationships between the development of the large production groups and, according to developments, large income groups, between the development of individual and social consumption and the development of investment, between human life and environmental conditions and economic growth. A conscious respect for these interrelationships in planning is conceivable in the case of various alternative developments. In the process there should not be any substantial disruptions in the interrelated macro-processes. There should, rather, be a harmonious development among them. Systematic regulation of the macro-processes thus always has both a genetic and a teleological character. It requires taking account of objectively caused pressures and the determination of alternative development processes.

In particular, the teleological aspect of planning (the aspect determined by desires) is important. For the macro-planning which we advocate should not be regarded only as an instrument to achieve a dynamic, balanced economic development, even though this goal has been placed at the top of the agenda. But if planning were to be restricted largely to this task, it would not differ very much from the planning systems existing in many Western industrial states, whose main purpose is to preserve the magical equilibrium of growth, namely full employment, stable prices, and an equalized balance of payments. Yet macro-planning ought to be much more than a mere auxiliary instrument used by the market to preserve the dynamic equilibrium; above all other things it should serve to humanize the economy, to integrate certain social and extra-economic goals more consistently into the course of economic development. At the same time it should represent the main instrument by means of which the population can consciously and democratically determine its own economic and social future on the basis of full information.

We might expect future macro-planning to overcome precisely this economic fatalism: namely the belief that economic misery afflicts peoples in the same way as natural catastrophes. In neither the capitalist nor the communist system are the broad masses of the population able consciously to determine their future economic situation, choose from among alternatives, and register their desires and interests in shaping the latter. In the new system, a broad consciousness-raising process concerning the opportunities and limitations, preconditions and consequences of fundamental economic decisions can become reality by means of democratic macro-planning. In an era of impending bureaucratic dehumanization of all economic apparatuses, it has indeed become the crucial demand of humanity. If for this reason we strongly emphasize the teleological side of macro-planning, this does not mean that we underestimate prevailing economic compulsions and laws.

Objective compulsions exist as a result of preceding economic development, which also sets the parameters for future development and leaves only limited scope for desired changes. At the same time, however, this scope means that there is both a possibility and necessity for freely-made decisions concerning future economic processes. These become all the more important the longer the time period is for planned future development.

Every plan is characterized by a certain duality. It is based on a synthesis of two apparently contradictory aspects. On the one hand there are statistics and evidence about the development in the past which, given the existing level of knowledge, can give rise to a scientifically grounded prognosis of development in the future. It is thus a matter of identifying the objective laws of development in the past and making a prognosis based on them; that is, it is a question of genetic research.

On the other hand, the plan also establishes the goals toward which economic policy is directed (these need not be goals defined authoritatively; economic policy can ensure their realization indirectly, by economic means). That is, it is a question of a teleological construction. In other words--in very general terms--every plan contains both a prediction of autonomous economic development and a projection of the goals set.

The goals of planning can, in general, be equated with the purpose of a plan, that is, those goals which must be realized in all the sub-plans of a planning system. Such generally expressed goals will of course represent the common substance of concretized, specified, and completed goals of the particular plans of the various planning periods. On the basis of the analysis and of what has already been said, the general goals of macro-planning, as we see it, can be formulated in the following manner:

1. maintenance of macro-economic equilibrium;

2. macro-proportional regulation of the development of consumption in accordance with the desired development of the quality of life;

3. regulation of the pace of economic growth;

4. preservation or transformation of individual income policies;

5. maintenance or attainment of the desired hours of work, occupational mobility, retraining (requalification), and medical benefits;

6. achievement of the desired equilization of different national and regional economic developments;

7. creation of the desired healthy environmental condi-
    tions and industrial and urban conglomerates;

8. securing the infrastructure and the energy basis of
    the economy and society; and

9. attainment of the desired educational, scientific, and
    cultural developments in society.

It is plausible that realization of these goals in the
sub-plans of individual planning periods will always have to
begin with recognized possibilities for the development of
production, if the desired development is not to become a
mere set of pipe dreams. In this sense, planning will
therefore always be undertaken on the basis of an analysis
of available forces of production and actual possibilities for
their development during the planning period on the one
hand, and the needs and interests which enter into formation of the plan and which determine the concrete goals of
future economic development on the other hand. Within the
framework permitted by the future development of production, based on its past development, various alternative developments are feasible. It will thus be a matter of which
needs and interests come to have a decisive influence on
the preparation and selection of the plan and are expressed
in its concretized goals.
Organization of the preparation, presentation, and selection of the plan must be such that the broad masses of
the population are able to discuss fundamental variants of
future economic developments, that the mass media are en-
listed in the service of such discussions, that various interest groups are formed and that their representatives
take an active part in the preparation of the plan. Minority interests must also be allowed to air their views publicly
and must be consulted with regard to alternative plans. It
is thus important that macro-planning be democratically organized. In no event must undesirable powerful groups be
given the opportunity to manipulate the plans in their own
interests or to pass off their partial interests as being
those of society as a whole.
If the market mechanism is to continue to function to
the fullest, planning must not encompass production and investment activities. Enterprises must continue to have full
responsibility for the determination of the development of
their production and investment. The goals incorporated
into the plan can be realized by means of certain distribution processes, that is, the distribution of gross income or
the national income among certain income groups, and a
distribution process of this nature can be accomplished by
appropriate economic policies. The goals of the plan should

be realized by means of indirect steering instruments, that is, basically a state economic policy adapted from the outset to the goals being pursued. The instrument for achieving the goals of the plan is thus not regimentation of production, which would be an obstacle to any market-oriented independence and responsibility on the part of the enterprises, but economic policy conforming to the market which, by means of income regulation, would guide production and investment toward the plan goals.

Distribution always constitutes the link between production and consumption. In contrast to the capitalist past, in which distribution processes did not develop in accordance or agreement with productive potential and social consumption goals, distribution processes would now link fixed consumption and life goals with an optimal development of production and would harmonize these two basic processes. However, while determination of the aims of the plan by means of democratic organization represents only the teleological side of planning, determination of the process of distribution can not only be adapted to the goals set, but must also be derived from the most objective and reliable information possible regarding opportunities for production. What is involved here is the genetic aspect of planning which, by means of analytical and scientific methods, must examine whether the goals to be set are attainable under existing economic conditions.

Planning must thus be organized in such a way as to allow scientifically based analytical methods to combine with goals that have been democratically worked out right from the preparatory stage of planning. On the basis of scientifically forecasted macro-proportions of future production and democratically established macro-proportions of needs, clear conceptions regarding necessary redistribution processes must be developed. Economic policy instruments must produce demand corresponding to the aims of the plan. It will thus be in their own interest, for market-oriented enterprises to develop production to meet that demand. The market will thus be steered indirectly, through the processes of distribution. In this way the desired development of production will be achieved without weakening or even undermining the enterprises' market interest and market responsibility.

The old Marxist notion (which however is often found in bourgeois theory as well) that developmental goals can be systematically achieved only if production, or at least investment--whether directly or via taxation on finances (credits, subsidies, etc.)--is regulated, is mistaken. It ignores the fact that any outside influencing of production, or even investment, in the enterprises of production will necessarily undermine intra-enterprise responsibility for efficiency and the meeting of demand. An enterprise which does not itself decide upon its investments cannot be made accountable for disproportions in market supplies or for lack of efficiency in production. Responsibility is borne by those who decide upon investments, which in the case of economically indifferent decision-makers always means that economic responsibility will be greatly diminished.

The goals pursued according to plan are always goals concerning a certain development of the standard of living, national and social security, investment-determined economic growth, regional equalization, etc. (see the plan goals). Realization of such goals always signifies the surfacing of a corresponding demand for certain groups (macro-proportions) of consumer goods or investment goods. This demand for its part is influenced by corresponding amounts of income on the part of the respective income recipients (social groups or institutions). If income distribution can be guided in such a way that the desired future development of demand evolves in conformity with the goals of the plan, production and investment will also move in this direction without having to be directly regulated.

This then has the great advantage that the productive enterprises, motivated by their own profit interest, will continue to be as flexible as possible in attempting to meet market demand for individual products, as well as to create new demand for individual products, and to outstrip their competition in new product areas, technological progress, cost-reduction, etc. Their initiative and responsibility will not be dampened; on the contrary, a knowledge of the goals of the national economic plan enables enterprises to gain a reliable impression regarding future demand. Their work with quota controls in the process of income distribution will facilitate further initiatives by the enterprises toward the development of production and productivity without income distribution having to depart from the projected goals of the plan. Similarly, the central planning authority need not issue directives for productivity increases and the like (which only leads Eastern European enterprises to cover up their capabilities and reserves) because the enterprises themselves, like any normal market enterprises, will be interested in optimizing their efficiency.

Furthermore, regional decentralization of planning-- which makes possible a better accommodation of the specific economic and social requirements of individual countries and regions--can be more consistently preserved with a system of planning essential aims and distribution processes than it can be with a system of production planning. There must be a central agency only to determine those distribution processes, whose income results have to be ensured by means of a balanced development within the entire national economy. Determination of the distribution processes, the

income results and utilization of which are to meet the specific requirements of individual regions, will consequently
be decentralized. At the same time central steering of regional equalization processes can be ensured without state
direction of investment activity.

Planning of the macro-proportions of consumer and
living standards and of the corresponding distribution processes thus makes it possible to retain the indispensable
working of the market mechanism while subordinating it to
broader social and democratically-determined developmental
goals. It represents a purposeful linkage between the market and the plan which makes it possible to avoid centralist
bureaucratism and to utilize the advantages of both the
market and planned economies, given the corresponding ac-
tivation of the interests of broad strata of the population.
We will now examine the methods and organization of this
planning.

THE ORGANIZATION OF PLANNING

Planning procedure must be organized so as to provide
reliable information about the tangible, quantitative and
qualitative state of production as well as its actual potential
for development--information which, on the other hand,
would accord with alternative development goals and with
the various social needs and interests. Since these mutually influence each other, it would be necessary to organize
the work of both aspects of planning so that a mutual linkage is maintained, and that the planning process takes
place with their progressive interaction.

This presupposes special planning methods. In any
event, the methods of formalized econometric plan formulation at the highest levels of government, assisted by officials and experts (technocratic planning) cannot alone suffice. Rather, cooperative planning will be required which,
from the outset, would place particular emphasis on the
work of commissions which, on the teleological side of planning, would consist of representatives of the various interest groups. Pierre Masse, one of the heads of the French
planning system, calls planning methods used in this way
the discretionary method or discretionary planning.[14] This

---

[14] Massé, P., Discretionary or Formalised Planning. Materials of the Congress of the International Economic
Association, Vienna, 1962; see also P. Massé, Investitionskriterien. Probleme der Investitionsplanung (Munich: 1968).

must not of course be taken to imply that there is no need at all for models of the plan prepared by specialists with the aid of econometric methods. In reality the point is to combine both methods, although the cooperative method is the decisive one because it alone facilitates the democratic inclusion of interests right from the plan-formulation stage.

The commissions working on the teleological side of planning should facilitate the formulation of the developmental goals which we would call quality-of-life goals in the broadest sense of the term. Naturally, they may be organized differently in different countries, at different times. For the sake of simplicity we will give only one example of how they might be organized. Since the individual sectors of quality-of-life development must be synthesized before the higher stages of integration are entered they have to be subdivided into a number of subcommissions:

Quality of Life Commissions:

1. Private Consumption Commission with a subcommission for consumer trends and formation of savings, wage development, and consumer protection.

2. Labor Development Commission with a subcommission for work and leisure, labor mobility, and job satisfaction.

3. Social Consumption Commission with subcommissions for social security, education, science, health and sports, cultural affairs, administration, security and justice, defense, transport and communications, infrastructure and energy, housing and urban development, and environmental protection.

4. Regional Equalization Commission with subcommissions corresponding to regional organization.

Each individual commission and subcommission should be constituted so that its members meet two requirements: that of special expertise and that of specific interest representation.

The first requirement means that the commission member would have to be familiar with the problems of the relevant commission, to be trained in related fields, to have produced initiatives or published proposals on the matters involved, and the like. The second requirement, which must be linked with the first, is the representation of significant large interest groups in the commissions. These include both political and other large interest associations such as the trade unions, farmers' associations, cultural organizations, youth organization, etc.

It would be a matter for parliament to define rules for the composition of the planning commissioners and, in each case, to establish the distribution of the number of representatives of the political parties and other large organizations in the planning commission. The parties and organizations would then elect and delegate their representatives. Consideration might be given to including even the representatives of the smaller initiative groups and minorities, for example, with a given number of signatures on petitions coming from the public. The economic council, to be mentioned later, would carry out the organization of the planning commission and oversee its work.

In due time, research institutes for the individual sectors of quality-of-life planning could be developed as well as for special interest organizations; these could constitute both a scientific and interest-based source of support for the work of the commission. As a result there would be improvements in both the inclusion and selection of the commission members themselves and in their preparation and bases of discussion and consultation. More and more people--not only specialists but also interested laypersons--could be involved in conceptions and proposals for development. In this context, an important role would also be played by the mass media, which would initiate and facilitate public discussion concerning future developments. The commissions, and the public backdrop against which they operate, may be understood as the further organizational development of current spontaneous citizens initiatives which, when utilized and canalized in this way, would produce an actual effect on society.

To this, market economists repeatedly retort that the results of discussions in commissions do not correspond to the actual sum of individual preferences which ought to be expressed by the committee members. This objection would be valid if the commissions were supposed to decide upon the detailed structures of the supply of goods, that is, if they were to replace the sum of individual demands on the market with a collective decision based on a majority vote. This would however amount to a collective assault on the individual and his needs (though for the moment we will set aside the undemocratic manipulation of needs by giant monopolies). Our proposal would, however, retain the market with its mechanism based on individual consumer preferences.

Let us now consider the other, the genetic side of planning. This is not a matter of incorporating idealistic conceptions but of recognizing precisely what the actual developmental tendencies or possibilities for changing the na-

ture of production might be. Here again, commissions
would have to be formed. These would, however, have to
be made up of technological and economic branch research
institutes right from the outset and in far greater measure.
In many countries, branch institutes of this kind are already evolving, and their conscious further development
would be the necessary precondition for macro-planning. It
is not necessary to describe the branch structure here,
since in all industrial states it will ultimately be bound up
with statistical measurements, economic policies, and planning developments. For each branch a commission would
have to be constituted whose members would be composed of
the representatives of the competent research institute as
well as planning experts from the enterprises of a given
branch. The most important criteria for the selection of
commission members ought to be as precise an understanding as possible of the productive preconditions of the
branch and technical-economic training for the execution of
analytical and prognostic work.

Along with the regular productive branch commissions,
three synthesizing commissions would be important for the
development of production, viz. commissions for Group I
(Investment Goods), Group ID (Investment Goods for the
Public Service Sector), and Group II (Consumer Goods). It
would thus be a question of synthesizing the development of
production in three commissions which would be required to
account for the most important macro-proportions. As is
well known, these three commissions cannot be regarded
simply as a merger of existing branches, since the division,
for example, into Groups I and II, runs right through many
enterprises. Apart from the productive branch commissions, additional commissions would be required for foreign
trade, domestic trade, and the financial and credit system.
Above all these branch commissions, a general synthesizing
sectoral production commission must be constituted.

Above the two synthesizing sectoral commissions there
would be a main planning commission whose purpose would
be to coordinate both aspects of planning (sectoral commissions) and to undertake the actual preparation of macro-
plans:

Main Planning Commission

Production Commission   Quality-of-Life Commission

The planning commissions should be composed of representatives of practical economics, the research institutes,
science and the interest groups, and staffed by only a rel-

atively small number of officials. For the individual
subcommissions, one or two secretaries each should suffice.
The sectoral commissions and the main commissions would
have at their disposal a scientifically based and a modern,
technologically equipped planning apparatus for all their
calculations and evaluations.

Furthermore, there would be an economic council
which, as the government's economic policy organ, would be
responsible for the organization of the commissions, plan
preparation, and plan realization, and to which the main
planning commission would therefore be subordinate. As the
executive organ of the government, the economic council
would be responsible for establishing the necessary conditions for planning activity. In particular it would have to
provide for a maximum degree of planning democracy. This
includes especially the stimulation of economic policy discussions among the population. Specifically, this would mean
supporting initiative groups, ensuring possibilities for the
flow of publications and information between the planning
commissions and the population, presenting two or three alternative plans for public discussion, etc.

The intention is to link the economic policy and political discussions taking place among the population, as well
as the selection of the medium-range (four to five years)
macro-plan, with political elections. The preparation of two
or three substantially different plan alternatives, as we
shall see, would be realizable within the framework of the
kind of planning aimed at here. For the purposes of political discussion, an account of the basic qualitative and
quantitative ends and means of projected alternative development may assume a generally comprehensible form. With
the aid of the political parties, other interest organizations
and the mass media, broader discussions could be initiated.
If particularly important social requirements, partial developments, problems and larger projects are dealt with, right
from the outset and constantly in the public eye, the population might be expected in time to develop an interest in
and understanding of the discussion surrounding various
complex national economic planning goals and developments.

There already exists a state in which the population
democratically makes decisions regarding individual politi-
cal--and economic--measures and on measures taken by the
government. That state is Switzerland. This significant
beginning of a democratic decision-making process can be
regarded as a manifestation of the democratic planning process which we advocate. The defects of the Swiss referendum must, however, be overcome. It is neither complex
enough, nor are alternative economic proposals presented.

Complex planning of distribution attempts to expand
and deepen the advantages of the direct popular plebiscite

into important governmental economic policy steps, and to give the people an opportunity for complex self-determination in the area of economic development. The preparation of two or three complex developmental alternatives relating to the quality-of-life of the population, in which different growth rates would create quite different living conditions in the future, could represent a significant step in the extension of economic democracy.

If for the time being we conceive of the different plan alternatives in such a way as to realize that they involve, in particular, different proposals for the rate of growth of private or social consumption, the more or less rapid solution of growing problems of transportation and agglomeration, changeover to different new energy resources, change or lack of it in level of social security, or the maintenance or reduction of prevailing working hours, together with new arrangements for leisure time, then it is evident that decision-making is not nearly as simple as many politicians today imagine. Politicians are convinced that the majority of the population would always choose the alternative that promised the most rapid growth in personal consumption. It must be remembered, however, that political discussion of complex conceptions would here, for the first time be possible. Such discussions could have a restraining effect upon the previously customary political demagoguery in the sense of simple goal preferences which ignore the further consequences for the population and loses it.

For instance, one consequence of a relatively more rapid increase in individual consumption in the near future, combined with a lower investment quota, would be a slower increase in growth rates in subsequent years, whereas a somewhat slower, direct increase would facilitate a more rapid growth later on. Also, different goals--for example, urgently needed urban renewal, more tranquil and healthy living conditions, overcoming traffic chaos during rush hours--would require correspondingly differentiated growth rates. It is not at all the case that the majority of the population would always opt for a more rapid, direct increase in individual consumption. But they first have to be better informed. Today already, many growing social problems weigh upon the majority of the population more than does an insufficiency of private consumption. This tendency will be even more pronounced in the future.

This brings us back to the fundamental question of whether the population in industrially advanced countries is mature or immature, or whether they can or cannot judge when given a choice of various alternatives. Everything will depend on this fundamental evaluation, one which at present can scarcely be confirmed or refuted on the strength of scientific evidence and which plays an important role in the subjective experiences and attitudes of the evaluator (which is not to say that scientific evidence cannot be produced at all or might not later be furnished).

Anyone who disputes the capacity of the people to evaluate different alternatives for development will also have to reject any public, political selection of the macro-plan by the people from among their own alternatives. We consider just such a possibility for choice--in the course of which positions for this or that alternative would be taken by political parties, and discussions about basic future economic developments would become part of the electoral process-- not only as a decisive step toward increasingly resolving complicated economic problems but also as the precondition for preventing future extremist political developments. Even at the risk of the population choosing an alternative that later proves to be less favorable than another, decisions about the future must be placed in its hands, rather than in those of a power elite (which, moreover, is no less susceptible to error).

The entire population learns from increasing experience as well as from the mistakes of past political decisions. This learning process augments the people's interest in economic policy. The longer alienated and uncontrollable authorities make decisions regarding the development of economic policy independently of the people, the longer the people's disinterest, (and their immaturity which is inferred from it), will last. However, the more the broad masses of the population gain an understanding of certain macro-economic interconnections as a result of discussion of the plan, the less they can be misled by purely emotional appeals.

If the decision regarding a new four-five year macro-plan is combined with political elections, then an election victory of a certain party or party coalition would also mean the election of their alternative plan. Since preparation of the various alternative plans in the democratically constituted planning commissions would have already taken place on the basis of the differing ideas of and attitudes toward economic policy of the various political parties, the entire planning process would also mean a further democratization of political life. In this case, the parties would have to prepare their conceptions of future economic policy in a much more responsible manner than they do today, since they would be forced to make more than just soft political demands and promises; they would have to consider the means and consequences of achieving certain goals, and/or the other solutions at the expense of which they would have to be accomplished. Participation of their representatives in the planning commissions would ensure that the necessary information was communicated to them in good time. To objectify political election campaigns in this way would impede the activities of those parties that rely particularly strongly on emotions, aversions, people's passions and on exploiting these through popular demagogues or readily produced revolutionary visions.

The definitive approval of the future macro-plan would also be accomplished by the newly elected parliament. With its mandate, a new government would have to carry out the economic policy embodied in the plan. The government would only empower the economic council to concretize and to implement this economic policy from the organizational point of view. To be sure, the economic council's competence and relative independence must not lead to a situation in which political responsibility for the development of the economy eludes the control of the government. Governmental decisions will be necessary particularly in the event of changes in the plan, which adapt it to actual economic developments. However, since this problem is connected with the methodology of planning and the temporal duration of the plans, we will return to it later.

THE CONTENT OF PLANNING

We will now take a closer look at those economic processes whose future development is to be regulated by the plan. In the process, however, the whole problem of distribution and redistribution of the national income will be deliberately simplified to make it more comprehensible to the uninitiated reader.

In the actual operation of economic policy, certain linkages are established between macro-quantities whose quantitative equilibrium is of crucial significance to the development of the national economy. The term macro-quantities stands for the levels of certain individual phenomena within a national economy, for example, the level of all market products (goods) expressed as prices, the sum of all profits, the sum of the prices of all consumer goods offered for sale, the sum of the prices of all means of production offered for sale, etc. Between certain economic macro-quantities there exists a two-way connection, a reciprocal determination, a mutually conditioned relationship from which a balanced growth of interconnected macro-quantities proves to be necessary if the national economy is to develop harmoniously and without serious disruptions. However, if decisions relating to the rise of individual economic phenomena are made in the individual enterprises in such a way as to prevent a balanced development of the sums of these phenomena and hence the macro-quantities linked to the economy, serious disruptions will occur in the development of the national economy, for instance crises, mass unemployment, inflation, large unsatisfied demands, etc.

Thus there is, for instance, a connection between the sum of all consumption-oriented incomes and the sum of all prices of available consumer goods. If at a given point in the development of a country these two sums are not equal in size, then either there will be an excessive supply of consumer goods, which will subsequently produce a crisis, or there will be an excessive demand for consumer goods, which will give rise to inflation.

In the capitalist economic system, all individual economic phenomena come about on the basis of decisions made in individual enterprises, yet no one is in a position even to weigh beforehand the required future macro-quantities and macro-relationships, to say nothing of coordinating the separate decisions. Thus, this economic system, repeatedly and necessarily generates serious macro-disruptions, crises, and inflation, with all their fateful social and economic consequences. In order to prevent these macro-disruptions, the future macro-quantities must be influenced or regulated so as to develop an equilibrium without the enterprises' decisions on independent market production being determined by the plan. In order to ensure the required balanced growth, it would be sufficient merely to regulate the income side of development in the plan, in such a way that it attains a balance in relation to the projected development of production.

When we speak of production, we mean simply the production of goods for the market, that is, products which are sold for a price and which in general also realize a profit. These are predominantly of a material character, but this does not necessarily have to be so. Services can also to some extent be sold as goods, and in this sense are counted as part of production. This production of goods or production for the market must be distinguished from those services which are not sold in the market, but which primarily represent state services to society or services available free of charge to the population. The costs of these are pre-eminently met from public revenues or expenditures. If we therefore speak of the gross value of production (gross production), then we mean the value of total market production, expressed in prices (without state-financed services).

Total proceeds from market production are not identical with the net value of production unless all goods are sold. These proceeds are made up of the value of the objective costs of production (including objective capital costs) and the newly created value. The objective costs of production consist of material costs, in the broadest sense of the word (used raw materials, semi-manufactures, etc.), and depreciation of machines, buildings that house production, and other equipment. The gross value of production, less the objective costs of production, makes up the net value of production (net product), which equals the newly created value. This newly created value constitutes either the income of an individual enterprise or, as the sum of all incomes of the productive enterprises, the national income. In contrast to the concept of national income prevailing in bourgeois economics, we do not make a distinction between net product at factoral prices and at market prices, because the total proceeds of all goods sold (at market prices), after subtracting the objective costs of production, constitute, in our view, the national income.

Just as the individual enterprises' income under capitalism is pre-eminently divided between two primary income components, wages and profits, so these also constitute the aggregate primary components of the national income. Even in the reformed economic system, these two primary income components must exist, irrespective of how profits are distributed and utilized. It is a matter of the undistributed-- that is, expressed in gross values--wages and profits (in short, gross wages and gross profits). The national income, which originates in market production, is thus primarily made up of the two large income groups: gross wages and gross profits.

In contrast to capitalism, where these two income groups express a social contradiction, and hence the division of the enterprises' incomes into gross wages and gross profits is the result of a distributive struggle, in the new system this distribution process should be regulated by the plan. Wages represent an income which is used overwhelmingly for consumption. Only relatively small portions of wages are transformed into taxes and net savings. Profits, on the other hand, are incomes used to a lesser extent for consumption, while a relatively larger portion is transformed either directly or indirectly (by means of the formation of net savings) into investments. Therefore, if the economic relationship between consumption and investments--one of the most important macro-relationships for balanced development--is not to be left to chance, then the relationship between gross wages and gross profits must be regulated by the plan.

However, given the enterprises' market autonomy, one can only make one prediction with respect to the growth of gross production and the national income. But, with the aid of a method to be explained later and subject to the planned regulation of incomes and demands, this prognosis can be made with a substantially greater degree of reliability than is the case in contemporary capitalism. This prognosis of production growth also contains a prognosis of the total size of gross investments necessary for growth. By gross investments we mean the purchase of means of production for market production. A portion of these gross investments constitutes substitute investments, that is, the purchase of the means of production which are intended to replace the means of production that are used up in production (objective costs of production). The other portion of gross investments is made up of the net investments, that is, the purchase of means of production which are needed for the expansion of production (prognosticated production growth).

The prognosis of production is thus for the present a prognosis of the future (in individual planning years) scope of market production, of the accruing objective costs of production (thus of the required substitute investments), of the national income produced, of the required quantity of productive labor power, and the required amount of net investment. If this prognosis is, for the time being, made in terms of constant prices and wages, then at the same time it will provide an initial overview of how much of the national income must go to gross wages (quantity of labor power multiplied by constant average wages in individual planning years) and how large gross profits will be.

This initial prognosis of the division of the national income into gross wages and gross profits is of course subject to change, first on the basis of a correction of wages with a view to a necessary increase in average wages, and second on the basis of a balanced growth of prices for qualitative product development (while precluding any inflationary development). The determination of the increase in average wages is in itself an important regulator of the allocation of the national income, upon which will depend not only the growth of consumption but also the size of profits (presupposing a growth in the national income). In this way, therefore, the tentatively projected primary allocation will be corrected. But for the time being let us disregard these corrections and further pursue the allocation of primary income by means of which derived income and ultimately consumption and investment income are generated and whose relationship is of great significance to the attainment of a balanced macro-development.

Taxes, which represent the state's most important revenues, must be diverted from both gross wages and gross profits. Since in Figure A

Figure A

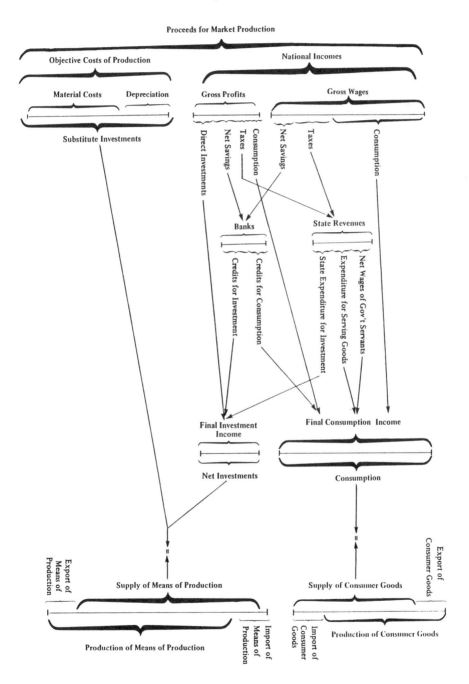

we will more closely illuminate the distribution and redistribution processes, for simplicity's sake we will ignore the
indirect taxes imposed by the state, or combine them with
taxes on net profits. On account of these taxes, primary
incomes decrease while state incomes (revenues) are generated. These state revenues are expended in the individual
sectors of the state services sector, as has been described
in the preceding chapter. Proposals for the allocation of
the projected profits, after subtracting the projected net
investments (which basically must be covered from out of
profits), must be worked out by the quality-of-life commission. How much of this is allocated for the increasing of
average wages in production, and in which proportions the
latter is distributed among the individual sectors--this for
the time being will be a matter for discussions and consensus in the quality-of-life commissions.

From the aspect of balanced development, however, of
particular importance is how much of the state's expenditures are spent on the purchase of consumer goods and how
much for the purchase of means of production. We must
take this opportunity again to point out that means of production only includes those goods used in the production of
market products (goods). All other goods, not only those
that are personally consumed but also, as durable goods,
used by the state service sectors (for example, schools and
their furnishings, administrative buildings and their furnishings) are, from this viewpoint, consumer goods. Their
utilization does not create any new market production.

Both groups, production of the means of production
(Group I) and consumer goods production (Group II) are
interrelated, not in a substitutive, but in a complementary
relation. Neither group can develop independently except
on a temporary basis
 in the long term the growth of the one depends on the
growth of the other. The chief planning commission must
follow and regulate this relationship. For this reason, the
proportions of state expenditures allocated between consumption (purchase of consumer goods) and investments
(purchase of means of production) is of primary importance
and must be regulated.

However, it must be stressed that state expenditures
for investment goods are relatively small. Basically these
include only the subsidies granted to various production
enterprises or new, large production enterprises established
with state assistance (for example, generating stations and
the like). Most expenditures by the state are however
consumptive in nature, since such absurd consumer goods
as weapons must be included in this category. For planning purposes, however, it would also be important further
to break down the state expenditures for consumption in all

service sectors into those spent for wages (salaries) of public employees and those with which objects are purchased for the fulfilment of the services in the institutions concerned.

With their wages, public employees buy consumer goods, form net savings, and pay taxes. In order not to have to draw too many complicated lines on our figure A, we have simplified the wages of the public servants and entered them as net wages (after deduction of taxes and net savings) which are used only for consumption. Although the goods that the service institutions purchase in order to carry out their activities are indeed not means of production (do not contribute to production for the market), they do have a character somewhat different from that of normal consumer goods (are not directly consumed by people but rather are used to render services). We will term them material goods for the carrying out of services (or service goods for short). During the process of planning, it would be particularly important to bring the production of these goods into balance with the material expenditures of the service sectors. In Figure A we have, again in simplified form, subsumed these goods under the group of consumer goods and also included their purchase by the state service sectors under the category of consumption.

A further mechanism for redistributing primary incomes is the formation of savings both from wages and from profits, and their concentration in the system of banking and other savings institutions (and in the system of insurance institutions which, for simplicity's sake, we have omitted here). However, since savings are not only formed but drained (withdrawals and utilization of savings) every year, we must subtract withdrawals from savings (assuming that the latter are greater than the former), which brings us to net savings. Of course the passive interest earned by the banks must be included as part of the drain of savings. Net savings reduce consumption from both wages and profits. To be sure, savings from profits can be partially utilized directly for net investments, while another part is concentrated, as net savings, in the banking system.

Net savings in the banking system are transformed into credits. The need to preserve the macro-equilibrium also requires an equilibrium between net savings and credits, and within these, between net savings from wages and credits for consumption, as well as between net savings from profits and credits for investment. From the credits for consumption, consumer goods are purchased and from credits for investment, means of production are bought. We will deal with the significance of the savings-credit equilibrium and the preconditions for realizing it in a later chapter. Here we will consider the savings and credit system only in general terms, from the aspect of equilibrium maintenance. In order not to complicate our Figure A even further, we have left out savings by the state and credits to the state. These will be taken into account in our discussion of credit.

To sum up, we now see with the aid of Figure A: the division of proceeds from market production into material costs of production and national income; the primary division of the national income into gross wages and gross profits; the redistribution of the latter into the portions that constitute taxes and net savings (among the latter are included direct investments), which proportionately reduces consumption from out of wages and profits. From out of taxes (state revenues), a portion is expended on consumption and a portion on investments. Also from net savings, consumption and investment credits are generated in the banking system. Thus both primary incomes (or proceeds) and derived incomes (state and banks) give rise to two final income groups: final consumption incomes and final investment incomes. These constitute the final demand for consumer goods and means of production and basically must develop, in the long term (apart from minor and short-term departures), at the same levels as the prices of the two supply groups, available consumer goods (production minus exports plus imports), and the available means of production (production minus exports plus imports).

If several variants of distributing and redistributing national revenues are prepared, each on the basis of relatively reliable prognoses of growth, a variety of quality-of-life goals can be envisioned. The macro-equilibrium can be maintained in each variant of the plan. Both the generation of excessive profits and final investment income can be averted, and final investment incomes can no longer be completely transformed into actual investments because, due to relatively retarded consumption, there must be a decline in investment activity. The crises necessarily set off in the process--first in production, then in the entire economy--can be prevented with the aid of macro-planning. But macro-planning can also help to prevent the generation of too small profits and final investment income which--particularly under the conditions of falling capital productivity (given a demand for objective capital that grows faster than national income and profits)--lead to falling investments and ultimately to a crisis. Primary incomes, and ultimately the relationship between the final investment incomes and final consumption incomes, can be adapted to the optimal relationship between the production of the means of production (investments) and the production of consumer goods (consumption).

The development of inflation can also be prevented through the plan. So far, we have described income flows both as productive and affected by the distribution process, which is why we have largely presupposed constant prices. In order to arrive at the final income groups-- whose equilibrium should be reached with supply groups corresponding to the specific nature of their use--it is necessary to take account of the possible uses of the credit system to influence developments. The peculiarities of the credit system make it possible to create incomes the size of which do not always correspond to the actual creation of use value in production. An increase in incomes vis-a-vis the actual use-values triggered with the aid of credit creation will result not only in a general inflationary rise in prices but normally certain shifts between various income groups as well. Incomes from profit can grow at the expense of incomes from wages, wage incomes at the expense of profit incomes, incomes of the active part of the population at the expense of pension recipients, incomes of debtors at the expense of creditors, etc.

At this point it should be emphasized that such an inflationary development can only occur if the demand for credits exceeds the normal development of income. A supply of credit, however low interest rates may be, cannot by itself create an inflationary development of income. For any increase in credit, which involves exceeding the scope of certain final income groups in relation to the value of the group of goods corresponding to it, will result in price increases. Only if debtors are willing to continue to take out credits despite these price increases, can inflation get underway. In this case either it is the state which, in certain situations when it is raising credits, consciously takes such price increases into account, or it is private entrepreneurs who count on being able later to pass on their costs (investment or wage costs), which are financed by borrowing, to consumers in the form of higher prices.

The banking system can thus contribute in two ways to income redistribution. First, it may do so in an economically positive manner by transferring those portions of certain legal subjects' income coming available through savings formation to other legal subjects by means of credits. In this way incomes from certain income groups and production groups can be transmitted to completely different final income groups and production groups. The borrowers thus gain the enjoyment of the actual value of the goods which the savers temporarily do without. Second, in an economically negative way, credits may be created in such quantities that the incomes thus generated exceed the value of production and services on which they are based, and prices rise. For this reason, all income earners receive a lesser value for their purchases (and this includes borrowers)

than they previously would have received for nominally
equal incomes. In the process, however, certain sellers of
goods can, by means of temporal adjustments, gain in real
value at the expense of certain buyers.

One must constantly bear in mind that the banks do
not know (and have not at all tried to know) which kinds
of credit creation will induce additional money into circulation corresponding in real values to growing production,
and which kinds of credit creation will only produce an
auxiliary, inflationary demand for products, without a corresponding increase in production.

In the first case the credit system positively helps to
increase the quantity of money which is necessary for rising production, rising sales of goods and hence rising incomes. Producers who, for example, want to employ more
workers in order to increase production, need more money
for additional wages before they can obtain larger incomes
from sales out of their expanded production. Credit creation here helps to expand the money supply which is
needed for greater production of goods and greater circulation of goods (given, for example, an unchanged rate of
circulation of money). In the second case, for various reasons, an additional demand for money is produced which is
also satisfied by creating credit but which is not accompanied by a corresponding expansion of goods production and
goods circulation. An increased demand for goods, produced by the creation of credit (the supply of which has
not increased) leads to a rise in the price of the goods.
When the scale of production expands, driven by prices,
then an increase in money supply is also required (assuming an unchanging rate of circulation of money), but this
produces an inflationary development. However, if the development of incomes is regulated by the plan, such inflationary increases in demand and prices, that is, negative
creations of credit should be prevented.

In the course of observing this circulation model, the
Sayrian illusions, which continuously appear, could be reinforced and it might seem that in fact income cannot be generated without first selling the goods that produce the incomes, so that incomes themselves represent confirmation of
the production sold. In other words, the mere fact that
the incomes, which are used to buy the production, are
somehow generated by this production creates the impression that production is already sold. All circulation models
constantly invoke this illusion. In reality, however, they
are only able to suggest a linkage that is correct only in
the long term. If individual production groups are to be
sold, they must ultimately be matched by value equivalents
to final incomes assigned to a definite purpose, as they are
produced by the distributive processes. This does not

mean, however, that wherever distribution is determined by factors other than the requirements of optimal needs satisfaction, circulation breakdowns cannot and will not occur.

But we are also concerned with countering the illusion that savings formation causes macro-disturbances. It is all too easy to explain the missing transformation of goods into money and an increase in savings as the expression of a falling propensity to consume and to deduce from this the problem of liquidity preferences in periods of falling investment readiness. However, savings formation is not the cause of the big disruptions in circulation because every expansion of the wage quota at the expense of the profit quota could bring with it a more rapid increase in the consumption quota than in the savings quota. The needs of the population are far from satisfied, and even in the wealthiest countries a far too great a percentage of the population live in conditions of poverty. If in reality excessively high savings did produce a crisis, it would suffice to raise the wage quota in order to produce an increase in consumption. In the Western industrialized countries, however, it is at present the too low investment quotas that, given stagnating or falling capital productivity, are a brake on efforts to overcome the crisis.

In times of falling capital productivity, objective capital costs must grow faster than national income. This also demands a growth in net investments--equaling growth in capital costs--in order to ensure a certain growth in national income. However, when consumptive final incomes grow as rapidly or even more rapidly than national income, then investive final incomes must grow substantially more slowly than objective capital costs. This produces an increasingly smaller growth in objective capital and hence an even smaller growth in the national income--including stagnation and absolute regression. This alone invokes a recession and increasing unemployment.

Moreover, if the demand for credits on the part of threatened entrepreneurs grows faster than the supply of credit, and this trend is further enhanced by the states' mounting debts (given excessive consumptive expenditures), the result is a rapid increase in interest rates. This produces an even more rapid decline in investments and a general crisis situation. The basic cause of all this is the negative development of profits and final investment income--which does not correspond to falling capital productivity--and/or a too rapid growth of consumption.

Regardless of whether it employs a falling wage and investment quota in periods of growing capital productivity or a falling profit and investment quota in periods of falling capital productivity, capitalism has no economic policy able to ensure the development of primary and final incomes in conformity with capital productivity. So long as national income is distributed through a process of conflict, without taking heed of the future, and in the context of antagonistic wage and profit interests, there will always be dangerous disruptions in the macro-equilibrium.

Only the planned regulation of consumption and investment can prevent both an insufficient and excessive development of consumption and better coordinate private consumption and public services.

In contrast to the production groups (I and II), which produce goods and which always must have the corresponding equal quantities of the final incomes belonging to them, services are distributed free of charge among the population according to need. They have an increasing effect on people's quality of life, and the planning of their total scope as well as the scope (proportions) of their individual internal sectors. They are therefore a decisive component of quality-of-life planning. It is clear, however, that the scope of these services depends in particular on how many of the consumer goods can be diverted to cover the removed net wages in the service sector, and how many objective goods are produced for the service sector.

At this point let us again refer to those nonsensical fears, already mentioned, that further growth in production in the highly developed industrial countries will be difficult due to inadequate demand and saturation. Even if a general saturation were attained with respect to privately used consumer goods--which we consider unlikely for some time to come--the need for social services would continue to grow well into the future. And if for this reason average private per capita consumption were in fact to stagnate, more and more service-sector employees would require consumer goods at an increasing rate, and the need for material service-sector goods would grow even faster. At present it is quite impossible to predict future needs for quieter, healthier housing; parklands; sport, recreational, medicinal and social conditions; new and faster means of transportation that at the same time are less destructive to the environment; and educational and cultural institutions of an entirely different nature. In these respects, our society is only in the initial stages. All measures toward rationalization and labor saving can therefore only further this development toward the meeting of society's needs, since they enable it more rapidly to meet the need for labor power.

The fear that such a process of meeting society's needs cannot have a secure tax base is essentially incorrect because taxes are diverted from the total production of goods. The growth in services demands a corresponding growth in consumer goods production for the service sector and hence again more means of production for consumer goods production. This also causes the tax base, as well as the redistribution of tax revenues, to grow. The fact that under present conditions it is difficult to increase taxes by means of relatively lowering net wages and net profits is in fact the best proof that private demand is not yet saturated and thus that private net incomes must further increase and be met by production.

If private consumption were in fact sufficient for the entire population so that the stagnating quantity of consumer goods met the private needs of a stagnating population size, the scope of services could only be expanded at the rate of the growth of productivity in production, which would save labor in this area. But this would only mean that taxes could again increase at the expense of savings from wages, which again would facilitate the redistribution of consumer goods in favor of the growing number of service-sector employees. Savings of labor and consumer goods made in production would work to the advantage of the additional work force in the service sectors. Only once the demand for both ceased to grow--that is, if consumption and public services actually stagnated in scope--would all productivity and efficiency increases lead to hours-of-work reductions (which is not to say that the latter could not occur sooner).

In any case, the stagnation of needs is by no means the right concept to explain a stagnating economy in crisis. It would be far more plausible to argue the point on the basis of problems arising from the lack of various raw materials, energy, etc. or difficulties of retraining and redistributing the work force. However, these too are merely problems of an economy in which the development of incomes and consumption take place spontaneously and without planning in which the need to regulate the pace of growth and processes of distribution, and in which the education and professional training of people in accordance with the productive possibilities and needs of the future are not recognized and attended to in good time.

What is completely incomprehensible from the perspective of planned economic development, however, is the fear that rapid technical development poses a threat to jobs. If labor saving were accomplished on such a huge scale that restructuring and job transfer into other branches and occupations seemed practically impossible (which, given planned development, seems dubious) then the self-evident solution would be a planned, universal reduction in hours of work. In the event of substantially reduced hours of work, all those able to work could, with the aid of the most modern technology, not only find work but at the same time produce more--which, in terms of the national economy, means consuming more.

In branches which achieve considerable labor saving, shorter hours of work and implementation of several shifts would permit the full utilization of modern technology. In the process of course the scope of technology would be adapted to estimated demand (which capitalism cannot do). In branches without recent technology but with a growing demand for their products or services, it would be possible to pay the growing work force (given shorter hours of work) out of prices. In branches without recent technology, where demand is stagnating, falling, or growing only slowly, the work force would stagnate or change correspondingly. Thus, if hours of work are reduced, all employees can find work in the growth branches, and the nature of their work will go from capital-intensive to labor-intensive (especially services) and from less qualified to more qualified. However, this reallocation of labor, bound up with ambitious retraining and enhanced qualifications, can only be effected with the aid of macro-planning; otherwise it could only once again be executed in an entirely inhumane manner which would debase generations. People ought not to be content with the gloomy forecasts of so many economists who are able only to think in terms of the capitalist economy, predict that the number of jobs will decrease in future.[15]

The same also applies ultimately to the ecological development. However much has been written and said about the devastating consequences of spontaneous, uncontrolled industrial growth to human beings and to nature and about the looming perversion of our environment, nothing is going to change so long as growth in production cannot be regulated by plan to exceed the investment quota. Only where investive final incomes are indirectly regulated in such a way that growth in production can ensure both full employment and ecological aims, do instruments for the ecologically sound development of production evolve. The ecological aims would then, with the aid of the already mentioned subcommittee for the quality of life, environment division, be directly incorporated into the plan goals and thus would be binding on the regulation of income distribution.

[15] P. Massé, Discretionary or Formalised Planning, Material des Kongresses der internationalen oekonomischen Association (Vienna, 1962), also see P. Massé, Investitionskriterien. Probleme der Investitionsplanung (Munich, 1968).

PLANNING METHODOLOGY

The methodology of the plan must also be adapted to the goals of the plan and the manner in which they are set. We have already said that the determination of the future quality of life should be regarded as the most important goal of planning. This will have to be approached in both qualitative and quantitative terms. The most important changes in the quality of life can be quantified through changes in overall private consumption, individual sectors of social consumption, development of hours of work, determination of leisure time, shaping of the environment, and the like, and hence can also be planned in these macro-quantities.

The quantified goals of planning would include growth rates of consumption, organized according to the already mentioned subcommissions for the development of the quality of life, as well as these consumption groups' share in the gross product (consumption quotas). Total consumption would be divided into two major groups: private consumption and social consumption. Private consumption, as a qualified goal, would not be further disaggregated; any subdivision of private consumption accrued for planning purposes would only amount to a series of non-binding prognosis as far as the planning organs were concerned. On the other hand, for the above mentioned subcommissions the subdivision of social consumption, that is, the pace of growth and the share of the individual sectors of social consumption, would take the shape of quantified goals. The organized, quantified development of consumption forms the core of the quality-of-life plans which, in the form of qualitatively set tasks, would be of a broader nature.

The qualitative tasks of the individual sectors of social and private consumption, of the development of work and working conditions, of regional equalization, etc. should be verbally expressed. Their realization would have to be ensured with the aid not only of quantified plans but also of further statutory measures (for example, in the spheres of hours of work, job protection, consumer protection, environmental protection, etc.). The quantification of the development of consumption as a quantified goal of planning thus forms the core of the planned development of the quality of life.

The distribution processes will serve as the direct means of achieving the planned differentiated growth in consumption. The most important means for the realization of the planned consumption goals are: primary income formation in the market enterprises (gross income) and its division into gross wages and gross profits, the redistribution of these primary incomes by the state and by means of savings and credit processes, and the formation of the final income quantities upon which a certain development of consumption and investment depends. The major precondition for the realization of this goal would be the planned regulation of the distribution and redistribution processes in such a way that the resultant final incomes ensure the planned development of both the private and individual sectors of social consumption and ultimately the necessary development of investment. The distribution processes can therefore be regarded as mediated goals of planning. And planning would have to be accomplished with the aid of the instruments of economic policy and by means of eliminating the existing struggle for distribution.

With the planned regulation of the most important distribution and redistribution process, society acquires certain leverage processes with the aid of which it can indirectly influence many additional processes dependent on the development of incomes, so that it can predict its future development with far greater reliability than is the case with existing prognoses. The distribution processes will then be overwhelmingly defined, with the aid of quota planning, in quantities of macro-economic relationships. This will allow, on the one hand, for balanced proportional development without, on the other, wrenching the future development of income away from the unpredictable development of the productivity of the individual enterprises. Thus, in this respect, there exist, in terms of the plan, very strongly, weakly, and more weakly regulable processes, and hence conversely less reliably, reliably, and very reliably predictable processes. We will therefore speak of the planned regulation of different degrees of effectiveness, which also implies that the distribution processes most important to the economy must be planned so as to achieve the highest degree of effectiveness.

On the basis of distribution, the flow of expenditures from state revenues provides the preconditions for the planned fulfillment of the social needs of the population. The amount of the production costs of the individual sectors of public services which the state finances (above and beyond the relatively small share paid directly out of the incomes of the population) determines the scope of the various services available to the population. Given a determinate total scope of consumption, the quality of life is crucially determined by the relation of social consumption or the value of the services to private consumption, or by the share of social consumption in total consumption, as well as the shares of the individual service sectors in total consumption.

In addition, of course, such factors as hours of work and/or leisure time, job satisfaction, popular participation, quality of leisure time organization, scope of people's opportunities for self-development, and the like, play an important part. It is however evident that these additional factors can be very strongly encouraged by the development of various service-sector spheres (for example, education, culture, scholarship, health preservation, sports, housing, environmental protection, etc.). Thus, the structure of consumption will crucially shape people's quality of life, and it would be the task of the plan goals to quantify the democratic planning of these quality-of-life conditions.

The various concepts would be expressed in two or three alternative plans, from which the population, thoroughly informed about each, would choose democratically. But the various alternatives of the planned development of the quality of life and consumption are themselves the outcomes and compromises of democratic discussions carried out in the quality-of-life commissions by representatives of diverse interest groups and involving different conceptions for the future.

Any deliberation about future goals of planning in terms of quantitative and qualitative change in quality of life, if it is to amount to more than mere pipe dreams, requires an overview of the macro-results of production capable of realization in the future, that is, an overview of possible increases in production, mass income, surplus income, and overall consumption. On this basis, it would be possible to contemplate how best to improve consumption and one's way of life and which structural changes in consumption, in social security, etc. should be aimed at. But at the same time any statement of future possibilities requires production to develop so as to fix the available investment funds, which in turn depends on anticipated income distribution; and any deliberation about the structure of production depends on conceptions about the structure of consumption. Hence the mutual interdependence of production and consumption also produces a mutual interdependence between the production commission and the quality-of-life commission that gives rise to the need for a linkage between econometric and discretionary plan methodologies.

At the outset of preparations for a middle-range (four to five-year) plan will be the econometric method in particular, and the main planning commission will use it to produce an initial projection of the possible development of the economy. Since this task is based not only on starting data and the extrapolation of past trends, but also on already accepted long-term projections (15 to 20 years)(which we will discuss presently), it will furnish an important foundation for further planning activities.

The initial projection should represent an attainable basic variant of a four to five-year development of the

economy which rests upon extrapolations of past growth,
presupposable changes in individual economic quantities,
and the most important goal variables that can be formulated on the basis of the long-term projections. These basic
variants would constitute the starting point for the work of
the planning commission; its goals and assumptions would be
altered in the light of individual proposals made by the
sectoral commissions or would serve to help prepare various
alternatives. The basic variant must therefore already display the goal variables, preconditions, and means that, on
account of the total task of planning, will be contained,
with different quantities, in the alternative plans. In order
to democratize the process of plan determination, it would
be necessary to prepare from two to three alternative
plans; practical experience based on two initial alternatives
should show whether, in view of the expenditure of labor
and time, it is still possible to prepare the desirable third
alternative.

The sectoral production commission and the sectoral
quality-of-life commission would have to work hand in hand
in the preparation of two or three alternative plans based
on the initial concept of the main planning commission, and
they would have to work toward iterations (step-by-step
rapprochement). Every possible change in the growth of
production, productivity, the national income, profits and
the scope of production (in comparison with the initial conception) provides an opportunity for the quality-of-life
commission to consider changes in the development of consumption. And all the changes in the structure of consumption undertaken by the quality-of-life commission require examination by the production commission and possibly
changes in its conceptions of the structure of production.

We consider the preparation of extrapolated global
functions of production as a foundation of growth to be too
imprecise and unreliable and hence unsuitable for our macro-planning. Concrete increases in production are the expression of various qualitative changes of many factors of
production and thus not only reducible to the quantitative
expansion of the two major factors of production: capital
and labor.

In order to arrive at a conception of anticipated
growth we will undertake practice-related analyses of what
is technically prepared in the individual branches of production and what will change production in the near future.
The situation today is that most enterprises--large as well
as medium sized--must prepare for their technical and technological innovations years in advance and prevent the competition from finding out what these are. They are therefore capable of transforming the future conceptions of
production technology into anonymous economic data which

would produce substantially more reliable coefficients of growth.

As well, the technical-economic branch research institutes whose activities we are taking into account, would have at their disposal relatively reliable information about the conditions of growth in the branches. The reformation of the prepared qualitative technical changes into economic growth data must not signify a one-sided inconvenience to the producers but on the contrary should open realistic future perspectives (information on the growth of the market, state contracts, structure of consumption, etc.) for the enterprises, perspectives valuable for their own decision-making (about investments, innovation, etc.). The representatives of the enterprises would thus take part, in their own interests, in the work of planning and in the transformation of their technical preparations for production into economic data.

Basically, it would be necessary only to work the fundamental coefficients of growth into as simple and uncomplicated form as possible. It would be a matter of collating data concerning the expansion of capital, which is necessary for growth of total production, and the other factors that this requires: investments, anticipated increase in the number of personnel (development of population, immigrant labor, etc.) as determined by studies, and increase in productivity as expressed as capital productivity. Only on the foundation of these basic data could further data be generated, in particular about the projection of material usage, quantified and grouped according to branch. Initially, quantities would be calculated in constant prices (basic prices) and would only include real growth.

With the aid of the input-output method, the sectoral production commission would have to estimate the interconnections between the individual branches of production in the light of their assumed consumption-oriented structure of production. To this end, the capital costs anticipated by the individual branches--given the qualitative changes in production--would have to be broken down in such a way that its structure corresponded with the input-output matrix. The productivity increases attained in each branch (in which one could then see the changed coefficients of material and machinery requirements) would facilitate a more reliable and dynamic calculation of input-output figures.

In this manner the production commission will gain an impression of the potential growth of production in relation to the need for increases of capital and hence of size of net investment required, of labor and thus of potential net profit, despite the fact that the increase in consumption, together with its structure, as well as the internal production nexus connected with it, is only provisionally assumed (projected by the chief planning commission). If the conception, thus gained, of the potential profit increase indicates prospects for an increase in profits in comparison to the initial projection, it will present the quality-of-life commission with new considerations regarding possible further increases in consumption and how they might be distributed.

At the same time and in the same manner as the production commission calculated total production and with it, total profit in the planning period, the quality-of-life commission should prepare a balanced structure of production, both as a branch structure (in accordance with the input-output matrix) and as a higher aggregation in the structure which we have been considering. This latter structure in particular is important to the deliberations of the quality-of-life commission. It provides first impressions about possible increases in private and social consumption, and of course the previously envisaged structure of production and hence of envisaged growth need not be accepted by the quality-of-life commission, who may propose structural changes.

This first projection of profit increase (whether made by the chief planning commission or production commission) provides crucial starting data for the quality-of-life commission, since it constitutes the basis of all considerations concerning the utilization of the increase in profits. In the process of plan preparation, the initial assumptions about profit increases express only the anticipated growth in productivity and increase in the material volume of production underlying the profit figure, but without consideration of price. In the course of further plan preparations, the production commission would have to take account of the price projections made by the individual branches. However, since one of the main goals of overall macro-planning is the elimination of inflationary development, the future price changes under consideration should also be limited and basically should only allow for substantial shortages and increases in use-value (product innovations). The estimated rises in profit would thus largely express the available real increase in products for the growth of net investments on the one hand and of consumption on the other.

A portion of the growing profits is of course continuously transformed into net investments, the amount of which is considered and calculated by the production commission in its projection of the growth of production. However, the projection of the growth of average wages, given the predicted growth in productivity, is already one of the responsibilities of the quality-of-life commission. The production commission, in its calculations, starts initially from the constant wages of the basic plan and has to project the growth of the labor force, in terms of these constant wages, into the sum of future wages. One of the most important tasks of the quality-of-life commission is to plan wage growth in terms of two or three alternatives. We will deal separately with this wage planning below.

On the basis of price and wage projections, a conception will develop about the primary income distribution of estimated national income into gross wages and gross profits. It is anticipated that a portion of gross profits will be utilized for net investments, since these net investments affect projected growth. The other portion of gross profits is used basically for consumption. In the course of planning estimates, some notion naturally develops about which portion of net investments will be financed directly from profits and which portion will be financed by means of redistribution via the state budget and the credit system. For the time being we will regard net investments as a whole (on the basis of direct considerations of production) and observe how the distribution and redistribution process is planned with respect to the development of consumption.

At the same time, the subcommissions must begin to deliberate on the necessary social consumption. Expanded public services normally require more, namely additional labor power. The growth in wages associated with this must of course also be calculated in accordance with the estimated increases in average wages, with the result that again limits are set on the growth in average wages. Improvements in social security are also linked to the growth of wages. Since any increase in social incomes must be met from the consumption fund, here again limits are imposed on the growth of wages. For all these reasons, deliberations about wage increases in production cannot occur independently of considerations of the development of social consumption.

The quality-of-life commission must, in its deliberations on the nature of consumption increases, take account of these different relationships, that is, it must simultaneously allow for the way in which growth or the newly distributable consumption fund are utilized. There exist certain pressures which induce growth in average wages but at the same time there is no clear quantitative process by which they are determined. Average wages should grow in a certain relation to productivity, but this does not mean that they must grow at the same rate. Only where the growth of wages has managed to prevail, through struggle, against the growth of profits, has the conception of a productivity-equivalent growth of wages developed. However, where the entire society democratically determines the distribution, it can and should also voluntarily decide on the manner in which it wants to utilize the increase in the consumption fund. Thus, for instance, the preparation of two or three alternative plans will enable society to differentiate among them by means of different growth rates of average wages. This need not be so, however.

The work of the quality-of-life commission thus amounts to the preparation of two or three alternative versions of those distribution processes that would give rise to proportionally different consumption matrixes. Later, we will discuss the possibilities of determining individual distribution and redistribution processes and hence the quantities of primary and derived income groups up to the origin of the final incomes provided for by the plan. But for the moment we are concerned with comprehending cooperative planning work between the production and quality-of-life commissions in the course of several iterations. The formulation of any two or three alternatives of final incomes and the development of consumption will of course require corresponding changes in the structure of production and necessitate other investment considerations, and hence renewed examination and balancing of accounts in the production commission. This gives rise to new concrete measures or corrections in the consumption fund, in the required number of workers in production, and the like. On the basis of these, further changes in the weighed distribution and consumption processes must be worked out and estimated in the quality-of-life commission. We will now turn to an individual examination of the regulation of the most important distributive processes.

DETERMINING WAGES

As already noted, planning of the growth of wages is the most important instrument for planning the regulation of the overall development of income. The sum total of all wages in the national economy represents the decisive share in the sum of consumption-oriented income. Even if compensated for through taxes and state expenditures, such measures cannot, for the most part, compensate any longer for substantial deviations of the sum total of wages from the proportion necessary to maintain equilibrium. Moreover, since the development of wages in production affects all other consumption-oriented income groups, each of its deficiencies has an accelerating effect. Thus, a planned maintenance of equilibrium requires that macro-economic planning of wages be centralized and stable and that the planned development of wages be compulsory.

This brings us to one of the most basic preconditions of macro-economic planning. If a majority of working people and the trade unions which represent them, cannot be convinced of the necessity of planning the development of wages, with the possibility of democratic choice from among several alternative plans, a balanced development of the economy could not be assured and the devastating cyclical crises and periods of inflation could not therefore be overcome.

Freedom to negotiate wages can be meaningful only under conditions where the development of profits is not planned, where capitalist investment and consumption out of profits are alienated from wage earners, and the struggle for wages takes place in opposition to alienated profits. Under such conditions, direct wage interests not only will necessarily emerge as the strongest factors as against general considerations about the well-being of the national economy, but individual branches, groups of professions, or trade union associations will also constantly make attempts to break out of uniform, cohesive, or coordinated actions by trade unions within the framework of the state as a whole.

One of the most interesting attempts to put into practice a uniform, cohesive wage policy in the context of a market economy with a predominance of private capitalist enterprises has been the Swedish system of wages and benefits negotiations in which the central trade union association LO (Landesorganisation) participates in centralized wage negotiations with the Central Association of Swedish Employers SAF (Svenska Arbetsgivar-foreningen). Even at this level it was recognized that the total sum of wage increases should be negotiated centrally before being distributed, according to the principle of equality among individual branches and occupations. This is understood as the solidarity principle of wage policy. The concretization of wage increase consistent with stability is brought about by means of consensus-building within the union. Even those conflicts which subsequently lead to decisions on wage increase differentials are settled within the trade unions themselves.

The behavior of most trade unions in developed industrialized countries is less pronounced than in Sweden, but the same in principle. Many governments attempt to influence wage negotiations by marshialing economic data, prognoses, and the art of moral persuasion (spiritual massage). The aim of all these interventions is to bring wage increases into line with projected growth in productivity.

Yet all such attempts, even though tried in countries practicing national economic planning (France, Holland, Norway, et al.), have failed again and again due to:

1. the contradictions between forecasts and the actual development of production;

2. the contradictory nature of wage and profit interests which comes to the fore particularly in times of unfavorable development of productivity;

3. the absence of objective criteria and democratic decision-making precedents concerning distribution of incomes;

4. the trade unions' need for legitimization, deriving from the fact that their members evaluate their success in the struggle for wages not in terms of objective economic criteria, but in relation to the successes of other trade unions, branches, etc.

If, instead of this, all developments in income were to be linked by plan to development of real productivity growth; if this planned regulation of the growth of incomes and consumption were to conform substantially to criteria which would be democratically debated and chosen, and subject to control by the public, and if this were to occur under conditions in which the social tension between wages and profits were eliminated; this would be a situation conducive to planning for rising wages. Beginning with this precondition, we will as already noted, confront its political implications at the end of our analysis.

A distinction must be drawn between short-term and long-term criteria for determination of wages. Short-term criteria are essentially determined by the situation of the labor market. Only if wages within individual occupations or wage groups depart in the short run from long run average wages can the relation between supply and demand be established in certain occupations and for specific skills. In the long run, certain differences prevail in the remuneration of different occupations and occupational groups (wage groups), and these more or less reflect objective standards of evaluation and criteria. In the short run, however, a more rapidly growing demand for certain occupations compared to their supply (and vice versa) can lead to a rise (or decline) in their wages in relation to the long-term level of this wage along the entire wage scale. But as soon as this occupation becomes more accessible, and supply and demand are again in balance, the wage paid to this occupation will swing back to its long-term point in the wage scale.

The planned differentiation of wages among individual professions or wage groups, has to take account of significant short-term market situations and in certain periods

must make allowance for situations of more rapidly rising
supply or demand within individual occupations by transferring them into higher wage groups (and vice versa). But
this only makes more important the long-term criteria of job
valuation used in arriving at wage differentials, which
would also longer sustain an equilibrium in the relationship
between supply and demand.

There are objective qualities of work which most people
would value identically or similarly. Otherwise a spontaneous increase in long-term wage differentials among different
categories of work in the labor market would not be possible at all. Evaluation of the physical and/or intellectual
difficulty of an occupation, its satisfactory nature, creativity, status, responsibility, its varying degree of jeopardy to
health and the like, given the different costs and varying
amounts of time required to attain the necessary training
(education, schooling, learning, experience, etc.), gives
rise to a dominant societal valuation from among the mass of
subjective value judgments which is expressed in the persistence of relatively long-term pay-scale differentials.

Wherever a relatively long-term regularity is to be
found it is a reflection of certain basic recurring linkages
that constitute the object of scientific research. Thus, research into the general foundations of wage differentials
and their psychological, technical, productive, socio-economic, cultural, ideological, and other causes, has been
gaining significance in society. It can and does furnish increasingly widely respected criteria and bases for the nego-
tiation and determination of wages. And it provides for
wage groupings and/or wage scales accepted, or directly
worked out by the trade unions.

In a free society where people can express their different interests and have to determine democratically how to
realize them, they also have to be able to form groups and
organize along the lines of their different interests. Therefore, even in the system we envision, all working people
should be organized in trade unions, which would help determine the actual development of wages. Even though
these trade unions would no longer have to be regarded as
organizations of struggle with the purpose of defending
wage interests against profit interests, they should continue
to bear a special responsibility in the process of determining wages.

The question is how to resolve the contradiction between two basic sets of demands in a new way. Both correspond to the interests of the working people, yet conflict
with each other. On the one hand, there is the demand for
a democratic confrontation of interests in the determination
of wage levels and wage differentials on the part of the
workers' own interest organizations. On the other hand,

there is the demand for a balanced development of the economy in order to do away with crises and large-scale unemployment, an aim which requires subordination of the development of wages.

This would not mean the abandonment of democratic interest representation and interest confrontation in the determination of wages. This interest representation would, however, be subject to certain new rules of behavior and organizational forms by means of which the overriding interest in equilibrium would be realized. Concretely, this would mean that the calculations of growth in the consumption fund described above would have to be regarded as the point of departure for all discussions relating to wage increases. It would be primarily the Commission for the Development of Wages that would work out the appropriate proposals. This body would, for the most part, be comprised of representatives of all the major trade unions and labor specialists. Its task would be to examine alternative methods of bringing about consumption increases by means of wage increases in collaboration with all other quality-of-life commissions. Inclusion in this organization would facilitate an understanding of all the important interrelationships and various possibilities for increasing consumption by means of wage increases as well as discussion as to how to find the best alternatives.

Only after the growth rates of average wages have been established in this way--perhaps in two or three alternatives--would they be concretized and distributed within the trade unions according to individual branches and professions. Ongoing intra-union discussions, based on the latest findings of labor research, would determine whether to automatically distribute the overall growth rate of wages equally among all wage categories. That is, they would determine whether to retain existing wage differentials or whether to differentiate growth rates, thus altering the existing wage groups with their pay-scale differentials.

In this way, the principle of democratic representation and confrontation of interests in the determination of the development of wages could be linked to the principle of subordination of wage growth to a planned maintenance of equilibrium. This would mean determination of wages both from bottom to top (from periphery to center) and from top to bottom. Preparations for centrally planned wage increases would result from discussions within the trade unions, and implementation of the accepted, planned wage increases based on a concrete, universally binding pay rate and wage-group scales would be guaranteed and supervised by the trade unions themselves.

This however presupposes the existence of trade union organizations which are united, at least to the extent that all branch trade unions or other trade union associations would submit to jointly and democratically adopted resolutions concerning the development of wages and the pay scale and act together against all violations. Only if the trade unions adhere unanimously to such democratic rules of the game in their actions would it be possible to create the most important preconditions necessary for a planned maintenance of economic equilibrium. This would mean the realization of, for instance, the wage-policy solidarity advocated by the Swedish trade unions--which could not however be implemented under conditions of capitalist income distribution and in the face of lack of interest on the part of wage earners in the development of profits and investments in the enterprises. The Swedish unions have also been unable, under existing conditions, to establish a link between solidarity in the development of wages and the principle of performance required by the market.

PLANNING PROFIT-SHARING

We have already explained in several places why the principle of wage solidarity, though necessary, cannot in itself guarantee remuneration geared to performance. In order to establish the incentives for performance of all the occupations necessary to society, despite the great differences among work activities and a relatively rigid division of labor, there has to be a system of wage differentials. This system should ensure that the various occupations which a society needs are learned and practiced. In other words, since there are still great differences in the attractiveness of individual occupations and work activities, and since these deter people from many kinds of work, there must be a system of differential compensation in order to create an interest in performing all these different kinds of work.

What is involved here is a kind of compensation that merely reflects objectively existing differences among occupations (as established by the division of labor) and takes no account of the market performance of the production and work collectives. The latter should, in this sense, establish compensation equal to what prevails in the national economy, beyond the individual branches (or horizontally) for occupations and jobs requiring the same amount of effort, training, responsibility, and social attractiveness, and which thus merit the same remuneration. Changes in the scale of occupations, especially those relating to effort, training, responsibility, and attractiveness, would require corresponding changes in these wage differentials.

However, if compensation were to be made solely in accordance with these criteria, this would ignore a very important aspect of work, namely its use-value to society as defined in market terms. This aspect is evident in the fact that different enterprises though making use of equivalent amounts of equivalently remunerated labor, may realize differing profits. These profit differentials, as the expression of differences in use-value and productive efficiency must, as has already been explained, enter into the remuneration of the individual co-worker/co-owners--given the existence of the desired capital participation or capital neutralization. This brings us to the macro-economic aspect of profit-sharing. The question is, how to ensure macro-economic equilibrium if profit-sharing in individual enterprises is linked to concrete, differentially developing profits, the actual amounts of which cannot be predicted?

Where the performance of an enterprise is equivalent, profit-sharing would be expressed in an equal rate of profit (in accordance with calculations to be explained later) and should be as equivalent as possible in per capita terms; whereas in the case of unequal performance (unequal rate of profit) it should be differentiated. Thus, the problem is to find a method of calculation, established by plan, that can account for per capita sharing, given an equal rate of profit, in all branches, as well as making allowances for situations of differing rates of profit. This would then represent the socially required, efficiency-oriented level of profit sharing (always assuming a development of the rate of profit geared to efficiency, as will be explained below).

The possibility of constructing a generally valid formula (a binding coefficient) which all enterprises would use in calculating their profit sharing out of net profits, provides the instument by which the desired portion of net profits established by the macro-plans for distribution to the co-workers would be regulated.

The coefficient x will have to be determined by the quality-of-life commission. Establishment of the proportions between guaranteed wages which do not depend on profits, and profit-sharing is among the most important decisions on economic policy. It must first be determined what share of the total consumption fund is to be utilized in the form of wages and what share in the form of profit-sharing. These proportions should also be projected in terms of a number of variants. However, the level of profit-sharing decided on must also be in proportion to estimated profits. The respective proportions of presupposed gross profits will be mutually adjusted.

But the regulation of profit-sharing cannot be accomplished as directly as in the case of wages, since it is necessarily dependent on the actual development of profits, while the development of wages is linked to the utilized

quantity and qualifications of labor and does not depend on
market performance (profit). Wages also have to be paid
continuously by the enterprise, independently of market results, in accordance with work done and thus the amounts
to be paid in wages are calculated at the same time as is
the requisite quantity of labor.

If profit-sharing were planned, the amount of net investments would be assured, and these, defined in accordance with anticipated growth in production, would constitute a crucial precondition for this growth. However,
investments themselves would not be planned irreversibly
since--in light of all the arguments above--they would first
have to be determined by the enterprises. Planning for
limitations on income for consumption would, however, ensure that consumption would not rise at the expense of required investment, thus preventing inflation and assuring
the establishment of equilibrium. If, therefore, it is established in the overall plan for the national economy that the
part of net profit represented by the profit sharing fund
should constitute a certain percentage:

$$\frac{\text{national-economic} \quad \text{profit} \quad \text{sharing} \quad \text{fund}}{\text{net profit in the national economy}} = ps$$

then this coefficient ps would be binding in all enterprises
for calculation of the profit sharing fund:

PS = ps . NP/tc . W

PS = Profit sharing fund of the enterprise

ps = coefficient established for the national economy

NP = Net profit of the enterprise

tc = total capital of the enterprise (fixed assets and liq-
       uid capital

W = total wages in the enterprise

The enterprises themselves would determine the distribution
within the enterprise of the annually calculated profit sharing fund. But if the enterprises decide to increase investment on their own at the expense of incomes for consumption (essentially at the expense of profit-sharing), they
should not be prevented from doing so. In the first place,
we see a more rapid development of investment at the expense of profit-sharing as the exception. And second,
such developments, though they may threaten to upset the

equilibrium, can be relatively easily corrected, as we shall also see later on. But it is more difficult to correct the contrary development (a too rapid growth of income for consumption at the expense of income for investment). This is the reason for the obligatory nature of the profit-sharing quota as far as the enterprises are concerned: it may fall short, but must not be exceeded.

PLANNING THE DEVELOPMENT OF PROFITS

We have already noted that the development of profits can be more or less reliably forecast. Aggregate gross profit in the national economy is, on the one hand, the result of forecasts of production and productive factors as well as of the projected development of prices in the production commission; and the planned development of wages in the quality-of-life commission on the other hand, assuming iterative cooperation between the two commissions. We have said that relatively reliable predictions concerning the development of the factors of production and productivity can be made by making use of analyses of branches.

If an inflationary development of demand can be prevented through regulation of income for consumption, it can also work against price increases. The rise in prices for new or scarce products should be balanced out by price decreases for outmoded or superfluous products.

It is, nevertheless, necessary to take account of the possibility that the actual development of profits may depart from forecasts. Such deviations may be due to the unpredictable initiatives of individual enterprises and entrepreneurs, and their productivity- and profit-enhancing effects. They may also result from individual mistakes and shortcomings in the development of production and the losses of profit resulting from them. They need not, however, lead to disruptions in the macro-equilibrium, provided that two conditions are present, namely where a surplus or shortfall in the projected growth in profits leads to a proportional acceleration or slowdown in the growth of consumption, and modifications in the proportions of distribution can be made relatively quickly. The demand for consumption would increase or decrease more or less automatically with growth or reduction of profits on the basis of the co-workers' profit-sharing quota. The greater profits are, the greater will be the profit-shares utilized primarily for consumption. In order to increase its equilibrating influence on consumption, the emphasis on profit-sharing should be increased wherever possible. This can be accomplished if, for several consecutive years, profit-sharing grows more rapidly than average wages. This should continue until profit shares average roughly 5 to 10 percent of basic wages in the national economy. Such proportions would increase the efficiency-stimulating effects of profit-sharing without undermining wage differentials as incentives for choice of job and occupation.

However, if the equilibrating effect of compensation for work is to be realized, it must be accompanied by the kind of utilization of private profits which promotes equilibrium. We have already explained the distribution of profits in private enterprises. From these profits, as of a certain profit level onwards, a portion would be transformed into neutralized capital. This upper limit on profits cannot be specified, first of all, since it depends upon the differing standards of consumption in individual countries, and second, since it involves a political decision. Nevertheless, the systemic goals we envision would be served if, on the basis of global calculations, an upward limit on profits could be established that, in addition to net profits (after deducting taxes, social security contributions, and interest on external capital), would guarantee a general profit-sharing for co-workers throughout the economy and, beyond this, a share of profits which could not be used to form neutralized capital to provide sufficient motivation for private entrepreneurs.

Profits remaining after deduction of profit shares would be distributed in the following manner. Up to a certain amount, remaining profits would be given entirely to the private entrepreneur. Any surplus above this minimal remaining profit would be subject to a planned division into neutralized new capital and an additional profit share for the private entrepreneur.

The division of this surplus in the private firm, above and beyond the minimal remaining profit --henceforth profit surplus --would be accomplished with the aid of a coefficient x. This coefficient x should be an integral part of the macro-plan, and would be binding on all private enterprises making a profit surplus. This coefficient x, multiplied by the profit surplus, produces the percentage of newly formed, neutralized capital in this profit surplus, as well as a remainder that is also placed at the disposal of the private entrepreneur.

Since private entrepreneurs would always receive a certain percentage (determined by x) as a supplement, they would have an interest in this profit surplus. After all, the neutralized capital formed out of profit surpluses would not be capital estranged from them, but capital belonging to the firm, binding it to its co-workers through their interests. Even if this neutralized capital were to be administered in trust by an elected board of co-workers, it would

be available to the firm's management for utilization in
production.   As long as the private entrepreneur is also
the manager of the enterprise, it is he who will have to determine the actual utilization of funds.   But his decision
will be in harmony with the interests of the co-workers inasmuch as any increase in profit would result in both rising
profit-shares for the co-workers/co-owners and in an increase in the profit surplus and hence ultimately a share of
the profits for the private entrepreneur.

What is involved is a planned calculation of the coefficient x and explanation of the socio-economic aspects that
should be taken into account in calculating it.   The minimum remainder of profit (from which neutralized capital has
not yet been formed) should actually be of an annual
amount roughly equivalent to the annual salaries of the
managing personnel.   Although there are admittedly great
individual differences in the remuneration of managers,
there is no way to establish this basic entrepreneurial profit-share without reference to actual or estimated average
managerial salaries.   This planned fixing of a basic entrepreneurial profit-share would not mean that the entrepreneur would be compelled to consume all of it, though he
could do so if he wished.   But fixing this amount will establish an upper limit beyond which the transformation of
profit surpluses into neutralized capital will be assured.

The division of profit surpluses with the aid of x
should be done in such a way that the proportion of newly
formed neutralized capital in the profit surplus grows with
its absolute growth.   Therefore, the more the profit surplus grows in absolute terms, the greater x will be.   There
must always be a portion of the entrepreneur's profit-share
supplement from out of the profit surplus that can be utilized for consumption, so that it will grow in absolute term
while decreasing relatively, as a share of the profit surplus.

The production commission has, first and foremost, to
forecast the anticipated development of profits of private
entrepreneurs in the alternative plans.   Simultaneously, the
process of calculation of the need for net investments to
cover assumed growth in production and profits will be in
progress.   In this way the necessary data will be generated
for the requisite division of profits, especially from the
perspective of need for investment.   This is, to be sure, a
global perspective, which can only be differentiated according to the average varying capital composition of individual
branches.   The approximate need for investment funds of
individual branches (irrespective of whether they are co-
worker companies or private firms), and thus of the part
investment will play in the gross profits of the branches,
should therefore be foreseeable.   Structural shifts in actual
investment requirements as opposed to this forecast can be

corrected by the credit system as well as by the market mechanism.

It is evident that co-worker profit-sharing would replace the dividends which have gone to the owners of private capital, while in firms where appropriation of private profit continues, it appears as a long overdue feature. At the same time, however, the system could not function if there was profit-sharing in addition to wages in one sector of production, while in the private sector wages were paid only according to scale. In order to achieve general profit-sharing in the surviving private sector as well, deliberate tax relief for private enterprises is needed in order to provide for both profit-sharing and adequately motivated entrepreneurial profits. During periods of low profits, there would be a percentage of profit-sharing, financed by tax write-offs, which, however, would have to fall progressively to zero as profits increased. The resultant entrepreneurial profits would rise more rapidly than the profit-sharing portion paid by the enterprises in order to maintain the entrepreneur's interest in a growth of profits.

It is now obvious again that the quality-of-life commission's deliberations concerning distribution of the fund for consumption or its growth toward the residual income for consumption has to take account of all its complementary and substitutive connections. If the amount or growth of a particular final consumptive income group is under consideration, all other groups have to be taken as given, so that the available remainder of the consumption fund is taken into account. If this amount is considered insufficient for the income group under discussion, any increase in it will have to be realized through a relative reduction of other residual income groups. In the process, account will have to be taken of all existing complementary relationships.

Any acceleration in the growth of consumption from out of profits, for example, will therefore have to take place at the cost of slower growth in other final incomes for consumption. Either average wages, and the social expenditures of government bound up with them, will have to increase more slowly, or the increase in manpower in the service sector, and hence in social consumption, will have to be slowed down. In the final analysis, all these kinds of growth in consumption must be dampened in certain mutually balanced proportions. Thus, for example, determination of the extent of consumption from out of profits as well as its growth is dependent upon all other consumptive final incomes. Thus, given levels of gross profit, the entrepreneur's share of the profits is limited by net investment on the one hand and wages, profit-shares, and taxes on the other hand. The size of entrepreneurial net profits can also be controlled through various opportunities for manipulation of these wages, profit-shares, and taxes.

The division of the profit-shares of enterprises into net investments (in the form of neutralized capital) and entrepreneurial profit-shares destined primarily for consumption will then be assured by means of the entrepreneurial profit coefficient. Even if the private firms' profits were to increase more rapidly or more slowly than anticipated, consumption from out of profits would correspondingly rise or fall in proportion. The gradations and progressiveness of coefficient x would then have to be adjusted more according to the motivational effect of the supplement to entrepreneurial profit (after deducting neutralized capital).

PLANNING REDISTRIBUTION BY THE STATE

Together with a development of wages established by plan, the profit- sharing quota and the division of private profits, the determination of state revenues and expenditures has a decisive influence on the generation and utilization of final incomes. Redistribution of incomes by the state has, in recent decades, not only increased quantitatively but has also come to determine significantly the qualitative standard of living of the population. In the process of macro-planning, special attention will have to be paid to the qualitative and quantitative development of this redistribution. It is precisely these redistributive processes which can be planned most precisely and firmly.

The largest and most significant sources of state revenues are taxes. We will not go into the history of taxation in the present context, since countless economic studies have already been devoted to this topic. In contrast to this, we will ignore the wide diversity of forms and sources of taxation in the various industrialized countries of the world and go on to develop a concept of taxation most appropriate to the general requirements of the system we envision. What we are aiming at is a system that is simple, understandable, and readily amenable to planning, the main task of which would be to acquire revenues for the state in quantities determined by planned expenditures (predominantly to cover planned social consumption). However, a distinction has to be made between a system of taxation conceived as a system of goals and the realistic transitional measures aimed at the establishment of such a system of goals. To begin with, we will describe the taxation system as the most simple conceivable set of future goals, one which could be implemented on the basis of a new system already in place for some years.

A community already operating with large co-worker enterprises, in which the profits of private enterprises would thus already be in the process of transformation into neutralized capital, where co-worker profit-sharing would be indirectly regulated, where wage differences would be consciously established in annual pay scales, and where a continuous, non-cyclical development of production is ensured, would no longer find it necessary to use taxes as a means of income redistribution. Differences among incomes would, for the most part, be managed directly (with the aid of pay scales and profit-sharing), and attention would be paid--as we have seen--to differences in work and performance. Under such conditions, taxes could basically be transformed into a simple and uniform (equal percentage) tax on all incomes. The sole exception would be the tax on monopolies which we will consider separately.

The significance of a value-added tax or similar kinds of indirect taxes (sales tax, etc.) could also increase. However, in the system here advocated, the market mechanism would yield differing income levels which could not-- and, within certain limits, should not--be eliminated despite the general (direct or indirect) regulation of wages and profits. This is why a direct tax on incomes cannot be dispensed with. Although it is desirable that profits increase, for example, through the lowering of costs, etc., it is necessary that the uniform tax be paid simultaneously from out of these increased profits. But if there were only a value-added tax or sales tax, different profit levels could not be taxed appropriately. For instance, two firms with equal sales but substantially differing costs and profits would pay the same amount in taxes. Even if their profit differentials were proportionate to their respective benefits to society and were, in this sense, desirable, all profits would still have to be taxed simultaneously using the same percentage.

With the exception of a monopoly tax, therefore, a simplification of the tax system is conceivable in the future. This would mean a uniform income tax without progressive taxation and basically eliminating double taxation. The notion that higher incomes should be subject to progressively increasing taxes in order to cover social needs arises from a system in which there is no direct and indirect predetermination of income differentials and in which large, spontaneously emerging differences are supposed to be equalized ex post facto. But if such income differentials are predetermined in the process of planning the development of wages, of profit-sharing, and of forming neutralized capital-- which are basically necessary only as work and performance incentives--then it would be possible to tax these incomes by a uniform percentage.

The transition from spontaneously emerging wage differentials to a democratically established pay scale will, however, take some time. And since it would not be possible immediately to equalize all large incomes (that is, those not commensurate with performance and perhaps monopolistic) of independent entrepreneurs without employees, the transition to a system with a uniform tax rate would also take a long time. Until then, the tax system would at least have to be progressive. Any political decision to implement the proposed reform of the system would thus always involve a transitional period. During this period, individual reforms would have to be coordinated and developed in terms of the established system of goals.

Either way, however, the planning of future taxes and other state revenues would have to be subordinate to planned state expenditures, that is, to the desired proportions of final income. In particular, the proportions of private and social consumption, that is, the share of social consumption in total consumption, would influence the amount of state expenditures. State expenditures for public services would, as already mentioned, have to be brought into a subsistence relationship with the growth of private consumption by means of wage increases.

The decision concerning the number of employees in the public service sector which, at a planned level of gross as well as net wages, should require a planned share of private consumption, provides a first approximation of necessary state revenues and expenditures. Further considerations in this immediate context will relate to the material goods needed for public services. A decision favoring a certain amount of growth in public services means not only that additional manpower must be hired but also that material costs will increase and thus necessitate correspondingly larger governmental revenues. These of course reduce net wages and other taxed incomes. They must therefore be taken into account in any considerations regarding the proportions of private and public consumption.

Apart from public services, the quality-of-life commission would have to deal with the growth rate and share of total consumption of the other state expenditures having predominantly to do with consumption, its social tasks, its subsidies to business, and its direct expenditures for consumer goods used by society as a whole (roads, paths, etc.). In addition to these, finally, there are state expenditures for investments. These together account for the total of all state expenditures. Naturally, reflections concerning the growth of state expenditures take the form of concrete considerations of desired growth of the individual departments of the public services and governmental activities (which can be derived, for example, from our organizational schema). The individual subcommissions of the quality-of-life commission which deal with social consumption

will examine the growth of the individual departments with a
view to determining what improvements in the quality of life
may be necessary. If, however, these reflections are no
longer to have the simple form of calculation of financial
needs, as has hitherto been the case, but rather to strive
to achieve development under conditions of equilibrium,
then they must constantly be translated into basic equilibrium aggregates.

It is therefore not enough to discuss how much additional funding will be needed and how much will have to be
raised in taxes in order to keep up with growth in state
expenditures, in the spheres of social security, education,
health, infrastructure, and defense, for example. These
expenditures will still have to be divided into those specific
final income groups whose growth stands in a complementary
or substitutive relationship to the growth of other final income groups, and which, taken altogether, will have to be
equalized in relation to their corresponding production
groups. It is therefore necessary to determine how much
additional manpower will have to be engaged in general,
given a certain amount of growth in public services. This
has to be done keeping in mind the necessary wage increases in the national economy as a whole and the remaining complementary or central state expenditures for consumption and the auxiliary consumption fund. Once a
decision has been made as to the planned growth of average
wages throughout the national economy, very limited scope
will remain for decisions concerning an expansion of the
number of employees in the public services.

A final and completely differently constituted state expenditure has hitherto been set aside for state subsidies of
investments. In contrast to subsidies serving to cover
costs (which will probably exist for some time to come,
since they very often result from crucial non-economic, political, environment-protective, and similar factors), the
question arises here as to whether investment subsidies will
need to be taken into account at all in future processes of
planning and regulating the development of income. In our
view, such investment subsidies would be reduced though
they cannot be done away with completely. In some
branches where the prices of products are relatively low
due to the prevailing productive technology, but where for
various reasons this technology has to be changed substantially (for example, in the area of energy production where
there is a shortage of the fuels being utilized), the necessary investments could not be made by the enterprises, not
even with the aid of credits. Given existing prices, the
required level of profitability of production made possible
by new technology could not be assured. Since prices cannot be raised (in view of the predominance of the old pro-

duction methods), the required new investment could be assured only by means of governmental investment subsidies.

It is, therefore, only by analysis of such individual and non-market conforming situations that notions of future needs for governmental investment subsidies can take shape. In the system advocated here, they would represent only justifiable exceptions. No doubt they would mean a draining of investment-oriented incomes (profits) exogenous to the system, and their redistribution to the benefit of those branches unable to ensure the development of investment either from out of their own profits or credits. If then the profit quota is indirectly planned so as to guarantee the necessary growth of investment in all branches, redistribution by government should indeed take place only in highly justified exceptional cases and would be planned in advance. This would imply a simultaneous determination of the additional amount of government revenues to finance such planned investment subsidies.

The maintenance of equilibrium in proportional macro-planning presupposes not only a normal, fiscally balanced planning of state revenues and expenditures; it also requires that government expenditures, classified according to the particular way in which they are to be utilized, be equalized by the production groups to which they correspond, as well as that part of their supply of goods which corresponds to the value of government expenditures.

PLANNING REDISTRIBUTION THROUGH CREDITS

With the credit system, we enter into a sphere of redistribution processes where forecasting by plan is most uncertain and where prognosis has to rely exclusively upon estimates derived from previous developments. This point will be further substantiated later. Although such uncertainty exists, it should be possible to prevent disruptions in the equilibrium in this area as well. Opportunities to do so are available: the development of primary, and most secondary incomes can be regulated quite well. Apart from this, some new methods of regulating the development of credits will be indicated.

First of all, future savings would be estimated on the basis of a planned increase in incomes. Here, a distinction among four kinds of savings must be drawn.

1. Savings from wages (including co-worker profit shares) and income from public sources;

2. savings from private profits and income from assets;

3. savings realized by enterprises from write-offs and profits;

4. savings realized by governmental institutions, public service institutions, unions, and associations.

In order to estimate savings on the basis of past developments, as well as future corrective measures, it will, of course be necessary to include savings within the banking system in our schema. The question that arises here immediately is whether this is at all possible where banks and savings institutions are involved. By this we mean that, with the aid of modern technology, such a classification and registration of savings would be possible without too much red tape, and indeed that certain basic trends in this direction already exist. Without it being necessary to violate bank secrecy or to restrict personal liberties, it would be possible to request certain basic data when savings or checking accounts were opened, which would indicate where future debits and credits could be classified among the four groups. Using modern techniques of accounting and reporting it would be possible, without much difficulty, to maintain running tallies of the inflow and outflow of savings within individual bank and savings institutions. Once this system had been operating for a period of time, it would be possible to estimate future savings much more precisely. As will be shown, however, even mistaken estimates would not be of great consequence.

The most important facilitator of future estimates of savings must be seen in a planned and relatively continuous development of incomes as well as in a planned protection of investment-oriented incomes. On the one hand, once wage increases become more uniform across the board (after the elimination of cyclical fluctuations and large-scale unemployment), this would lead to a more balanced development of net savings from wages. And on the other hand, the production commission's forecast--which would be necessary in any case--would make possible approximate estimates of future savings and demand for credit in the individual branches. Forecasts of the utilization of privately appropriated profits would be the least reliable, at the outset. But here too, a macro-economic regularity in the growth of consumption and savings should emerge after a certain period of continuous outflow of these profits on the basis of the regulation of the division of profits.

We can thus, first of all, estimate the amount of savings from private incomes and from the incomes of the enterprises and institutions relatively precisely. Second, classification of savings formation as well as rapid determination of any deviation from the forecast, would make it possible to carry out corrective measures in time, particularly in the development of credits, as will be discussed later.

The total extent of net credits, to be explained below, would not exceed the total amount of net savings. Net credits must however also include other kinds of bank expenditures. In order to cast some light on how credits might be regulated we now turn to a more detailed explanation of the complicated system of incomes and expenditures in the banking system relating to the desired maintenance of the equilibrium.

It must always be remembered that all losses from the proceeds that enter into the sphere of the banking system flow back out in the same amounts and must again enter into proceeds. Otherwise the equilibrium between the constantly renewing supply of goods and the monetarily-defined supply of goods would be disrupted. Hence if the actual gross product is to be completely sold, that share of proceeds which--in whatever form--flows into the banking system during a planning year must correspond to the money flowing back from the banking system.

This picture of inflow and outflow characterizes the transformation of actual control over money: money flows temporarily into the sphere of the circulation of goods and back out again. Money constitutes the proceeds from the sale of goods and must be utilized again for the purchase of goods in order to become the proceeds of the next seller of goods. This process can take place, without any change of venue, within the banking system or even within a single bank. This is accomplished by means of deposits, that is, by payments for goods from one current account to another. Money then leaves the realm of circulation (where it has remained even in the process of intra-bank transfer from one account to another) and enters into the bank's sphere of liquidity formation and returns, quantitatively changed, to the circulation sphere again. But as soon as the sellers of goods transfer a share of their proceeds to the banks--whether in the form of credit repayments, interest payments or savings--there is no longer any automatic guarantee that these money losses will return to the sphere of circulation in the same amounts in order to yield the proceeds necessary for the complete sale of actual production. In the banking system, proceeds are in a system of redistribution from out of which they can return to the circulation process, both in smaller and larger amounts than required by actual production, and this can give rise both to disruptions in the sale of goods as well as inflation.

If in what follows we regard the flow of money between the banking system and the proceeds functioning as circulation funds in rather simplistic terms, it is because we are abstracting from the monetary relations between the banking system and outside countries, since we are speaking of equilibrium in the domestic market. This presupposes an equilibrium between additional foreign demand in the domestic market and the indigenous share of incomes flowing into foreign markets. The flow of money into and out of the banking system cannot be equated with the assets and obligations of the banks because a different kind of consideration is involved here. Some monetary flows will be active and some passive as far as the banks are concerned. The decisive criterion is shrinkage or growth in the amount of money required for the sale of actual production, which is accomplished by allowing monies to lie dormant or by expanding the money supply.

If we start from the assumption that the amount of receivable interest and other service charges of the commercial banks is equivalent to the banks' passive interest plus costs and profits, it follows that gross credits must equal credit repayments and net savings if the inflows and outflows are to be equalized. If we subtract from the banks' annual credits an amount corresponding to annual credit repayments (irrespective of whether these repayments relate to debts from past years or the current year), we arrive at net credits. Given a balanced inflow and outflow of money to and from the sphere of circulation, then, credit repayments for the year will be immediately transformed into new credits to be used for the purchase of goods. Only the amount which develops above and beyond this reproduced credit will be designated as net credit. To be sure, this should only serve to explain the equilibrium. From this point on, we will again refer to credits as a whole.

Net credits must equal net savings. Of course banks can expand their liquid capital from out of profits for credit purposes, which they have to do at the expense of investment. This would mean that net credits would be greater than net savings. But there would be no change in the equilibrium of the national economy, since although demand for goods would be diminished, in monetary terms, by demand for investment goods on the part of the banks, it would expand by the corresponding demand for credit arising in this manner. Since, however, in actual practice banks also make investments from out of profits for the expansion of their own banking network as well as--indirectly--for industry, we have not added this portion of profits to credits.

In today's market-economy system, the demand for credits by business and private households can at certain times be substantially higher than net savings, thus leading to an excessive demand for goods (in relation to actual pro-

duction). The banks have the possibility of using deposits
to create excessive credits, which can result in an inflationary increase in the monetary supply. If to this we add
the credits that the central bank can potentially grant directly to the state, the amount of credit needed to produce
an equilibrium may be even further exceeded. It will suffice thus to produce inflation if this kind of rising demand
for credit on the part of entrepreneurs, the people, and
the state is assured to the banks. However, excessive demand for credit on the part of government need not necessarily be the factor that sets off inflation. Rather, as already shown above, it may be a demand for credit
preceding income formation and later repaid from increases
in income, which can develop as a result of upward pressure on prices.

Everywhere, where prices can be increased, even if
only in individual branches, because demand exceeds supply, and wage increases (for example, in order to attract
more employees in a situation of full employment) ultimately
translate into across-the-board wage increases, the result is
that all goods can be sold at higher prices. In such situations, the development of credit is not the cause, but
rather the indispensable precondition for inflation. Without
national economic planning, the banks cannot judge, in each
individual case of demand for credit, whether the credit is
to be repaid from rising incomes realized by real increases
in production, by socially desirable increases in quality and
product innovations, or by inflationary price and wage
hikes. It would ask too much of the banking system, as
well as the central bank, if they were expected actually to
prevent inflation. If the decline of inflation experienced in
times of crisis, that is, when investment activities are declining in absolute terms, were put forward as evidence for
such a possibility, this would be tantamount to self-decep-
tion.

In order to prevent an inflationary generation of credit
it would be necessary, first and foremost, to know the actual amount of net savings. This may include not only
savings and term deposits but also the portion of sight deposits not utilized for the purchase of goods during the
planning year. This cannot however be determined solely
within the purview of the banks, since in granting credits
from a portion of their sight deposits, they are concerned
only with the recipients' capacity to repay. Even if the
banks were to grant such credits in relation to the floor
rate of sight deposits not threatened by the danger of non-
liquidity, the credits thus generated might exceed the
quantity of goods actually available to meet the demand for
credit.

Only when more extensive studies have been done will we be able to say what percentage of sight deposits will be required, on average over the longer term, to sell a certain quantity of goods, and what percentage of them will form an actual surplus for the owners of the sight deposits if in a given year no goods are sold. Only this part of the sight deposits really constitutes savings and would thus be transformed into additional credits. As already stated, short-term credits, which are repaid within a given year, can be transformed back into new credits, since their repayment amounts to a postponement of consumption. Savings from sight deposits can therefore also be utilized in theory for longer-term credits, provided they represent actual savings, and are not utilized by their owners to pay for goods during the given period. But since a good deal of uncertainty is associated with determining whether or not this is the case, in actual practice priority will have to be given to the transformation of savings from sight deposits into short-term credits, a process which might be repeated within the same year.

It is not enough, however, to adjust the global development of credit to the formation of savings. The problem is to harmonize macro-production with macro-income groups. Let us assume that the development of primary incomes together with planned redistribution by government were already able to maintain equilibrium. The banking system would then basically not have to effect any redistribution among macro-groups. At least such redistribution would be the exception. This means that savings and other sources of inflow into the banks from consumption should flow back into incomes for consumption in the form of credits and other outflows from the bank. The same applies to investment and governmental incomes. In other words, credits for consumption should correspond to net savings and credit repayments (including interest) from wages and private profits. Credits for investment should correspond to net savings and credit repayments from enterprise profits. Credits granted to government should correspond to net savings and credit repayments by government.

We must now take note of the possibility of shifts among these groups due to various causes. These include, first of all, planned, exceptional shifts and, second, unwanted shifts precipitated by an inability to comprehend sufficiently precisely the organization of savings and credits. Planned shifts will conceivably occur, especially between credits for consumption and government credits. If in certain periods the plan calls for the exceptional state of affairs in which government expenditures exceed government revenues, that is, if an increase in current government revenues is not desired, then redistribution would be planned by means of government credits at the expense of part of credit for consumption. In this event, credits granted to the government would be approved by the central bank, but the state bonds issued for these credits would have to be exchanged for credits from the central banks at the expense of a percentage of credit for consumption. Since government credits are largely spent on wages in the public service sector, a shift of this kind is conceivable without having to change the structure of production. Where government credits are to be spent on durable material goods, however, they will require a corresponding change in the structure of production.

Although enterprise savings would be generated primarily from out of profits, these savings would also include savings from tax write-offs. Borrowers could realize net investments from such write-offs. From the point of view of the national economy, these net investments by individual enterprises arising from savings made through tax write-offs represent a substitute for utilized investments (that is, are substitute investments). When, after a certain period of time, those who have realized savings through tax write-offs then, reclaim their savings in order to reinvest them, from their point of view they are making substitute investments. In terms of the national economy, these are actually investments for expansion. Since tax write-offs from debtor net investments and their credit repayments have accrued to the banks in the meantime, the latter can readily pay out the originally saved tax write-offs to the holders of the savings. In this manner, the credit system would enable the written off long-term investment goods to contribute to the acceleration of net investment.

Let us now sum up. There are savings whose character as deferred consumption (because they derive from consumption-oriented incomes) can be reliably ascertained in the banks. These are savings from wage incomes and social incomes. Private net profits, in the system advocated here, are also basically incomes from consumption, and savings derived from them can be separately ascertained. Savings realized by the state, public institutions, unions, associations, etc. are also essentially savings from incomes for consumption and as such can be reliably ascertained. However, the sources of one form of savings cannot be ascertained in accordance with this income classification, namely savings from sight deposits. Here, specific analyses would have to be used to determine the average percentage of consumptive incomes and/or loans (in the sight deposits of the enterprises) would have to be estimated against savings from sight deposits.

All these savings or net savings from consumptive incomes would be retransformed into net credits for consump-

tion.   It is easier to ascertain the amount of net
consumptive credits granted to private persons separately
in the banks. This is more difficult, however, in the case
of credits granted to enterprises.   But it is relatively simple to estimate the percentage of short-term credits accorded to enterprises for payment of wages, which are therefore
classified under credits for consumption, and the percentage used for material purchases which thus must be seen as
investment credits.   The only shift of credits from one
evaluation group to another still possible should be from
consumer credits to government credits.   Since, however,
short-term government credits will be utilized primarily for
purposes of wage payments, shifts of this kind would not
be problematic.   Middle- and long-term government credits
(to the extent that they exceed government savings) utilized primarily for establishing services and institutions
(including perhaps those for military purposes) must be
granted at the expense of long-term credits for consumption.   Their predetermination by plan should also be coordinated with timely correctives to the structure of production (information provided by the planning commission to
the concerns affected).

A forecast of all these movements of savings, credits,
and other monetary flows into, out of, and within the
banking system would have to be prepared by a special
banking commission as a subcommission of the production
commission.   In this commission, representatives of the central bank and the large commercial banks would predict and
calculate the redistributive processes of those incomes that
are earned with the aid of the banking system in collaboration with the other production commissions and the quality-
of-life commission.   In the banking commission, the difficult
task of estimating the development of net savings, particularly from sight deposits of net credits would have to be
carried out, as would the preparation of binding regulations
for granting credits with a view to the overall economic
equilibrium.   As in the case of all other distribution and
redistribution processes, this would have to be done with
reference to the alternative plans.

The elimination of major cyclical fluctuations would also
mean that fluctuations in the bank rate would disappear or
at least be greatly reduced.   An absolute decline in consumption and subsequently in investment has always been
linked to an accumulation of temporarily superfluous liquid
capital, which has normally brought interest rates down.
But even the lowest of interest rates cannot overcome non-
existent market prospects or stimulate investments--a fact
which most dramatically reveals the weaknesses of monetarist theory.   However, the moment rising consumption based
on rising investments, higher productivity and rising real

wages has resulted in excessive stimulation of the demand for liquid capital, interest rates have always increased as well. Their fluctuation has not been the cause, but rather a result of the contradictions between income distribution and investment requirements.

For this reason, it may be assumed that the discount rate could also remain relatively stable. For in the system we advocate, the requisite investment quota would be assured by means of direct regulation of wages and profits in relation to the planned need for investments. Most investments could be covered by auto-financing (with the aid of planned profit quotas), and a redistribution of investment funds by means of credits would primarily serve to change the structure of production. Consumption credits to enterprises (wage credits) aside from wage savings and consumption credits could, for their part, accelerate changes in the structure of consumption of the population toward long-term, relatively expensive consumer goods. Such structural purposes of credit would not require any significant changes in interest rates. On the contrary, a relatively stable interest rate can only help make the efficiency calculations of all investment decisions much more reliable.

This would however limit only large fluctuations in the interest rate caused by the cycle of production and the hitherto desired anticyclical changes in the discount rate. But minor interest rate fluctuations due to the supply of and demand for credit cannot be eliminated. Savings will also always be subject to minor fluctuations. For this reason, it will also be impossible to predict precisely the amount of net savings. Diminished net savings must lead to a corresponding diminution of credit, and vice versa. If the total amount of net credit can be made to approximate optimally the total amount of net savings, then the development of credit will contribute to the desired equilibrium.

PLANNING FOREIGN TRADE

We now turn our attention to the problem of foreign trade and foreign monetary relations in the context of our reform of the system. It should be emphasized, right at the outset, that nothing of substance in this sphere would be changed. Just as the existence of many independent, and some very small states must be assumed for the foreseeable future, the systemic changes we advocate within individual states cannot change anything of substance in relations with other states in which there has been no reform of the system. For this reason, we will demonstrate only that reform within individual states is not made impossible by external economic relations, and indeed may be advantageous even to countries retaining the former system. This is not to say, however, that simultaneous reform in several industrial countries--for instance, among members of the EEC--would substantially lower the risks of foreign trade.

Foreign trade is about market relations, that is, the productive activities of individual independent enterprises seeking to satisfy market demand with their goods. As with production for the domestic market, this demand cannot be predicted with certainty and is thus fraught with some degree of risk. It may be that competition in foreign markets is greater than at home, and that foreign markets are more difficult for the individual entrepreneur to assess than the domestic market. But for all that, foreign trade generally holds out prospects of higher returns or at least increased profits due to additional turnover. Enterprises thus show more willingness to take greater risks on their own responsibility in export trade. None of this will change in the future.

The overall development of imports and exports has to be forecast in the macro-plans, on the basis of past development. The export prospects of individual branches would be worked out with the aid of branch analyses in the branch commissions and of special forecasts of foreign market perspectives. On the basis of these, both the anticipated share of exports in the production of individual branches and the aggregated exports of the Macro-Groups I and II, as well as global exports, have to be forecast. Assuming equilibrium in the balance of trade for the time being, imports balanced by exports at price levels expressed in domestic currency must be divided between Groups I and II, and a forecast made of its subdivision by branches. Since these forecasts exhibit a relatively low degree of reliability, we have to consider in particular what developments might be triggered by a gap between forecast and reality.

Even under the proposed new system, both reverses and booms relating to sales in individual enterprises and branches cannot be predicted insofar as foreign markets are concerned. So long as there is no macro-planning in countries with which foreign trade is being carried on, a country that has already implemented macro-planning has to be prepared for certain disruptions originating abroad. Complications occurring in individual enterprises or branches can be dealt with relatively easily. A decline in exports of one or more branches will first result in a restructuring of domestic production, perhaps even short-term unemployment, and subsequently lead to a corresponding decline in imports. Since the reduced exports would attract less foreign exchange, the higher cost of foreign exchange, presuppos-

ing flexible exchange rates, would slow imports. This would
also correspond to a temporary reduction in domestic production. Conversely, unexpectedly high exports in some
branches would increase the inflow of foreign exchange,
make this foreign exchange cheaper, and increase imports.

If the macro-plan were therefore to assume equilibrium
in the balance of trade and a certain percentage of exports
in domestic production, as well as their equalization by imports, then unexpected departures from export forecasts in
several branches need not lead to macro-disruptions. The
excess or shortfall in exports would then have to be offset
by exports or a shortfall in the exports of other branches.
If this were not possible in the short run, equilibrium in
the balance of trade would require equalization by a shift in
imports. More exports than anticipated would require corresponding increases in imports, and vice versa.

The structural adaptation of imports to domestic demand is assured by the market mechanism. In this case,
the market mechanism also ensures the adjustment of the
two large product Groups I and II, including exports and
imports of them, to the development of domestic demand. If
more investment funds than anticipated are exported, more
investment goods will have to be imported in order to offset
planned domestic demand for investment. If more consumer
goods than anticipated are exported, more consumer goods
will have to be imported to meet the planned demand for
consumption. If on the other hand fewer investment and/or
consumer goods than anticipated are exported, and if this
shortfall cannot be replaced by other exports, so that domestic production has to decrease at least temporarily, a
corresponding decline in imports would also be required.

This decline in imports would have to be divided into
investment goods and consumer goods, corresponding to the
makeup of domestic profits. This subdivision of declining
imports into investment goods and consumer goods can only
be effected by the market mechanism since no planning
body is in a position to establish the quantity of reductions
in imported consumer and investment goods made necessary
by a decline in export production.

It would be desirable and feasible, given an overall
view of the development of foreign trade, to speed up the
adaptation of imports to exports. The more rapidly a decline in exports or rise in exports is offset by a decline in
imports or rise in imports of the same value, the less likely
it is to give rise to domestic disequilibria. The usual
methods of equalizing the reaction of imports to changing
domestic demand and varying exchange rates, function too
slowly for the most part. In the intervening period, the
domestic equilibrium is disrupted by an oversupply of
goods. The larger and more widely distributed export

losses are, the greater the oversupply naturally will be, a state of affairs which can ultimately lead to a recession.

If, given flexible exchange rates, the response of exchange rates to all inequalities in the balance and trade and--as will be shown later on--the balance of payments were to occur more quickly, then the adaptation of imports to unexpected changes in exports would be more rapid and hence result in fewer losses. Given flexible exchange rates, declines in exports result in decreased currency flows, which sooner or later must lead to an increase in the foreign currency exchange rate. If large foreign currency reserves are available, however, the response of exchange rates might be rather long in coming. Moreover, many economic experts still have an aversion toward frequent changes in exchange rates. If exchange rates reacted more rapidly every time exports diverged from the forecasts contained in the macro-plans--perhaps even within an internationally accepted framework--imports could more rapidly be adjusted to changes in exports.

Should an industrial country experience an export surplus which cannot be offset by imports because the surplus of profits made abroad are not utilized either by the population for consumption or by businesses for investment, then certain basic decisions would have to be made:

1. It might be decided that developing countries need this absolute surplus of the production of an industrial country, that is, the people of that country decide in a process of democratic choice and decision-making to equalize permanently their surplus of production and exports by means of capital exports for the benefit of the developing countries.

2. If above and beyond this increased development aid there exists a disequilibriated active balance of payments, this may be symptomatic of an intensive and insufficiently heeded need for security on the part of the people. Savings are excessive (savings exceed the investments required for planned growth) because the people are striving to establish greater security for old age, illness and possible unemployment. Given adequate productivity and quality of production, the surplus from production can easily become an export surplus. In any case, this model applies only to a few industrial countries and then only in old-style capitalist systems. One possible solution would be to plan for utilization of surplus savings (beyond those needed for investment) as credits taken out by the state, for instance for improved social security, and expect increased imports.

3. If despite increased development aid and adequate social security, there still should be an excessive savings quota

(surplus incomes) realized by an export surplus, a raising of wages at the expense of the profit quota might be con- sidered either as a universal measure or for the lowest wage categories (that is, wage leveling).

4. The excessive surplus income quota could however also be caused solely by excessive profits realized by powerful exporting enterprises. Profit rates that are relatively too high (substantially exceeding their investment needs) occur in these exporting enterprises, and transformation of their profit surpluses into savings and supplies of credit in the banks does not lead to credit-granting and investment by other branches and firms. The latter no longer invest, since they find no sufficient demand. A universal wage hike at the expense of the profit rate could hamper the in- vestment activities of most enterprises having a low profit quota. In such cases, all evidence points toward a special draining off of excessive profits made by powerful export- ing enterprises by means of a special monopoly tax to be considered later on and utilization of these funds to in- crease the expenditures of government for consumption.

5. Only if none of these methods worked to eliminate the excessive surplus income quota, which over the long run can develop only from an export surplus, would a reduction in working time be implemented. Only then would there be sufficient reason to conclude that a national economy was producing more than it could use for consumption and in- vestment (including considerable development aid). If in- creases in development aid, social security, wages, and other expenditures of the state for consumption do not lead to a utilization of excessive savings and of surplus in- come from export surpluses as investments, that is, if sur- plus value is produced, the obvious conclusion is to reduce working hours correspondingly.

   A passive balance of payments that is not in economic equilibrium, is in evidence either where imports of goods and/or services are greater than exports, or where capital exports are greater than capital imports. Equalization of this passive balance as a precondition for its subsequent progressive planned maintenance is far more difficult than for an active balance of payments. A passive balance of payments can result from different causes in different countries and economic systems, or depending on whether exchange rates are firm or flexible.

   Given firm rates of exchange, countries with overva- lued currencies (for example, the United States and Eng- land in recent decades) have been able to show passive balances of trade over the longer term. That is, they show a surplus of imports usually expressed either as an equally pronounced or even more pronounced passive balance of payments. Excessive imports and inadequate exports were, among other things, symptoms indicating the overevaluation of these countries' currencies. For domestic importers, the import of considerably cheaper goods from abroad paid off; for importers in other countries imports from countries with overvalued currencies was too expensive and thus less attractive. And the export of capital from countries with overvalued currencies increased constantly since other currencies could be purchased cheaply and used advantageously in making foreign investments. As a result of this capital export surplus, the economic passivity of the balance of payments increased even more rapidly than the balance of trade, although from an accounting perspective every balance of payments appeared to be equalized.

The implementation of flexible exchange rates thus led necessarily to devaluation of these currencies. An equilibriated balance of payments or, in particular, balance of trade nevertheless remained more difficult to achieve and took some time. Over the longer term, import surpluses usually led to a rise in the living standard of the countries concerned that was more rapid than warranted by the productivity of their labor. Whether import surpluses are paid for by long-term credits or by foreign exchange and gold from diminishing reserves, the presence of these import surpluses always means that the country concerned will for a time live beyond its actual productive means. In overcoming this reality under new conditions of flexible exchange rates, it is often difficult in the short run to lower imports and along with them the standard of living to which people have become accustomed. But the necessary growth in exports is retarded by excessively high wage costs and the resulting limited competitiveness of goods in many foreign markets.

There are, however, causes of passive balances of payments which cannot be eliminated by flexible exchange rates. Such causes include, first of all, those related to an excessively low level of industrial development in the Third World. Here exports often cannot be increased sufficiently because their industrial base is too weak and their volume of exports too narrow. Given an often limited range of exports, especially of countries with monocultures, the flexibility of these countries in times of low or declining demand is too narrow given their limited number of export goods and their susceptibility to price fluctuations is too great. But political pressure for accelerated industrialization and rising standards of living for the people require increased imports which often can be paid for only with credit or economic aid.

Imports of finance capital can help to equalize the passive balance of payments of developing countries if they represent an inflow of foreign currency earmarked for certain purposes in the developing country, for instance for construction, floating capital (wage payments, purchase of domestic materials, etc.). Capital utilized for the purchase of foreign machines or which enters the developing country directly in the form of these machines, does not help directly to improve the balance of payments, but may do so indirectly by increasing exports. In the long term, however, this importation of capital can only contribute to the equalization of the balance of payments if the exports generated by capital imports, and the proceeds from them, are greater than the imports required for their production plus capital transfers (transfer of profits, tax write-offs, etc.), that is, monies flowing abroad deriving from the capital imports. In the present context we are, of course, dealing with the balance of payments and abstracting from the other economic and political implications of the importation of capital into developing countries.

We have mentioned only the special problems of developing countries relating to balance of payments in connection with our reflections about the causes of passive balances of payments. But these problems will not be pursued any further, since our entire conception of reform is oriented to industrially developed countries. Therefore the special problems of the developing countries cannot be solved now. If however, we are concerned with planning the equalization of balances of payments as a precondition for the establishment of equilibrium in reformed national economies of industrialized countries, we have to indicate the causes of passive balances of payment in the East bloc states. One important indicator that their economic systems are in need of reform is the very fact that most of these countries rely on long-term credits from Western industrial countries and, moreover, are able to prevent an even more passive balance of trade only by means of extraordinarily huge losses incurred at the expense of their own populations.

If we disregard partial reforms in the organization of foreign economic relations of some East bloc states (for example, of Hungary, or minor ones of the GDR, etc.) and consider instead the foreign economic relations of the classical socialist system, which still exists in the Soviet Union, we will note the same losses in efficiency that are characteristic of domestic relations. Due to lack of interest on the part of state foreign trade organizations and enterprises engaged in production in the aims of achieving maximum efficiency in their foreign trade relations, and because of their contempt for market prices, competition, and converti-

bility of currency, these trade relations continually result
in substantial losses.   Exports of industrial products in
particular increasingly suffer relative price losses in Western markets.   This results, first of all, from their structural, qualitative, and innovative backwardness; second,
from a low level of interest, bureaucratic rigidity, and im-
mobility of the sales agencies; and, third, from inadequate
packaging, lack of spare parts, inadequate services, poor
advertising, and much more.   In light of all these shortcomings, export trade can function only when promoted by
markedly low prices which, when the relatively high costs
of production are taken into account, are often well below
cost and thus represent pure losses.

But unnecessarily high prices are also often paid for
with imports from the West.   Lack of competition among im-
porters--import trade is carried out by absolutely monopolistic foreign trade organizations in each branch--and the
same bureaucratic disinterest in the relationship between
price and utility of the imported products frequently leads
to import prices that are excessively high when compared
with their own export prices.   The East bloc states are
constantly afflicted by declining terms of trade which, however, are difficult to discover since the calculations that go
into them are not officially published.   These losses cannot
be calculated from the outside in light of rigid, non-economic exchange rates, of non-comparable use-value exchange, and of completely different price relations in East
and West.   But they are obvious to all experts in the East
bloc states and partially ascertainable--though with some
gaps--from rising state subsidies to the foreign trade organizations, which are not separately published either.

Deteriorating terms of trade mean that from year to
year larger quantities of some products (with the exception
of exported raw materials, oil, natural gas, etc.) have to
be exported in exchange for a given quantity of required
imports from the West.   If the same quantity of certain
products were always exported, imports would decline in
absolute terms from year to year.   If then the quantity of
imports were to remain constant, a growing deficit in the
balance of trade would result due to the price.   This could
be offset only by resorting to reserves of gold and foreign
currency as well as by increasing debts.   All this applies
to most East bloc states, since, despite increased exports,
produced at a loss to reduce the deficit, the gap in their
foreign trade balance remains.

The foreign trade organizations, which buy increasing
quantities of export goods from domestic production enterprises at domestic prices can, to be sure, re-sell some of
the comparatively decreased quantities of imported goods at
home for higher prices.   But to some extent they have to

calculate constant, administratively determined prices for these. Relatively increasing quantities of exported goods, exchanged for constant quantities of imported goods, both calculated at constant domestic prices (though only for part of the imports), leads to deficits for the foreign trade organizations, deficits which then have to be offset by government subsidies. De facto rising prices of many imports and growing subsidies for foreign trade deficits mean increasing losses to the people, who of course must in the end bear the burden of every loss of efficiency.

In this manner, very large deficits accumulate in the balances of payments or trade of the East bloc states. Sometimes these become visible in the form of increasing credits (and in the case of the Soviet Union, outflows of gold). Sometimes, however, they are concealed by exports sold at a loss which are carried out at the expense of the real income of the local population. It is obvious that in light of this constantly increasing passive trade balance, foreign exchange cannot be freely sold but must be administratively allocated. This foreign exchange is allocated to foreign trade organizations in conformity with administratively established import plans. This very often--when export goals are not met (due to insufficient foreign exchange proceeds)--leads to cutbacks in planned allocations.

A planned equalization of the balance of payments in the new system would therefore require, first and foremost, an adjustment of imports to forecast export opportunities. The relative decline in imports which will be necessary in some countries will be facilitated by a corresponding adjustment of the development of incomes to production supplies actually available. The same would apply to countries requiring higher imports which would be able to obtain these more easily by stepping up incomes for consumption. If, as a result of income regulation, global demand for goods from domestic production (minus exports plus imports) were always to correspond to predicted supply, and if the same could be achieved for incomes from investment, it would not be a difficult economic problem to use the market mechanism structurally to harmonize supply and demand. But the prerequisite of export-import equalization is that exchange rates should react flexibly and rapidly to differences developing in the balance of trade and balance of payments. In any case, limitation of import or export surpluses as well as capital outflows and inflows that are out of equilibrium by market means, using flexible exchange rates, is to be regarded more positively than any kind of administrative control on foreign exchange. Such limiting measures would be used only in the most essential, extraordinary circumstances, arising for the most part in the wake of extraordinary political events, that is, in situations in which changes in the exchange rate are no longer of any avail.

PERIODIZATION OF THE MACRO-PLANS

We have by now dealt with the most important distribution and redistribution processes. It should thus be clear that these processes can not only be translated into the necessary statistical categories, but can also be planned or relatively reliably forecast in terms of several alternatives. Even where actual developments deviate from forecasts, these would be rapidly detectable so that the necessary correctives could be made to other planned distribution processes in order to forestall possible macro-disruptions. This would require that planning be understood as an ongoing activity including constant confrontation between the actual development of the economy and the goals of planning, as well as the continuous modification of the plans whenever necessary. This brings us to the temporal organization and periodization of planning, to the realization of the planned goals by means of economic policy, and to the possibility of economic development deviating from the plans and to possible ways of correcting these plans.

Up to this point, we have been concentrating on middle-range planning which--on the basis of all experience and knowledge to date--is intended to operate for a period of four or five years. This is a period which allows for reliable predictions of the quantitative and qualitative development of production. This is the period planned for by the enterprises in terms of most of their investments, technical innovations, structural changes, product innovations, etc. It is, therefore, also possible to make relatively reliable forecasts for this period of additional amounts of capital and labor required as well as of anticipated changes in capital and labor productivity in the individual branches and in the production process as a whole.

During this period of time, however, many important changes in the macro-structure of consumption or quality of life can also be prepared or carried out. Changes in the proportions between total private and social consumption, and among individual sectors of the public service will also take place during such a period, not only by means of corresponding changes in the structure of investment in production but also perhaps by means of differentiated expansion of buildings and institutions of public services.

Within a period of roughly five years, however, the additional specialists and university graduates needed for the expansion of particular sectors of production or services can be trained. And general reductions in working hours, along with changes in the rhythm of production, logistics, transportation, etc. which they would necessitate, would also require about this length of time.

Five years, therefore, represents the approximate period of time during which many important changes in the structure of production and services, as well as consumption take place. These structural changes have a decisive influence on the quality of people's lives. Not only will they appear as the goal of middle-range planning; they must also be assured by means of the planned distribution processes, that is, by changes in the amounts and structures of income. A relatively reliably predictable growth in the gross and net product is assured, in this period, by the necessary amount of investment that results from the planned distribution of gross profits as a guaranteed amount. It is also covered by the forecast increase in the labor force and the planned development of education and training. Planned wage increases, profit-sharing, consumption shares from private profits, state revenues and expenditures, and regulated consumption and investment credits will give rise to those residual income groups corresponding to the forecast macro-production groups and make possible the desired changes in the structure of consumption.

Five years is thus a period of sufficient length to implement important changes in the development of the economy and life. Yet it is not so long as to make forecasts mere conjectures. Just as in the domain of production, many changes will be prepared and implemented during this period, so must society also be able to foresee these changes in their overall context and to pursue them consciously. Yet this period is not long enough to effect larger and more fundamental changes in society. Preparations for many such changes must begin ten to twenty years beforehand if they are to be realized without great losses or in order to avoid chaotic conditions.

If for instance society desires to maintain the necessary supply of energy given a certain rate of population growth and given the objective needs and level of production determined by this supply, it must predict the development of disposable energy resources for decades to come and, when facing the prospect of their depletion, take appropriate measures in good time. However, such measures must be decided upon at least fifteen to twenty years before they are needed. To be sure, there are plenty of analyses of existing energy resources and their development. What is missing, however, is an opportunity for the entire population to choose democratically from among several alternative solutions. This decision must be made on the basis of an awareness of all important and nowadays predictable consequences of various alternative solutions.

The evaluation of all important interrelationships and consequences can no longer be the preserve of relatively small groups of scholars. It will now require large groups organized at the center in which specialists from all important areas of life are provided with all necessary data, facts, and opportunities to acquire information. They will have to carry out evaluations not only of usable substitute sources of energy but also of the probable costs of obtaining them, their effects on health and the environment, and their dependence on other large-scale economic and social processes. Other solutions would have to be seriously considered, such as a somewhat reduced population, changes in needs, transformation in the processes of distribution, etc. Needless to say, such considerations would have to stay close to reality rather than turning into wish-dreams.

From such analyses and determinations of the important interrelationships--and in no other way--could proposals for alternative solutions emerge relating to economic and social consequences, advantages and disadvantages. Yet even such thorough and comprehensive analyses of a particular area would not be sufficient to make a well-grounded and responsible decision. Since the development of energy might, for instance, be fundamentally tied to growth in regional production, the development of the transportation system, the growth of cities and agglomerations, extensive changes in the landscape (river diversions, canal construction, lake creations, etc.) which for their part could be prepared for and carried over at least as long a period. If fundamental change in all imaginable areas of human life were considered to be necessary, none of these could be analyzed and decided upon independently of the others. They would all have to be taken within the given context, recognizing their mutual interdependence. Also, first and foremost, the costs of their complexity cannot be ignored.

Where such complex analyses and evaluations of future changes are not available, but where the people gradually become aware of the need for them, the result is insecurity, anxieties, and tensions, and along with them, emotionally colored exaggeration and action. Anxiety then begins to gain the upper hand. Studies will be to no avail, whether carried out by individual scholars or small teams, ad hoc commissions of political parties, or even ministerially appointed groups of experts to provide a background for government literature prepared for political purposes. There can be no broadly considered and evaluated future to the problems of the future as long as solutions and limitations on information, knowledge, confrontation of interests, and linkage to actual practice--inevitable even for innovative small teams of scientists--result in uncertainty about the future, or where solutions to weighty problems looming on the horizon have to be subordinated to the needs of momentary popularity and transitory political coalitions. Thus the bases for mistrust and demagoguery will remain.

The many warnings of serious scholars about the future, initiatives of concerned citizens, and appeals for moderation of individual heads of state and prominent party members can only be regarded as evidence of the growing necessity for democratic, complex, long-term programs in the industrial states. Neither individual scholars, whatever their scholarly talents, nor ruling political elites, and certainly not anonymous bureaucratic apparatuses are competent to make determinations regarding vital future developments. This is the case since when such decisions are made, (which of course involve a certain amount of uncertainty and error) only the population as a whole can assume responsibility and must make its decisions democratically from among alternatives. Even though this may not reduce the possibility of mistakes, but rather may even increase it, the people must have the opportunity to learn from their mistakes and experiences and thus avoid faulty decisions.

As with middle-range planning, long-term projects for the most important spheres of technical, economic, and social life would also be developed by individual commissions made up of specialists of different opinions and interests. The number of such commissions would be considerably smaller than for middle-range planning, since the number of technical-economic domains whose development would have to be worked out and realized in the long term is also much smaller. Thus, it would probably be necessary to have commissions to work out the following long-term programs:

(1) development of energy resources
(2) new means of transportation
(3) urban development
(4) environment
(5) regional development
(6) exploration of space.

Experience would show which additional areas would require the working out of long-term programs. In order to coordinate the work of individual commissions and programs with each other and to ensure mutual agreement among them, a superior, synthesizing commission would be needed to execute the complex long-term program. Two or three alternative versions of this long-term program would be planned in order to give the people the opportunity to make a democratic choice. These two or three alternative versions of the overall, long-term program could be distinguished by different, mutually interrelated alternatives in each individual area, or merely by different developments of one or two areas.

A chronological linkage between decision-making with regard to the long-term program and the choice of a mid-

dle-range plan, and political elections could be established.
There is a tension between the need for a consistent, una-
bridged long-term and middle-term developmental outlook,
and the need to allow the people to decide democratically
about what this outlook should be, a tension which would
have to be resolved by narrowing the outlook. In order to
make sure that both a 15-year and a five-year projection
would always be possible, it would be best to prepare a
new initial year annually for both the long-term program
and the middle-range plan. If this is not done, the pas-
sage of a year would shorten the long-term outlook to 14
years and the middle-range outlook to four years; one year
later it would be down to 13 and three years respectively.
This narrowing outlook might, nevertheless, have to be
taken into account, since it would be difficult for the people to make decisions each year concerning extension of the
plans and program for a further year.

In our opinion, however, a sacrifice of democratic decision-making would be more serious than the lack of a projection for a few years. Without a referendum on the
course of the development, there would be no real voluntary support for the government's planned economic policy,
a policy which of course would contain measures that would
not be popular among all groups in society. Without democratically conducted referenda there would be no control
over the correspondence between the aims contained in the
plan and government policies, no process of learning from
experience on the part of the people, no self-determination
for nations and people. Simply to transfer responsibility
for decision-making to parliament would already amount to
alienation of the population from the entire planning process
and would conjure up the danger that the aims contained in
the plan will be influenced by small but strong groups.
There can be some hope for success of planned economic
policy only if it is preceded by broad public discussion
promoted by all the mass media, if political parties and
groups advocate clear alternatives, if opinions and counter-
opinions are confronted, and if the people can make a majority decision, in free elections, in favor of one alternative
and its proponents.

A loss of outlook could be tolerable under the following
circumstances. Let us assume that the long-term program
is for 15 years. The middle-range five-year plans must be
viewed as embodiments of the long-term programs, though
their substance will of course be broader and more complex.
Long-term decisions to change, for example, the transportation system, cannot be made outside the context of the
five-year plan. They must be incorporated into it to the
extent that the planned creation of residual incomes ensures
the development of investments in production and a classifi-

cation of state revenues and expenditures with which the specific tasks of changing the transportation system can be realized in the coming five years. The process of concretization would still allow for the possibility of various kinds of diversification in detail. Thus, if a long-term program for changing the transportation system were to be accepted, it would necessarily be carried out in terms of basic, general contours. Naturally, this would not preclude various specific changes, and hence diversification in the several alternative plans, for instance in the speed of construction, in technical innovation, in aesthetical forms, etc.

A new five-year plan would always have to be adopted at least two years prior to the expiration of the preceding five-year plan. During the third year of the current five-year plan, a projection of only two more years would remain. Given the proposed contents of the plan, however, this would not be as serious in its consequences as in the dirigiste planning of the East bloc states, where the experience so far has been that the new five-year plan has not even been adopted until the fifth year of the current plan, or indeed, often after its expiration. Therefore, of course, enterprises have an increasingly short-range outlook in the final years of the current plan, and in the fifth year they have virtually no idea of what to expect in the next few years.

Such a lack of outlook is naturally devastating. Although it gives rise to significant losses, it cannot be altered as long as the development of production and investment is governed exclusively by the central plan in a dirigiste manner. The extraordinarily wide gap between production planning and the actual development of production makes it quite impossible to prepare any kind of plan a number of years in advance of the expiration of the preceding plan, since the planning agency cannot reliably predict the actual state of production at the end of the five-year plan, even though that actual state of production must be the basis for further development of production. Since the five-year plans deviate increasingly from actual developments from one year to the next, this kind of planning has to resort increasingly to dirigiste one-year plans, thus entailing disastrous losses in perspective.

With macro-economic distribution planning, it should, however, be possible to submit a new five-year plan two years before the end of the current one. This would ensure that enterprises would not face an uncertain future in the present-day market economy. Nowadays enterprises do not know what kind of wage and profit increases they will have to deal with in a few years, how the market will grow, and what kinds of investments they will require. Their estimates, which are based on past developmental trends, are so unreliable that they are hardly more than pure speculation. If each new five-year plan, two years prior to the end of the one preceding it, were to establish firmly the future growth of wages on the basis of the predicted increase in the gross and net product, as well as determining state revenues and expenditures, the enterprises could predict the future market in good time and yet reliably to a degree never attainable in the past. This would also reduce the risks entailed in their investment activities, which would at the same time retrospectively make the planning of investment needs in the macro-plan more precise.

Moreover, since production forecasts would be much more reliable for years beforehand, in light of the planned assurance of the continuous development of incomes and the market, the approximate state of production at the end of the fifth year could be predicted as early as the first or second year of the current five-year plan. Since, as already noted, the enterprises would have to make preparations for technological changes in production many years in advance, the growth in production for the subsequent five-year plan, with its investment and labor requirements, could be predicted at that time.

It would be even easier, at that time, to make decisions regarding potential and desirable growth in private and social consumption and thus the distribution and redistribution processes. In this way, the future security of the enterprises would be substantially increased, even though in the third year of the plan would only be a plan outlook of two years. The attempt to achieve continuity of development, which would involve beginning work on the new five-year plan right from the start of the current five-year plan, would in itself constantly improve the enterprises' prospects and increase their security.

And finally, the existence and further development of a long-term program on an ongoing basis would have similar effects. It too would have to be worked on constantly. When a new five-year plan is submitted for democratic choice, decisions would be made concerning a possible extension of the long-term program for another five years. Any extension of this kind would naturally be based on the most current findings and experiences from technical and social developments and would be incorporated into the program proposals. Significant new findings could lead to the scrapping of current long-term projects. To be sure, any basic changes in long-term programs worked out earlier would necessarily have to be justified by costs-benefit analysis. This would indicate which projects, buildings, and other works already begun would be sacrificed if the long-term program were to be changed or at least modified. It would also show how such changes would effect increased

costs and whether these could really result in gains in the
light of estimated increased benefits. Naturally, in this regard, the people could be asked to choose from among conflicting alternatives.

At the end of the first three years of each five-year
plan, the people could be presented with a choice among alternative new five-year plans, as well as alternatives for
continuation of the long-term program (for five years). Tying this choice to political elections would mean that the
people's representatives in parliament would be selected at
the same time as the alternative five-year plan advocated by
the winning party or party coalition. The government
formed by this party or party coalition would have an obli-
gation to attempt to realize the goals of the plan by means
of an economic policy which would already be basically predetermined by the plan. The government would have to
have an economic council--perhaps confirmed in office by
parliament--at its disposal for the actual organization of economic policy measures, for a constant confrontation of the
actual development of the economy with the aims of the
plan, in order to make minor changes in some measures,
and to organize all ongoing operations under the plan, as
well as new operations which would always be starting up.

The economic council, which would be responsible for
organizing the planning process, would also have the responsibility of organizing the planning commissions which
would be necessary. In order for these commissions to be
assured of both an accumulation of experience and an inflow
of new ideas and concepts, an attempt must be made to ro-
tate the commission members so that half the members would
change after each five-year plan. Political parties, established mass organizations, and cultural associations should
send their delegates to these planning commissions in accordance with an established formula. Aside from this there
should also be some role for the representatives of smaller
initiative groups that emerge as a result of significant new
proposals for development. In this way, the planning commissions would tie the initiative which is being fostered on
the part of the people through their direct representatives
to the initiatives of politicians through the government and
economic council.

MACRO-PLANS AND ECONOMIC POLICY

The specifications of the distributive macro-plans alone indicate that basically they should be realized only by means of market-conforming instruments of economic policy deployed by the government or its economic council. Only in the area of state-financed services would investments be structurally determined by the fact that funds for invest-ment-building will be divided among individual sectors, which, for their part will have binding quantitative and qualitative tasks directly assigned to them. In this man-ner, most of the developments envisioned in the long-term programs will be assured. However, no investment or pro-duction tasks will be assigned to the economic enterprises, and their decision-making will be oriented to assumptions about the development of the market, the consumption-re-lated aims of the published macro-plans and the planned ec-onomic policy measures of government (as contained in these macro-plans).

The economic policy of the state, which is crucial to the macro-plans, is made up, in particular, of:

1. wage policy,
2. profit-sharing policy,
3. entrepreneurial profit policy,
4. fiscal policy,
5. credit policy,
6. currency policy.

All these are actually power-political acts of will aimed at achieving certain quantitative results of economic pro-cesses. The objects of these policies are primarily distri-bution and redistribution processes whose quantitative un-folding in the macro-plans has already been laid down and the execution of which must be guaranteed by the govern-ment or economic council by means of binding and controlled regulations and directives. We have already dealt with these distribution and redistribution processes and will re-view them here only briefly as objects of economic policy.

Wage policy must ensure the planned growth of average wages as provided for in the plans for each of the years of the five-year plan. This presupposes that the working people have been properly classified into wage categories corresponding to the actual work they do, and that pre-scribed wage differentials are adhered to. The wage scales worked out by the trade unions for the individual branch-es, together with the wage increases proposed by the plan-ning commission (perhaps after negotiated modifications) and integrated into the macro-plan, would thus be the basis for a binding government wage policy. It will then be in the trade union's own interest to adhere to these wage scales and regulations. The controls may thus be implemented by the trade unions rather than by state authorities.

In any case, a balanced development of the economy would require that wage regulations be adhered to, inasmuch as possible deviations for them within individual enterprises will require state intervention if they cannot be remedied by trade union demands and criticisms. In any event, a scarcity of labor could not be used to justify a departure from wage scales. Such shortages would usually be taken into account, by the general trade union commission, now representing not only wage earners but now co-owners of capital as well, who have an interest in market conformity and they would be built into the wage differentials established by the commission.

Regional differences in labor scarcity would also be taken into account by means of differential supplements or deductions incorporated into wage scales. Frequently recurring shortages would have to be recorded on an ongoing basis and lead to modifications in the wage scales which could be announced every year. The market mechanism would thus have an immediate effect. Arbitrary deviations within individual enterprises, must not, however, be allowed to occur, since this would undermine the wage discipline necessary for wages related to performance and equilibrium. If the trade unions are unable to adhere to wage regulations within individual enterprises, the state would be compelled to use fiscal means to tax away that portion of wages exceeding the normal level.

Since the prevailing trade union majority will have an interest in adhering to wage scales, the trade unions themselves could relatively easily uncover any attempts to subvert the pay scales (faulty classification into work categories, artificially low rates for piecework, etc.).

Profit-sharing policy will have to guarantee that profit-sharing by all co-workers in the enterprises is maintained in accordance with the profit-sharing coefficients and calculation formulas stipulated in the macro-plans. This makes it necessary to calculate profits within the enterprises uniformly by means of appropriate regulations to record them, convert them to statistics, and to exercise control over them. It is indispensable that the development of profits be visible to all. Indeed, the co-workers in the enterprises will insist on this. All kinds of potential concealment of profits must and can be revealed and thereby eliminated. This includes even tax write-offs of investment funds provided for by law.

Depending on the average life of the various objects of production, the regulations governing tax write-offs wil contain differential but binding depreciation coefficients.

An enterprise will have to adhere to these norms for depreciation irrespective of how long it makes use of some particular means of production or how soon it phases it out. If an enterprise wants to make more rapid technical progress by replacing its machines or other objects with new ones before the old ones are completely depreciated, it will have to finance this new investment (over and above the insufficient depreciation allowance) from out of profits. In this way, first of all, any attempts to conceal actual profits through higher depreciation will be avoided, and second, any inflationary cost increases will be prevented. Although technical progress will not be retarded in this case, it will no longer be possible for it to take place at the expense of consumers. Much like the classification of working people in accordance with scales of wages and benefits, the various means of production will be classified into depreciation categories, making it relatively easier to control how records of their depreciation are maintained.

The emergence of co-worker enterprises or capital-sharing can substantially reduce, if not completely prevent, the often-mentioned practices of multinational concerns of suppressing profits in certain countries in order to evade taxes and effecting de facto illegal capital transfers. The most frequently used method of profit-suppression is the manipulation of the accounting prices used between the parent company and its affiliates or branch plants in different countries. The delivery of semi-finished goods, etc. from one branch to another is billed at prices that are much lower than current market prices. Given the great complexity of relations within these concerns, it is very difficult to control this from the outside. In this way, the supplier enterprise lowers its prices while the receiver, given its relatively low costs and the fact that it sells the finished products at market prices (moreover, often at monopoly prices), realizes very high profits. If the concerns want to suppress these profits again, they can claim excessively high tax write-offs. The end result is an excessive development of investment and capital in the target country to the detriment of profits and development of capital in the country from which capital transfer is made.

Such practices often lead to tensions between governments and multinational concerns. They are very difficult to uncover from the outside. But if the co-workers within these firms had an interest in profit-sharing, this could lead to a more effective control from within, since the manipulation of profits downwards would also lower the profit shares of co-workers. In any case, to prevent such practices once and for all, it would be necessary to establish legally binding regulations fixing internal accounting prices within concerns--a subject which we will deal with later.

Adherence to such regulations could then be relatively easily controlled from within.

In co-worker enterprises the alienated profit interest beyond the enterprise that today exists at the centers of multinational concerns would disappear. Even the top managers of the central authorities, who are charged with the exercise of joint technical-economic tasks for the concern, would not be able to exercise definitive control over capital. Their profit-sharing would be contingent upon the demonstrated profits derived from the prices of their particular services. Every transfer of capital from one country to another would have to be made public and would take the form of long-term or indefinite credits for new ventures subject to approval by the supervisory councils. Movement of capital would thus not be out of the question, since it would bring larger profit shares to the co-workers from interest on venture capital and from profits thus enhanced. But it would not, first of all, establish ownership of the new enterprises concentrated in the hands of the suppliers of capital and would thus not lead to any accumulation of power (for example, in the developing countries) in the hands of the multinational firms. And second, it would only take place with the consent of the co-workers and the states affected.

If actual profits were openly and formally registered, then performance-motivated profit-sharing by all co-workers in market enterprises would be guaranteed by means of the above mentioned formula. If profits were laid out in this way, remaining amounts of private entrepreneurial profits-- required for consumption and hence an incentive to the entrepreneur--would be assured politically.

This brings us to entrepreneurial profit policy. As we have already shown, these profits will be determined by plan, (1) by establishing maximum amounts of net entrepreneurial profits (after deduction of taxes and co-worker profit-sharing) which cannot be used to form neutralized capital; (2) by determining the coefficient which defines the development of neutralized capital from profit surpluses (above and beyond net entrepreneurial profit); (3) by instituting tax relief for excessively low profits which, after payment of profit-shares, would leave a low and insufficiently motivating net entrepreneurial profit. These three measures will have to be incorporated globally into the macro-plan, including the total sum to be added to net entrepreneurial profits in the form of tax relief. Concrete tax reductions, along with the control of the development of net profits would, however, belong to the economic policy activities of the government or economic council.

Fiscal policy would have the function of fixing and assuring state revenues and expenditures as determined by

plan. The relatively long-term tax system would be taken
as given in the plan, and tax revenues and other state
revenues globally planned on this basis. It would be the
task of fiscal policy, first, to establish a long-term taxation
system and, second, to fix and assure planned overall state
revenues in the short run while maintaining the planned
overall taxation of wages and profits in doing so. At the
same time, the planned classification of personnel and material expenditures, as well as other planned government
expenditures, in accordance with the individual service sectors, must be adhered to.

There would be a change in the tax system only if the
structure of incomes should change substantially and each
revision would remain in force for an extended period of
time. Progressive income taxes will be necessary so long as
rapidly increasing incomes, independent of the market, can
be earned by independent professionals (doctors, lawyers,
artists), incomes not affected either by the tax on entrepreneurial profits or by the monopoly tax. A uniform rate
of income tax could be imposed wherever possible to guarantee a differentiation of all income groups in accordance
with their performance. The tax on profits must, however,
be retained, even given a uniform tax rate, since profits
develop differently under the influence of the market
mechanism. At the same time, along with this, indirect
taxes can take on increasing significance. A monopoly tax
would be needed when profit differentials reflect not only
differences in performance but also, in the form of excessive profits, represent monopolistic domination of production
and the market. Tax relief for private profits will be required where the implementation of profit-sharing for co-
workers results in residual profits too small to provide incentive to entrepreneurs. The political decision to adopt
these various tax reforms, their proportions, their differentiated development, etc. all belong to the fiscal policy of
the government.

Credit policy would have the task of seeing to it that
the development of credits tied to savings, the movement of
the discount rate, and the productive supply of state credits are all maintained. If the granting of credits in the
banking system as a whole is ensured in relation to credit
repayment and formation of net savings in accordance with
the various income utilization groups, then inflation can be
prevented. A central role in the process will have to be
played by the central state bank, which will now have to
concentrate more heavily on a balanced development of
credits and will not be able to rely solely upon regulation
of minimum reserves. Control of the money supply cannot
be ignored either, since increases and decreases in hoarding (cash build-ups) can contribute to unbalanced income

formation. It follows from this that it is not chance variation in hoarding of cash, but rather an unbalanced development of distribution and redistribution processes which would be regarded as the main cause of periodic and long lasting macro-economic disruptions. For this reason, the banks will have to pay special attention to the regulation of redistribution.

Changes in the discount rate will continue to be made by the state bank in the sense of credit supply and demand. Forecasts of the formation of and demand for credit derived from production forecasts will make possible a more rapid recognition of disparities between the amount of credit required and the development of savings. The discount rate should therefore react more flexibly to all disparities. Fluctuations in the discount rate could be more flexible, but, assuming continuous economic development, they would stay within a substantially narrower range and thus without severe fluctuations. With a general spread of co-worker enterprises replacing stock companies, the absolute average amount of the discount rate could decline substantially in the more distant future in contrast with the situation in the past. But its total elimination cannot be envisaged for as long as the market mechanism has to continue to function, and this will be a very long time.

The issuance of government bonds will continue to play an economic role. There will always be a market for government bonds as long as state credits on the one hand, and long-term, fixed-rate monetary investments on the other hand, are necessary for development of the economy. In fact, in the possible event of limitation on, or abolition of the system of stock ownership in the more distant future, the significance of government bonds should increase. The state bank in particular will have to ensure that all government credits involving an increase in the volume of government bonds are offset by correspondingly reduced credits on the part of commercial banks. The significance of the open market policy would decrease with a continuous, non-cyclical development of the economy. This would not, however, mean its total elimination, since unexpected deviations in the circulation and hoarding of money cannot be ruled out, and in such cases the open market policy can be used as a relatively rapidly working instrument of equalization.

Currency policy will have the primary task of protecting the reformed system within the country against economic disruptions from abroad. The adaptation of imports required to deal with unanticipated changes in exports as well as changes in capital inflow or outflow can be accomplished quite effectively by revaluing the currency upwards or downwards. Decreases in exports require flexibility in the devaluation of currency to help slow imports and foster exports. Upward revaluation, on the other hand, is used when exports increase excessively and/or imports are inadequate. In certain countries and situations, however, the flow of capital from and to the outside can conflict with the currency valuation that is necessary. Excessive capital inflow can hinder or prevent a needed currency devaluation, and a needed upward revaluation of the currency can be blocked by excessive capital outflow. In such situations, changes in the exchange rate do not suffice and additional measures have to be taken (restraining capital inflow or outflow by means ranging from economic to administrative measures). Here again, a forecast, well-balanced balance of payments will make it easier to control the actual development of this balance and to use effective methods flexibly to combat disequilibria.

Economic policy should naturally not only seek to safeguard the processes of distribution and redistribution established by plan, to bring about its realization; it should also constantly compare the actual development of the economy with the expectations of the plan on the one hand, and corresponding changes in the means used to achieve planned goals on the other hand. Actual development would have to be determined statistically on as short-term a basis as possible, at the very least semi-annually but on a quarterly basis for the most important data, if possible. We have already mentioned in several places, changes in economic policy as compared with its planned development. Now we will point out some further possible deviations of actual planned development, as well as the changes in economic policy which they would make necessary:

1) Productivity in production rises more slowly than foreseen. Both gross and net production, and hence national income as well, are less than had been forecast at a particular point in time. This would automatically lead to a contradiction of profits and thus smaller profit shares. Should the decline in consumption which goes along with this not be sufficient, then wages would have to increase more slowly than foreseen in the original plan. The decisive criterion would be actual growth registered in the production of consumer goods.

2) Productivity rises more rapidly than predicted. In this case, profits and profit shares would also grow more rapidly than anticipated. Should it prove necessary to step up consumption more than investments because a rapid rate of growth is no longer desired, wage increases would have to grow. This could even be linked to an acceleration of growth (I) of consumer goods production, (II) vis-a-vis production of the means of production. The wage quota (including profit-sharing) would increase in this case.

3) Savings from out of wages grow more rapidly than foreseen. Because of lower interest rates, consumer credit should automatically expand accordingly. In particular, long-term consumer credit (mortgage credit) should expand more rapidly, and would be followed by an increase in construction (single-family homes, better apartments, etc.). If credits for consumption cannot be sufficiently increased, either the lowest wage categories will have to increase more rapidly (leveling) or more rapidly increasing exports involving a corresponding increase in capital exports would have to be decided upon. The first would be an attempt to compensate for the gap in consumption by increases in the lowest wages (in comparison to II). The second would seek to export surplus of production by means of capital exports (economic aid and the like).

4) Savings from wages grow more slowly than foreseen. An appropriate contradiction of credit for purposes of consumption should suffice, and would be easy to accomplish in such cases. However, if demand for credit for consumption from production (credits for wages) were to continue to be greater than opportunities for credit, a slower growth in wages would have to be considered.

5) The savings of the enterprises increase more rapidly than expected. This would be a manifestation of the fact that production will have to be restructured to a greater extent than had been foreseen. Greater investment savings in certain branches would have to be offset by greater investment credits to other branches and by lowered interest rates. If, however, investment credits could not be increased, an accelerated growth in wages and a higher wage quota would have to be the aim.

6) The savings of the enterprises grow more slowly than had been assumed. In this case, investment credits would have to be decreased proportionally along with an increase in interest rates. If demand for investment credits subsequently remains greater than the availability of credit, a thorough analysis of actual investment needs would be required and would be carried out with the help of the production commission. If the commission finds that there is an actual shortage of investments in relation to the growth of consumption, then a slower increase in wages and a declining wage quota would have to be considered. But if such a rapid growth in production were not desired, then investment credits would have to be reduced by even higher interest rates.

7) Exports increase more slowly than expected. This would require the decrease in exports and/or decline in capital exports as already mentioned. Second, however, analysis of export reduction would have to be carried out with the help of the production commission. If the analysis shows that the reduction should be maintained over the longer term, then production would have to be rapidly re-structured. This could be accomplished either by tempo-rary, <u>one-time</u> shifts of credits for consumption to cheap investment credits (which would also reduce the demand for consumption to the extent of the required reduction in im-ports), or by means of governmental investment subsidies. The goal of the restructuring would be to create a substi-tute for reduced production, either for exports or for in-creasing domestic sales.

8) Exports increase more rapidly than had been pre-dicted. This requires a corresponding rise in imports in order to compensate for reduced supply on the domestic market. But if the increase in exports does not take place at the expense of the domestic market and if the increased incomes are transformed into growing savings, so that im-ports cannot be increased, then capital exports would have to be increased proportionally (in the form of economic aid and the likes).

Possibilities for deviation from the anticipated develop-ment of the economy are of course even more numerous. They cannot all be dealt with here. But a brief examina-tion of the most significant of them has demonstrated that, given the processes of distribution and redistribution es-tablished by plan, economic policy should be in a position to intervene quickly in the event of mistaken forecasts and to avoid more severe disruptions in the equilibrium. An essential precondition would, however, be an as up to date as possible or short-term statistical survey of all fundamen-tal economic processes and a rapid analysis of these.

This should be possible, without an overly large bu-reaucratic apparatus, using modern reporting techniques and information processing, with computer storage and clas-sification. Even classification of particular types of prod-ucts into the requisite macro-groups, along with the income (proceeds) subcategories and developments, could be real-ized using today's technology. The collection and evalua-tion of these data in a highly modern and qualified planning organization (which would serve to support both the plan-ning commission and the economic council--for planning and for modifications of economic policy) could be carried out at relatively low cost and still operate more efficiently than to-day's extensive bureaucratic organizations in the East and, increasingly, in the West as well.

The entire problem of the relationship between centralized and decentralized economic policy cannot be dealt with here in greater detail. We can only make the following basic observations which are important for an understanding of macro-planning. Macro-planning, as everyone knows, must encompass the entire national economy, since production, based on the division of labor, is spread out throughout the country. Moreover a significant portion of production has to go to satisfy foreign demand. It would therefore be desirable to develop a world system of macro-planning, although this is of course politically impossible. But even a macro-plan for the entire market of the European Community would be a great step forward. Unfortunately, at this time there are significant obstacles even to this. A planned maintenance of the development of an equilibrium of final incomes and production within the entire EEC could only benefit the people in this area. This would not necessarily mean restricting the national sovereignty of the individual peoples, since they would all be able to participate democratically in the top coordinating bodies, and in the preparation of joint alternative plans. To be sure, this would require the subordination of all states to a democratic choice of plan with the entire area of the EEC--something which seems unrealistic for the foreseeable future. But it would be extraordinarily advantageous if all states in the EEC could commit themselves to systemic reform, especially involving macro-planning of distribution. Even if each sovereign state had its own macro-plan, mutual coordination of economic development would be facilitated. At present, there is still a danger that the EEC, with its economies and systems, might drift apart somewhat.

In particular, however, if all members of the EEC -- who maintain extensive mutual foreign trade relations--were able to overcome cyclical developments, they would eliminate the danger of transferring crises from one country into another. Forecasts respecting foreign trade would become more reliable for all of them. And their mutual exchange rates would not have to be altered so often, which would facilitate the planning of production. On the strength of a development of this kind, a later transition to joint macro-planning in the entire EEC area would no longer seem so unrealistic.

Balanced development of the economy within a state can be ensured only if the regulations governing distribution and redistribution processes apply to the entire national economy. At the same time, however, the peculiarities of individual regions must be incorporated into the plan in advance. The recognition of these peculiarities is of course political in character. Therefore, special attention must be paid to formulation of the particular developmental requirements of individual regions (sub-states, autonomous regions, cantons, etc.). The representatives of such regions will come together in the previously mentioned regional subcommissions of the central quality-of-life commission, where the particular demands of individual regions will have to be confronted, implemented, and coordinated.

Peculiarities may have to do with a wide variety of distribution processes. But these should be understood only as a means of achieving an equalization of economic and living standard among the regions. This means that they can be considered as a means of accelerating the development of production and consumption in economically backward regions, or on the contrary as a way of bringing about slower growth and shifting industries into and out of overtaxed, overcrowded centers and regions. From this viewpoint, one might consider, for example, special wage supplements or allowing higher net entrepreneurial profits, cheaper credits, and/or more government investment subsidies in underdeveloped regions. In overindustrialized regions, special tax increases and the like would be conceivable. Each peculiarity would of course have to be estimated in advance and incorporated into the appropriate final income group in the national economy, in order not to jeopardize the equilibrium of the national economy.

The emphasis of regional economic policy would lie in the domain of government revenues and expenditures, just as it does today. Regional political agencies generally have the right to collect certain government revenues (special taxes, payments, fees) directly and/or to receive a percentage of central government revenues. Similarly, they can make decisions on their own responsibility concerning the utilization of these funds in certain areas. Such regional independence would be maintained or perhaps extended even further. As far as the development of equilibrium is concerned, the only important aspect would be that all these incomes and expenditures would be estimated according to the schema we have presented, namely according to primary and final income groups, and incorporated into the planned income groups in the national economy so as to ensure an equilibrium among them. While actual political decision-making can therefore be highly decentralized, the planned equilibrium of all final incomes (whether arising from centrally or decentrally decided redistribution processes) must be achieved centrally for the entire national economy, since all final incomes can be utilized for purchases in the total domestic market of a state.

5

THE REGULATED MARKET

MARX'S CONCEPTION OF THE MARKET UNDER SOCIALISM

Given the division of labor in advanced society, the satisfaction of economically limited needs requires market relationships. Those involved in the cooperative production of enterprises are willing to work for other consumers, who are strangers to them, on an ongoing basis, as long as this enables them to obtain all the products, services, and objects of need required for the satisfaction of their needs and which represent at least an equivalent amount of work on the part of the others. It is not only a matter of performing a certain amount of work. Rather, this amount has to provide an optimal utility for the other people with a minimal expenditure of labor and means of production.

Neither creation of use-value nor potential minimization of expenditures in society can, however, be measured and comprehended centrally. Neither can the development of use-value, technical progress, and the potentially increasing relative economies of labor, materials, and energy be centrally ensured. At the present stage of the development of work, these societal requirements in the invidual productive cooperative can only be realized by means of the market mechanism. But they are ignored in the Marxist theory and practice of the Soviet socialist economic system.

Marx's original notion that in the Communist system market relationships would already disappear at the initial, lower stage (nowadays called the "socialist" stage), with socialization of the means of production, has not been realized. Marx's ideas have, however, been negated by "socialist" practice in two respects and for two different reasons. First, they have been negated in a progressive way, that is on the basis of more recent, more accurate knowledge which has transcended Marx; and second, in a regressive way by the bureaucratic essence of the "socialist" system and its power-political aims. In order to explain this, it is necessary to reconstruct briefly Karl Marx's conceptions in two separate clusters of ideas.

First, in several places in "Capital," but mainly in his critique of the Gotha Program, Marx expresses unambiguously the conception that instead of an exchange of goods among private owners of the means of production, products (consumer goods) would be directly distributed by associated producers on the basis of common ownership of the means of production and solely according to work performance.[1] Products would no longer be commodities, since they would no longer be the fruits of private labor and hence only indirectly of social labor. Rather, they would be the result of work performed according to plan that would be directly social. The total amount of labor that a society would have to expend for production ("past labor" materialized in the means of production and living labor), would have to be distributed for the manufacture of individual products in such proportions that the quantity of the end product would suffice for anticipated social needs.[2] These products could then be distributed directly by means of social distribution agencies and certificates for work performed (purchase vouchers).

Second, Marx augments his conception of the elimination of the exchange of goods with a second basic idea: In the initial, lower stage of Communism ("Socialism") where labor has not yet become a primary vital need, but still remains a mere means of sustaining life,[3] consumer goods would be distributed among producers according to the amount of work they have done (and after deductions from their work for the social fund). Marx compares this form of distribution with the kind of production of goods in which the labor value of the goods would be established by the exchange of average (as the average tendency) equivalent value.[4] In contrast to this kind of goods production,

---

[1] Cf. Marx-Engels-Werke, 19 (Berlin, 1962), pp. 19-20; MEW 20 (Berlin, 1962), pp. 264-88; Karl Marx, Das Kapital, vol. 3 (Berlin, 1964), p. 859.

[2] "Only where production is subject to a genuine predetermined control by society does society establish a connection between the quantity of societal working time related to the production of certain articles, and the quantity of societal needs to be satisfied by these articles." Marx, Das Kapital, vol. 3 (Berlin: 1973), p. 197.

[3] "In a higher phase of Communist society . . . when labor is no longer just a means of making a living, but has itself become the primary life need. . . . " K. Marx, "Kritik des Gothaer Programms," ME Werke, vol. 19, p. 21.

[4] Cf. Marx, "Kritik des Gothaer Programms," p. 20.

in the lower phases of communism (phase 1), labor value (that is the socially requisite quantity of materialized and living labor of differing quality, translated into time for simple work) would be directly calculated in advance for individual products. At the same time, each individual worker's amount of work would be registered[5] and in proportion to it--after deductions--each would be able to take consumer goods representing an equivalent amount of work from available supplies. Deductions from the work output of each individual would serve to provide for the needs of society as a whole: Replacement and expansion of production funds, reserves, costs of administration, educational and health needs, funds to provide for those incapable of working, etc.

These are in essence Marx's conceptions, which, in addition to eliminating all market relationships, place primary stress on the labor-equivalent distribution of consumer goods at the lower stages of Communism.

"Socialist" development in practice shows, above all, that elimination of the categories commodities and of money is impossible. While Lenin was still able to justify the continued existence of market relationships due to the existence of small private agricultural producers, Stalin formally had to retain market relationships, and they have continued to in their formal existence to the present day.

It has proven unfeasible to calculate the value of labor directly. Only by means of money and prices has the distribution of products among consumers been able to function at all. The term "formal market relationships" is supposed to mean that although products are bought and sold for money and at certain prices, the function of the market mechanism has, nevertheless, been eliminated. Before we go into the problems bound up with the market mechanism, we will demonstrate how the bureaucratic practices of "socialism" represent a regressive departure from Marx's ideas.

Although market relationships still prove to be necessary (though not only in the formal manner just described) and although we will show later on why Marx's notions of eliminating the market were oversimplified and unrealistic, it should be stressed that his idea of distributing consumer

---

[5] "Secondly, after abolition of the capitalist mode of production, yet retaining social production, the determination of value remains predominant in the sense that the regulation of working time and the distribution of societal work among the various productive groups, finally the bookkeeping in this regard will be more essential than ever." Marx, Das Kapital, vol. 3, (Berlin: 1973), p. 859.

goods among the working people in proportion to their work is consciously disregarded by the bureaucratic rulers. To be sure, verbally, the "socialist law of distribution according to work-performance" is constantly talked about,[6] but in reality, the actual distribution deviates from this theoretical demand. Although unequal quantities of work done by workers with differing qualifications is compensated by means of wage groups and wage scales, which correspond in essence to the demands posed, prices, however, do not reflect true labor value, or even its modified form, price of production.

The centrally determined prices of particular products or whole categories of products (for example, agricultural products, etc.) deviate so variably and fundamentally from the costs of production (and thus from an assumed value of labor or price of production as well) that it is in no way possible to speak of distribution or compensation in terms of labor-equivalence. The working people in Soviet agriculture in particular have not, for decades, been paid according to labor-equivalence. Rather, they receive a relatively much inferior amount for their work than does the urban population, since they have to pay substantially higher prices for industrial products (in comparison with the costs of producing these) than they receive for their agricultural products.

The arbitrary, bureaucratic distortion of prices, which funnels off indirect taxes of differing magnitude for the state financing of politically determined priority tasks, fundamentally contradicts Marx's conception of an equal deduction from the labor value of each associated worker to make up the social fund. The bureaucratic, power-determined distortion of prices has unpredictable consequences for different strata of the population, represents a violation of the development of their consumption, and is hardly more than an absolutized further development of monopolistically dictated prices.

Only by means of such monopolistic state-dictated prices was it possible to carry out an excessively rapid forced build-up of heavy industry and armaments industry at the expense of a Soviet agriculture that was plundered and impoverished for decades. A backward agricultural system kept the Soviet Union constantly dependent on imports of agricultural products from capitalist countries and brought the population such a low standard of living that an armaments industry, however big it may be, cannot make up for it. Only the use of feudalist repressive measures

---

[6] Cf. Politische Oekonomie des Sozialismus (Frankfurt a.M., 1973), p. 230.

(prohibition on leaving the country, forced labor in agriculture, etc.) has it been possible to keep agrarian workers
in agricultural production.

The pursuit of power-political goals by the political
bureaucracy is thus also the real reason for monopolistic
state dictation of prices and elimination of the market
mechanism. If the market mechanism were really to function
(even subject to limitations that would preclude a capitalist
development), then substantial disproportions in the structure of consumption and production, resulting from decades
of strangulating entire branches, would be completely unthinkable. The economic policy actually practiced in the
Communist states thus stands in fundamental contradiction
to Marx's conception of the law of value,[7] as well as of the
essence of the market mechanism, although this already
represents a great simplification of this market mechanism
compared with its real function in a highly developed economy.

If the positive function of the market is understood
only in the sense of the Marxian law of value, then it signifies something like this: Under capitalism, the value (labor value) of goods is transformed into their price of production. The surplus value created by the entire system of
production is manifest in the form of an average profit, the
level of which is determined by the relationship between the
totality of surplus value and the totality of invested capital
in an economy.[8] This rate of profit for the national economy, pro-rated as the particular capital of an individual enterprise, would then yield the average profit of this enterprise. Production costs plus average profit would then
constitute the price of production of the total production of
this enterprise. Given conditions without monopolistic
impediments to hinder the free flow of capital (conditions of
more or less perfect competition, which Marx did not explain in greater detail), any deviation in a branch's rate of
profit from the average rate of profit in the economy would
lead to competition and induce migration of capital across
branches, and this would, sooner or later, lead to an
equalization of rates of profit.

If the rate of profit is higher in a particular branch
than in the overall economy, free capital will increasingly
be drawn into this branch. This would increase production
and supply of goods in relation to demand. The ensuing

---

[7] Cf. K. Marx, Das Kapital, vol. 1 (E. Berlin, 1968), p.
49ff.

[8] Cf. K. Marx, Das Kapital, vol. 3 (E. Berlin, 1974), pp.
33-220.

decline in prices of goods would bring about a decline in the rate of profit, bringing it closer to the rate of profit in the economy as a whole. On the other hand, in branches showing a rate of profit lower than that of the overall economy, production would decline relatively, first through bankruptcy of the most backward firms and second, through the outflow of free capital (capital newly formed from profits); and, by causing a decline in the supply of goods in relation to demand it would aim at price increases and thus again at a shift in the rate of profit, bringing it closer to the rate of profit of the economy as a whole.

This notion of a constant tendency toward equilibrium of the rate of profit among branches leads Marx to conclude that the law of value, as modified for capitalism, governs the essence of exchange relationships under capitalism. For him, any deviation of average profits from surplus value is merely a manifestation of the capitalist pursuit of profit. Apart from these differences between profit and surplus value (which balance out in the economy), it is the socially requisite quantity of labor (past and living) which determines the price of production by means of the market mechanism (constant fluctuations of market prices around prices of production and with expansion and contraction of production and supply of goods bound up with the flow of capital). Instead of allocating labor time spontaneously, yet always ex post, among individual branches and adjusting the proportions of demand, socialism would anticipate need and adjust labor allocation ex ante to the structure of needs.

Here, however, Marx in the first place, saw capitalist property and the interest in exploitation as the primary source of a development of production governed by the market and by the profit criterion. Second, he simplified the function of the market mechanism, restricting it to the mere proportional allocation of labor (allocation of resources). And third, he assumed a perfect market, in which monopolies would be the exception. These simplifications by Marx have, however, turned out to be seriously mistaken in light of the actual experience of "socialism." In order for these shortcomings to be transcended, they must be theoretically explained.

We have seen in particular that even after the elimination of capitalist property, production cannot be concretely determined by central state authorities. These authorities have to be content with the establishment of highly aggregated global planning tasks (apart from, to some degree, the priority tasks of greatest political significance). The concretization and transformation of these into comprehensive, detailed decisions concerning the development of production must be left to the enterprise managements in an industrially developed economy.

However, as we know, interests do prevail in all human decisions and Marx was not able to take this problem of interests into account. Lenin then very quickly recognized, on the basis of his earliest experiences, that unless the distribution of consumer goods among the workers is linked to the efficiency of their work, there can only be disinterest in efficiency and in the development of work itself. For this reason he increasingly called attention to the importance--even in socialist enterprises--of utilizing the material interests of the workers in the development of work. Along with transition to the NEP (New Economic Policy), differentiated compensation began to be linked to work performance (quantity and quality of work) and to increases in the scale of production, and records were kept of the enterprises' costs of production and development of profits (the so-called Chorastschot).

Later, Marxist economic theorists recognized that planning and centralized control of the development of production costs no longer sufficed. Enterprises were increasingly interested in maximizing gross output (gross production), even when this led to excessively rapid increases in the costs of production. Complicated bonus incentives linked to relative economies of costs, were devised, which also involved increases in gross production, productivity, etc. The more diverse the production to which incentive bonuses were paid for improvements, the more the enterprise managements were confronted with contradicting interests. Where it was not possible simultaneously to promote incentives for all production processes (for example, increase in gross production together with simultaneous relative reduction in costs), the enterprise managements worked out systems that made it possible for the highest increases in wages and premiums to be attained (for example, lower bonuses for lower cost economies, but higher bonuses for more rapid growth in gross production, etc.). This system of premiums further promoted the interest of enterprise managements in concealing their own capabilities (formation of reserves) from superior planning instances by distorting information. This interest, however, was always an interest held not only by the managements of enterprises, but also by the entire production collective.

The history of the innumerable reorganizations of the planning system in the East Bloc states have always been linked to a great variety of changes in the system of incentives.[9] Because the bonus systems were one-sided and

---

[9] Cf. L. Bress and K.P. Hensel, Wirtschaftssysteme des Sozialismus im Experiment--Plan oder Markt? (Frankfurt, 1972); J. Kosta, J. Meyer, S. Weber, Warenproduktion

contradictory and because they thus senselessly encumbered the development of production, the idea keeps cropping up that the different aspects of the development of production (increase in the scope of production, cost economies, improvement of quality, flexibility of structural changes corresponding to needs, etc.) should be regarded from the point of view of profit maximization. This, however, has worked only under certain market conditions (which will be discussed in greater detail). The implementation of these conditions, however, runs up against intense opposition from the ruling bureaucracy; and their realization, in all their complexity, also causes difficulties, primarily resulting from dogmatically rigid, ideological thinking. Some East bloc states therefore retain their internally contradictory systems of differentiated premium-incentives; in others, premium funds tied to the development of profits have evolved.[10] All this takes place, however, under conditions such that a maximization of profits cannot and will not be the result of a socially requisite development of production aiming at optimum results.

The experiences of "socialism" demonstrate strikingly that a highly efficient development of production cannot be attained without getting direct producers--even socialist ones--interested in this development.[11] The efficiency of the economy is and will remain the basis for the satisfaction of increasing needs, whether these be individual material needs or other economically limited needs. As long as a "socialist" society has to order the individual needs-satisfaction of a large majority of the population and keep them within limits by means of income restrictions and income differentials, and indeed, as long as a large number of workers are prepared to do extra work in the form of

---

im Sozialismus. Ueberlegungen zur Theorie von Marx und zur Praxis in Osteuropa (Frankfurt, 1973).

[10] Cf. U. Fox, "Oekonomische Hebel als Instrument der Planung und Leistungsmobilisierung im polnischen Industriebetrieb," in Osteuropa Wirtschaft 2 (1974), p. 89ff. F. Vagi, Die betriebliche Interessiertheit und der Mechanismus ihrer Durchsetzung in den Staatsguetern (Budapest, 1977); G. Hahn, "Lohn und Praemie in der oekonomischen Stimulierung der Betriebe," in Die oekonomische Stimulierung der sozialistischen Produktion (Berlin-East, 1970), pp. 268-82.

[11] Cf. J. Slama, P. Sokolowski, H. Vogel, "Technologische Luecke zwischen West und Ost: Fallstudie Computer," in Osteuropa Wirtschaft 2 (1974), p. 120ff.

moonlighting in order to realize a higher income, this society will not be able to dispense with efficiency in the economy.

Put in general terms, greater efficiency thus means an
increase in output in relation to a given input, that is in
relation to the available means of production and living labor (available manpower multiplied by time worked). Regardless of how this efficiency is expressed in terms of
value (gross product, net product, or profit, in comparison
to the value of the means of production and/or labor), its
increase is always primarily dependent upon qualitative improvements in the means of production, organization of production, qualifications of the workers, etc., which we collectively refer to as an increase in efficiency.

If, therefore, antipathy toward an economic conception
of increased performance and efficiency is widespread in
various intellectual circles in the West, this may indicate a
misunderstanding of the concept of economy (equating it
with increases in the quantity and intensity of labor,
growth of production, etc.). More often, however, it indicates an aversion to the kind of increase in efficiency in
which innovations, as well as technical and qualitative
progress lead not to an increase in the amount and intensity of labor but, on the contrary, to relative economies of
labor; they thus become the precondition for greater consumption per unit of labor and/or for the reduction of
working hours.

However, such antipathy toward efficiency and performance goes against the fundamental interests of a majority of the working people. This is true, not only in the
Western states, but also in the Eastern "socialist" countries. Its consequences would be to reinforce differences
in living standards, in economic limits to the meeting of
needs, and the still relatively long and arduous work day.
As has always been the case in the past, the propagators
of a mood of "anti-efficiency" are truly no "friends of the
people."

Hostility toward technological progress and qualitatively
improved performance, however much it may be associated
with humanitarian solutions, remains anti-humane as long as
it does not show other feasible ways of reducing work and
making it easier, while simultaneously satisfying the needs
of the broad masses of the people.

It has indeed long been clear to the rulers of the Soviet bloc countries that economic efficiency is important.
Nor are they unaware that little can be achieved without
enterprises having a material interest in increasing production. But even up to the present day they have refused to
recognize that highly efficient and simultaneously needs-oriented production is not possible without a market mecha-

nism. Here, however, lack of understanding of this complex set of problems coincides with ideological prejudices bound up with a fear of losing positions of power. This is due to the fact that market-controlled enterprises operate independently.

If we are to understand the significance of the market mechanism for socially necessary development of production, then, Marx's views will not suffice, since they only lead to the simplistic conclusion that in place of indirect distribution of labor by the market under capitalism, planned distribution of labor according to social needs would have to be achieved under socialism. The development of theory and practice has also come to a halt in mid-stream in the Soviet bloc countries. It is becoming increasingly evident that not only the capitalists may have a specific interest in growth of profits but also that only by means of the profit motive can socialist producers too acquire an interest in the needs-oriented, highly efficient development of production. However, such a profit interest presupposes the market mechanism, even in an economic democracy, but which is as complete as possible in its operation and unrestrained by capitalism.

IMPROVEMENT OF THE MARKET MECHANISM

If the market mechanism is really to work:

1. Prices have to establish themselves parametrically to the market in accordance with the relationship between supply and demand.

2. There must be competition among the producers impelling them best to utilize the potential development of efficiency and use-value, as well as inducing them to establish competitive prices.

3. The incomes of those who make decisions regarding the development of production must be dependent on market results, whereby state readjustments, subsidies, etc., which do not conform to the market, should be regarded only as publically justified exceptional phenomena.

We will not reiterate the various well-known theories of prices and markets, but rather will concentrate upon those explanations necessary to an understanding of the characteristics peculiar to a non-capitalist, regulated market mechanism as a component of the projected new economic

system. Just as a market mechanism already existed much
earlier, when there was no capitalist production with wage
labor, so we will also maintain its necessity in an economic
system where the social antagonism between wage and profit
interests would be essentially overcome.

At the outset of the present study, we attempted to
explain that, above all, the objectively existing antagonism
between people's interest in maximal satisfaction of their
needs and their interest in minimization of the most unplea-
sant remaining work makes the market mechanism necessary.
This antagonism of interests will continue as long as existing working conditions continue to prevail. These include
relatively long working hours, rigid division of labor, great
differences among work activities with regard to effort, attractiveness, creativity, authoritarian management, etc. on
the one hand, and on the other, the necessity of an economically limited meeting of needs as a manifestation of the
relative scarcity of goods, resulting in unavoidable differences in consumption among social strata.

If we assume the necessity of performance-related income, this means, in the light of our explanation so far,
that part of the compensation of co-workers is tied to the
profit of the enterprise. Only as the profits of an enterprise develop can there take place the socially necessary
synthesis between the maximum potential creation of use-
value and the maximum potential efficiency of production.
In the long run, therefore, interest in profit optimization
cannot be abandoned; but profit optimization does not--as
already explained--exclude democratically made decisions to
depart from profit maximization in the employee-owned enterprises. The optimal development of profits should, however, manifest the potential long-range maximal development
of efficiency. But this can only be attained with a truly
functioning market mechanism.

The question now arises as to which means are to determine the size of gross profit in a market economy and
whether objective social requirements or subjective desires
and interests are to have a decisive effect on the size of
profits. Along with this, the old economists' controversy
reemerges as to whether profits are necessary at all under
conditions of market equilibrium, or whether interest is not
the only manifestation of capital utilization, with profit representing only surpluses of income exceeding interest, as a
manifestation of market disequilibria (higher demand in relation to supply), dynamic profits or monopoly profits. We
do not pretend to have the only right answer to these
questions. Nevertheless, we have to present and justify
our position here, since our concept of necessary market
regulation in the reformed system is based on it.

In our view the requirements of social development always make something like a surplus in the economy of a
community or nation necessary.   The producers have always
had to produce more than they consumed in a given period
of time (for example, a year).   First, they have needed reserves in order to survive.   Second, the working and producing people have always had to support a large number
of people who could not yet work (children), or who could
no longer work (elderly, sick, incapacitated people). For
this, let us set aside for a moment the highly ideological
problem of what is to be considered as productive work.
Third, finally, in a dynamic economy it has also been necessary to produce more means of production (investment
goods) and consumer goods than are consumed each year,
in order to continuously expand the productive basis (investment goods and labor) and to increase production.
Since the population viewed over the long run and on a
worldwide scale has increased, economic development has up
to now been predominantly a dynamic development.
  As soon as a market and money economy begins to un-
fold, the surplus takes the form of profit, wherever products become merchandise, that is, when they are produced
for the market, for sale.   All who take part in production
or in its preliminaries, organization, management, control,
etc., produce more than they consume personally or in production.   The magnitude of consumption is, in each case,
productively and socially determined, which always also includes differences in consumption that are determined by
the division of labor and relations of ownership.   Seen from
the perspective of the national economy, a considerable
portion of the sum of all profits goes to those products
required for the life of all people who do not take part in
production, the formation of reserves, expansion of the basis of production, and expansion of non-productive social
arrangements.
  The fact that all social efforts and needs have to be
implemented by means of the activity, needs, interests, and
wills of individuals should not thereby be overlooked.   Society does not have a life of its own apart from individuals,
but rather becomes social through individuals.   The individual is always both part of society and simultaneously
transcends it.   He is thus a tangible individual general en-
tity and simultaneously a unique individuality.   Subjective
activity expresses the objective, general characteristics of
needs, interests, and activities which a given society im-
poses upon its members.   But it is also always an activity
of completely inimitable and unique individualities which
constitutes what is distinctive about the subjective.   With
regard to profit, this means that the amount of profit is always primarily determined by social requirements (social

needs, needs relating to reserves, protection, defense, and
administration, but also those required for growth, etc.)
and imposed upon the entrepreneur from outside, as it
were. At the same time, however, it is the fruit of particular, individual entrepreneurial action and activity.

Thus, there exists, in each case, a certain average
relative magnitude of profit, which can be understood in
relation to the whole of production as a reflection of the
surplus product required by society. At the same time,
however, particular, concrete profits will always deviate
from this average size. They will be larger or smaller as a
result of individual entrepreneurial activity. Even though
profit has always had to meet certain social needs, it has at
all times contained elements that satisfied the private needs
of its owners, meaning the consumption and reserve needs
of entrepreneurs and their families, as well as their needs
to increase production, and to secure and increase their
markets. In this way, profit becomes the driving force behind private entrepreneurial activity.

If in future, decisions regarding the distribution and
utilization of profits are social, and capital that is newly
formed out of profits is progressively transformed into neutralized capital, the personal profit motive (which cannot be
eliminated at the present stage of meeting of needs) will
also coincide more and more with the social profit need
(surplus product need). However, what was once a purely
theoretical postulate, has long been the most fundamental
lesson of the "socialist" system, namely that, only where
those who make investment decisions also can gain personal
shares in the profits (or suffer losses in these shares), will
decisions actually be carried out with a far-reaching sense
of responsibility. Purely bureaucratical and materially disinterested decisions are made in the most irresponsible
manner. This undeniable experience leads to the conclusion
that all investors of capital should continue to be profit-mo-
tivated in future under the reformed system.

The overall magnitude of total societal gross profit and
the macro-rate of profit will be pursued by means of distribution planning (planning of wages). The macro-product
will no longer be the result of a purely spontaneous development determined by a struggle over distribution. Rather, the surplus product in the form of profit would be purposefully assured on the basis of macro-economic
pre-calculation of societal needs and required net investment, including the profit-sharing and entrepreneur profit
shares required as incentives. At the same time, this
means the determination, by plan, of overall gross profit
and of net profit in relation to total need for capital.

The planned overall size and rate of profit are based
on a prognosis of the anticipated branch structure and de-

velopment of profit in the individual branches. This prognosis must not, however, become more than a construct that, though significant, is only <u>provisional</u>, since it cannot predict reliably enough the <u>precise</u> development either of demand structure or efficiency potential in production. If this important prognosis were to become the definitive plan, it would mean that market-conforming distribution planning would turn into the dirigistic planning of production, with all its initiative- and efficiency-stifling bureaucratic consequences. The actual development of profits must continue to be the result of the actual development of the structure and efficiency of production and investment.

The actual size of profits and profit rates in the individual branches and enterprises will therefore also develop differently, first, according to the varying development of efficiency and costs, and second, according to the varying market tendencies of individual products and product groups. All new capital would then be invested in the interest of the investor so as to yield the highest possible profit. It would thus be supplied, first and foremost, to those branches in which the highest rates of profit already prevailed or were rising most rapidly. Whether this new capital is already neutralized capital (derived from the profits of existing productive enterprises or branches), or private capital (formed from private savings or profits) those who invest it will and should be interested in its maximal utilization, that is, a utilization that is as efficient as possible. Whether the investors are private persons or collectives and their representatives, both should either gain or lose according to whether they have applied the capital more or less effectively, more or less to the benefit of society.

Here, it is simply a matter of developing the market mechanism better than is the case in contemporary capitalism, and of making the organization and rate of profit into a more consistent expression of the development of efficiency and use-value. In other words, the issue is the social <u>performance</u> of the individual enterprises. On the one hand, the interest of all producers must continue to exist as a direct interest in as high a rate of profit as possible, since this means an interest in maximally high cost economies in relation to profits or maximum increases in profit in relation to capital. All increases in the rate of profit will also lead to increases in profit-sharing and net profits for the entrepreneur and vice versa. On the other hand, however, all deviations of the actual profit rates of individual enterprises from the respective profit rate in the national economy should, as far as possible, only be the reflection of an above- or below-average efficiency and use-value creation of their operation. So far as possible, they should not reflect monopolistic advantages, domination of the market, manipulation of production, informational advantages, or any similar disadvantages.

Markets in the new system will be preponderantly heterogenous markets, just as they are today, with clearly planned wage incomes and clearly defined state economic policies. The transparency of markets can, however, be improved in comparison to existing conditions. Macro-distribution planning alone, with its branch commissions, analyses, and prognostic procedures, with its prognosis of distribution of income and with the programed state economic policy, makes it easier for every entrepreneur to gain an overview of the development of production and the kind of market to be anticipated. Their forecasts of the structure of demand for a relatively long time will be considerably more reliable than is the case nowadays, and it will make the structural decisions of the enterprises easier. Knowledge of the planned volume of investment in particular branches will help to avoid the establishment of unnecessary capacities, without sacrificing the interest of individual enterprises in overtaking competitors and winning market shares. Continuous information about the development of actual rates of profit within the individual branches would be institutionally promoted and would become a statutory function of the banking system. For all new capital investments, when making the decision as to whether enterprises should invest in their own branch or in another one, it would be important not only to have a thorough market analysis, but also a knowledge of the developmental trend of the rate of profit.

Just as the transparency of the market would have to be increased, competition would simultaneously have to be intensified and consciously promoted by the government or the economic council. Competition has been brought into disrepute by Marxism, partly due to the often antisocial and ruthless behavior of entrepreneurs in the early capitalist period, and partly to an unscientific, ideological representation of competition in many socialist writings. If, however, we understand competition as the market efforts of individual enterprises to overtake other enterprises and win larger market shares by means of better adaptation to the market, technical and technological improvements, product innovation, increases in productivity, cost reduction, greater and more efficient investments, etc., then this has to be recognized as a type of behavior which is still socially necessary and advantageous at the present stage of development.

The purpose of competition is not to destroy competitors, but rather to overtake them by means of better and more flexible performance, which works to the benefit of consumers and thus, of course, for one's own income as well.[12] In this sense, the term "contest" is probably more appropriate, even though, admittedly to change the vocabulary cannot alter the phenomenon itself. Under prevailing conditions of work and consumption, however, no more effective incentive exists for the socially required qualitative development of performance, and any abandonment of market competition as a principle causes irreparable losses and damages to society as a whole. After all, the absence of market competition has set back the "socialist" states far behind those states with market economies in the development of their economic efficiency and quality. The beneficiaries are not the population, but only an idle, parasitic bureaucracy.

Lenin himself once coined the term "socialist competition" and his emphasis on material incentives and necessary wage differentials, probably indicates that he had some idea of the significance of a performance-oriented policy in the socialist system. However, he did not recognize the significance of such motivations for the entire enterprise. Or he was no longer able fully to overcome ideological barriers built up over decades. Since then, understanding of material incentives has remained confined to the domain of individual compensation. Even "socialist competition" has become a very formal and barely effective means of motivating workers to fulfill or exceed the plan, while it does not contribute in the slightest to raising the efficiency of enterprises. The problems bound up with the structure of production, innovation, technical progress and reduction of costs, in their reciprocal interdependence and in their profit-related manifestation, have remained completely divorced from the interests of those affiliated with the enterprise and cannot be promoted by any kind of competition within the enterprise.

The political leadership in the Soviet bloc states has not yet recognized (or will not recognize) that individual enterprises also have to face the pressure of market competition, since without it, they, as absolutely monopolistic producers, will be influenced in all their decisions only by their immediate producer interests. An absolute monopoly exists wherever a single administrative authority or management makes decisions involving the development of production of all enterprises in a branch, or whenever it divides up the productive tasks among all branch enterprises, and compensation and performance of the enterprise

---

[12] Cf. W.A. Joehr, "Die Rolle der Konkurrenz in der modernen Wirtschaft," in Zeitschrift fur Nationaloekonomie, offprint from Vol. 26, Nos. 1-3 (1966), p. 90ff.

collective depend upon fulfillment of these tasks. Under such conditions, the individual enterprises cannot develop an interest in taking their own initiatives to improve market supplies. Even in those countries where profit-sharing or profit bonus funds have been established (GDR, Rumania, etc.), there is no competition among several independent enterprises within each branch to increase their market share and no free market prices, with the result that the profit interest must produce only negative effects. If profits are increased through market control and manipulation on the part of absolute monopolists at the expense of consumers, yet no competitor can challenge and pose a threat to this monopoly situation and activity, the profit interest in the development of production will produce strong antisocial tendencies.

The activity of every independent enterprise can only be challenged by the activity of other competing enterprises. Only by means of such competition can the fruits of all producers be objectified and subjected to consumer evaluation and selection. Only in this way can all potential increases in use-value and efficiency be discovered. No supra-enterprise administrative body, no method of supra-enterprise control can uncover the potential of a productive enterprise with regard to product improvement, flexibility of the micro-production structure appropriate to needs, technological innovation, improvement of the organization of production, relative cost economies, etc. If this were possible, enterprise management bodies would actually be superfluous, which--in this case--of course could also be said about the supra-enterprise bodies. Only competitors who are really interested in increasing and realizing their profits by increasing their share of the market and achieving relatively top prices can, time and again, perceive new possibilities within a branch which other enterprises have not, or not yet uncovered. Orthodox Marxist ideology ignores this positive and irreplacable effect of market competition or it suppresses it, and stresses exclusively its negative consequences (displacement from the market, bankruptcies, unemployment, etc). However, it conceals the consequences to the population of the abandonment of market competition, and it avoids openly comparing the advantages and disadvantages of market competition. It cannot be entirely excluded that some, less enterprising, miscalculating enterprises will be pushed out of the market when the task of social production consists of satisfying human needs as well as possible and with the lowest relative cost expenditure, but where this is possible only given optimal initiative and performance on the part of individual production collectives. If such displacements from the market were to be completely excluded, the result would be that all enterprises, even the least productive, least effective, and incurring the highest losses, would be kept alive by state subsidies. Even outright flawed production, which increases supplies of unnecessary products on the market rather than consumption, would be protected by subsidies. Under such a system, in the final analysis, steady profits from enterprising and efficient enterprises would be redistributed to bad enterprises. In the long run this can hardly lead to anything but a gradual exhaustion of interest in efficiency within all enterprises.

THE MARKET MECHANISM AND MONOPOLY

Theoretical and practical discussions surrounding the concept of monopoly, the characteristics of competition-limiting monopolization, and possible measures to prevent monopolistic developments have been going on for decades. They have yielded an immense flood of valid findings as well as oversimplified or false points of view. These discussions and theories cannot even be listed here, let alone reproduced. We will limit ourselves to describing the new opportunities that the reformed system would provide for combating monopolistic developments disruptive of the market mechanism. To this end, however, we will also have to present our views on the essential manifestation of a negative development of monopoly.

We consider it, first and foremost, to persist in our distinction between micro- and macro-monopolies.[13] If we define "monopoly" in general as a priority or exclusivity in production or sales (or purchasing) of merchandise, then micro-monopoly refers to the exclusivity of individual products on the market, which--at least for the time being-- cannot be imitated, and for which it is difficult to substitute. For this reason they can also usually be sold at high monopolistic prices containing a relatively high profit ratio (portion of profit in the price of one single product). Macro-monopolies, on the other hand, involve a preponderance of giant concerns, within branches of production, having broad product groups. The capital intensity, mass production, and extent of supply of these mammoth concerns or combines usually makes possible a control of the market within the affected branch such that the rate of profit realized by them (relation of profit of the concern to the invested capital of the firm) substantially exceeds the average rate of profit in the national economy in the long run.

---

[13] O. Sik, The Third Way, p. 149.

We do not consider micro-monopolies to be detrimental, nor do we believe that they substantially impair the market mechanism. To be sure, an exclusive patented product or a product with a popular brand may not be subject to competition, or only to weak competition for a time. Its price will therefore often be substantially higher in relation to costs than is the case with most other goods. Competition is thus limited in this case, and micro-monopolists sometimes can also realize profits for a long time which they would not have realized given unrestricted competition. Nevertheless, micro-monopolies do not cause any serious disturbances in the market mechanism. The relatively higher profits realized by these means are an important motivation for inventive and innovative activity and, for the most part, do not last very long.[14] Even in the case of patented products, rarely will 18 years elapse,[15] before competition develops for their producers. Well before this, products with a substitution effect will appear, which have price-dampening effects and often lead rather quickly to the end of monopoly profits.

Macro-monopolies, however, constitute the real problem. In their case, it is not a matter of relatively short-run, temporary increases in income. They realize long-run, constant, and often accelerating, above-average profits which can no longer be seen as reflecting a correspondingly higher creation of use-value for society. Of course, macro-monopolists can also realize profit increases by means of micro-monopolies (and, for the most part, the attention of the public is directed at these, as for instance the products Valium and Librium of the firm Hoffmann-LaRoche, etc.). However, this is not the decisive source of their monopolistic profits. The range of products of macro-monopolies is usually very broad, and the portion of monopolized products (that is micro-monopolies) in their total production is very small. Distinctly homogenous markets are exceptional phenomena in practice. For the most part, similar goods (heterogeneous markets) or even quite dissimilar goods, with substitutable use value (for example, automobile and train) compete. Seen in this way, an absolute majority of the products of macro-monopolies are under competitive pressure, and yet they register monopolistic profits.

---

[14] Cf. F. Oppenheimer, Weder Kapitalismus noch Kommunismus (Stuttgart, 1962), p. 80.

[15] In the patent law of the Federal Republic of Germany the inventor is granted the right to exclusive exploitation of the invention for 18 years.

We regard monopolistic profits as the decisive manifestation of the existence of a monopoly and must therefore explain these in further detail. First of all, however, it has to be noted that--as opposed to the usual concept prevalent in bourgeois economics--although we do not dismiss the distinction between monopolies and oligopolies, we do not consider it as important as this theory normally does. Absolute macro-monopolies are a distinctive rarity and probably occur only as state monopolies. They signify the domination of a certain branch of production by a single concern (collective combine, trust, state combination, etc.), in which a single supreme management body makes decisions about the distribution of production and about marketing. While these monopolies are universally typical of the Soviet bloc states, it is difficult to find them in the West (salt monopoly, etc.). Apart from this, many macro-monopolies, as defined here, do exist, since we term most so-called oligopolies as macro-monopolies, because they are able to realize monopolistic profits on the basis of the scale of their production and control of the market.

A monopolistic profit can only be recognized with reference to the national economic rate of profit. If we take the relationship of total gross profit to total invested capital in a national economy, we obtain the quotient of the rate of profit in the national economy. In all concerns whose individual rate of profit is substantially larger than the rate of profit in the national economy, and this relatively, over the long run (if not permanently), then this indicates the existence of monopolistic profit. This rate of profit must not be confused with the profit quota. The profit quota is determined as the portion which gross profit (or net profit as well) represents in total production, expressed in terms of prices, whether this be of the entire national economy, the production group, the branch, or the concern. The rate of profit, in contrast, refers to the relationship of gross profit (or net profit as well) to total invested capital--and again, of the national economy, the production group, branch, or concern.

The difference is primarily and decisively one of the differing rate of capital circulation. While the rate of profit of two concerns can be the same, even though they are in different branches with differing rates of circulation of their floating capital as well as their wage capital, the profit quota in their respective annual products may differ substantially. The smaller amount of floating capital and/or wage capital required by the concern with the higher rate of circulation will realize a correspondingly smaller profit (given the same rate of profit) than the concern which, because of a lower rate of capital circulation, requires a larger amount of floating and/or wage capital and must therefore also realize higher profits.

It follows from this that monopolistic profit cannot be detected in the profit quota and therefore not in prices: either in the total price of the whole of annual production, or in the prices of individual products. Even a profit which, in relation to the total price of annual production or to costs of production, need not differ substantially from the profits of other concerns in the same relation, can, in reality, be a monopoly profit. In the same way, however, a relatively high profit quota need not always indicate monopolistic profit, even though this is one of the determining features of micro-monopolies. For macro-monopolies, however, only the rate of profit is decisive, just as decisive, in fact, as it is for capital utilization itself. What capital pursues, and must pursue, is maximization of the rate of profit, since it alone indicates maximal exploitation of invested and long-term capital. Profit maximization by itself does not mean much, if for instance the capital required to achieve it is greater than elsewhere where the same level of profit is realized. Maximization of the rate of profit under capitalism thus corresponds with the self-interest of the owners of capital. But it can also correspond to the interest of society, if it really expresses the maximization of efficiency.

Just as, in every new investment, capital orients itself to possible developments of the rate of profit, and to this end strives to obtain and evaluate all available information, so there is a prevalent tendency toward the formation of a national economic average rate of profit. If no macro-monopolistic impediments existed, a more or less balanced rate of profit would develop as the long-range span (from-to) of the rate of profit, despite an imperfect market (heterogeneous goods and incomplete market transparacy), indeed, despite the existence of micro-monopolies. Of course this remains only a speculation, but one which corresponds to the logic of the interest of capital and the market mechanism.

Neither the notion of an exchange of equivalent use values, as in Walras, where the ideal national economic equilibrium of the exchange of goods expresses an equalization of the marginal utility and marginal costs of all varieties of goods, nor the Marxian conception of a national economic exchange of goods, in which use-value (utility value) is the pre-condition for exchange and this results in the prices of production, stand in the kind of opposition to each other that the ideologues of both camps like to construct. Both conceptions express more or less the same market tendency, even though they place their emphasis on different factors, and each side's philosophical explanation of the essence of this exchange process emphasizes the opposing side of this internally contradictory process.

In Marx's case, the philosophy of general labor value led to a profound but one-sided elaboration of the productive aspect of exchange value (prices) as the sole determining exchange value. He took only insufficient account of the equally important consumptive aspect of exchange, and established the need satisfied by use-value only as a general precondition for exchange.

The theorists of marginal utility, with Walras at their forefront, who brought the theory of marginal utility into a macro-economic equilibrium model by means of a simultaneous statistical system of equations, have thoroughly worked through the consumptive evaluation aspect of the exchange process proceeding from the philosophy of human needs. Their theory analyzed the evaluation of use-value by buyers and the developmental tendency of utility evaluation with the aid of Gossens Laws and--in contrast to the widespread reproach of "subjectivism"--has discovered what is universally valid and therefore objective in these evaluations of millions of people. Yet for all that, they oversimplified the productive aspect, and above all the wage and capital interest, with their crucial influence on the level of exchange value. They also sought to explain this aspect exclusively in terms of utility evaluation (use-value of labor and the means of production derived from consumer utility). If we disregard this one-sidedness on both sides and in particular their respective philosophically-based overemphases, we will quickly recognize a common rational core in the macro-economic equilibrium theories of Marx and Walras which we need in order to understand the essence of the market mechanism. Even if we are not in a position to measure use-value, the hypothetical but correct explanation of Gossens' first law will enter into our thoughts time and again. Falling marginal utility under conditions of increasing satiation (even though differing elasticity is to be noted in demand for different products) corresponds to general experience. If then, in determining use-value, emphasis is not placed on marginal utility, but rather this marginal utility is regarded as itself fixed through the respectively given exchange value (market price), it will always be the case that marginal utility and marginal costs will balance out in an equilibrium. That is to say, the marginal utility of a commodity could continue to decline to zero if the commodity were evaluated without reference to its previously fixed price. However, the explanation that the scarcity of goods makes satiation impossible where the marginal utility would fall to zero, overlooks the fact that this scarcity is, in the case of most goods, not a given of nature, but rather depends primarily upon the scale of human production.

If we try to recognize objectively the factors upon which production has primarily depended hitherto in the

course of historical development, we will very quickly see
that human labor must be mentioned in the first place. The
quantity of use-value produced depends on its scope,
whereas the availability of raw materials, energy, etc., limited by nature, has not played such a decisive role, nor
will it over the long run. Until the Middle Ages, labor was
almost exclusively the determining factor, since the means
of production were primitive and could be relatively easily
acquired. With machine production in factories, however,
the era of capitalism began, since acquisition of the costly
new capital goods required the protracted accumulation of
relatively large quantities of finance capital. No one gives
up this finance capital, which means sacrificing of consumption, into the productive sphere for long without receiving
an appropriate amount of interest. Thus, along with labor,
finance capital has become one of the determining factors
upon the scope of which the volume of available goods, and
hence their relative scarcity, depends.

This means, however, that wages and capital value, as
well as the socially and capitalistically requisite surplus
product in the form of profit, together determine the
amount of value that has to be created in production. Up
to now, they have also decisively determined the limit below
which prices can fall only temporarily. And it is only to
this price that marginal utility could fall, since a lower
marginal utility could no longer maintain production. The
price thus determines the lower limit of the fall of marginal
utility, and marginal utility determines the quantity of production which will still be consumed at this price and which
thus has some utility.

Although marginal utility theorists see the equalized
exchange value as determined by the balancing out of marginal utility and marginal cost, these marginal costs also
contain capital costs, wage costs, and interest. However,
where there are several firms in a branch, it is the marginal firm, that is, the firm incurring the relatively highest
costs, whose costs (including interest) will still have to be
covered by the price. This means, however, that this conception (apart from its philosophical foundation) does not
contradict Marx. In Marx's view, an equilibrium price is
determined by the average production costs (capital costs
plus wage costs), to which, however, a national economic
average profit would also have to be added. This, however, necessarily exists despite the notion that interest is
contained in the marginal costs. All firms which produce
the same product at lower cost (average costs as well as
marginal costs) than the marginal firm will also realize more
than interest alone.

If we thus understand interest as the minimum profit
which a sum of capital has to yield, then this means that

the average production, with costs that are average for the branch, also has to yield an average profit that is higher than interest. It is the profit which guarantees the necessary net investment (after deduction of taxes) and the consumption of the entrepreneurs (owner salaries) which the owners must strive to attain if they would seek to prevail in competition, with the aid of investments. Newly invested finance capital will never aim at the minimum amount of interest in the calculations of investors. Rather, it must guarantee a profit that is at least average for the branch, which will be the object of all considerations relating to capital allocation among branches.

If in a branch a rate of profit is realized that is higher than that of the majority of other branches, it will also, in the first instance, attract new finance capital. Now whether this higher rate of profit has been realized by reducing production costs or by rapidly rising demand in relation to supply, is not decisive. In either case, the influx of capital will lead to increases in production and supply, and to decreases in prices and profits. In this way, the rate of profit will again fall to the rate of profit prevailing in the national economy. Conversely, a profit rate lower than that of the national economy reflects either higher production costs or rapidly falling demand (in relation to supply). This will lead to bankruptcies of the weakest firms as well as to the flight of finance capital, with the consequence that production will decline in absolute terms. On this basis, prices and profits will again rise gradually in the direction of the average profit rate in the national economy. Thus, with the help of the free flow of capital, not only does a tendentially equal rate of profit form, but with the help of this mechanism the branch structure will adapt most reliably, flexibly, and with the most efficient utilization of capital--provided that there are no monopolistic impediments to the free flow of capital.

If one wanted to calculate the average rate of profit for the national economy, even in a present-day capitalist economy, as the relationship of the total gross profit to total invested capital, it would naturally be necessary to try to uncover all concealed profits, which occur primarily through manipulating depreciation, profit transfers, economically vague bookkeeping categories, etc. In theory, we can determine these rates of profit post factum. The same should then hold in ascertaining the long-term rate of profit of individual branches or of the firms which dominate production in a single branch, (in branches with several firms, the profit of the firms with average conditions of production; in oligopolistic branches, those of the oligopolists). Comparison of these branch rates of profit with that of the national economy over an extended period (several years) should then suffice to uncover monopoly profits. Rates of profit that are substantially higher than the rate of profit of the national economy are to be understood as a manifestation of monopoly profits.

If competition among branches is really to function, free capital has to flow very rapidly, in particular in branches with substantially higher rates of profit, and, sooner or later, must lead to a falling rate of profit. If, however, certain branches or individual firms within certain branches receive long-term or constantly above-average rate of profit, this suggests that no competitive capital is flowing in over the long run, and the firms in question have to be regarded as macro-monopolists. It is not crucial whether one or several highly concentrated large firms, trusts, or even a cartel of several firms is involved. What is crucial is that an above-average rate of profit, whatever its origins, is not being lowered by means of price reductions for the benefit of consumers. Thus, equilibrium prices are reached across the whole range of production, which substantially exceed not only the current rate of interest, but also the higher average profits in the national economy.

This then is not the dynamic profit of the leading firm described by Schumpeter, which after a certain time lag, is always overtaken by eager competitors. For a development of this kind would be market conforming and should always reduce the rate of profit through the pressure of competition: either by the overtaking firms expanding production, thus forcing the leading firm to lower prices and further reducing its rate of profit; or by prices remaining constant despite rising production (actually already a sign of inflation, since prices in fact ought to fall), but then all the competing firms could also raise their rates of profit to the level of the leading firm. However, if the rate of profit of the whole branch should still be above average, production would have to rise again through an influx of capital under conditions of competition so that ultimately equilibrium prices would again fall, thus benefiting consumers, and would facilitate the realization of a profit not exceeding the average level in the national economy.

To be sure, if macro-monopolies are to be comprehended, various other characteristics can be included as auxiliary characteristics, such as the share of the market of large firms, their degree of concentration, obstacles to entry into the market, cartel agreements, forms of cooperation that turn into non-competitive concentrations, etc. However, none of these traits alone warrants the conclusion

that a macro-monopoly exists.[16] It is not possible to determine the dimensions of a market share in such a way that
to exceed them clearly signifies the presence of a monopoly.
To be sure, a high degree of concentration is also a widespread trait of monopoly, though it need not always be
present. Even medium-sized firms can behave like cartel
members, with unwritten (hence unprovable) agreements.
The absolute degree of concentration which has to exist before we can speak of a monopoly cannot be established.
Cooperation among several firms can have a positive and
competition-promoting effect. But at a certain degree of
intensity, it can just as well impede the market access of
other firms and thereby stifle the competitive effect. The
size of the oligopolies alone can deny market access to other
firms, since only new firms of comparable size would really
be able to enter into competition. In such cases, however,
the result would have to be devastating competition due to
a large oversupply from increased production. As a rule,
this will deter would be capital investors or company
founders. Barriers to market access may therefore be more
difficult to grasp and do indicate definitive traits of a monopoly.

On the basis of what has just been said, we consider
any attempt to infer the existence of monopolies from monopoly prices to be futile. Individual prices in a market
economy will always basically be equilibrium prices (a balancing out of supply and demand) though they may contain
high, as well as relatively low profit quotas. Whether a
profit quota is excesssive and represents a monopoly profit
is not something that can be determined from the profit
quota itself. Branches with a lower rate of capital circulation will show relatively high profit quotas in their prices,
which need not represent an above-average rate of profit.
In the same way, an enterprise can, for example, realize a
rate of profit that is only at the average for the national
economy, and yet set up its production program so that it
realizes relatively high prices with high profit quotas for
certain products but then realizes correspondingly low prices with low profit quotas for other products. This kind of
arrangement of prices can bring about a normal, average
overall profit, can conform fully to the market, and therefore should not be prohibited by administrative measures.

As we will see, these arguments are not intended to
rule out consideration of various traits from which monopolistic tendencies can be inferred. They are, however, intended to indicate that their utility for drawing such

---

[16] Cf. E. J. Mestmaecker, Europaeisches Wettbewerbsrecht
(Munich, 1974), p. 383f.

conclusions is only a limited one. Accordingly, we consider the existence of <u>long-range</u> <u>rates</u> <u>of</u> <u>profit</u> <u>that</u> <u>are</u> <u>sub-</u> <u>stantially</u> <u>above</u> <u>the</u> <u>national</u> <u>economic</u> <u>average</u> for certain firms as the decisive characteristic of a macro-monopoly. Under the reformed system, these would serve as the primary basis for decisions regarding anti-monopoly measures, though where possible the decision-making process would be augmented by additional criteria.

LIMITS TO THE PREVENTION OF MONOPOLIES

Even under the reformed system of co-worker and mixed enterprises, macro-monopolies cannot be ruled out. As long as there must be independent firms having a profit interest, it is to be expected that some firms would develop into macro-monopolies if certain counter-measures are not taken. These monopolies may be the result of either spontaneous development not consciously intended by the firm or of conscious entrepreneurial activities.

Since individual firms are never equal in size they will realize profit volumes that are also unequal in the initial stages of any reformed system. This is due to their unequal rates of growth and differing degrees of concentration. In principle, this tendency need not, and should not be altered, since up to a certain point concentration can have progressive technical and economic effects. Beyond a certain size and degree of concentration, however, the preconditions for the formation and maintenance of monopolistic profits as well as monopolistic behavior will emerge on a scale to which the firm had not previously aspired.

For all that, purposeful attempts to monopolize cannot be ruled out either. These seek monopolistic domination of the market with the aim of securing monopolistic profits in the course of striving for their own growth, as well as by means of mergers (amalgamations), co-operatives, or written or unwritten modes of cartel-like behavior. Whether or not they are intentionally created or whether they are established in the form of giant individual firms or oligopolies and cartels acting like huge firms, identifiable macro-monopolies should be regarded unfavorably. They must be prevented or their negative consequences overcome.

What would the negative consequences of a macro-monopoly in the reformed system be? The existence of <u>monopoly</u> <u>profits</u> must be mentioned first and foremost. It has three negative implications:

1. Monopoly profit, as substantial and long-term excessive profit, will be passed on to consumers through excessive prices. Though the prices of the

macro-monopolies' individual products might match normal competitive prices, the prices of their other products will be substantially higher. In the final result, the totality of the prices of all products of a macro-monopoly will be higher over the long run (or permanently) than when only the average rate of profit for the national economy is realized in this lump sum price. Macro-monopolies also have to reduce the amount of production in the same proportion to which they raise the monopolistic prices, since only when supply is relatively reduced can the relatively higher prices be realized (since an increase in supply would cause prices to fall). Consumers, whose incomes derive mostly from non-monopolistic funds, therefore get substantially less use-value when they purchase goods at monopoly prices than they would if there were no monopolistic prices and profits. This would have to be regarded as exploitation of the consumers by the macro-monopolies.

2. Monopoly profits make possible a kind of profit-sharing by co-workers and private entrepreneurs which is no longer possible to view as compensation for extraordinary performance. Enhanced performance means expenditure of more intellectual and/or physical resources, greater efforts in the innovation of products, production procedures, increases in use-value and/or relative cost economies. This enhanced performance is limited in duration, and earns an increased compensation that is also of limited duration. This therefore corresponds with a temporally limited increase in profits and a similarly limited increase in profit-sharing. If, however, this higher profit is not reduced by price reductions after an appropriate period of time, the profit-sharing payments paid out of it can no longer be regarded as a form of income corresponding to performance. These payments would detract from the entire performance-related incomes policy.

3. Monopoly profits substantially increases the profit differential between large and small firms. Even at the same rate of profit, the profit position of smaller firms is at a disadvantage in comparison with the greater absolute profit of larger firms. This is so because, after deduction of profit-sharing payments and entrepreneurial net profit, less remains to the small firm for net investments, research activities, etc. Therefore, the greater ab-

solute profit surpluses (in excess of profit-sharing)--assuming the same rates of profit-- or continually recurring temporary dynamic profit increases, which cause price decreases that work to the benefit of consumers should suffice for the development of the larger firms. Monopoly profits would rapidly enlarge the gap between the large and small firms, thus leading to an increasing dependence of the small firms, and finally to the elimination of them, one after the other, just as under capitalism.

Aside from monopoly profits and their negative effects, one further negative after effect of macro-monopolies needs to be mentioned. Macro-monopolies exhibit two different, alternating developmental tendencies, which suggest that no monopoly can manage to do away with competition absolutely and permanently; at best it may temporarily and relatively preclude it.

In certain periods, the macro-monopoly has less control of the market. It will be at least constrained by potential competition, which develops when the same, or similar goods with a substitution effect appear. To be sure, it has to be regarded as a macro-monopoly, since it obtains a long-term, relatively high rate of profit. However, rising competition threatens these monopoly profits and would sooner or later force price reductions that would also lower the monopoly profits.

In this situation macro-monopolies will employ both socially useful means and unfair, no longer market-conforming means in a battle to preserve their monopoly profits. The beneficial means are found in efforts to bring about rapid technical, technological, product innovative and other improvements that promote efficiency. These aim at driving a competitor out of the arena, or at maintaining one's share of the market at previous monopoly prices. The negative forms of struggle mainly involve a wide range of means of applying pressure on customers (not to buy from the threatening competition), on its suppliers of raw materials (not to supply the competition), on influential politicians (for example, to establish customs barriers or other measures against foreign competition, etc.). Even purposeful price reductions of limited duration and dumping prices aimed at destroying smaller competitors and troublesome outsiders, figure among these forms of monopoly struggle.

However, there are also conditions under which the macro-monopoly has firmly established its position, feels no competition--not even potential--and is relatively easily able to control the market. Inflation is one of the conditions favorable to macro-monopolies. Here the macro-monopoly can maintain its monopoly profits without substantial further efforts. On the contrary, it will not be much interested in increasing efficiency and production, since this could also expand production and supply and lead to price reductions. Even the buying out and "burying" of inventions is characteristic for this period. Under inflationary conditions it is that much easier to increase profits by raising prices rather than by strenuous and risk-laden innovations. The macro-monopoly can raise its prices more rapidly in an inflationary period than can other non-monopolistic firms, thus increasing its rate of profit at the expense of the non-monopolies, despite general increases in costs.

In this way, macro-monopolies have a contradictory effect on development. At certain times tendencies toward technical and economic progress and toward more rapid quantitative and qualitative development predominate in them. At other times however, tendencies toward stagnation and hostility toward innovation come to the fore. The negative forms of struggle used by macro-monopolies and their occasional stagnation effects are additional negative consequences that create a need for anti-monopolistic measures in the interest of society.

If we assume a monopolistic rate of profit to be the decisive indicator of a macro-monopoly, the question legitimately arises as to whether macro-monopolies cannot be prevented completely. In our opinion, though it may be possible to use certain measures to counteract them, their emergence cannot be entirely prevented.

To be sure, it is generally known that concentrations of capital based on accumulations of profit are what make the emergence of macro-monopolies possible. However, since it is not possible to determine the level of concentration at which macro-monopoly begins, and since, in our opinion, this level of concentration may be present in two or three large firms within the same branch, it is not possible to prevent the emergence of macro-monopolies merely by placing limits on concentration.

It would be far more feasible, then, for merger plans to be kept under scrutiny--as is already being done under the capitalist system--since, as is generally known, market-dominating macro-monopolies can also emerge from them. But of course not every merger needs to lead to a weakening of competition. Rather, medium-sized firms may fuse with the aim of defending themselves against a macro-monopoly's gaining too strong a market position. A merger of several medium-sized firms can prevent their impending displacement from the market by large competitors and an ensuing elimination of competition. Thus, one can require no more than state supervision of merger proposals, their obligatory registration, and an examination of anticipated con-

sequences of every merger. Only if a merger would clearly
lead to market domination and thence to macro-monopoly,
should it be administratively disallowed.

Obviously, no attempt should be made to abandon the
prohibition of price cartels. To be sure, there will always
be shortcomings in the supervision of cartel-formation,
since many of the oligopolists' most successful modes of be-
havior--by means of which they mutually maintain price sol-
idarity--keep supply so low that it has no price-dampening
effect. Such behavior is possible in the absence of written
agreements, or when such agreements are kept secret.
Even cooperation among independent firms, which usually
serves to increase productivity and thus has to be welcomed, may suddenly slow down production with the aim of
maintaining prices. This would produce cartel-like effects
which, however, could not be ascertained from the outside.

The new system must however reject any attempt to
eliminate cartel-like price agreements by means of price
controls, since no price control agency is in a position to
determine market-conforming criteria for the price levels of
individual products. The price controls implemented in
countries with market economies were precipitated by an inflationary development. As such, however, they were not
able to prevent the real cause of the inflationary development: disturbance of the macro-economic equilibrium by incomes that were rising rapidly in comparison with real production. Instead, attempts were made to combat the
symptom of inflation: rising prices.

If the government is not in a position to check inflation by eliminating its fundamental causes, price controls (a
braking mechanism which is not in itself market conforming)
cannot be completely ruled out. This is particularly so if,
during persistent inflation, it is primarily the monopolies
who raise their prices quickly and thereby further accelerate the general rise in prices and incomes. If price controls are taken only for what they can be, that is, as a
relatively weak braking mechanism which cannot basically
eliminate inflation, they can be accepted on these terms.
For governments, from whom one of course cannot expect
any systemic critique, price controls no doubt have a mere
alibi function.

Price controls can dampen rising prices only for a very
limited range of key products which are of relatively constant quality and can thus be controlled. Goods like energy, fuel, building materials, transportation, rents, basic
foodstuffs, etc., however, have a crucial influence on the
real income and consumption of the population. Supervision
of their prices is thus often a political necessity. Since,
however, the population's range of consumption is substantially broader than this, consisting of tens, indeed hun-
dreds of thousands of kinds of products, the   impetus of

prices cannot be checked--analogous to what occurs in the Soviet bloc states.

Qualitative changes in products (often only of a formal character) make it impossible to control broader ranges of product types, since price must always be tied to a particular product quality and can be circumvented with every change. It would naturally be senseless to prohibit changes in products, since this would lead to general stagnation. Thus in times of an inflationary rise in income in which total demand is rising faster than real supply, price increases may be checked for some kinds of products. But prices of the bulk of the other, uncontrollable products will rise all the more rapidly.

Thus, the more the prices of goods are controlled and their growth administratively checked, the more the system has to be transformed into an instrument, whose criteria are purely subjective, and which is out of step with the market. No central price control agency can ascertain price relationships in their constant state of flux as well as is done by the relationship of supply and demand. If the price is to be an equilibrium price, it must be able flexibly to reflect unpredictable fluctuations in supply and demand relationships. Or it has to be able to bring about flexible changes in the proportions of production in market-oriented firms by means of its potential for change. However, the moment prices are as much as slowed down under conditions of increasing supply, without production being sufficient to compensate flexibly for varying demand surpluses, unsatisfied demand, that is, gaps in supply, will necessarily result. This is characteristic of the "socialist" planned economy. However, all demand surpluses then give rise to a black market, and thus ultimately lead to forced price increases after all.

Price controls can thus be understood less as an effective emergency measure, and rather more as a political issue. Even when combined with equally blind wage controls, the combination is not an effective anti-inflationary instrument. Even in the capitalist system, wage controls are only a means of retarding inflation, since they cannot eliminate the antagonism between wages and profits. Both sides will and must blame the other side for the income ups and downs. There can be no objective determination of income distribution as long as the antagonism of interests between profits and wages prevails, the capital alienation of the working people is not overcome, and the distribution of income is not objectivized by means of generally accepted, democratic distribution planning.

We have had to return to the problem of distribution in order to show why price controls have been introduced in present times at all, and in order to combat political illusions which purport to see them as a weapon against monopolistic price-fixing. Although we see them as a very limited auxilliary measure against a capitalist inflationary development, we consider them to be utterly useless in the struggle against monopoly prices as such. If the necessity of market-determined equilibrium prices (which no central authority can determine properly) is recognized, then there is a possibility of preventing those developments of monopolistic rates of profit which lead to relative constraints on production and higher monopoly prices. It would naturally make more sense to prevent the emergence of the productive basis from which market domination and the formation of a monopolistic rate of profit grow. We have already shown, however, that there is no objective criterion which would reliably make possible a recognition of monopoly-forming levels of production and concentrations. The corresponding administrative decisions would, however, have even worse consequences than would be the case with administrative determination of prices.

Where there are no monopoly profits, even a high degree of concentration does not have antisocial effects, since prices as well as profits would correspond to real creation of use-value. Neither would stagnation be probable in this branch, since the sale of goods at non-monopolistic prices does not promote anti-productive tendencies. On the contrary, the interest in temporary profit increases promotes efforts toward more and more improvements in efficacy.

Monopolistic profit rates thus remain the decisive indicator of a macro-monopoly. Unfortunately, they cannot be recognized until they are already present, and a macro-monopoly thus already exists. It is, of course, possible to observe especially carefully each intended merger between larger firms, whose rates of profit correspond to that of the national economy. It would then be possible to detect very quickly any change to a monopolistic rate of profit. However, a development toward concentration cannot be curbed as long as there are no monopolistic profits. It is thus necessary to consider primarily measures which would lead to a dismantling of monopoly profits. The more effective these measures are, the more reliably they will actually be able to detect and reduce monopoly profits, and the more strongly they will also be able to work against intentional efforts to form monopolies. This alone can deter monopolistic developments in the enterprises.

PROMOTION OF COMPETITION AND MONOPOLY PROFIT TAX

High monopoly profits can occur in particular when an unstoppable production merger (trusts, combines, secretly cartelized oligopolies, etc.) is unanimously bent on, and in a position to manipulate the supply of production in entire branches. In such cases, production can be lowered to price levels which would bring in obvious monopoly profits.

If at the same time, an inflow of capital that could threaten the manipulation of supply is forcibly prevented then anti-monopoly policies must seek primarily to thwart the manipulation of supply. In such cases, the market mechanism alone no longer suffices since, as we have shown, monopolistic production mergers, once in existence, are so large and powerful that any new firm lacking comparably strong capital backing does not stand a chance of competing.

At the present stage of development, the state represents a political and economic force sufficiently powerful to promote an anti-monopolistic development of competition under certain circumstances and using a certain strategy. It must be emphasized, however, that this cannot be carried through consistently in capitalist systems, and anti-monopolistic policies in operation here are less successful, indeed often a farce. First of all, in the absence of a macro-distribution plan, there is no way reliably to detect monopolistic profits. They are usually noticed too late, if at all, and hardly lend themselves to quantification. Second, the necessary development of profit cannot be socially assured, and every private firm sees its profits as a guarantee of their struggle against possible competitors as well as against the unions. Third, monopoly profits give the macro-monopolists enormous economic power. This lends itself to rapid translation into political influence which is then used to weaken anti-monopoly policies to the point where they are harmless.

In the reformed system, profit would in general be distributed in such a manner that neither a private person nor a firm would be able to amass so much that concentrated political power would be able to grow out of it. Even though there will be private entrepreneurial profits, they will be restricted so as to meet the consumption needs of the entrepreneurs and provide the necessary incentives, but they will not be suffcient for purposes of political manipulation. Profits in the co-worker owned enterprises are thus subject to constant public control and cannot be misused for political purposes. However, since it is precisely the large firms, who once tended toward monopoly, that are organized in the form of the co-worker-owned enterprises, this kind of pressure against anti-monopolistic policies will disappear in the reformed system.

Besides, in the new system, profit has a deliberate and planned social function. Personal incentives toward enterprise and efficiency are part of this, while antisocial abuse of profits should be prevented. Right from the planning stage, the quality-of-life commission, mentioned frequently above, has a decisive influence on the distribution and utilization of profit, especially since determination of tax policy also falls into its domain. This planning also constitutes the basis of the ongoing check on profits required by the anti-monopoly policy and, above all, of the monopoly taxation policy to be discussed later on. This does not mean that the commission could carry out this check by itself, since controls are governed by the economic council and can only be carried out by authorized taxation officials. However, a special sub-commission, which would exclude any representatives of the producers, would be appointed by the economic council to oversee the entire anti-monopoly policy. Macro-planning is based on advance calculation of the need for investment. And even at an average rate of profit in the national economy, the net profit secured by means of the distribution plan should guarantee a profit to all branches showing motivation and the will to invest. If this rate of profit is exceeded as a result of entrepreneurial initiative, amounts for investment as well as for incentive (co-worker and entrepreneur profit shares) can naturally be further increased. The monopolistic freezing of these extra profits by means of manipulation of production and the market should, however, be avoided in any case. Control of the development of the rate of profit will be made easier by macro-planning, mainly because the average rate of profit in the national economy will be planned. A continuously exercised control over the national economic rate of profit makes possible the timely discovery of all deviations in the rates of profit of all branches and individual firms. As already mentioned, this of course necessitates a statutory system of bookkeeping which gives access to all categories necessary for a calculation of real profits. The registration and summarization of the development of profit, automated if possible, would, at the right time, provide the data required for all necessary anti-monopolistic measures. Verification of the correctness of all profit figures by competent state authorities is, of course, not to be ruled out, but it would fundamentally serve the interest of the coworkers of all firms. For the registration and control of the rate of profit, in addition to the uniform calculation of profits, a uniform estimation of the capital of the enterprises is important. As we have already explained, all capital income transferred out of the enterprise (including, for example, interest) must be calculated as part of gross profits. The type of capital estimation is then a matter of convention.   The procedure we have proposed is derived from a purely economic consideration, which could be modified for reasons of accounting technicalities or other specific considerations.   What is important, however, is the basic economic (correctly motivated) calculation of the rate of profit, <u>as well as</u>, in particular, the <u>uniformity</u> of the system of calculation and accounting throughout the production system.

The calculation of capital requires first and foremost a determination of fixed assets (fixed capital) at the beginning of each year.   We have advocated the method or net asset calculation, which seems to be appropriate for recognizing the real development of the value of productive capital.   With this method, the fixed assets, divided into several main groups (for example, land and buildings, machinery and mechanical appurtenances, plant and office furnishings) are calculated at their acquisition prices after deduction of the binding annual rate of depreciation. Depreciation rates will be prescribed by law and enterprises will have to adhere to them in the calculation and posting of capital. Depreciation will always be deducted from the acquisition value (purchase price) of an individual facility, that is, from the residual value of the facility still being utilized in the domain of production (that is, integral to profit and loss calculation rather than used up) as well as from the value of new facilities added in the preceding year.   Added to the current annual total capital value will be the balance remaining from the previous year, after depreciation of the old facilities, which in the new inventory will be reduced in the amount of the discarded equipment to the extent of their remaining value, and increased to the extent of the newly added facilities at their value at acquisition.

The objective floating capital will be calculated in its productive form at inventory time.   The latter of course includes supplies on hand as well as materials being used in production (processing) or already in finished form (half-finished and finished products).   Also included here, however, must be that amount of finance capital demonstrably needed to purchase the necessary materials to complete the production recorded in the inventory and which cannot be paid for out of receipts.   This amount of finance capital cannot be left out of consideration, since firms with particularly long time lags between production and sales--for instance shipyards--cannot have all the materials on hand necessary to finish production that has been initiated.   The additional required capital should be included in the calculation. All purchases of materials made out of profit receipts count as replacement and/or extension of the calculated floating capital. It is gross profit that is tracked in calculating rates of profit.   And since this includes interest on outside capital, the outside capital (credit) required to complete the production in progress at the time of inventory must also be included in floating capital. What has previously been said about the additionally required finance capital which the enterprise would have to invest out of its own assets also applies here. But on the other hand, credits taken out during the year to expand supplies or production, must already be viewed as net investment and be calculated in the following year in the form of expanded floating capital.

Wage capital must be calculated in its requisite finance capital form at the time of inventory. The finance capital (the enterprise's own, or credit) which must be available so that the firm can pay the wages of those workers needed at the time of inventory, and which--with exception of the first weekly payment--does not derive from revenues during the payment period, will be calculated as wage capital. The first week's or month's (for those paid on a monthly basis) payment can be calculated as wage capital even if it derives from this week or this month (highest rate of circulation of wage capital). All further weekly or monthly payments paid out of current revenues can no longer be viewed as wage capital. In the case of firms where a number of weekly or monthly payments do not derive from the revenues of this period (low rate of circulation of wage capital) the entire amount of wages will be calculated as wage capital until such time as the first amounts deriving from revenues are utilized. Any increase in the labor force during the year, including the necessary expansion of wage capital (the enterprise's own, or credit) will be viewed as net investment, which will appear at the beginning of the next year as expanded wage capital.

In planning the rate of profit for the national economy, which constitutes a decisive criterion for calculation of monopolistic rates of profit, rigidly fixed quotients alone cannot be used, but rather it is necessary to work with a range between two quotients. Assuming a national economic rate of profit of 25 percent, for example, an upper limit to the rate of profit to be tolerated would have to be established, based on specific plan calculations, say, 30 percent. The range of variation in rate of profit established for the national economy need not fix the lower limit to a scope of variation. The lower limit of the actual development of profits in the firm can lie indefinitely below the rate of profit calculated as average for the national economy (in our example 25 percent). While the upper limit of tolerance (in our example, 30 percent) can, of course, also be exceeded, it will be used as an important criterion for certain measures.

   The upper limit of tolerance for variation in the rate of profit should not be primarily a manifestation of uncertainty in the estimation of the rate of profit for the national economy. It should be estimated as accurately as possible and will be constantly refined, primarily on the basis of ongoing statistical calculation. Deviations of a few percentage points above the national economic average in the actual rates of profit of individual branches and enterprises will, however, have to be tolerated for the time being. However, it should still be possible to exceed this limit of tolerance as long as no administrative cutoff is permitted to restrict the development of profit in firms. If measures conforming to the market are used against a development in profit rates that lies above the limit of tolerance for a predetermined length of time, they should be seen as conforming to the market inasmuch as they represent substitutes for an inadequately functioning or monopolistically limited market mechanism.

   It should always be kept in mind that under conditions of competition, that is, where there is an unhindered flow of liquid capital to all branches, rates of profit substantially above the national economic average would not be possible over the long run. The period of higher profits would be limited to the time needed by new capital to establish a competing firm or to expand an already existing smaller firm. Thus, if in a majority of branches the average firm (dominating market volumes) should, for example, attain a rate of profit oscillating around 25 percent, whereas 30 percent or more were registered in one or a few branches, profit-oriented capital would, sooner or later, flow into the latter branches and dampen their rate of profit.

   But if macro-monopolies prevent such an inflow of capital through their control over the branches concerned, and no firm, no bank, and no private individual thus dares to make their capital available in these branches, then it would be entirely market conforming for the state to take measures to support and facilitate a building up of such competition.

   To do this, it would be necessary, first and foremost, to establish a period of time as the criterion for determination of a monopoly rate of profit. As already mentioned, it should include approximately that period of time necessary (expressed as the average for the national economy) for potential competitive capital to establish a competing enterprise. We are here assuming, for the time being, a period of three years. In this regard, however, empirically based corrections could still naturally take place. This assumption would mean that exceeding the limit of tolerance of the profit rate for over three years would be an indication of the presence of existing monopoly profits. Whether a single dominating firm or several firms (oligopolies or even several medium-sized firms) are involved here, is not crucial. Either way, as is now clear, the branch concerned will be protected against profit-inhibiting competition by a macro-monopoly.

The economic council can now propose to the anti-monopoly commission the following measures to promote competition:

1. State support for outsiders in the monopolized branch.

2. Support for newly established firms in the monopolized branch.

3. Support for price-reducing imports of products in the monopolized branch.

These measures of state support would, for the most part, take the form of cheap state credits or temporary tax reductions for those outsiders, newly founded enterprises or importers, who would contribute to overcoming the monopoly. Which of the three forms would be used would depend on an analysis of specific conditions within the branch. Thus, for example, calculation of elasticity of demand in the affected branch would have to play a substantial role. Only where there was an elastic or at least neutral development of demand would there be any point, for example, in expanding supply. Thus, only where it is anticipated that the expanded supply, together with simultaneously falling prices caused by competitive production (or imports), would bring about a corresponding rise in demand, would a decision be made in favor of this kind of subsidized competition.

The results of the analysis would already be important in determining whether subsidized competition would really be viable without subsidy after a certain period of time. In no case should a permanent state subsidy evolve out of competition-promoting state support. The latter should be viewed only as a temporary start-up incentive impulse in a market previously dominated by powerful macro-monopolies. The analysis should, however, also show convincing prospects for the autonomous existence of a firm initially supported by the state. Should this not be the case, or if it were concluded that the market would in future, suffer from oversupply, subsidized competition should be abandoned. That is to say, a market oversupply would give rise to devastating competition, in which case either the new firms or the old macro-monopolies would be eliminated. This would mean a serious loss to the national economy and would bring about grave social consequences.

Since state-promoted competition is not feasible in all cases nor always advantageous in the long run, one can also propose a general and automatically functioning anti-monopoly instrument, namely a special monopoly profit tax.[17] It would be applied by means of a special tax assessment rate and special method of calculation wherever a monopolistic rate of profit is determined to exist over a three-year period on the basis of the ongoing calculations of rate of profit. Thus, as soon as a firm's rate of profit exceeded the limit of tolerance for three years, the special monopoly profit tax (monopoly tax for short) would automatically come into effect. Its function would be to drive down the monopolistic rate of profit to the level of the national economic rate of profit over the course of several years.

Calculation of annual monopoly tax would be done by means of a special formula. The firm's rate of profit could not, however, be reduced to the level of the national economic rate of profit within the space of a year, since this would be intolerable for the firm. The taxation would thus have to continue for several years while the rate of profit would gradually be reduced to the desired level. As soon as the level of the national economic rate of profit was reached, the taxation would stop automatically.

Therefore, if it is ascertained that a firm has realized an actual rate of profit higher than the limit of tolerance of the national economic rate of profit for three years of observation, the extent to which the actual rate of profit of the firm exceeds the national economic rate of profit is to be understood as a monopoly rate of profit. It should now be possible to reduce this monopoly rate of profit over the course of several years (period of adjustment) by means of a monopoly tax coefficient and special tax calculation. The monopoly tax should be designed in such a way that the monopoly tax would increase progressively along with the rate of monopoly profit and decline progressively as it falls. The desired, yet economically bearable rate of reduction of the macro-monopolies' profit rates would be calculated cooperatively by the planning commission, the monopoly commis-

---

[17] W. A. Joehr already saw a means of combating monopoly profits not matching performance in a progressive taxation. Even though our monopoly profit tax differs from his tax conceptions, it pursues the same anti-monopolistic purpose. Cf. W. A. Joehr, "Die Konzentration als Problem der Theorie der Wirtschaftspolitik," in H. Arndt, ed. Die Konzentration der Wirtschaft (Berlin, 1960), p. 1,327.

sion, and the tax authorities.[18]

The reduced profit results from deduction of the monopoly tax from the profit of the macro-monopolistic firm. To be sure, this reduced profit will still represent a monopoly profit--though a reduced one. The enterprise's reduced rate of profit has, at any rate, fallen in the direction of the planned national economic rate of profit, though it still lies above it and thus represents a reduced monopoly rate of profit.

The reduced rate of profit will be prescribed to the macro-monopolies as a maximal rate of profit for the current year, that is until the next tax assessment. The purpose of monopoly taxation is not to derive income for the state, but rather to put pressure on the macro-monopolies to lower their monopoly prices. Prescription of a maximum rate of profit is actually a substitute for the lack of pressure which ought to result from an influx of competitive capital. The macro-monopolies would now be compelled to reduce their prices, give up monopoly profit, and reduce their rate of profit to the national economic average. They can, of course, also increase their net investment and production in order to effect price reductions and arrive at the national average rate of profit.

Net investments in this controlled year could not, however, reduce the rate of profit, since they will be made out of profits and attributed to them. It is, therefore, not

---

[18] The monopoly tax rate is calculated as follows:
$$TxMo = f \cdot pre \cdot prMo$$

TxMo = Tax rate levied on that part of the rate of profit of the monopolistic enterprise which exceeds the average rate of profit in the national economy

f = Coefficient set by the plan, regulating the speed with which monopolistic rates of profits are to be pushed to the average level in the national economy

pre = Rate of profit of the enterprise

$$= \frac{\text{profit of an enterprise}}{\text{total capital of an enterprise}}$$

prMo = Monopolistic profit rate of the enterprise=amount by which the profit rate of the enterprise exceeds the profit rate in the national economy.

possible to avert price reductions by means of investments.
Otherwise, it would indeed be possible to avoid the monopoly tax with the most absurd and unproductive investments.
The adjustment period begins with monopoly taxation after
the three-year calculation of monopoly profit and ends with
the reduction of profit to the level of a national economic
average profit. During this period the macro-monopoly can
itself contribute to the reduction of the period of taxation
only by passing on profits to society through price reductions. If the price reductions are so far-reaching that the
rate of profit already actually falls to the required national
economic level after the first year of monopoly taxation, the
adjustment period will be ended. The firm can now again
raise its rate of profit for three years and exceed the limit
of tolerance. If, however, the macro-monopoly reduces
prices during the current year only to the point of meeting the prescribed or maximum rate of profit, and thus
shows a reduced monopoly profit, the adjustment period will
continue. In the second year, calculation of the monopoly
tax assessment continues according to the same formula.
Since, however, the monopoly rate of profit was lower than
in the previous year (has not exceeded the rate of profit
prescribed as maximal), the new monopoly tax will come out
smaller. This will induce macro-monopolies to reduce their
monopoly rates of profit as far as possible, if they cannot
eliminate them immediately. The lower the monopoly rate of
profit is at the beginning of every year of the adjustment
period, the lower the monopoly tax will turn out to be in
accordance with the given method of calculation.

If we assume, purely for theoretical purposes, that, in
each year of the adjustment period, the macro-monopoly ad-
heres to the reduced--that is, achieves the maximum rate of
profit, the rate of profit will decline year by year as a result of ongoing monopoly taxation, until it matches the national economic rate of profit.

As macro-monopolies learn that it hardly pays not to
keep to the maximum rate of profit and that this surplus
amount beyond the target rate of profit will be taxed away
in any case, they will be induced not to exceed the maximum rate of profit.

We find that pre and prMo in their mutual interplay
are the dynamic elements of the tax formula. If the monopoly profit rate prMo=0, the monopoly tax rate TxMo also=0.
If prMo rises above zero, the tax rate then rises progressively and declines again correspondingly when the monopolistic rate of profit is reduced. The amount of the monopoly tax is determined by multiplication of the monopoly tax
TxMo by the total capital of the enterprise.

Since it will not be possible to establish this maximum rate of profit fictitiously, either by net investments or by write-off manipulations, it can be expected that it will be realized by the necessary price reductions. Given the continuation of monopoly taxation, price and profit reductions may in any case be anticipated instead of monopoly tax payments. That is, one can hardly expect payments of monopoly tax for many years. This is also the decisive argument against fears that the monopoly tax could inhibit technical progress and interest in increased profits.

It must not be forgotten, first of all, that the limit of tolerance allows profit increases, in the first instance, without countermeasures. Second, the limit of tolerance can be exceeded for three years in a row, so that profits can be very high during this period. Both of these factors can certainly motivate a maximum growth of profits by means of technical progress, increases in use-value, and improvements in efficiency. Then, however, it is only fair, from the point of view of the national economy, to regard the three years exceeding the limit of tolerance as sufficient compensation for extraordinary performance. No permanent compensation should come out of it. On the contrary, the macro-monopoly should be forced, as in the case of a perfectly functioning market mechanism, to earn the fruits of its extraordinary performance and special compensation.

It may be contended that a good firm can constantly produce extraordinary results, and in the space of a single year, implement price reductions (that is, as it were, passing on to society the fruits of its extraordinary performance), but simultaneously again realize many new increases in use-value and efficiency and thus once again achieve a higher rate of profit. However, even this argument cannot be recognized. The basic criterion of a well-functioning market mechanism is not simply that it manages to effect some kind of price reductions, but rather that it produces a tendency toward the equalization of profits in all branches. The more perfectly the market mechanism functions, the more flexibly and rapidly would tendencies toward differential profit rates be neutralized by tendencies toward equalization. A firm which forges ahead within its own branch will be overtaken sooner or later if there are no monopolistic impediments. And a branch which overtakes other branches in its average rate of profit will be pulled back to the average for the national economy by an influx of capital, if there are no monopolistic hurdles. Constant expansion and contraction characterize a functioning market mechanism. Where one of these two processes begins to predominate at the expense of the other, the entire mechanism is jeopardized.

Thus, market conformity is only achieved when a monopoly firm is artificially transformed back into a competitive firm through the mechanism of monopoly taxation. The
macro-monopolistic firm should reduce not only a number of
its prices, but also its rate of profit. Once the latter falls
to the level of the national economic rate of profit, this
means that society actually receives the fruits of extraordinary performance, for which extraordinary compensation
was paid for a determinate period. Subsequently, a claim
can again be made for additional extraordinary performance.

Thus, under the proposed system, when, after two
years of excess profits (above the limit of tolerance) a firm
reduces its prices and rate of profit during the third year
on its own initiative to the national economic average, the
monopoly tax will not be imposed. And, from that year onward, the firm would again have three free years to increase its profits. The reduction in profit rate can, however, be achieved only by price reductions and not by
capital increases. Since the rate of profit will be calculated
every year, and net investments can be realized each year
only out of registered profits, it cannot be used to lower
the rate of profit.

With each year's net investments, the assets of the
next year will naturally be increased. However, since at
the same time the scope of production also increases, the
capital expansion alone does not bring about any reduction
in the rate of profit. If, on the other hand, the rate of
profit falls substantially, either as a result of reductions or
of a possible decline in the productivity of a branch, this
has to be recognized. It is to be stressed, however, that
the decline in productivity cannot then be the manifestation
of a general decline in productivity in the national economy,
in other words, of a general reduction in the national economic rate of profit. Only in the event that the rate of
profit of the branch concerned approximates the national
economic rate of profit, will this be recognized and the firm
again have three years time.

It is clear that competition-facilitating measures will not
become superfluous with the introduction of a tax on monopolies. Both means must be combined. It will not always
be easy to advocate competitive production, especially if its
prospects are uncertain. It can sometimes be more promis-
ing to advocate competitive imports. If, however, neither
the one nor the other holds out any promise of success, the
monopoly tax will always work, in the final analysis, as the
crucial instrument. The market thus can be perfected for
the benefit of society. In the process, the negative economic and social effects of the capitalist market mechanism--
which are manifest in the form of cyclical macro-disturbances and massive unemployment--will be overcome by means of

democratic   macro-distribution   planning   and   capital
neutralization.   Both of these reinforce the positive operation of the market mechanism, which is indispensable at the
present stage of development.

6

REFORM ASPIRATIONS AND POLITICS

NEW HORIZONS OF ECONOMIC DEVELOPMENT

The reformed economic system, with its three fundamental pillars of capital neutralization, macro-distribution planning, and the regulated market mechanism, ought to, and can make it possible to implement the following new principles, purposes, and structures of the economy:

1. Macro-distribution planning, as envisioned here, permits two or three alternative variants. If these can be prepared and the ideas of different interest and opinion groups taken into account, this will allow the <u>further</u> <u>and</u> <u>significant</u> <u>democratization</u> of industrial societies, it can contribute to their <u>postindustrial</u> <u>humanization</u>,and can increase their <u>attractiveness</u> <u>throughout</u> <u>the</u> <u>world</u>.

2. Such planning would enable society to make economic development something more than mere profit-making. Growth would cease to be an end in itself and would instead become a consciously regulated means of achieving democratically determined objectives. The economic <u>future</u> would no longer confront people as blind fate but could be <u>systematically</u> <u>managed</u> <u>in</u> <u>its</u> <u>fundamental</u> <u>development</u>.

3. The purpose of any economic activity, namely continuously improving the satisfaction of human needs, should not be downgraded but rather consciously emphasized. The reforms, however, would block any one-sided manipulation of needs by monopolistic production interests and provide a new basis for the <u>growing</u> <u>number</u> <u>of</u> <u>people's</u> <u>non-economic</u> <u>interests</u> in the economic sphere as well.

4. Needs such as a <u>stronger</u> <u>feeling</u> <u>of</u> <u>security</u>, <u>job</u> <u>satisfaction</u>, <u>personal</u> <u>fulfillment</u> <u>and</u> <u>self-realization</u>, <u>environmental</u> <u>protection</u> <u>and</u> <u>preservation</u> <u>of</u> <u>nature</u>, <u>more</u> <u>humane</u> <u>arrangements</u> <u>of</u> <u>working</u> con-

ditions, equality of opportunity and reduction of
social inequalities, increase in leisure time and enrichment of personal interests will increasingly
complement people's material needs. Their realization and satisfaction can only be effected by institutional changes in the micro- and macro-spheres of
the economy.

5. True equality of opportunity for people will only
    come about where the differences between the liv-
    ing conditions of individuals right from childhood
    can be considerably minimized. Income differen-
    tials, which result from differences in occupational
    training, job qualification, and labor intensity,
    particularly in white-collar activities, can be
    strongly reduced, though not yet eliminated. The
    incomes of the weakest social strata can be raised
    more rapidly. Planned decision-making concerning
    the distribution of profits, enhancing social securi-
    ty, economic and educational development coordi-
    nated by plan, reorganization for increased leisure
    time, the changed self-consciousness of people in
    the co-worker enterprises--all this can contribute
    to the reduction of social inequalities and greater
    equality of opportunity.

6. Economic growth can be systematically regulated in
    such a way that various diverse goals do not come
    into conflict. The reduction of differences in social
    consumption and life inequalities within one coun-
    try, and on a world scale, will remain the primary
    objective for some time. At the same time it is
    possible to coordinate this objective with the calcu-
    lable growth resources on earth. Growth need no
    longer destroy the natural habitat of man but, on
    the contrary, should ensure an improvement of the
    ecology. It must be coordinated with the develop-
    ment of the population, which will ultimately re-
    quire not only the regulation of economic growth
    but also population growth. Without macro-plan-
    ning, these contradictory developmental objectives
    would necessarily result in grave situations of con-
    flict.

7. Full employment and the right to work for each and
    every individual can be guaranteed by planning for
    the provision of investment funds and the deter-
    mination of economic goals. Full employment does
    not necessarily require economic growth, however.
    Only where the pursuit of other objectives makes

this desirable can the development of investments ensure the required creation of jobs. Where society opts for slower growth, and where the resultant lower investment activity does not create jobs for all, the systematic reduction of working hours should be planned for. Whatever level of consumption and quality of life society opts for, investment and working hours can be regulated in such a way as to ensure basically full employment.

8. At the present stage of development, society cannot do without individual initiative and the entrepreneurial spirit. Ideologically motivated suppression of private entrepreneurial activity results in great economic losses to society. Even with a system of macro-planning, there will still be an element of risk in entrepreneurial ideas and activities. For this reason, there should be not only appropriate profit motives but also guarantees of private property.

The right to private ownership of productive values and the appropriation of profits does not, however, have to be equated with the infinite accumulation of wealth from capital income. It can be assumed that despite fixed maximum limits on private profit-shares and the planned neutralization of newly generated capital from profits, a sufficiently strong incentive for entrepreneurial activity will remain. Indeed, the indispensable entrepreneurial initiative may well be enhanced since the corresponding guarantees would dispel fears of expropriation.

9. The creation of a profit interest on the part of all the working people in market-oriented enterprises can substantially increase the efficiency of production and investments. Capital and profit are no longer alienated economic forces in opposition to wage interests but are transformed into immediate objects of the working people's interests and linked to their wage interest. In this way they acquire a broad interest in the qualitative development of the enterprise's production and market performance. The working people will view capital as the basis of their own economy, and their indifference toward its utilization, growth, and investment activity will be overcome. Investments will no longer have to fight against wage and consumption interests but can be planned to harmonize with these interests.

10. The working strata will increasingly regard profit as the monetary form of the surplus product, required to generate net investments for planned economic growth, for most societal needs, and for the indispensable motivation of private entrepreneurs and co-workers (profit-sharing). This conception of profit arises from publicly planned and announced distribution and utilization of profits, from the direct experiences of profit-sharing, from limits on the appropriation of private profit, and from the widest availability, in the enterprises, of economic information and education about profit utilization. Making public the development of profits can eliminate the distrust of profits and contribute to people's identification with the objectives of their enterprises and, as a result, with the objectives of the economy as a whole.

11. Wage increases will no longer have to be gained through struggles against the interests of capital owners, but will be determined by plan in accordance with the growth of consumer goods production. Trade unions will participate decisively in the planning commission (quality-of-life commission) by preparing wage-group catalogues for the economy as a whole and some alternatives for wage growth. The volume of wages in production and in the market-determined service sectors will be coordinated with enterprises' net profits, with social expenditures, and with other consumptive incomes. The occupational groups, and/or wage groups and wage rates (and in this context wage differentials between the various wage groups) will be determined on the basis of long-term evaluations of different jobs in terms of the physical and mental stress bound up with them, as well as the differing preparation and training they require. The short-term relationship between supply and demand on the one hand, and certain occupations and qualifications on the other should be taken into account. Sectoral trade union representatives and labor researchers should work, in the wage-planning commissions, toward the flexible modification of wage groups and wage differentials in accordance with the development of the economy, the workers' interests, and the market. They should do this in collaboration with the production commissions of the economic sectors.

12. <u>Social security</u> is recognized as a <u>vital right of man</u> <u>in</u> society and <u>is planned in accordance with the</u> <u>development of wages</u>. Since national income is dis-tributed according to the plan, all social expendi-tures from state revenues can be made in line with annual requirements. Taxes, which every income earner pays in proportion to his level of income, always include social security contributions--the aggregate of which is pre-calculated on the basis of social income payments during the planning period. Since there are no cyclical fluctuations in produc-tion and income, and no mass unemployment, the requisite social incomes can also be assured from annual revenues without undue fluctuations. In determining the real growth of wages in terms of the planned consumption fund, the proportional growth of social incomes is taken into account. Thus unsatisfied social income claims will no longer occur, and the insecurity facing individuals in old age and in times of illness--an insecurity unwor-thy of human dignity--will be overcome.

13. <u>Socially met needs will in future increase in signifi-cance</u>. In particular, new structures of living conditions in urban planning and modern innova-tions in transportation will become the foremost goals of work and production; they will attempt to create healthier, cleaner, quieter, more ecological-ly-oriented living conditions for people, and to overcome their isolation. All this can no longer be provided for out of individual incomes, but must be assured by the plan from out of collective (munici-pal, state, etc.) revenues. Thus, to the extent that in the near future differences in income and consumption become inevitable as motivations for work of varying intensity, to that extent will equalizing tendencies emerge in the form of collec-tively satisfied needs.

14. Productive activity must continue to respect the principle of efficiency as decisive, and hence opti-mization of profit will remain the dominant motiva-tion. Yet at the same time new objectives in so-cial work activity will gain in importance which, with the aid of the <u>democratization and humaniza-tion of the work process</u>, will create the conditions under which people's <u>job satisfaction and their identification with the enterprise will develop</u>. All means and methods of overcoming the monotony of the division of labor, the wholly authoritarian

compulsion to work, and the alienation from the
goals of work and production can, in the long run,
also lead to an increase in productive efficiency.
Unavoidable job losses due to technological progress and changes in the structure of production
need not lead to degrading unemployment but can
be solved in a humane manner on the basis of democratic decision-making within enterprises, if necessary at the cost of short-term profit losses.

15. The formation of self-steering group work and of a
    democratic management style in employee-owned
    companies can contribute most decisively to over-
    coming alienation from work and from other human
    beings in the process of production. Man can
    most readily overcome his feelings of individual
    isolation and insignificance vis-a-vis his fellow man
    if he experiences identification and support in his
    work group, because it is here that he spends a
    relatively large part of his life. Alternating be-
    tween rank-and-file and supervisory work within
    the group, including democratic decision-making
    about work processes for the attainment of tempo-
    rarily and quantitatively set production results for
    the whole group, as well as democratic coordina-
    tion of work groups and departments within the
    enterprises, could not only trigger new productive
    initiatives but also develop the abilities of all indi-
    viduals more fully and enhance their feeling of
    being important to society, as well as their job
    satisfaction.

16. Perfection of the market mechanism makes possible
    income formation more in line with performance and
    a more effective distribution of the factors of pro-
    duction. As long as economically limited needs and
    the principle of efficiency exist in an economy
    based on the division of labor, the market mecha-
    nism will be indispensable. It forms a natural cy-
    bernetic system that guarantees the automatic coor-
    dination of producer and consumer interests in the
    economy. The greatest danger to, and limitation
    on this system is represented by the monopolization
    and bureaucratization of production and product
    distribution. Perfection of the market mechanism
    consists in particular of intensifying market
    transparency, promoting competition, and systemat-
    ically restricting macro-monopoly profits.

17. Reduction of macro-monopolistic profit rates with the
    aid of a monopoly tax provides a functional substi-
    tute for the missing tendency toward equalization of
    profit rates among sectors and among enterprises.
    Although it is difficult to ascertain in advance
    macro-monopolistic concentrations and behavior as
    well as their constant feature, monopoly profits,
    the worst negative effects of monopolies can be
    overcome through the elimination of monopoly
    profits. The development of profits will thus more
    consistently reflect the differing performances of
    enterprises and function as an incentive to such
    performances. This also facilitates the universal
    implementation of profit-sharing for all employees of
    market enterprises as a kind of performance-orient-
    ed remuneration that is beneficial to society.

POLITICAL PRECONDITIONS FOR THE REFORM

The new economic system has the advantage that it
need not be implemented overnight, and that it would not
immediately change the lives of the broad strata of the
population in any fundamental way. It is for this reason
that we have emphasized reform of the system, rather than
revolutionary transformation.

Revolutionary movements and theories will only emerge
and gain a foothold within a system when an absolute majority in society experiences unbearable living conditions
and their political interests are increasingly in contradiction with the interests of the beneficiaries of this system. Under these conditions, ideas will always emerge
geared to changing the social system as rapidly and radi-
cally as possible, including the use of violent means. For
at that point the support of a majority of the population
and of society will be assured. Of course the understandable emergence of such revolutionary ideas does not mean
that their application in practice would always result in
social change advantageous to the broadest strata of society.

Our theory of the Third Way does not reject revolutionary transfers of power in countries where the suppression of democratic freedom does not allow for any other
kind of power turnover. But even where these political
conditions are present, it still regards the precipitate restructuring of the economic system as dangerous, since it
will always be bound up with grave and disastrous economic losses suffered by the broadest strata of the population. In countries with a democratic political system,

then, conditions do exist under which the necessary support of the majority of the people for long-term economic reform could be won. But even if this were not possible, the economic reform we are seeking could not be realized through any revolution led by a minority, since a precondition of the reform is voluntary support by the broadest strata, and the extension and intensification of existing pluralist democratic forms.

Reform of the system thus requires the formation of a political majority which can legislate the various laws required and create the legal preconditions for institutional changes in the economic sphere. It is assumed that in most Western democratic states economic reform could be achieved through laws which would not contradict the existing constitutions. Should this not always be the case, modification of certain constitutional laws by the required political majority would of course be essential. It is questionable whether the political majority required for such an economic reform can always be secured by one or a number of existing political parties, or whether for this purpose completely new political movements would be necessary. This problem cannot, however, be examined within the scope of this study and must consequently remain open. Yet it would be necessary in any case for a party or parties to adopt a policy of economic reform such that their program could actually explain the basic tenets of this reform to their supporters. Only political movements whose members are able to make intelligible even the most complicated economic and social interconnections and to familiarize the widest sectors of the population with them on the basis of their experience, can carry out such great tasks as the reform of entire economic systems. Nowadays it is largely the Communist parties in the Western states which, with the support of their members, conduct well- organized and widespread persuasion and agitation throughout the population. The fact that they are nevertheless unable to gain the greater social support they seek, or even to gain an absolute majority, is due neither to any lack of political effort nor to the strength of bourgeois counter-propaganda, but primarily to those long-term objectives for societal change which these parties have so far pursued. We will return to this point later on. It should be emphasized here that reform of the economic system, although it requires a long-term and concentrated effort of education and persuasion within and outside the parties that have set such a reform objective for themselves, can only be successful if the reform is in fact directly related to the experiences and emerging desires of the broadest strata of the people.

Although we have stressed the possibility and necessity of gradual change of the economic system, we have to

emphasize at the same time the interdependencies of the
individual fundamental   processes with each other, which
gives rise to a certain complexity of the reform process as
a whole.   If these were not properly taken into consideration, there would   be unforeseen consequences which would
subsequently provoke partial changes to be discredited.
Hence the necessity for complex reform   processes in which
the individual stages can be prepared and   implemented
periodically over a longer term, but which must   always be
considered in their reciprocal effects and which must   be
consciously pursued with due regard to their infinite interconnections.   The parties which have made reform their
goal should therefore incorporate these complexities into
their party program and lead their members to an understanding of the fundamental interconnections.

    A programed reform will of course have to be elaborat-
ed much more concretely than can be done in this basic
theoretical work. It must reflect the particular economic and
political conditions of each country and will especially be
adapted to the state of political consciousness of the population.   Though reform can thus appear in countless concrete variations, it should respect the following fundamental
interconnections.

    The neutralization of capital, by means of which the
contradiction between owners and non-owners   of capital as
well as the working population's alienation from   capital is
to be overcome, is a fundamental process.   In this way   the
nationalization and bureaucratization of enterprises can be
substantially counteracted.   It is also a way of proceeding
which will not deprive enterprises of their capital resources, as is   the case, for example, when supra-enterprise
capital participation funds are formed.   It further allows
the   establishment of mixed enterprises up to a certain extent of production. But the decisions according to which
capital companies or large enterprises ought to be transformed   into employee-owned companies, and the approximate time period   within which this should occur, are matters which belong to the   party programs.   Whether the
neutralization of capital is to   occur only by means of
transforming net investments or   immediately by gross investments, and the volume of profits at   which this capital
neutralization is to take place, must also be politically determined.   In any case, capital neutralization does   not
harm the enterprises, or cause any disruptions in productions and investment; nor does it result in economic losses.

    The realization of employee profit-sharing is a funda-
mental process without which the contradiction between
wage and profit interests cannot be eliminated.   Without
profit-sharing, the employees of the enterprises will remain
indifferent toward the performance of the enterprises in the

market, its productive efficiency, and the surplus value which it creates. Profit-sharing is also a condition necessary to employee interest in investment and the increase in profit resulting from it. Only in this way can the one-sided, limited interest in wages and consumption be balanced and linked to an interest in the generation of capital. How extensive profit-sharing should be depends, however, on the size of the entrepreneur's private net profits and on the possible remaining dividends for private stockholders, and for this reason is a matter for political decision.

It is regarded here as fundamental to preserve private net profits, up to a certain level of profit, for entrepreneurs whose personal activity is important in establishing and managing their enterprises. Only by completely ignoring the importance of personal interests and entrepreneurial initiative and activity can their removal be demanded. However, problems such as how high entrepreneurial net profits as a percentage of gross profits should be, at which point the neutralization of capital and profit-sharing should begin, and thus the question of limits to entrepreneurial net profits must be determined politically. These shares need not remain constant, and for this reason changes from time to time are matters for political decision. Finally, the same applies to the payment of dividends to private stockholders. Here a distinction should be made between small stockholders, private owners of stock portfolios, and public institutions as stockowners (for example, pension plans and the like). Also subject to political decision are the temporal and quantitative aspects of the transformation of these differentiated payments of dividends.

The introduction of macro-distribution planning is a fundamental process without which the neutralization of capital and profit-sharing cannot produce the anticipated results. If the development of wages and profits and the distribution of profits for purposes of investment and consumption depended only on spontaneous struggles of interest and power, no precautions could be taken against the cyclical development of inflation and crisis. But, on the other hand, without capital neutralization and profit-sharing, the systematic determination of income distribution cannot work. The preparation of macro-distribution planning requires time, however, and its determination is a political decision. The number, composition, and membership size of the planning commissions, and their relationship to the government, the economic council and parliament, as well as to the political parties, mass organizations, and action groups must be determined.

Determination of the planning periods and their coordination with political elections (selection of alternative plans), the relationship between long-term programs and medium-term distribution plans, the kinds of ongoing controls and plan adjustments as well as their relation to economic policy, all these must be adapted to concrete political conditions and therefore decided politically. In particular, one must take into consideration the time that will be required for the standardization of bookkeeping in the enterprises, for the organization of automated transmission and processing of information, and for the registration and collection of the necessary statistical and economic data. Another important item is the establishment of technological economic sectoral research institutes for the objectivization of production forecasts; this should not be overlooked during the political process of preparation.

Finally, the problems involved in a possible fusion of the plans of several countries are an eminently political matter because they depend on the options available in both foreign and domestic policy. The simultaneous introduction of economic reform in a number of countries that are closely integrated economically (for example, the countries of the EEC) could be declared a political goal in the programs of related parties in these countries. If this goal could be achieved, the reliability of forecasts concerning foreign trade, production and income could, of course, be greatly increased, thus resulting in economic and social advantages for the people. The coordination of plans, and ultimately even joint planning, sould be regarded as long-term political goals. Even if this simultaneous development of macro-planning were advantageous in countries which maintain intensive economic relations, it would not be a precondition for the development of reform in one country, and therefore is not regarded as a fundamental process.

One fundamental process, finally, is the introduction of market regulation. Only if the generation of monopolistic incomes can be substantially restricted using such tools as strong competition and monopoly-profit tax, and if the development of profits more consistently reflects actual differences in enterprise performance, can employee profit-sharing achieve the expected positive results. The promotion of competition can, however, be introduced earlier than the taxation of monopoly and requires only political determination and implementation by the institutions concerned, the setting of criteria and the necessary funds from the public treasury for the active promotion of competition. The taxation of monopoly, on the other hand, is tied to macro-planning since it entails planning and control of the rate of profit in the economy as a whole, without which monopoly profits can neither be recognized nor taxed. Establishment of the duration of a period of equalization and exemption and of the rate of monopoly taxation is also a matter for political decision.

We have attempted here to show briefly what would be required for further concretization of the reform model in the reform program of a political movement. It would of course be necessary in particular to get the widest possible political support for the more concrete, temporary measures, with their projected complex effects and the economic and social advances which they are intended to bring about. This would necessarily involve our diverting (directing?) attention from a narrow (but necessary) scientific exposition of the systemic reform, toward a more universally understandable explanation the reform, in these terms, is presented as essential to bringing about the mature economic and social improvements (see preceding chapter).

Meanwhile most segments of the population have come to desire the new economic goals and socio-economic improvements, several points of which we have described in the preceding chapter. But since without macro-planning and its prerequisites these goals will remain in the realm of wishful thinking, it should be possible for not just one but several political parties to advocate the reform. To realize the reform would provide the various parties with the possibility of transforming their concrete proposals for economic growth, income distribution, and the solution of social, educational, ecological, and other problems into their own varieties of planning. In other words, only after macro-planning exists can the various political parties clearly define themselves and advocate complex and realistic development objectives. This would be the road leading from promises to be realized in the future to calculated, realistic plans for the future, and would thus signify a rationalization of politics.

Nowadays, there are wings, groupings, or fractions in almost all political parties that are not content merely with short-term political successes, but are searching for real and long-term solutions to economic and social problems. They are aware that great dangers are involved in procrastinating on these problems, in the current opposition politically exploiting them against the ruling parties, and in the opposition's equal inability to solve them once it gets into power. The longer the present system remains unable to overcome its crises and their accompanying mass unemployment, inflation, social insecurity, perversion of the environment, youth problems, the greater will be the danger of extremist political reactions. Since the more far-sighted people, who are less confined to thinking in day-to-day terms, and who can be found in almost all parties, are aware of this danger, and since their number is on the rise, it is conceivable that they will be able to recognize the need for fundamental reform and bring it about

within their parties.   Without having   to abandon their
differing ideas about concrete solutions and steps in the
developmental process, a number of parties could   adopt a
common resolution, expressing their willingness to   realize
the economic reform.

In the trade unions too, there are forces on the rise
in search of fundamental solutions.   There are, of course,
also   Communist forces within the unions seeking systemic
change along   the lines of the Eastern model.   However, by
far the largest   number of non-Communist trade unionists,
and even a growing   number of Communist trade union
functionaries, reject the Soviet   economic and social system
and are searching for other non-capitalist development alternatives that do not follow the Soviet Communist pattern.

The growing struggle for codetermination and employee
capital-sharing may be viewed as a symptom of this search
for fundamental   solutions.   At the same time, however, one
recognizes that this   alone cannot abolish all the system's
diseases.   It might even be   said that many unionists,
lacking complex alternatives to the two   currently existing
basic systems, retreat into purely pragmatic   union activity, although that does not satisfy them either,   because
they also see the growing political dangers.

The possibility cannot be discounted therefore, that
even the trade unions will produce groups advocating this
reform of the   system, a development which would considerably enhance prospects   for its transformation into political
programs.   In fact, no   stratum of society can any longer
be said to be for or against   such an economic reform.
What was said about the parties also   holds true here.   The
members of the various social sectors   increasingly fall into
two groups: those who only live from day to day and are
satisfied with immediate improvements in their level   of consumption; and those who are concerned about the future,
who are increasingly apprehensive about the irrationalism
and lack of perspective of present-day life, and who are
searching for more fundamental solutions to society's problems.   That part of the   population which is no longer content with short-term and often   demagogic promises and
which seeks more fundamental changes--not, however, oriented toward communism--has rarely ever been so   large
and growing as it is at present.

Among the workers, short-term wage and consumption
interests naturally predominate because their real incomes
are the lowest in society.   But concern about keeping their
jobs, about the state of the economy, and the survival of
their firm is also strong in many workers.   Most workers
will support a reform which promises convincingly to prevent crises and mass unemployment.   Furthermore, long-
term planning of the development of wages, which includes

substantial participation by their union representatives, is much more in their interest than annual struggles over wage increases whose actual value during inflationary periods is often questionable. Profit-sharing under conditions of capital neutralization, and seats for elected representatives of the employees on the boards of directors or for elected partners in the private enterprises can only be welcomed. In particular, the formation of self-steering work groups and a democratic style of carrying out work activities will find strong resonance among workers.

Commercial and administrative employees and the technical intelligentsia in enterprises could come to support capital neutralization and profit-sharing even more strongly than the workers. Among these groups, who have a far better insight into their enterprise's economic situation than do the workers, and who moreover display a stronger need for identification with their enterprise, co-ownership and participatory decision-making would be very attractive. Particularly within this group in the large-capital companies the question often arises as to why the profit must go to stockholders who are alienated from the firm, and why they themselves cannot make decisions relating to the development of the firm. They have a much deeper and more accurate understanding of the enterprise's developmental needs. Their initiatives for increasing efficiency, improving the working climate, and for self-directed group work would be of great importance. At the same time, however, it is the members of this sector who perceive the growing contradiction between increasing production on the one hand, and perverting the environment and worsening living and transportation conditions on the other, and who, for this reason, ought overwhelmingly to support the idea of macro-planning.

One might expect to find a strong interest in macro-distribution planning among public service employees, a category that is very large nowadays. It is the employees in the school system, in scientific institutions, public hospitals, social institutions, public security, the legal sector, cultural institutions, as well as employees in the whole private and public information sector, entertainment industry, etc., who experience the contradictions between obsession with technological progress and the compulsion to consume, on the one hand, and man's isolation, insecurity, and fear, on the other hand. They have to service that sphere of their fellow man's life in which the contradictions of this life most often surface; they have to find answers to questions and fears, they experience directly the reactions to the daily flood of information; they see the desperate and the stranded, and the rebels and anarchists among those who are fed up with the results of this socie-

ty. Their search for new social conditions in which the
great questions   about the goals of further development
could be posed openly and   solved democratically should
make them receptive to macro-planning.   Furthermore, the
need for long-term perspectives on   one's own activity and
the systematic provision of funds for one's   institutions--
which are always first affected and cut back by public austerity measures in times of crisis--speaks for macro-planning.

Basically, wage earners might be expected to show a
rather   positive attitude toward economic reform if they can
be   made aware of the changes that are realizable, and if
the reform's advantages to both the capitalist and the Communist system   can be demonstrated.   Much will depend on
whether the opponents   of such changes succeed in appeal-
ing to people's natural conservatism and fear of complex
changes that cannot be experimentally verified, and in mo-
bilizing these against the   reform.   All social change has
and must have its opponents,   because certain strata and
groups will always fear a loss of   advantages and privileges
which they enjoyed in the old system   and which they associate with it.   At the same time, there will always be ideologues whose whole intellectual development and   previous
activity are chained to the old system, and who, for   this
reason, will mobilize all their ideological weapons against
any changes in it.   Before speaking about the anticipated
opponents of the reform, however, we want to present a
few   thoughts on whether the remaining category of the
self-employed   and entrepreneurs as a whole will have to be
counted among the   opponents of the reform.

If people were to be judged only on the basis of their
economic positions and interests, it would be necessary to
come   to the conclusion that a reform aspiring inter alia to
limit the private appropriation of profits and advocating
planned distribution, must provoke hostility on the part of
all who are owners of capital and recipients of profit.
This would, however, be an all too simplistic conclusion.
For   many reasons, one might instead expect some private
entrepreneurs   to advocate the reform.   The old Marxist
characterization of the   bourgeoisie as a class consisting of
nothing but exploiters, who   are therefore the enemy of
any socialist transformation, has   three deficiencies: first,
it underestimates the entrepreneurial activity in society;
second, it uses the term exploitation in an unscientific manner; third, it originates in a conception of a socialist society without entrepreneurial initiative, without   individual activities developed outside of bureaucratic   regulations.
This ideology and its political practice must   necessarily
provoke opposition not only on the part of   entrepreneurs,
but of all people who value freedom and democracy.

By contrast, the reform advocated here proceeds from a recognition of the societal importance of entrepreneurial initiative and activity which cannot be replaced by any bureaucratic system of decision-making. In general it must be emphasized that entrepreneurial activity, in addition to highly valued specialized knowledge, requires a considerable readiness to take risks. We would not, however, stress readiness to take risks as such, because what seems much more important is the endeavors of the owners of new enterprises, whose future simply cannot be accurately predicted, to reduce risk as much as they can. This, however, requires considerable mental work and effort because it implies that a great deal of information, analyses and evaluations must be made available, that technical and economic options and requirements of the enterprise must be thought out, that organizational questions, and very frequently ways of raising additional capital, must be solved, that public regulations must be known, that linkages with all competent authorities and public offices have to be established. All this work, the objective of which is the future successful operation of the enterprise with the greatest possible reduction of risks, cannot be accomplished by just anybody, and especially not by any bureaucratic organ. The latter assumes no risk at all and is indifferent toward risks to society.

It is a gross ideological oversimplification to believe that all wage-earners regard entrepreneurs and only entrepreneurs as exploiters and are unable to recognize the importance of real entrepreneurial activity. Recognition of the social function of private entrepreneurs as well as the necessary profit motivation for the projected economic reform are in accordance with the goal of improving the life of the broad strata of the population by increasing efficiency and by the simple prevention of unnecessary economic losses. But it is precisely this goal which also requires that the development of private profits be systematically limited and their distribution regulated if the profit interest is not to jeopardize the further development of society in a human direction.

All past experiences demonstrate, however, that all entrepreneurs do not by any means pursue only their profits to the exclusion of all else, without paying heed to the wider and more fundamental economic and social context. Many are increasingly disturbed about the inability of the existing system to guarantee continuous, balanced, and non-exaggerated growth as well as permanent full employment; about ever more threatening pollution and destruction of our environment, problems about which there is a good deal of talk but for which solutions are lacking; about the one-sidedness and mindlessness of the ideology of consume-

rism which does not make man happier but rather more
lonely; about the restlessness and opposition of youth who--
-despite, or perhaps because of, so much material wealth--
leads some in desperation to anarchism and terrorism.   It
can be assumed that these concerns and the search for
their causes lead more than just a few entrepreneurs to
ideas that go beyond their immediate profit interest.   If
they could gradually be convinced that the fundamental deficiencies of the capitalist economic system can be overcome
by means of a democratically determined and planned distribution and utilization of profits, subject at the same time to
guaranteed and sufficiently motivating profit-shares for private entrepreneurs, then gaining their support for reform
of the system should not be entirely impossible.

In fact, a sizable number of entrepreneurs are already
experimenting with a form of capital-sharing, codetermination, and self-steering group work.   This is a sympton of
the maturation of new socio-economic relations in the sphere
of production.   The initiators of such changes are aware,
however, that this alone does not go beyond the bounds of
pure experimentation and that the number of such enterprises is not increasing quickly enough, nor is the economic
system as a whole being transformed in this way.   Some
entrepreneurs are hesitant because they do not know which
of the experiments will prove valuable in the future, and
many would not oppose employee sharing in capital and
profits if this were a universal, legally defined trend that
benefited the economy as a whole.

As far as many managers of large capital companies are
concerned, not only is there no reason to reject capital
neutralization and employee profit-sharing, but there are in
fact positive reasons for adopting these policies.   This can
be ascertained from numerous presentations on these ideas
and the discussions that followed them.   In these circles,
the contradictions between stockholders' interests (dividend
interest) and the interests of employees (wage interests) is
quite frequently felt to be an impediment, and linkage of
the wage and capital interests of employees is regarded positively.   Furthermore, these economically trained people
very quickly grasp the overall economic relationship between wages and profits and thus recognize the potential of
macro-distribution planning.   Practical experience here prevails over ideological prejudices.   Only a few of them still
hold the old macro-economic theories with which they were
brought up and which stand in the way of conceptions of
reform.

In the Western industrial states, prospects for winning
over a majority of the population for a reform of the system
are thus by no means negligible.   However, everything will
depend on which parties stand behind it and which political
and ideological counterreactions are encountered.

PARTIES AND REFORM OF THE SYSTEM

Under relatively democratic conditions, where the interests of minorities cannot be asserted by suppressing the fundamental interests of the majority and certain rules of the democratic game must be respected, it is more difficult to carry out more fundamental changes in the economic system which will always negatively affect the interests of certain groups. These changes are conceivable only if they receive the democratically expressed support of sufficiently large popular majorities. A precondition, however, is a realization on part of the majority of the people that the fundamental transformation of economic conditions is in accord with their interests.

This is the point at which Marxist revolutionary ideologues interject that under conditions of political dominance by certain groups or classes with an interest in preservation of the status quo, the majority can never recognize their true interests. The same is said to be true of present-day capitalism where the working class and the rest of the working population in the capitalist system have been unable to realize their true long-term interest in achieving a socialist society. Manipulation of their consciousness by the grand-bourgeois ruling class, using all available means to shape consciousness (school education, religion, culture, mass media, etc.) has been so great that the majority of people consequently act contrary to their real interests.

This argument serves as justification for a revolutionary overthrow by minorities. It is maintained that the large majorities had not yet far enough advanced to be able to recognize their long-term interests. The revolutionary minorities, backed by Marxist theory, were acting as a vanguard representing the broad masses and fighting for their interests. They would only receive their support once the ideological influence of the old classes was broken and the masses' socialist consciousness had developed sufficiently. Until then the revolutionary minority had to assert its power, if necessary by dictatorial means, which meant that even for some time after the revolution the so-called dictatorship of the proletariat had to be maintained.

This line of argument is today still employed by official Marxist ideology in the Soviet sphere of influence, as well as a number of Western Communist parties faithful to Moscow and many radicals who call themselves Marxist and revolutionary. The majority of the large Communist parties in the West, however, have abandoned this position. We stress this line of argument here not only because it is part of the ideological arsenal of the Communist parties in the Eastern bloc states, but also because we regard it as fundamentally mistaken in certain respects. Revealing the theoretical error it contains will better enable us to support our ideas about a democratic reform of the economic system under conditions of bourgeois democracy.

It is certainly true that any politically organized interest group continually attempts to influence as many people as possible and to win them over to their side, while not hesitating to disguise their own various interests in order to deceive those whose interests differ. Despite this concealing of interests in the political power struggle and despite the periodic deception of entire strata of the population regarding the real fundamental interests of different political parties or their centers of power, it is not true that the majority of members of large social groups, strata, and classes could, in the long term, be so deceived that they would be unable to recognize their own fundamental interests and their true political representatives. By conceptualizing interests in this way, communism, in the form in which it dominates the Eastern bloc states today, perpetrates its grossest ideological deception--even contradicting Marx's theory in the process. That this itself is a result of its own power interests has already been indicated at the outset.

In reality, people's basic interests, especially their economic interests, develop independently of the political power struggle, that is, these arise from their needs. However, those interests that motivate people the most and result in extraordinarily strong acts of will are always highly conscious interests. People always know what they want and do not want; what they want more and want less; when it is and when it is not worthwile to engage in a certain activity; which activities they do, and do not want to engage in. Of course, it will take some time for any new opportunity--that is, any new object, any new satisfaction of needs, any newly discovered opportunity to satisfy a new need through a certain activity--to enter into the sphere of interests of various persons. Once discovered, the development of interests will not be long in coming if this new need-satisfaction stimulates sufficiently intense feelings and a strong demand.

The same applies to politics, whether one likes it or not. Any new opportunity to achieve the satisfaction of certain needs of broad social strata better or more quickly--particularly those needs which have been transformed into their interests--will, one day be discovered with the aid of political struggle and proposed changes in the economic and social system proposed here. After all, ideologues and politicians are the ones who espouse certain group interests, prepare proposals for their realization, and create political interest groupings which will then set off the political struggle. Other political groups with contro-

versial interests have always attempted to use ideological
and political means to prevent the formation of such new
groupings. In the long term, however, they have never
succeeded where the new political ideas, goals, and means
really corresponded to the interests of the groups in question.

It is not true that the large majority of the population
in Western industrial states, which is made up of wage-
earners, could not be won over for socialist changes because they did not realize that socialist changes were in
their fundamental interest, or because the opponents of socialism were able to lead them away from their true interests. Rather, the fact of the matter is that they do not regard socialist goals as serving their interests. When
political parties begin to advocate socialist changes during
election campaigns--and of course long before--time and
again these represent demands that, if realized, would either move directly towards Eastern-type economic systems
or would not be distinguished from them clearly and unequivocally enough. Demands for nationalization put forward
by Communist parties, and frequently by socialist and social-democratic parties as well, necessarily give the impression that these parties' conception of a socialist economic
system is not very different from that of the Eastern bloc
states.

Meanwhile, however, far too many wage earners in
Western industrialized states have become aware of that
system and all its basic flaws. The world of today offers
sufficient international contacts, provides people with a
veritable flood of information, and, through the mass media,
awakens their political interest to such a degree that they
have everywhere acquired an adequate knowledge of the
Soviet economic and social system. Communist propaganda is
no longer capable of papering over the situation. Rejection
of this system deeply permeates the ranks of the workers.
In West Germany, many people also know the Eastern
system through information received from relatives and
friends in the GDR. An aversion to Soviet socialism is
widespread among all strata of wage earners. But in the
other Western industrial states, not only the grand- and
petit-bourgeoisie but broad strata of wage-earners, are not
interested in socialist economic development following the
Eastern model.

Thus, the fact that the Communist parties cannot reach
such broad strata among the wage-earners cannot be dogmatically explained by asserting that they do not know
where their interest lies. On the contrary, far too many
working people have long understood that elimination of the
market mechanism and introduction of state-controlled planning can only mean a growing bureaucracy with rapidly

widening supply gaps, uneconomic waste, and poor product innovation. For an increasing number of wage earners, entrepreneurial initiative is no longer something merely to be ridiculed or maligned. In the face of the economic results in systems where entrepreneurial initiative has been eliminated, Communist polemics about exploitation increasingly appear as empty phraseology.

This does not mean, however, that wage-earners agree with the capitalist system and all its great social disparities, unemployment, insecurity, and lack of perspectives. As long as they are not offered a different alternative, and as long as they are consistently faced with an either-or choice, a large number will--at the most critical moments--prefer the more efficient, freer capitalist system.

The significant changes in most Western Communist parties, hich today are labeled "Euro-Communist," are largely an expression of the actual development of interests among the working classes in the West. These parties have understood that information about the Eastern system of oppression, and the fact that people there are deprived of freedom, has sunk too deeply into the consciousness of broad strata of the population in the West. The powerful Eastern bureaucrats--who have long since lost any ability to consider the views and feelings of their people, believing instead that anything can be solved by censorship, police, and cannons--are incapable of understanding the reactions of Communist parties in the West, who have to vie for people's consciousness under conditions of free information. Only bureaucrats, for whom nothing is important but the atmosphere within their own power apparatus, can fail to see that the occupation of Czechoslovakia, for instance, ultimately cost Communism more than they think it has gained.

Commitment to pluralist democratic conditions, even in a socialist system, is thus for most Western Communist parties a first necessary reflection of the actual development of interests on the part of nearly all segments of the population in their countries. They have realized that most working people do not have any political interest in a one-party system within which any trace of opposition, any political dissatisfaction, all attempts to associate with other like-minded people, and any public criticism outside party confines are prohibited. "But an even worse evil than the opposition between poor and rich is the opposition between freedom and slavery--the opposition between a New Class, the ruling dictatorship, and undesirable fellow citizens, banished to concentration camps or elsewhere."[1] Lack of

---

[1] K. Popper, in : A.T. Ferguson, ed., Chicago 1976.

interest in such a system, and consequently interest in preserving a pluralist democracy, is today characteristic of the interests of the broad masses. Any realistic politician must respect this, regardless of which ideological and political development he himself has undergone.

However, most of the Communist movements that have turned away from Soviet Communism and criticize it fundamentally--such as the Trotskyites, the more consistent Euro-Communists, supporters of Rudi Dutschke and the like--have come to a standstill mid-way along the road to an understanding of Soviet Communism and the causes of its failure. Their criticism of Soviet bureaucracy is not only sincere but also correct insofar as they regard it as a dictatorship of the bureaucratic apparatus over society. Moreover, this insight is developing--at the present time in various ways--into a recognition of the need for political democracy under socialism. However, in their understanding of the fundamental shortcomings of the Soviet economic system they have not penetrated deeply enough. In this domain they continue to be caught up in certain illusions which are generally characteristic of communist thinking and have their roots in the aforementioned simplification of Marxist theory.

The fundamental deficiency in the conceptions of a socialist economy, that is so widespread among Communists, is that they do not adequately understand the problematic of interests, and of the related role of interests in social production and economic activity in general. Whenever advocates of this position reflect on the socialist economy, they overwhelmingly believe that its present deficiencies are only the result of planning and the bureaucratic decision-making system, and that this all will change as soon as the workers themselves and the rest of the working population prepare the plans for enterprises and the economy. One thus arrives, at best, at an understanding of the present contradiction between the interests of the ruling bureaucracy and the interests of the people, without being able to proceed further. Very little account, if any, is taken of the problem of contradictions between partial interests of enterprises and the interests of society, between immediate producer interests and consumer interests, between economic and non-economic interests, and in this context the whole problematic of markets and market plans.

Far too many Communists simply avoid the difficult field of economic problems and move only in the sphere of abstract philosophical concepts which buttress their conception of socialism. Consequently, they can turn to the concrete political struggle: to questions of strategy and tactics. Economic problems are dismissed with reference to general terms such as "socialist consciousness," "socialist

morale" and the like. While they therefore still recognize
the role of "material incentives" to socialism in accordance
with Lenin (who is no different from Soviet ideologues),
they are embarassed and already divided with respect to
the categories of "profit" and "profit-interest." Yet no concrete new theories have been emerging. The far more complicated problematic of market prices, competition, monopolies, investment and business initiatives, subordination of
market initiative to the objectives of the democratic plan
without restricting the former, etc. has to this day been
ignored by most anti-Soviet Communists since they have
simply been unable to overcome certain ideological barriers.
However, one can expect that all those sincerely seeking
solutions to the great problems of development of our times
will gradually arrive at new insights and changes in the
sphere of economic problems.

It is noteworthy that in most Euro-Communist parties it
is the workers in particular who are turning away from the
Soviet type of socialist economy and society, whereas certain intellectual circles--especially students--frequently oppose changes of a Euro-Communist type in those parties.
This confirms our thesis that economic development and the
value of increased material needs-satisfaction are often un-
derestimated by small, sectarian groups of intellectuals. Yet
the same groups overestimate the potential for political
change through revolution. Broad strata of the population, workers in particular--insofar as they can be won
over to socialist ideas at all--do envision a considerable improvement in their economic and social situation. The non-
economic interests of workers and employees (codetermination, job satisfaction, self-realization, and the like) are also
such that they do not see the Communist system as an attractive model for satisfying them. Hence it is very likely
that the Communist leaders--if they want to remain realistic
politicians--will gradually have to dissociate themselves from
those exclusive intellectual groups, since they are being
pushed into increasingly strong opposition to the Soviet
system by the broad strata of the population and their
evolving needs. They must, therefore, search for new economic ideas of their own.

Socialist and social-democratic parties have for decades
dissociated themselves from the anti-democratic and anti-human Communist system, and consequently most countries
have established a much broader basis among workers and
other wage earners than have the Communist parties.
Their struggle for important social improvements and the
incorporation of greater social security into the capitalist
system has periodically brought them to power in many
Western states. At the same time, however, during all those
decades they have fallen victim to their internal contra-

dictions and vague long-term goals, which is why they have
repeatedly been forced into opposition.

For many adherents of the socialist parties, and for
the younger generation in particular, everyday pragmatic
politics, with all its longer-term reform goals, is unsatisfac-
tory because it does not change the underlying foundations
of the capitalist system, and thus fails to alleviate its negative socio-economic effects. When these party critics outline their proposals for fundamental change, they contain in
many countries ideas which are reminiscent of, or closely
resemble Communist conceptions of socialism (nationalization
of various sectors, planning proposals not conforming to the
market, ideas of state regulation of investment,and the
like).

These vague notions of socialism, in the context of the
socialist tradition, frighten off those segments of the population who, because of their social status, could be potential voters for these parties, but who--being ideologically
influenced in the most diverse ways--reject any hint of socialism because they suspect the practice of the Communist
states behind it. Of course, the bourgeois parties and especially the most conservative bourgeois politicians consciously add fuel to, and fan these fears. Fear of socialist
tendencies on the part of some segments of the population,
as well as dissatisfaction with unresolved capitalist ills on
the part of other segments, have time and again led to the
downfall of socialist parties. In reaction to such developments, the social-democratic parties often turn even more
sharply away from any notions about transforming the system, thus unconsciously emphazing pragmatic, day-to-day
politics.

Some significant new trends evident in many socialist
and social-democratic parties, often developed in collaboration with trade unions, are their demands for codetermination and employee capital-sharing. Here a development is
being initiated that could contribute to a democratization
and humanization of the economy while simultaneously counteracting its impending bureaucratization. There is a danger that this positive process will become discredited, however, due to its inadequate sophistication, its insufficiently
considered economic interconnections, and its one-sided and
simplified views, it may produce results different from those
hoped for, and greatly disappoint the expectations bound
up with it.

If the processes of income distribution continue to fall
short of their objectives, codetermination will be impotent
vis-a-vis the capitalist cycle of unemployment and inflation.
If capital formation is pursued only in combination with
trans-enterprise participatory capital funds, the working
people's alienation from capital, investment, and enterprise

will not be overcome and investment problems will be further enhanced. If the problem of crisis is perceived only as a deficiency in capitalist investment activity, which must be overcome with the aid of trans-enterprise partici- patory capital funds, then solutions may give rise to dan- gerous and counter-effective process of bureaucratization. Simplistic and one-sided measures in discredit among the population, would then further impede the necessary, more complex reform of the capitalist system. Humane economic democracy could solve the dilemma which has confronted social democratic parties for decades: the dilemma between the acknowledged importance of private entrepreneurial ini- tiative on the one hand, and the socialist demand to tran- scend the contradiction between wage labor and capital on the other.

Reactions to the growing problems of economic and so- cial development are even more contradictory among the Christian democratic parties of the industrial states. Here we find a continuously increasing differentiation between those forces firmly committed to capitalist positions, which reject any reform at all, and those that see a great danger for humankind in the unmodified capitalist system. Natural- ly, this difference has very much assumed the form of a generation gap. Yet typically, a growing number of people from the older generation, particularly more religiously-ori- ented people, are joining ranks with the opponents of capi- talism. Among the defenders of capitalism are not only those who do not want to recognize certain problems of capitalism and downplay them for this reason, but also those who are accustomed to thinking only in terms of "either-or" and who consequently, because of their anti-Communism, can only arrive at a pro-capitalist position.

Underestimation of the faults of capitalism can be at- tributed to factors having to with both cognition and inter- est. Ignorance about specific deficiencies of capitalism and their causes, while attributable to one's entire upbringing, education, and sources of information is often bound up with one's own constellation of interests. It is self-evident that many private entrepreneurs who regard the success of their business as their life's work, and who have in most cases devoted great effort and toil to this lifework, do not want to hear any criticism of the system. For this system is, after all, what first made possible and then supported their entrepreneurial activity. Moreover, when these critics completely ignore their work and attack it in an unscientific and one-sided manner, one can readily understand their equally passionate rejection of such ideologies, which may lead to a completely uncritical attitude toward their own system. This does not make it any more scientific however.

Of course, such entrepreneurs will be, and always have been, willing to pursue their interest in preserving an unmodified capitalist system by supporting conservative political parties or by becoming politically active themselves. The conservatism of such parties, while not implying a rejection of various individual changes and social reforms, is nevertheless fixed on preserving all the fundamental principles of the capitalist system, along with an unequivocal renunciation of any socialist changes. The fact that socialist development also appears frightening to many people who are not entrepreneurs explains why even very conservative parties have been able to attract a much broader base of followers and voters than only the ranks of large and small entrepreneurs. However, within many Christian-conservative parties an increasingly powerful opposition has developed in recent decades against conservative defenders of capitalism, which may be interpreted as a reaction to the negative features of this system.

A growing number of Christian-educated and Christian-minded people are becoming conscious of the fact that the existing capitalist system is increasingly pushing people in a direction that is far removed from the basic conceptions of Christian morals and humanity, and that this system is not only incapable of averting the looming dangers threatening all mankind, but will sooner or later produce them itself. The one-sided, exaggerated trend toward consumption, which capitalism fuels, requires an exclusively materially-oriented people who see consumption as the purpose of life, and who can therefore be manipulated in this way. Man is intended to become the subject and object of a production machine in which not he himself but only his material, profit-maximizing products become the exclusive goal of and criterion for all activity. Yet it is precisely this one-sided, socially uncontrollable consumption mania of capitalist man (the other side of which is his ever growing isolation, spiritual impoverishment, alienation and desperation) that many Christian-minded people and particularly young Christians are finding increasingly intolerable.

Among these circles, one can see the dangers of capitalist society, where all new scientific knowledge and technological progress can degenerate and be transformed into a disaster for humankind. This results in problems for a society no longer able to heal the wounds of its far too egoistic economic organism with the medicine of the Christian moral code, compelling it to search for new, more humane economic principles.

Only these young Christians justified fear of Communist state bureaucracy, with its increasingly anti-human machinery of oppression, compels them to remain immobile and prevents them from going beyond their moral outrage. They find themselves in a dilemma, especially with regard

to their economic conceptions, helplessly searching for alternatives.   On the one hand, economists--often just as
Christian-minded--impose the eternal laws of the market
economy and join in condemnation of the regimented planned
economy.   On the other hand, the advocates of morality
and theology are teaching them love for humankind, self-
denial, devotion, and unselfishness.

However, it must appear schizophrenic to thinking
people, particularly the young, to behave for eight hours a
day according to egoistic principles and for eight hours
according to God's principles, and after all this to enjoy
eight hours of calm and unburdened sleep.   In reality,
however, these people's tranquility is not at all harmonious,
and their rebellion against a morally divided world as well
as their search for salvation have been increasingly taking
on political contours.

In its starkest form, one can observe the reflection of
capitalist discrepancies and hopelessness in the liberal
bourgeois parties.   They see themselves as the genuine
guardians of the freedom of private enterprise and the free
market economy, and have always fought against any state
encroachment on this freedom. But they are now becoming
increasingly aware of the fact that the free market economy has long since become a theoretical illusion; that it has
caused and given rise to enormous concentrations which
themselves increasingly restrict and undermine the free
play of the market mechanism. The adjusting equilibrium
inherent in the system no longer functions, and ubiquitous
state intervention, which is supposed to satisfy opposing
interests, is not really in a position to do so.   The only
result is a growing bureaucratism within the economy itself,
and an ever increasing fusion of economy and state. Anti-
monopolistic policies have become a farce, since they cannot
even expose, let alone eliminate, macro-monopolistic market
restrictions.

The attempt to rescue the freedom of the individual by
making the average person more wealthy and independent
must evoke an image of Don Quixote in a world of economic
giants. To allow the individual worker to accumulate a bit
more than he needs for daily sustenance, is not yet to
create equality of opportunity for all, let alone to subordinate the generation of capital to human needs. Still, the
positive attitude of liberal parties toward employee capital-
sharing and codetermination might contribute to positive social developments if it could be understood that at present
the freedom of the individual can only be ensured by subordinating actual communities of production to the democratically expressed will of economically equal individuals.

In the Federal Republic of Germany there is a growing
and widespread tendency on the part of many young people

toward an increasing discontent about the development of society, about the incomprehensible, uncontrolled and the mammoth, self-important structures in politics, economy, and society. Some dissatisfied youths have rallied, in their opposition to the capitalist system and the established political parties, to form a new political party, The Greens.

The party's name itself indicates that its establishment was a result of growing concern about the development of the human environment, of resistance to all economic and military developments that are leading to the further perversion of the environment and ultimately are threatening humanity itself. The politically active core of this party are unanimous in their view of the symptoms; but they are deeply divided in their analyses of the causes of overall developments today. Although they agree that many of the developments they oppose originate in the essence of the capitalist system and thus can only be eliminated by fundamentally changing that system, their agreement stops at a similar assessment of the Communist system. Just who "the enemy" is for this party is uncertain, which helps to explain its internal divisions.

Just as the party harbors differences in its analyses of the overall development, so too do members' views on the specifically economic problems and their possible solutions differ.[2] As a result, the party has no consistent position toward such important problems as economic crises, mass unemployment, inflation, the development of worker and social incomes, etc. So far, the party's proposals have been vague, unconvincing, contradictory, and in some measure naive. Until now it has been unable to go beyond thinking and propagating in terms of a part of the total system, namely the environment, as a political topic. It thus overlooks the fact that precisely the problem areas just mentioned are the ones that most affect the great majority of the population and, in times of crisis, push environmental problems out of most people's consciousness. Until the Greens are able to eliminate this vagueness and these inconsistencies in basic economic issues, they will only be able to address and win over a minority of the population and therefore will not be in a position to bring about any fundamental change in the ecological development.

However, if the Greens should come to realize, in the course of their increasing parliamentary and political experience, that they have to deal with the economic problems of the present age in a realistic and practical manner, then their success will depend on their ability to free themselves

---

[2] See W. Kaden, "Aepfel statt Apfelsinen, Grundig statt Sony," Der Spiegel, no. 2 (1983), pp. 34-40.

from two devastating illusions. The first of these is the illusion that people's economic needs and interests can be
feasibly limited by means of education and moral appeals
based on social ethics; this is supposed to bring about a
limitation on the growth of the economy.

The second illusion is Marxist in origin. The market
mechanism, it is thought, can be replaced by national economic planning, but with the difference that production
would be autonomous or cooperative and that national economic planning by the self-administering units would be effected from the grass roots without a state bureaucracy.

If the Greens would abandon their basic economic positions, and hence their basic illusions, they could, with
their critical attitude toward the present overall system,
become a motivating force for the future, in ways suggested
here. Yet we are entirely aware that if the Greens were to
abandon their fundamental values and wrong theoretical assessments they would lose much of their attraction to young
people and, as a political party, would be left without a
following. The Greens' following is primarily made up of
groups in the population whose activities are primarily "extra-economic," that is, not workers and clerks directly employed in the process of production, but more theoretically-
oriented groups such as high school and university
students and teachers. These groups, whose ideologies are
also anti-economic in orientation, necessarily come into conflict with economic reality and envision a radical and narrow-minded strategy of rapid transformation rather than
permitting the party to strike a course of step-by-step reforms aimed at a really humane and democratic economic and
social order. Therefore one must be skeptical about the
possibility of the Greens developing in the direction of the
economic reform program described in this book.

More and more, broad segments of the population are
becoming aware that capitalist society today is on the verge
of fundamental changes which could, however, develop in
diametrically opposed ways, thus making people either into
passive puppets manipulated by all-powerful apparatuses,
or the true benefactors and core of a more humane democracy. This development cannot escape the political parties,
and almost all of them show signs of differentiation and far-
reaching ideological changes. These parties of course differ in terms of their traditions, thought, and perceptions of
reality. Hence they will display the most diverse reactions
and proposed solutions. However, the most far-sighted
and systematic-thinking members and functionaries of these
parties seem to be increasingly converging on one point: a
realization that neither a conservative ossification of the
existing system, nor its transformation into a power-elitist
society can save humanity from catastrophe; only a more
profound and humane democracy can do this.

304 FOR A HUMANE ECONOMY

We too regard this as one of the most significant symptoms of a maturing economic democracy. Whether or not these transformations will in fact correspond in every aspect to the structures proposed here is no longer important. What is important, however, is the fact that an impetus has been provided through the presentation of economic and social relationships which may give rise to goal-oriented attempts to overcome the present fundamental shortcomings of the system by a more complex and far-reaching thinking of systems. As mentioned earlier, it cannot be the task of science to propose concrete social structures, since theory and living social praxis are two different matters. If, however, economics does succeed in demonstrating the interrelationships between fundamental economic processes, in describing conflicts growing out of unperceived interrelationships and in predicting in a convincing way the consequences of specific changes in the economic sphere, then it will be able to help actual politics and economic policies to find more feasible solutions and to avoid unnecessary simplifications or failed attempts.

Proposals to change the system into a humane economic democracy are most likely to be realized--and this also is expressed by the theoretical conception presented here--if the various parties searching for realistic solutions of present-day systemic problems could agree on certain basic principles for transformation of the system. Since the reformed system can only be a democratic one, and since macro-planning would also be truly democratic only if it involved pluralist clashes of interests and proposals for the future, then if several parties were to agree on the introduction of such planning with its basic principles, this would not imply that these parties had to give up their autonomy and particular position in society. But it would of course mean that all of them recognized the necessity of macro-distribution planning for present-day society, and therefore at the same time realized that the market mechanism alone cannot solve the problems that build up.

Basic principles such as linking the market to macro-distribution planning, linking capital- and profit-sharing to the market advantages of neutralized capital, regulating profit-distribution and restrictions of monopoly profits substituting for the market, and adjusting incomes while preserving business-motivating private profits are principles for which considerable support could be won after some years of educational work among the substantial, future-oriented sectors in all the parties mentioned. Whether as a result of appropriate changes in the programs and objectives of the established parties or the creation of new groupings and movements, the emergence of large and sufficiently strong political majorities would in any case be the precondition for economic reform by democratic means.

THE REFORM OF THE COMMUNIST SYSTEM

Like the reform of the capitalist system, the reform of the Communist system, which in the Eastern bloc states has developed in two stages, has matured. This system has indeed emerged on the basis of a socialist theory and calls itself socialist. The dispute about whether or not it is in fact a socialist system would in turn only be a dispute about conceptions of socialism for which no generally accepted criteria exist. For this reason, we believe that such a discussion would not be fruitful. We will therefore deal only with those concrete, ascertainable shortcomings of the system that we have been analyzing in the course of this work. In our view, these deficiencies are of such a negative nature and will turn out to be such growing obstacles to the satisfaction of human needs, that political dissatisfaction will increase on the part of ever broader strata of the population, and this will ultimately lead to a fundamental reform of the system.

In listing the shortcomings of the system, one has to mention first of all the well-known fact that here a political group has come to power which--resting on the aforementioned theory that workers and other working people are unable to realize their own interests--sees itself as the representative of the interests of the working people. Apart from the non-scientific character of this theory, the fact that in the Soviet Union, 60 years after the revolution, broad strata of the population are still not believed to be capable of knowing their own interests --interests which therefore must continue to be expressed a single political party--is in itself a manifestion of the profound contradiction between reality and the ideological justification of this situation.

Ideologically, of course, it is no longer claimed that the population do not know their interests. Rather, a complete harmony of interests is said to exist between the broad strata of the population and their Communist party so that there is no need at all for another party. Every dictatorship makes this same claim, whether control is exercised by one person, a clique, or a party--or rather, a party apparatus. Counter-evidence, in the form of a legal opposition, has never been permitted. So long as such evidence is not forthcoming, therefore, it is wrong to claim, as has always been done, that the people do not want an opposition.

Naturally, in the West the question may be, and is constantly raised about why the peoples' dissatisfaction in the Eastern bloc states does not manifest itself in greater resistance and insurrection. However, this is to pose a question which still cannot be scientifically answered: what level of dissatisfaction would have to prevail, what chances for insurrection would have to be present, and what would the nature of the dictatorship possibly have to be, before a visible opposition could develop, up to and including an armed insurrection? In any case, in history there have been dictatorships that survived for centuries before the people's pent-up dissatisfaction and anger manifested itself in open resistance and ultimately rebellion. At times it was an uncontainable desperation, at others persistent covert illegal preparations, at still others the extraordinary weakening of the police regime (for example, as a result of ongoing war and the like) that ultimately brought the situation to the boiling point and precipitated a successful rebellion.

In almost all Eastern bloc states, the broad strata of the population have in the past waged resistance--often sufficiently so as to be noticed on the outside--which has always been suppressed by the most ruthless and brutal violence. On the basis of these experiences, as well as their knowledge of widespread dissatisfaction and of the people's latent opposition to the prevailing political conditions, Communist rulers have reached the conclusion that truly democratic conditions must not be created. If the unity of interest between the people and the party were genuine, Communist parties would not hesitate to permit free interest- and opinion-groups.

Not only for the sake of Western Communist parties, but also in the interest of furthering socialism on a global scale, it would be preferable to introduce democratic rules, and within their framework demonstrate the leading role of the Communist party. An election victory of 60 to 70 percent, achieved in competition with several parties, would strengthen the party's external image considerably more than do the 98 percent victories registered by "unified candidates lists," which in reality amount to a one-party dictatorship. However, if the Communist leaders decide not to create such pluralist conditions, this indicates that they understand only too well the existing state of interest relations between the majority of the people and the party. It is not only that they fear competition from other parties as they decide on certain conceptions for the development of future economic policies, five-year plans and the like, but also that the autocratic party or party apparatus is afraid of losing its accustomed exclusive power forever.

First, it is simply too easy to make decisions about anything in society without having to debate and attempt to win votes, as in a democracy. Under such circumstances, people can for decades pursue careers and remain in top positions who, in a competitive political system with a real contest for votes, would either not stand a chance or have to be content with being part of a minority. The political and general standard of Communist functionaries, in countries where they enjoy autocratic power and a monopolistic position, is much lower than the average level of politicians in democratic societies. Any monopoly creates laws of mediocrity and below-average standards. It is, therefore, particularly these politicians' fear of real political conflict that leads them to cling to their political monopoly and its strenuous ideological "justification."

Second, not only the professional politicians and employees of the party apparatus itself are involved in all this, but also the whole broad stratum of functionaries in all spheres of society. In the economy, the educational sector, public administration, the military and security system, culture, etc., mainly Communists are entrusted with all responsible and, of course, highly paid management positions. Their political activity and reliability are decisive and, for this reason, they will always be preferred to people who, although they may have greater expertise and abilities, are not party members--or who at least do not appear active and reliable to the party apparatus. This practice triggers corresponding reactions and thus becomes the most important motivation for joining the party and taking part in extraordinary party activities. In particular, persons whose knowledge and talent are less than outstanding, but who nevertheless have great ambitions, pursue their career through the party.

Those with the most talent and character, on the other hand, come to realize the universal hypocrisy of this system, are turned off, and consequently attempt, despite personal disadvantages, to go their own way outside of, or even against the party. The distinction between party members, especially party activists, and non-members increasingly manifests itself in terms of different moral qualities, a fact which gradually also penetrates into public consciousness. The overwhelming majority of the population rightly regard Communist functionaries as political careerists. Particularly young people, who generally place greater value on the respect and friendship of people with good character than on their future careers, increasingly see this trend as a barrier to their joining the party. To be a Communist in countries where there is a communist monopoly of power, consequently, has a totally different meaning than in countries where Communists still have to struggle for power and are frequently even subjected to personal persecution. The original reasons for joining the party (devoted, unselfish,

morally strong class fighters) which originated in and were
sustained by such conditions of opposition and persecution
appear ludicrous when seen in the context of the practice
of Eastern bloc states.
Third, the privileges accorded to Communist functionaries,
particularly to those working in the party apparatus, are
consciously increased in order to tie them even closer to
the system, as well as to widen the gap between them and
the ordinary people. In a situation of general scarcity,
higher pay alone does not suffice to ensure people's material benefits. Rather, there must also be special allotments of
goods that cannot be obtained with money alone. Thus
preferential housing allocation for high-party functionaries,
in a situation of a dismal housing shortage where young
couples have to wait for years for their allotment, creates
an extremely strong incentive for party activities. The same
applies to preferential allocation of cars, various Western
goods, trips abroad, special medical services, separate, exclusive recreational facilities, and the like. That Communist
functionaries try to conceal these privileges, while workers
nevertheless find out about them, reinforces the latter's
envy and hatred of the functionary clique, and in itself is
proof of the immense gap between the new ruling stratum
and the population.
    All these factors make it impossible for Communists to
achieve real changes and improvements in the "socialist"
economy. Their betrayal of the people is great, and continuously becoming greater. The top functionaries' constant
appeals to the workers to produce more and better, while
stressing at the same time that they, in contrast to the exploited workers in capitalism, are working for themselves,
appears as a mockery and provocation. Today, the overwhelming majority of workers are aware that their standard
of living is considerably lower than that of workers in
Western industrialized states, that their top functionaries
basically live as well as the Western bourgeoisie, and that
great economic scarcity is caused not by their working less
but by the economic system which actually produces declining efficiency and use-value.
    Official Communist propaganda, of course, ignores all
fundamental deficiencies of its economic system and attempts
to downplay them in such a way as to make them appear to
be sporadic mistakes caused by incompetent managers of
isolated plants. They are desperately trying to disguise the
widespread and permanent existence of disproportions, efficiency drops, qualitatively inferior products, unsatisfied
needs, etc. and to suppress any scientific generalizations
relating to these phenomena. Not that the system may exhibit permanent faults, it is claimed, but only that particular people and managing organs are to blame for particular
mistakes.

Simultaneously, an attempt is made to emphasize the "great achievements of the socialist system" by continually citing growth figures in production, consumption, social achievements, etc. Again, not a single concrete comparison with Western industrialized countries may be made since an awareness would then suddenly dawn that, despite all "successful growth," actual productivity, per capita national income, and real wages have lagged far behind the level of comparable Western countries. Czechoslovakia, for example, as late as the end of World War II was keeping pace with many Western industrial countries in terms of industrial production, productivity, workers' real wages, etc.; today it has been left far behind on all counts. Such facts, however, must be concealed most stringently and must not be revealed to Czechoslovak workers.

Even if workers and employees are unable fully to comprehend the economic causes and interconnections of the economic deficiencies, they have nevertheless experienced such diverse and recurring economic losses that, for these reasons alone, they are increasingly distrustful toward the system and its official propaganda. They see the mindlessness of formal plan-fulfillment which, foregoing quality, pursues quantity with products of high material value. They see the permanent losses in production, caused by shortages of materials and intermediate products, which at the end of the month must be compensated by "plan-storming" at their expense. They have long realized the incompetence of most managers and superiors who, being political proteges, do not meet professional standards. As consumers, they notice mindless planning incapable of adapting supply structures to demand structures. They see waste of machines which, due to a constant shortage of spare parts, become inoperative and rust away. As a result of the--if only meager--imports from the West they become convinced of the incomparably lower quality of Eastern products.

In particular, above and beyond an interest in receiving wages for official work activity in "socialist" production, there is a growing interest in earnings from private activities. To farmers, work on their private plots has been considerably more important than work for the kolkhoz from the very beginning. With their private work and enough initiative, they can get not only additional goods for their own larder, but in particular relatively high monetary incomes from their sales in the market. Moreover, workers have also acquired an increasingly important second income source through the rapid development of the practice of moonlighting. The planned economy creates so many bottlenecks and unnecessary shortages that the scope for moonlighters' and black marketeers' initiatives is continually growing. There are constant shortages, particularly of services, repairs, building materials, spare parts for automobiles, etc. Thus the greater the demand for goods and services in relation to their supply, the higher the price, and ultimately the more profitable the additional nocturnal effort for the moonlighter or the risk to the black marketeer.

The energy that moonlighters expend is, of course, very great, and they accordingly try to conserve more of their energy during the day in the production of labor power, in order to be fit at night. It is worthwhile then to bribe even masters (foremen) or engineers (heads of departments) so that while doing less, they can charge for their full work load. Similarly, these supervisors turn a blind eye to moonlighters misappropriating large quantitities of materials from state enterprises for their illicit work. Higher-placed supervisors, without working themselves, in turn receive a share of the illicit incomes through bribery. The proportion of illicit workers to the working class as a whole is at present so high that by itself it impedes an increase in the work productivity of "socialist" production. Even a growing number of employees and civil servants are attempting to raise their incomes through supplementary work, predominantly by building private houses for relatives and friends.

The black market is continually expanding and the initiatives which it produces are often incredible. For some black marketeers it pays to ship fruit and vegetables by plane from Caucasia to Moscow where they still make a significant profit. The market mechanism thus succeeds, in spite of all police persecution, against the will of its political liquidators; meanwhile the state loses in taxes what it could have gained with official toleration and regulation. Moreover, this black market has an undesirable side effect in that it results in a de facto leveling of incomes. Basically, scarce and overly expensive goods and services are required and paid for predominantly by higher-income earners. This leads to a continuous redistribution of incomes to moonlighters and black marketeers, whose incomes frequently more than double. As a further consequence, many more demanding, qualified professions decline, and training or even university programs for these professions are unappealing because one can earn as much or even more without such strenuous professional training. This, in turn, retards the qualitative development of production.

More and more people are becoming aware of how inefficient the economic system is, and of the fact that, given labor intensity equal to, and plundering of natural resources even greater than, under capitalism, less economic use-value is created for the population. Under the pressure of this dissatisfaction, reform tendencies repeatedly emerge. It is almost laughable how, at certain intervals, nearly every decade, the same waves of public discussion and economic criticism are set in motion. Whenever the criticism and proposals of the preceding wave have begun to ebb, new economists, scientists, editors, and practitioners come along with basically the same criticisms, showing how planning results in material waste, a production structure not oriented to demand, low product quality, slow technological progress, and the like. Their proposals for improvement, in turn, always move in a similar direction: greater plant autonomy, fewer plan objectives, greater profit incentives, more decentralization of investment, etc. However, the central bureaucracy, fearing the loss of its influence, power, and basis of legitimation, has so far always managed to subdue these waves of decentralization in time, or--owing to inconsistency and lack of commitment--discredit them and then enforce recentralization.

But it would be wrong to believe that nothing had changed as a result of these waves of criticism and decentralization. It only appears as if the entire past has fallen into oblivion and that development has been circular. In reality, the number of people who keep in mind old criticisms and proposals is growing progressively; they are becoming aware that not decentralization as such, but its inadequate implementation, inconsistency, and one-sidedness, as well as the bureaucracy's power and interest in recentralization, have led to the failure of efforts in the past epoch. As the people accumulate such experiences, their related ability to generalize and analyze grows, and they gain a deeper understanding of causes and effects thus producing increasing political determination to carry out consistent changes. In Czechoslovakia, which is industrially far more advanced than the Soviet Union, it took two frustrated decentralization waves before the reform movement which developed into the Prague Spring, using new experiences and insights, could get off to a start.

The national bureaucracy alone could not thwart the realization of the movement's goals; it needed help from the Soviets in the form of intervention. The indigenous forces for reform had grown so strong, and the idea of reform so widespread, that they would have succeeded had it not been for external intervention. The experiences gained from this long-term objective and subjective preparatory period and its relevance to system reform can also be applied to the Soviet Union. Preparations there would naturally take much longer than in the Central European Communist states, because the Soviet Union, prior to the revolution, was economically and politically far less developed than most of the satellite states. Its capitalist economy was too weak and its experience of capitalism, as well as its stock of cadres to operate the capitalist system were correspondingly less advanced. The population's needs and expectations were not as highly developed. Its democratic traditions were non-existent, while the population had become deeply habituated to a centralized, all-powerful state and hence to the power of the bureaucracy.

Since then, the Soviet Union has become an industrially developed country. As a result of increasing international contacts, the population's needs and expectations are rising rapidly, and the younger generation in particular is more and more oriented toward Western ways of life--developments which cannot be halted despite all the counteractions taken by the political bureaucracy. Democratic experiences have not increased, but an awareness of Western democratic liberties is again growing progressively among the younger generation whose attitude toward Communist power is increasingly critical. The generation that lived through pre-revolutionary conditions is dying out, and propagandistic comparisons with Czarist Russia are very rapidly losing their effect. Marxism-Leninism is increasingly reduced to formal lip service trotted out and rendered to the bureaucracy; its influence on people's actual thinking has almost completely vanished because of the gaping contradictions between theory and reality. Pragmatism is increasingly prevalent in thought and action.

Negative experiences of one's own system, therefore, demonstrably produce critical attitudes, while further development in the West will produce ever more sharply contrasting criteria for that system to meet. This, however, does not mean adopting Western patterns uncritically in all spheres nor accepting tendencies toward the simple restoration of capitalism. Any simplistic pro-capitalism will be countered not so much by Marxist-Leninist propaganda phrases, but rather by real information about crises, unemployment, inflation, insecurity of young people, etc. prevailing in the capitalist system. It is particularly the workers' fear of these capitalist phenomena which inhibits their dissatisfaction with "socialism." Since they do not see any real alternative, they retreat into political apathy, attempting more and more to use their own initiatives (moonlighting and the like) to improve the situation in a purely egoistic, consumerist fashion.

But the stratum of people able to receive and reflect on more information is rapidly growing; their experiences, as already mentioned, are accumulating; they think more analytically and are able to comprehend linkages; they are also capable of gradually generating new conceptions of society and developing into an increasingly strong, conscious opposition. If the political bureaucracy were to react to this growing consciousness only by persecution and repression, the gap between the party and the population would very quickly widen. In such societies, hatred and anger grow and accumulate in the long run much more than fear. The number of rebels increases, and in new situations where the regime is weakened (economic, external relations, personnel, and similar crises) revolutionary situations very quickly develop. The assumption, however, that the political bureaucracy only reacts by repression to the aforementioned development of consciousness--which partly they do perceive--is too simplistic.

Part of the political bureaucracy is always observing the mood among the population, and as they begin to think about it, they are willing to carry out certain changes which might meet the demands of the population. This of course does not imply that they would give up their position as the ruling bureaucracy and, for example, would be willing to yield to anti-Communist currents. They will always hold on to "socialism" which to them means first and foremost that system in which the Communist party holds the power monopoly. Yet in contrast to conservative or reactionary sectors of the bureaucracy, this sector--let us speak of it as a flexible party bureaucracy--will attempt to win over the population. Flexible Communists simply have not given up the intention to win the people's support for party policies and to legitimate these policies. They are aware of the consequences of a widened gap between the population and the party and know that ultimately this would have to end in the overthrow of their rule. They are thus motivated by the justified fear of revolution to listen more closely to the political mood among the people, and to stabilize their dominant position by means of somewhat more flexible policies.

On the other hand, there is a decidedly more reactionary sector of the bureaucracy who have already lost all contact with the people, are basically afraid of them and incapable of finding a common language with them. It is those political bureaucrats who constantly move in political circles, that is, in the circle of bureaucrats close to them, and only think about the mood of these same bureaucrats. They are completely oriented toward the personal power struggle within the party; for this reason the only important things to them are any changes of mood within the party apparatus and among Communist functionaries. The mood among the people, on the other hand, is of less concern to them because they no longer have any illusions about the possibility of gaining their support. They are basically cynics and rely predominantly on repressive means to preserve their rule. They may be labeled Stalinists.

Even if this differentiation among Communist power bureaucrats largely depends on the moral qualities and intelligence of individuals, one can nevertheless also observe the influence of different areas of activity on these bureaucrats' political attitudes. There are very diverse areas for which party functionaries, and particularly the apparatus, are responsible. In certain areas they have to take much greater account of the population, or more precisely, they have certain political goals that can only be realized through this population. Examples are the economy, the educational system, culture, social-medical system, and the like. Heads and secretaries of these sectors cannot totally disregard the mood among the population, and have also realized that in this context one cannot govern by repression alone. On the other hand, heads of such sectors as inner-party organization, security, military, party education and propaganda, and the like are basically oriented only towards the political apparatus itself and thus not responsible for any repercussions among the population. The result will therefore always be a rather dogmatic, unrealistic attitude.

Western observers of the Eastern political landscape are often skeptical toward claims about political differentiation in the Soviet sphere because the phenomenon is seldom visible to the outside. Predominantly, one sees the principle of party unity elevated to a supreme principle and, while one cannot deny that there is some discussion before party resolutions are taken, one nevertheless believes that once these resolutions are passed, everyone unites in implementing the policies thus decided. The uniform implementation of these policies may be a fact for the outside, since party discipline is one of the firmest principles of party organization. However, this does not signify the elimination of progressive differentiation within the party, where the relationship of the population to the system and to the party is reflected in a different way. Of course, in the short term this differentiation manifests itself in a struggle over individual political and economic measures which occurs earlier than in the Central Committee. But it is predominantly the long-term struggle over the most crucial positions of power and which persons should occupy them, where the opposing wings are permanently engaged in a behind-the-scenes struggle.

For outside observers it is difficult to follow this struggle because they have no knowledge at all of the personnel differentiation and have little opportunity to look more closely into it. Even the so-called experts on the Eastern political situation, scholars of communism, and other specialists must rely to a great extent on official information and rarely learn anything about these differentiations in advance. A few months before the outbreak of the Prague

Spring, Western observers still did not have a clue about the imminent events, and interpreted the Czechoslovakia of the Novotny regime as one of the most Stalinist of countries. In reality, the process of internal differentiation within the party had been a vehement one for years, and the systemic transformations--the Prague Spring being one of these--basically had been consciously prepared for ten years beforehand. Even Western diplomats, who for years have been active in Eastern bloc states, only very rarely gain deeper insights into the differentiation and the internal power struggles in the ruling party.

This differentiation, however, is a long-standing fact and largely manifests itself in certain fundamental changes in politics and/or economic policy. Most frequently, of course, such political shifts occur at times when changes in the internal power constellation emerge. Thus a new appointment to the most crucial power position, that of the party's Secretary General (or First Secretary), as well as other secretary posts, is a manifestation of possible new antagonistic wings with fundamentally different political conceptions. The subsequent political shifts are thus not purely personal, fortuitous changes, but generally transformations fought out and prepared over a long period of time. However, since the struggle is not enacted in public, as would be the case in a Western democracy, it is not only very difficult to perceive, but also almost totally unpredictable.

Since the flexible party wing, to a certain extent, reflects the people's growing mood, in certain periods it will have an influence on the party's political turns. One can say that, as a rule, following a lengthy period of stringent centralization of planning and control of the economy, as well as of high priority on heavy industry, problems of declining efficiency, structural disproportions, qualitative defects, etc. will increase to such an extent as to produce a dangerous degree of dissatisfaction on the part of the people. It is usually in this situation that the more flexible politicians' influence increases and, as a consequence, a period of decentralization or limited liberalization begins, accelerating the production of consumer goods. After a few years of decentralization policies, the situation becomes too threatening for the reactionary Stalinists; and since in most cases they are able to turn the poor results of inconsistent partial reforms against their initiators, they are ultimately, through their political advances, able to bring about renewed recentralization.

As already mentioned, however, it would be a mistake to view this wavelike motion as a permanent continuous process. What is growing quantitatively, and at a given moment produces a completely new quality, is the consciousness and political mood of the population. In most satellite states, the population's consciousness has long become ripe for real democratization and humanization, and basically these are thwarted only by the Soviet imperial power, where the population's consciousness has been retarded. But the laws of development are also at work in the same direction there, and will sooner or later force quantitative changes.

There are, in fact, only three basic alternative developments. First, the Stalinist bureaucracy may succeed in preventing the imminent systemic transformation by means of great foreign policy success. In this way, one can for a time divert the population's attention and also temporarily contain their dissatisfaction. This basically means incorporation of further significant areas of the world under Soviet hegemony. This course, however, runs the risk of developing into a global catastrophe at some point. Although this possibility cannot be completely excluded, we may nevertheless regard this very factor as reducing the long-term prospects for the Stalinist bureaucracy within the Soviet system. However, in terms of what the West can do to counteract this development, there is no other option than to ensure the military balance of power while fostering the two other intra-Soviet development alternatives.

The second alternative development would be revolutionary development. This would have to occur if the political regime did not implement any economic reforms, if the population's standard of living and freedom increasingly lagged behind the West, and if the people's political dissatisfaction therefore further intensified. Such a development would also necessarily result in growing national tensions and conflicts: both within the Soviet Union, and between it and the other small Communist states. Since in the latter the people's readiness for, and pressure toward system reform is more developed, the regimes in these countries would, for the sake of self-preservation, increasingly seek more relative autonomy. These tensions and national contradictions would weaken the Soviet regime, and possible adventurist reactions on the part of the Stalinists might even accelerate the emergence of a revolutionary situation.

The third alternative development, which we consider the most likely, is the implementation of certain system reforms by the flexible party wing under growing pressure from the population. The flexible party bureaucracy is aware of the danger inherent in both Stalinist imperial policies and the stubborn, conservative ossification of the system. While at present these bureaucrats are not yet capable of conceiving of systemic reform, which really would fundamentally alter economic development, they nevertheless do acknowledge the necessity of certain reforms in the sense of far-reaching decentralization and strengthening the

market mechanism. They are also aware that without a
certain liberalization of the political realm, the two related
dangers will increase. Irrespective of how far-reaching or
limited this thinking may be at present, the logic of growing economic problems and popular political dissatisfaction
will further develop these conceptions. Under the pressure
of increasing dangers, in particular the Stalinists' threatening adventurist policies, the flexible bureaucracy may grow
into a real anti-Stalinist opposition movement.

The possibility of the development of such reforms
cannot, however, mean abandoning any revolutionary tendencies. In a totalitarian dictatorship the people can never
give up the struggle for their liberation using all the means
at their disposal. The stronger the resistance to totalitari-
anism and pressure for liberalization and system transformation on part of the most diverse population groups, the
easier it will be for the flexible bureaucracy to force such
reforms through. The more the reform conceptions are able
to assuage the population's (particularly the workers') fears
of capitalist restoration, the sooner will tendencies toward
systemic change mature. Emerging clusters of ideas which--
like those which once developed in the Czechoslovakia --
point to alternatives for a fundamental rise in economic efficiency and the people's standard of living, without at the
same time resurrecting the perils of capitalist crises, unemployment, and other capitalist processes, are of fundamental
importance for the political liberation movement in the Soviet
sphere of power.

The system model presented here, adapted in turn to
the specific conditions of the individual Eastern bloc states,
could ideally contribute to the envisaged reform development. One might far more strictly restrict the private entrepreneurial activity proposed here--for example only to
the sphere of small firms, the trades, small-scale services,
and the like, and to a certain number of hired employees.
Although we regard this as a loss from the perspective of
economic efficiency, and therefore also in terms of the population's standard of living, it would be understandable if
these restrictions were incorporated into the reform goals in
those countries where dogmatic socialist ideology has been
disseminated for so long and fear of capitalist restoration is
relatively strong. One may state with full conviction that in
the Eastern bloc states the proposed system of humane economic democracy, even without private entrepreneurial activity beyond the small firms, would bring about a leap forward in economic efficiency and value creation.

For these impulses, in their present form, are already
strong. They are directed toward: a transformation of state
bureaucratic ownership of the means of production into
neutralized collective ownership with profit-sharing by all

employees; democratic election of supervisory or
self-governing councils in all plants; transformation of bureaucratically controlled production planning into macro-distribution planning with democratic plan preparation and selection of alternatives by the population through pluralist
political elections; implementation of the market mechanism
with market pricing and strongly encouraged competition in
all sectors, along with the use of monopoly taxation and
other anti-monopolistic measures; admission of private business activity in the area of the trades, smaller-scale services, small trade, and the like; and all this would produce
enormous initiatives in the economy, increases in efficiency,
and an expansion of economic value that for decades has
been inconceivable in the Eastern bloc states. This would
not mean the re-introduction of capitalism, for it would be
entirely possible to control the development of profits, and
this control could be enforced even more reliably than in
today's expanding black market. From a certain profit level
upwards, the transformation of a profit surplus quota into
neutralized capital would be guaranteed, at the same time
preserving small producers' motivation for increasing their
profits. The detailed preparation of such a reform model by
progressive, anti-Stalinist forces in Eastern bloc states
may--just as it once did in Czechoslovakia --give a strong
impetus to the reform movement.

SUMMARY OF THE MAIN THESES

In their traditional forms, the capitalist market-economy system and the communist planned-economy system will lead to increasing problems of development, thus causing serious and ever more threatening dangers for people. The two systems' developmental deficiencies, though of different natures, can be overcome by means of up-to-date economies guided by humane and democratic goals. If this can be accomplished, then a new economic system may develop which eliminates the dangerous systemic antagonism between East and West.

In the capitalist system, the working groups among the population are increasingly alienated from the development of their economy. The processes by which the national economy is distributed--linked to interests, violent and blind to the future--lead to macro-economic cyclical disruptions in the form of economic crises and inflation, to private overconsumption in the face of public poverty, and to income formation not geared to performance. Mass unemployment, inadequate satisfaction of the needs of below-average income-earners, wasteful consumption, perversion of the environment, growing threats to living conditions, enhanced antagonisms between poor and rich, North and South--these are the ominous results of this development.

Due to these deficiencies, which lend themselves to ideological exploitation, the system is under a latent threat of communist overthrow which, however, is no solution but rather brings with it even greater economic deficiencies and undemocratic suppression of the population. The basic error of communist ideology lies in ignoring the role of the human individual, his interests, his initiative and activity on behalf of the development of the enterprise, the economy, politics, and society as a whole.

In the communist system, the practical realization of ideology is expressed in the concentration of all important decisions concerning every sphere of society in the central agencies and the apparatus of the Communist Party. In the economy, this means eliminating the independence of the enterprises, the competition among them, market prices and market-linked incomes, and the positive effects of the market mechanism in general. Total monopolization and bureaucratization with unprecedented losses in efficiency and economic backwardness are the results.

A solution to the capitalist dilemma and a preventative concept against communist developments can be seen, above all, in the far-reaching democratization and humanization of the economy, in overcoming the contradiction between wage and profit interests, in extending economic responsibility through capital neutralization, in linking the plan with the market, in implementing democratic, alternative distribution planning together with a regulated market mechanism.

The neutralization of capital means transferring constantly reforming new liquid and productive capital into indivisible assets of the enterprise collective. It is to be administered by trustees elected by the current collective of the co-workers of an enterprise. The big capital companies should gradually be transformed into co-worker companies based exclusively on neutralized capital. Medium-sized enterprises will be reformed as mixed companies in which private and neutralized capital are joined. Small enterprises will remain as private property.

The co-workers in all enterprises will share in the enterprises' profits. The profit-sharing fund and the transformation of profit shares into neutralized capital will be governed by a planned distribution formula for the entire economy. This distribution formula will also indirectly determine the profit shares which, as net entrepreneurial profits, are to continue to motivate private entrepreneurial activity. In this way, those profit shares required for net investments will at the same time be ensured.

On the basis of neutralized capital, a democratic system of management evolves in the co-worker societies with the goal of linking the necessary efficiency principle with the new principle of work humanization. Democratically elected supervisory councils, control over and the right to recall management, long-term determination of the enterprise's economic policies, provision of current information to all personnel, periodic accounting by the supervisory council, democratic management style and autonomous work groups should bring about increased job satisfaction, self-development, and co-worker identification with their enterprise.

Profit must remain the criterion of the development of efficiency, but profit-optimization rather than profit-maximization will be sought. Optimal profits are an expression of long-term, maximal efficiency despite short-term, democratic decisions to defer profits in favor of more humane solutions to structural and modernization problems. But all humane solutions must produce long-term improvements in effectiveness if income losses and economic dissatisfaction are to be averted.

The long-term goals of the development of the national economy will be governed with the aid of macro-distribution plans. Long-term programs and middle-range plans will determine the macro-structure of the desired development of the quality of life. This includes the determination of the pace of growth together with the necessary continuous and harmonious development of investments and consumption. The goals of quality of life and equilibrium must be ensured by distribution processes and macro-final incomes regulated by plan. Most important is the planned determination of wage increases, wage differentials, and profit-sharing quotas. Plan fulfillment will be accomplished by planned economic policy, income policy, fiscal policy, credit policy.

The preparation of the plans is accomplished by democratically constituted planning commissions. Two or three alternative plans should be worked out, giving expression to substantially different interests and conceptions for the future. The alternative plans will be subjected to a broad discussion in society, and the selection will be made through political elections. Linking plan selection to political elections once every four or five years can lead to a necessary degree of objectification of politics. It is the mandate of the government and/or its economic council to fulfill the plan chosen by the majority.

The concrete development of production and investments in the enterprises is determined by the market mechanism. One of the main goals of economic policy is the perfection of the market mechanism. Enhancing market transparency, increasing market competition, and the consequent restriction of monopolistic developments should lead to the elimination of entrepreneurial incomes not related to performance. The profit rates of all branches should be tendencially equal. If the profit rate of individual enterprises should depart from the profit rate of the national economy, this should only be as a result of different performances in the market. Monopoly profits that remain despite anti-monopolist policies, will be siphoned off by a special monopoly tax.

The reformed system will enable the working people to shape their lives and futures, according to plan and democratically, on the basis of a linkage between their own interests and those of society. The elimination of crises and unemployment can help to assuage people's insecurity and apprehensions about the future. The planned determination of growth, of urban development, of solutions to problems of transportation, of reshaping the environment, and of the development of education and leisure, can bring about a substantial change in the quality of life. The democratic codetermination in the micro- and macro-sphere of the economy, together with a degree of objectivity in politics, can prevent a threatening bureaucratization of society.

The implementation of the reformed system can only be accomplished on the basis of majority democratic decisions. All ideologies that assume the immaturity of the people and the exercise of decision-making powers by power elites in the final analysis serve to preserve the privileges of small, powerful groups and to alienate broad groups in the population from social institutions. Only on the strength of real advances in democratization and of a mature economic democracy can the threat of environmental polution, perversion of society, and other catastrophes be averted and hence ensure a more humane development of society.

INDEX

ABOUT THE AUTHOR

OTA SIK was born in Pilsen, Czechoslovakia in 1919. On completion of his university studies in Prague he was employed by the electronics firms of Ericson and Koreska from 1936-1940. He spent 1940-1945 in the concentration camp Mauthausen as a political prisoner. After World War II he studied at the University of Political and Social Sciences, Prague and in 1952 began his academic career as Professor at the Political University of Prague, then as Deputy Director of the Institute of Social Sciences there. In 1961 he was appointed Director of the Institute of Economics of the Czech Academy of Sciences as well as Head of the Government Commission for Economic Reform in Czechoslovakia. During the "Prague Spring" from April to August 1968 he bacame a Vice-premier in the Dubcek government and thus a leading force in its economic reform program. Forced into exile after the Soviet intervention, Professor Sik was appointed Professor of Comparative Economic Systems in 1970 at the University of St. Gallen, Switzerland, where he now lives and works. Among his works available in English are The Third Way (1974) and The Communist Power System (1979).

ABOUT THE TRANSLATORS

FRED EIDLIN is Associate Professor in the Department of Political Studies at the University of Guelph (Ontario, Canada). He studied at Dartmouth College, l'Institut d'Etudes Politiques de l'Universite de Paris, Freie Universitaet Berlin, and Indiana University, receiving his doctorate in Political Science from the University of Toronto. In 1968 and 1969 he was a researcher specializing in Czechoslovak affairs at Radio Free Europe in Munich. Among his principal research interest are impediments to the development of the social sciences. In addition to his book, The Logic of "Normalization": The Soviet Intervention in Czechoslovakia of 21 August 1968 and the Czechoslovak Response, he is the author of numerous papers and articles on Czechoslovak politics during 1968-1969, and on problems of social and political inquiry. He has edited Constitutional Democracy: Essays in Comparative Politics, and the Newsletter for those interested in the philosophy of Karl Popper.

WILLIAM GRAF is Associate Professor in the Department of Political Studies and Coordinator of the International Development Programme at the University of Guelph. He has degrees from the University of British Colombia, the Freie Universitaet Berlin, and the London School of Economics, and has taught at the University of Maryland and University of Benin (Nigeria). He is author of Elections 1979 in Nigeria and of The German Left since 1945, as well as editor of Towards a Political Economy of Nigeria. He is a regular contributor to The Socialist Register. His most recent work, The Nigerian State, is scheduled for publication early in 1986.